SHARING OWNERSHIP, PROFITS, AND DECISION-MAKING IN THE 21ST CENTURY

ADVANCES IN THE ECONOMIC ANALYSIS OF PARTICIPATORY & LABOR-MANAGED FIRMS

Series Editor: Takao Kato

Recent Volumes:

ADVANCES IN THE ECONOMIC ANALYSIS OF PARTICIPATORY & LABOR-MANAGED FIRMS
VOLUME 14

SHARING OWNERSHIP, PROFITS, AND DECISION-MAKING IN THE 21ST CENTURY

EDITED BY

DOUGLAS KRUSE
Rutgers University, Piscataway, NJ, USA

Emerald

United Kingdom – North America – Japan
India – Malaysia – China

Emerald Group Publishing Limited
Howard House, Wagon Lane, Bingley BD16 1WA, UK

First edition 2013

British Library Cataloguing in Publication Data
A catalogue record for this book is available from the British Library

ISBN: 978-1-78190-750-4
ISSN: 0885-3339 (Series)

CONTENTS

PART II: COMPARATIVE SYSTEMS OF OWNERSHIP AND PARTICIPATION

PART III: THEORY AND POLICY

LIST OF CONTRIBUTORS

Daphne P. Berry	Barney School of Business, University of Hartford, West Hartford, CT, USA
Joseph Blasi	School of Management and Labor Relations, Rutgers University, Piscataway, NJ, USA
David Ellerman	University of California at Riverside, Riverside, CA, USA; Center on Global Justice, University of California at San Diego, San Diego, CA, USA
Alban Hashani	Business School, Staffordshire University, Stoke-on-Trent, UK
Iraj Hashi	Business School, Staffordshire University, Stoke-on-Trent, UK
Charles Heckscher	Department of Labor Studies and Employment Relations, Rutgers University, New Brunswick, NJ, USA
Anthony Jensen	Business School, University of Sydney, Sydney, Australia
Derek C. Jones	Department of Economics, Hamilton College, Clinton, NY, USA
Tatiana Kachalina (Ershova)	Southern Federal University, Rostov-on-Don, Russia
Mark J. Kaswan	Department of Government, University of Texas at Brownsville, Brownsville, TX, USA
Sudha Kornginnaya	Besant Women's College, Mangalore University, Mangalore, India

Douglas Kruse	School of Management and Labor Relations, Rutgers University, Piscataway, NJ, USA
Christopher Mackin	Ownership Associates, Inc., Cambridge, MA, USA; School of Management and Labor Relations, Rutgers University, Piscataway, NJ, USA
Tom Malleson	York University, Toronto, Canada
Philip Mellizo	Department of Economics, College of Wooster, Wooster, OH, USA
Erik K. Olsen	Department of Economics, University of Missouri Kansas City, Kansas City, MO, USA
Jeffrey Pliskin	Department of Economics, Hamilton College, Clinton, NY, USA
Jaroslav Vanek	Cornell University, Ithaca, NY, USA
Dan Weltmann	School of Management and Labor Relations, Rutgers University, Piscataway, NJ, USA

FOREWORD

The series Advances in the Economic Analysis of Participatory & Labor-Managed Firms was launched almost three decades ago by Derek C. Jones and Jan Svejnar. Since then, Advances has been a leading forum for high-quality original theoretical and empirical research in the broad area of participatory and labor-managed organizations. While general and specialized journals publish work in this field, many do so only occasionally. Advances has been the only annual periodical that presents some of the best papers in the field in a single volume.

It is my great pleasure to present Volume 14 of Advances in the Economic Analysis of Participatory & Labor-Managed Firms. Advances has been making frequent use of guest editors. This volume is also ably edited by Douglas Kruse, one of the world's foremost experts on profit sharing and employee stock ownership. The 2008 financial meltdown and the ensuing Great Recession continue to remind us of the fragility of the traditional form of capitalism. It is most timely that this year's Advances is edited by Douglas, a major driving force behind the shared capitalism movement. I find it particularly satisfying and encouraging that Douglas has been able to include in his volume a number of excellent contributions from young researchers in the field. It is my sincere hope that this year's volume will further encourage young scholars to consider contributing to the future volumes of Advances.

The scope of Advances will also continue to reflect great changes in the realities of participatory organizations over the last few decades. Following the disintegration of the former Republic of Yugoslavia, the principal systemic example of self-management was replaced with diverse forms of participatory systems. In advanced market economies, many firms have been experimenting with new and innovative work practices aimed at promoting employee participation in decision making in the workplace (sometimes even at the top corporate level) and collective incentive pay (e.g., profit sharing, gain sharing, team incentive, employee stock ownership plans, and broad-based stock options). A complementary set of such practices are often called a "high-performance work system" or "high-involvement work system." In addition, a number of significant examples of worker cooperatives have flourished (e.g., Mondragon). In transition economies, the collapse of the former USSR triggered widespread experimentation with diverse forms of participation, in particular employee ownership.

Methodologically, Advances will continue to welcome papers utilizing diverse methodologies, ranging from conventional economic analysis (including both theoretical and econometric studies) to new institutional economics to behavioral economics.

I hope you will find this volume informative and stimulating and that you will consider contributing to the future volumes of Advances and sharing information about Advances with other interested colleagues.

Takao Kato
Series Editor

INTRODUCTION

The participation of employees in company financial performance and workplace decision-making continues to be a topic of live interest, debate, policy, and research around the globe. This volume contributes new studies to inform our understanding of the causes and consequences of such participation, along with theory and thought pieces to provoke deeper understanding of the potential value, meaning, and limitations of financial and decision-making participation.

PART I: EMPIRICAL EFFECTS AND CORRELATES OF OWNERSHIP AND PARTICIPATION

The first five chapters analyze evidence on the effects and correlates of employee financial and decision-making participation. Daphne P. Berry uses a strong research design in doing three in-depth case studies, comparing the largest U.S. worker cooperative with two companies in the same industry, one in the for-profit and one in the nonprofit sector. Her study is of particular interest because the main occupation – home health aides – is the second-fastest growing occupation in percentage terms in the United States and the third-fastest growing occupation in numerical terms, projected to add 706,000 jobs between 2010 and 2020 (Lockard & Wolf, 2012).[1] The growth is due in part to the aging of the population, creating higher rates of disability among many countries (Schur, Kruse, & Blanck, 2013; World Health Organization, 2011). Berry's key finding, obtained using both quantitative and qualitative techniques, is that caregiver job satisfaction is substantially higher in the worker cooperative than in either the for-profit or nonprofit firm. This is partly but not wholly explained by greater influence and participation in decisions at the cooperative firm – there appear to be other aspects of cooperative membership that enhance job satisfaction. Berry's study provides valuable insights into the viability and attraction of cooperatives in a fast-growing segment of the U.S. economy.

One of the biggest objections to group incentive schemes such as employee ownership and profit sharing is the free rider problem, which has come to be known by economists as the "1/N problem" since each person in a group of *N* members will directly receive on average only 1/*N*th of the value of his or her increased individual effort. This results in a strong disincentive for individual effort. If, for example, I can take an action that increases group output by $10 but I must share that among 100 people, then I receive only 10 cents of the increased value. If my personal cost is, say, $1 for taking the action, it does not make sense to do it. But if all 100 of us can agree to take such actions causing the group output to go up by 100 × 10 = $1,000, then the $10 we each receive is well worth the $1 cost in personal effort. The question then becomes how we can establish and maintain a cooperative agreement to take such actions. Such cooperation may be encouraged by workplace policies that foster a sense of membership and teamwork, and foster group norms that support cooperation. The importance of such norms in practice, though, remains an open question. Philip Mellizo contributes extremely interesting evidence on this question in a careful laboratory experiment, finding that participants operating under group incentives do have ongoing higher performance than those in a flat-rate compensation system, but the higher performance does not appear to depend on institutional or cultural factors. A useful and interesting twist in his experiment is that he accounts for risk aversion by allowing for payments to vary outside the control of group members, much as company profits are affected by market factors outside the control of employees. As he notes, a useful extension would be to consider cases where group incentives are established on top of market-level pay, reflecting the situation for most employees who own stock or participate in profit sharing where the group incentives may function in part as an efficiency wage. Mellizo's findings constitute a provocative challenge to standard theory about the importance of the 1/*N* problem and whether special efforts are needed to overcome it, suggesting instead that workers may develop norms on their own that support teamwork and cooperation when group incentives are available.

There has been a long debate over the effects of technology on workers' jobs – in, particular, whether and how new technologies result in deskilled jobs with less worker discretion or instead require new skills with greater worker discretion and opportunities for affecting performance. Derek C. Jones and Jeffrey Pliskin examine the growth in new computer and information technologies that accelerated in the 1990s, seeing how these relate to different forms of employee financial and decision-making participation.

Looking at firms in New York State, they find that those with employee ownership plans for nonmanagerial employees are more likely than other firms to use Internet technologies, suggesting that such plans may help to attract workers with the needed skills and build their commitment to improving firm performance with such technologies. A similar interpretation may apply to the finding that profit sharing and gainsharing are linked to a greater percentage of workers using information technologies, although the interpretation is complicated by the different measures of technology that are linked to employee ownership versus profit sharing and gainsharing. Jones and Pliskin conclude that that the growth of financial participation over the past two decades may be explained in part by the diffusion of new technologies, and the ongoing diffusion of these technologies is likely to shape the future growth of employee ownership and profit sharing.

Two chapters delve into the underexplored relationship of employee ownership and firm survival. Erik K. Olsen focuses on worker cooperatives in Chapter 4, summarizing the theoretical arguments that generally predict a lower likelihood of survival among worker cooperatives, and then reviewing the empirical studies that instead find higher rates of survival compared to conventionally owned firms. The findings are consistent across samples from five countries. Olsen concludes that the low incidence of worker cooperatives cannot be explained by lower rates of survival, but instead is due to low rates of creation. He concludes that there are a number of factors that may discourage the creation of new firms as cooperatives, but these factors are greatly reduced in the conversion of existing firms to cooperatives, which is how most ESOP firms are created. Given Berry's finding of higher job satisfaction under cooperative ownership, and the greater survival of cooperatives that implies greater job security for workers, the question of why more existing firms are not converted to cooperatives is a live one for future research. While there have been no studies of survival among U.S. cooperatives, my chapter with Joseph Blasi and Dan Weltmann contributes the first evidence on the survival of privately held ESOP firms. Consistent with two prior studies on publicly held firms, in Chapter 5 we report substantially higher rates of survival among ESOP firms compared to closely matched non-ESOP firms. The findings also point to higher sales and employment growth following ESOP adoption, and a much greater incidence of other pension plans among ESOP firms compared to non-ESOP pairs, indicating that ESOPs tend to supplement rather than substitute for other benefits. The survival findings are of particular note because they point not only to greater job security for workers but also a possible public policy rationale for support of employee ownership, if employee ownership does reduce the likelihood of unemployment with its broad economic and social costs.

PART II: COMPARATIVE SYSTEMS OF OWNERSHIP AND PARTICIPATION

The second part contains four chapters examining forms of ownership and participation in different economic systems. In Chapter 6, Tom Malleson reviews the well-known Mondragon system, which is the largest system of worker cooperatives in the world. He concludes that Mondragon's success shows that workplace democracy is clearly feasible and may be generalizable to other settings, and discusses the thorny issue of degeneration, making the point that the evolution of worker cooperatives may be dependent on the structure of the markets in which they operate. In Chapter 7 Tatiana Kachalina (Ershova) assesses the state of employee ownership in Russia, which has been in flux since a strong push to give ownership of companies to their employees following the breakup of the Soviet Union (Blasi, Kroumova, & Kruse, 1996). She describes the failure of the initial effort to establish broad-based employee ownership, and the subsequent effort to establish "people's enterprises" using what she calls a "Russian model of the ESOP." While there is only a small number of these enterprises now, Kachalina sees great potential for their expansion, and discusses the legal reforms that would further encourage their growth.

Employee ownership and profit sharing in Europe have been the focus of a substantial amount of research in the past two decades. In Chapter 8, Iraj Hashi and Alban Hashani use the latest employer and employee survey data from the European Union to analyze trends in employee ownership and profit sharing along with the company and individual characteristics that predict their use. Growing percentages of employees report being covered by employee ownership or profit sharing since 2000. These pay systems are more common in large firms, consistent with prior data and with Mellizo's finding that the $1/N$ problem is not a significant deterrent to cooperation. They are also linked to employee representation, training, and teamwork, consistent with the idea that these policies are complementary to financial participation.

Chapter 9 by Sudha Kornginnaya examines the value of decision-making participation for small farmers in India, under a promising program that organizes farmers into groups of 4 or 5 who meet regularly, support each other through shared labor, receive training and technical support, and are eligible for financial support. Over 700,000 groups have been established since 1995. Using both interviews and surveys, Kornginnaya examines the growth of this program and the factors influencing farmers to participate, and concludes that there is great potential value in expanding the program throughout India.

PART III: THEORY AND POLICY

The volume concludes with six chapters examining employee ownership from theoretical perspectives. A wide variety of workplace practices are often described as "democratic," and Mark J. Kaswan in Chapter 10 uses political theory to evaluate practices according to democratic norms. He distinguishes between "weak" democracy, where employees may have little input beyond a formal right to vote their shares, and "strong" democracy where workers have substantial control and direct input into decision-making. He finds that employee ownership is neither a necessary nor sufficient condition for a strongly democratic workplace, and that it is possible for conventionally owned firms to be more democratic than worker cooperatives. Kaswan also considers the powerful argument by Carole Pateman (1970) and other theorists that workplace democracy can have positive spillover effects on democracy outside the workplace by stimulating increased skills and interest in political participation. While some evidence supports this link, the empirical relationship is not a simple one (Schur 2003). Kaswan notes while some forms of strong democracy may be more effective in incubating civic skills, weakly democratic practices may have larger effects by being easier to implement and more widespread. As with the topic of firm survival, there have been only a few studies in this area, and there is tremendous value in further studies given the potential for broader social and political benefits that can justify supportive public policy.

Anthony Jensen in Chapter 11 contributes new theory on the emergence and behavior of labor-managed firms, informed by evidence from case studies of six firms. These firms are in three different economic and legal systems – in the United States, Italy, and Spain – that help shed light on the role of government, markets, and trade unions in shaping the structures and success of labor-managed firms. Along with these three macro factors, Jensen identifies three important micro factors: organizational design, governance, and human resource management policies. He questions prior models that focus either on macro or micro factors in explaining the appearance and success of labor-managed firms, and highlights the tensions that can exist among these factors that significantly shape the evolution of the labor-managed firm.

There has been a lively theoretical debate over the structure and effects of labor-managed firms since the Benjamin Ward article in 1958. One of the key theorists in this area, David Ellerman, discusses three issues with worker cooperatives in Chapter 12. One of these is the "horizon problem" in which worker-owners who plan to leave or retire may favor investments only if they have a short-term payoff, but Ellerman describes how this is solved by a system of internal capital accounts (as in Mondragon) that reflect the value of long-term investments. A second issue is active learning, which Ellerman argues will be more effective in democratic firms where workers have greater autonomy and rights. The third issue concerns entrepreneurship, which touches on the issue of starting cooperatives as new businesses as discussed by Olsen. Contrary to some critics who have said cooperatives are incompatible with entrepreneurship, Ellerman uses the example of Mondragon to make the case the cooperatives may in fact encourage entrepreneurship, since conventional forms of ownership may limit entrepreneurship due to a desire to maintain control of the firm's "offspring."

Employee ownership has been viewed using a variety of perspectives that are often based on political metaphors. Christopher Mackin in Chapter 13 examines common metaphors that view the firm as a family, bureaucracy, contested terrain, or democratic social institution, discussing how these shape one's understanding of the value of workplace democracy and the potential for its expansion. He notes that the growth of the employee ownership sector in the United States complicates the traditional view of workers as "guests" rather than partners in the firm, and such growth raises the issue of extending self-government rights for workers and managers from the political sphere to the economic sphere.

Charles Heckscher in Chapter 14 poses several provocative questions about employee ownership in the 21st century economy. He makes the case that the traditional firm with well-defined boundaries and ownership is becoming increasingly rare, being replaced by flexible cross-boundary collaborations that complicate issues of ownership rights. Heckscher reviews the growth of "value chains," nontraditional contingent work, and external stakeholder claims on firms that all complicate the issue of who may be entitled to ownership claims and what types of rights those ownership claims entail. He argues that new definitions of property rights are emerging that pose a challenge to advocates of employee ownership, who will need to think hard and strategize about the types of claims workers will be able to make for ownership and participation in workplace decisions.

Finally, in Chapter 15 we have a short research note by one of the founders of the field, Jaroslav Vanek. He has made enormous contributions to the field of participatory and labor-managed firms, particularly with his book *The General Theory of the Labor-managed Economy* (Vanek, 1970). In this research note he makes the case that free international trade – which is held to improve economic output and welfare under standard economic models – can lead to suboptimal outcomes and unemployment under conditions in today's international economy. Vanek argues that the negative effects of "destructive trade" can be counteracted by the establishment of worker cooperatives, which will not destroy jobs at home by moving to other countries. As an example he points to the Mondragon cooperatives which help create new jobs around the world without decreasing domestic jobs, and makes the case that economic stimulus funds would be better directed to creating support structures such as exist for the Mondragon cooperatives rather than spent on standard Keynesian stimulus of the economy.

Taken together, the chapters in this volume provide cutting-edge research and thinking on issues of financial and decision-making participation. It is noteworthy that we have empirical and theoretical contributions from young emerging scholars as well as established scholars, showing great promise for the future of the field. The development of new scholars – including several who authored chapters in this volume – has been encouraged over the past 4 years by a fellowship program coordinated through the School of Management and Labor Relations at Rutgers University, with over 80 fellows from around the globe who study broad-based employee ownership and profit sharing. The program receives valuable support from Dr. J. Robert Beyster and Mary Ann Beyster of the Foundation for Enterprise Development; the Employee Ownership Foundation; the Beyster Endowment at SMLR; and a number of other donors.[2]

Future scholarship in this area will not only have high intellectual benefits, but will help to inform corporate, labor, and public policy-making (see Blasi, Freeman, & Kruse, 2013 for a review of policy history and options). The continued growth of employee participation in ownership, profit sharing, and decision-making makes it likely that these will become even more important parts of the economic landscape in the 21st century, and they will be major factors in the ongoing evolution and policy regarding the employment relationship, corporate governance, and the economic and social health of societies around the globe.

Douglas Kruse
Volume Editor

NOTES

1. The closely related occupation of personal care aides is the fastest-growing occupation in percentage terms, and the fourth-fastest growing occupation in numerical terms.

2. The other donors include Adam Blumenthal, Lynn Feasley, Accurate Equity, Blue Wolf Capital Management, Joseph and Bonnie Cabral, Ray Carey of the Carey Center for Democratic Capitalism, Fidelity Investments, Dr. Caroline Huber, Linda Borden McKean and the Shrewsbury Foundation, Bill and Connie Nobles, the Rosen Ownership Opportunity Fund of the National Center for Employee Ownership, and Robert W. Smiley, Jr. The Fellowship Program can be viewed at http://smlr.rutgers.edu/beyster-fellows.

REFERENCES

Blasi, J., Freeman, R., & Kruse., D. (2013). *The citizen's share: Putting ownership back into democracy*. New Haven, CT: Yale University Press.

Blasi, J., Kroumova, M., & Kruse, D. (1996). *Kremlin capitalism: The privatization of the Russian economy*. Ithaca, NY: Cornell University Press.

Lockard, C. B., & Wolf, M. (2012). Occupational employment projections to 2020. *Monthly Labor Review*, *135*(January), 84–108.

Pateman, C. (1970). *Participation and democratic theory*. Cambridge, UK: Cambridge University Press.

Schur, L. (2003). Do jobs create active citizens? Employment and political participation. *British Journal of Industrial Relations*, *41*(4), 751–771.

Schur, L., Kruse, D., & Blanck, P. (2013). *People with disabilities: Sidelined or mainstreamed?* Cambridge, UK: Cambridge University Press.

Vanek, J. (1970). *The general theory of labor-managed market economies*. Ithaca, NY: Cornell University Press.

World Health Organization. (2011). *World Report on Disability*. Geneva, Switzerland: World Health Organization.

PART I
EMPIRICAL EFFECTS AND CORRELATES OF OWNERSHIP AND PARTICIPATION

CHAPTER 1

EFFECTS OF COOPERATIVE MEMBERSHIP AND PARTICIPATION IN DECISION MAKING ON JOB SATISFACTION OF HOME HEALTH AIDES

Daphne P. Berry

ABSTRACT

Purpose – *This paper examines job satisfaction and participation in decision making in three home health aide facilities with different organizational structures (worker-owned for-profit, for-profit with no participation or ownership by workers, and nonprofit).*

Design/methodology/approach – *More than 600 surveys were completed by home health aides across the three facilities. The author also engaged in participant observation during training sessions and other meetings and conducted a small number of interviews with caregivers and agency management.*

Findings – *Home health aides at the worker-owned, participative decision making organization were significantly more satisfied with their jobs*

Sharing Ownership, Profits, and Decision-making in the 21st Century
Advances in the Economic Analysis of Participatory & Labor-Managed Firms, Volume 14, 3–25

ISSN: 0885-3339/doi:10.1108/S0885-3339(2013)0000014002

than those at the other agencies. Results for the other agencies were not significantly distinguishable from one another.

Research limitations/implications – *This study involved respondents from one of each type of business. A study across several of each type of organization would allow more focus on the effects of the structural characteristics of the organizations.*

Practical implications – *In the United States, the work that home health aides perform provides a valuable service to society. On behalf of caregivers and those for whom they provide care, conditions of the work need improvement. If participative democratic workplaces provide better outcomes, they should receive more attention from lawmakers, the business community, and researchers.*

Social implications – *This research highlights the working conditions of the people (primarily women) who perform this work. The poor compensation received is a reminder of inequality in opportunity for some workers and of the value placed on this type of caring labor.*

Originality/value – *This research is unique in its focus on work environment and outcomes in home health care across nonprofit, for-profit, and worker-owned for-profit organizations. The findings of different job satisfaction outcomes from the others in the worker-owned organization and similar outcomes in the nonprofit and conventional for-profit organizations are also unique.*

Keywords: Job satisfaction; home health aide; participative decision making; worker-owned; worker cooperative

JEL classifications: M54; L23

INTRODUCTION

Reports on the consequences that an aging population has on a nation's resources have focused attention on the needs for new models of care for the elderly as well as those with disabilities in United States and other nations (BLS, 2012; Folbre & Nelson, 2000; Kinsella & He, 2009; Summer, Friedland, Mack, & Mathieu, 2004). Changing views of care are encouraging more home and community-based environments as alternatives to institutional care. Meanwhile, over the next few decades, the number of elders in the United States will increase by more than 100%, while the pool of women from which direct care workers[1] are usually drawn will increase by less than 10% (PHI National, 2012).[2] Therefore, in accordance with an aging population and an increased desire by elders and those with physical disabilities to remain at home, the need for home health aides – a subset of the "direct care" workforce – has also greatly increased. The (mostly) women who perform this work should be caring, well trained, in good health, and adept at managing personal relationships with both those they care for and the families of those they care for. In addition, a satisfied and committed workforce is important if the growth in the need for home care is to be met. However, the work environment in which most home health aides must perform their caring work is not conducive to the establishment and maintenance of a satisfied and committed workforce. In the words of the U.S. Bureau of Labor Statistics (BLS) describing home health aide jobs,

> Some aides go to the same home every day or week for months or even years. Some visit four or five clients on the same day. Others work only with one client all day. This may involve working with other aides in shifts so the client always has an aide. They may help people in hospices and day services programs and may also help people with disabilities go to work and stay engaged in their communities ... Home health and personal care aides had a higher-than-average number of work-related injuries and illnesses in 2010. Work as an aide can be physically and emotionally demanding. Aides must guard against back injury because they may have to move clients into and out of bed or help them to stand or walk. In addition, aides may frequently work with clients who have cognitive impairments or mental health issues and who may display difficult or violent behaviors. Aides may also face hazards from minor infections and exposure to communicable diseases ... (BLS, 2012)

The BLS description of these jobs provides some insight into the difficulty of working as a home health aide while leaving open the question of why anyone might choose a career in this field. As to why businesses might choose home health care, although margins are relatively thin, owners in the home care industry have found it sufficiently lucrative. In most of the United States, for-profit privately owned businesses (70%) far outnumber nonprofit (21%) or government-owned (9%) agencies (CMS, 2009). In New York state, nonprofit agencies (56%) outnumber government agencies (24%) and privately owned for-profit agencies (20%). Other institutional conditions, linked to the close relationship between the federal government as payer and regulator, bring pressures upon organizations and workers in this industry. Much of the funding for home health aide agencies comes from federal, state, and local governments.

Turnover is high in the long-term care industry in general. A 2007 report by the Institute for Aging Services (IFAS) included data from assisted living facilities, nursing homes, and home care agencies across states. Turnover rates ranged from 40% to well over 100% (over the 2002–2005 period) depending on the venue. This report and many others identify low wages, lack of benefits, lack of career mobility, and other poor working conditions among the reasons for the turnover (Banijamali, Hagopian, & Jacoby, 2012; IFAS, 2007; Karsh, Booske, & Sanfort, 2005; PHI National, 2013). Among factors contributing to poor working conditions are those also associated with low rates of job satisfaction and organizational commitment such as lack of inclusion in decision making about their work, lack of proper training, and poor relationships with supervisors. Castle, Engberg, Anderson, and Men (2007) are among those who call for an examination of the features or processes of the direct care facility (e.g., ownership, staffing mix) when studying antecedents to turnover.

Kruse, Freeman, and Blasi's (2010) shared capitalism research links certain compensation practices based on collective performance – including profit sharing and various forms of employee stock ownership – and participation in decision making at work to positive productivity outcomes, on average, in an organization. They find that the positive outcomes might be conditioned by "human resource policies, the quality of employee relationships, the nature of supervision, and how the job is constructed" (p. 29). In the home health aide industry, the few firms operating under a worker cooperative structure report several of the positive outcomes found by Kruse et al. (2010) for other employee-owned firms where high performance work systems are in place. Turnover for direct care workers in the home care industry is reported to be lower in worker cooperative agencies (Barbarotta, 2010; Lund, 2012). Cooperative Home Care Associates (CHCA), a home care agency in New York City, focuses on quality jobs for home care aides in support of quality care for clients. As a worker cooperative, they foster participation in decision making about how the business is run by those who perform the face-to-face work with clients – the home health aides. They also report consistently lower turnover than industry averages. Is there something about the worker cooperative organization form that results in an outcome of lower turnover? Is this effect repeatable despite the work environment and other realities of the job? Can home health aides experience job satisfaction despite their current exploitation in a system that needs them badly but compensates them so poorly?

In this study, I examine home health aide job satisfaction using data from caregivers from three organizations under different governance: a worker cooperative, a "conventional" for-profit home care organization (with no participation in decision making or ownership by caregivers), and a nonprofit home care organization. With surveys, participant observation, and interviews of workers and managers in these organizations, I examine home health aide responses to questions about their jobs and work environments. I begin by reviewing the role of the U.S. government as regulator and payer in the home care industry. Next, I describe the results of research on participation in decision making, job satisfaction, and turnover. And last, I empirically investigate the relationship between organization type and home health aide job satisfaction, and conclude with a discussion of the results.

FEDERAL GOVERNMENT ROLES

The federal government plays a key role in the home care industry as a payer and a regulator; its omnipresence determines much of the external environment of home health aide agencies in the United States. Local and state governments also play a role in regulating the agencies. Government presence is felt not only in the economic and regulatory realms but also in the social aspects related to how these jobs are perceived and valued by society at large (Boris & Klein, 2012).

In their study of the interface between changes in the aged population and in home health agencies' organization type, Swan and Estes (1990) address isomorphic processes in the industry. They note an increase in privately owned (for-profit) and system-affiliated agencies (chains) in the United States and attribute the increase to changes in Medicare policy (that allowed large numbers of for-profit providers to enter the market eligible for Medicare reimbursement), deregulation, competition, and cost containment efforts. Amidst new dominance of the for-profit organizations with their focus on efficiency, competition, and uncertainty reduction, legitimacy questions for once-dominant nonprofit organizations have been the impetus for them to organize and behave more like for-profits. Government requirements also drive agency processes and human resource-important factors. While funding mechanisms for Medicare and Medicaid differ, together they are the primary funders of home health care services in the United States (Cohen & Tumlinson, 1997). Those agencies receiving funds must comply with government requirements in areas such as agency job-type staffing ratios and reporting mechanisms in areas ranging from client care to caregiver time sheets. There are government-mandated minimum training requirements for home health aides for initial and maintenance certification. Collopy, Dubler, Zuckerman, Crigger, and Campbell (1990) point out, in addition, structural arrangements of home care that include complex referral and sub-contracting processes, made more complex by federal, state, and agency monitoring requirements, and limited, fragmented funding. Given the environment, Collopy et al. note that while home care may be considered an option for deinstitutionalizing those who need certain types of care, "the direct relation between caregiver and client is surrounded by an institutional thicket of inter-agency agreements" and at the provider level is "anything but deinstitutionalized" (p. 5).

Because the need for home health care has only recently become a national priority, much of the research in the direct care industry has focused on patient care in nursing homes. Nursing home aides share similarities in demographics and work environment with home care aides; however, key differences between the two exist. First, nursing home aides are protected by United States Federal Labor Standards Act (FLSA) wage and overtime laws. As of early 2013, the FLSA, which currently covers more than 130 million United States workers and is designed to prevent abuses by employers, still contains exclusions (DOL, 2008) that affect large segments of the low wage work population. Home health aides are among those who are specifically excluded from FLSA coverage, a holdover from the time when they were classified as babysitters (Boris & Honey, 1988; Seavey, 2007). Therefore, the difficult conditions of the work, as determined by the work itself, are exacerbated for this group of caregivers by even fewer protections and lower pay than available to others doing similar work in this industry. Another difference in the work environment of those who work in nursing homes and home care aides is that the latter work is (usually) done alone in a client's home rather than with other aides in a care facility. Home health aides therefore lack frequent contact with colleagues while at work. This can enhance feelings of isolation and make the job more difficult (Collopy et al., 1990). Government-mandated training sessions are the event at which many home health aides regularly see others performing the same work for their agencies.

Turnover, Participative Decision Making, and Job Satisfaction in the Direct Care Industry

High turnover in the industry is costly to a home care agency in lost hiring and training costs, lost productivity, and loss of knowledge about the needs and preferences of those cared for (Bishop et al., 2008; Seavey, 2004).

Therefore, identifying and addressing the sources of home health aide turnover is important to home care agencies. In Banijamali et al.'s (2012) research on turnover in the state of Washington, home care workers who left the industry cited the need for better pay, hours, and career opportunities among their reasons for leaving. The lack of health benefits and physical pain were also included as difficulties of the job. In short, these workers listed as reasons for turnover the very factors included in the BLS description of home health aide work provided earlier. Karsh et al.'s (2005) study of nursing home employees found that job satisfaction, along with demographic and economic factors, were significant predictors of the intent to stay with the organization. The study also identified factors related to the practices and environment of the organization such as training, cooperation, and teamwork as significant predictors of intent to stay. Job satisfaction, along with various other factors, is consistently identified as an important factor in turnover in the larger direct care industry of which the home health industry is part. Kahana, Kiyak, and Namazi (1997) identified age, length of employment, and job satisfaction, in that order, as the best predictors of the intention of nursing assistants to leave an organization.

Research also links participation in an organization's decision making to job satisfaction. Among those who desire to participate in decision making, the perceived participation or lack of it is associated with job satisfaction (Driscoll, 1978). Black and Gregersen (1997) found that the type of decision making involved mattered as participation in various stages of problem solving and resolution generated different levels of satisfaction. Witt, Andrews, and Kacmar (2000) also found that participative decision making is related to job satisfaction and that the relationship is stronger when organizational politics (negatively experienced) are high. They speculate that participative decision making may yield more positive outcomes in adverse conditions. Similarly, Scott-Ladd, Travaglione, and Marshall (2006) found a positive relationship between participation in decision making and job satisfaction. Such research supports expectations of higher job satisfaction in a worker cooperative-type environment, even perhaps under adverse working conditions.

Is the Organization Type also Important to Home Health Aide Job Satisfaction?

In research comparing the job satisfaction of employees in nonprofit and for-profit firms, Benz (2005) found that nonprofit workers were more satisfied with their jobs than were for-profit workers. The results could not be attributed to differences in pay or benefits, individual differences in workers at the firms, or concentration of firms in a particular industry. Benz's research pointed to benefits derived from the intrinsic motivation of the work performed in the nonprofit organizations. In their investigation of worker motivation, loyalty, and job satisfaction, Borzaga and Tortia (2006) also found that intrinsic motivations were important for increasing worker satisfaction. They attribute the differences found in various organizational forms (for-profit, public, various types of nonprofit, etc.) to the ability to satisfy workers in various ways related not only to wages, but also to internal labor relations and process aspects of their jobs. Mirvis and Hackett (1983), too, attribute their findings of higher job satisfaction in the nonprofit sector than in the for-profit sector directly to greater intrinsic rewards, decision making, and autonomy in nonprofit organizations.

In the current study, I expect differences in the nature of participation and associated processes and practices between the three types of organizations to have an impact on job satisfaction (and, possibly by extension, turnover). The worker cooperative for-profit (WCO) home care business strongly encourages worker ownership (although it is not mandatory) and actively seeks to ensure employee participation in organizational decision making. After a three-month waiting period, new home care workers are eligible to purchase a single share in the cooperative and only those who work at the agency may be owners. Not all owners are home care aides; some are administrative staff. Ownership by home care workers ranges from approximately 75–90% and each owner has one vote in the organization's affairs. Home health aides hold 8 of 14 seats on the organization's board of directors and therefore, participate in strategic planning and decision making about how surplus revenues are to be allocated. At the conventional for-profit (CFP) and the nonprofit organization (NPO), while employee input is sought through surveys or "suggestion box" input, frontline home care employees are not active participants in any way in governing the organizations, nor are they owners.

Proposition. Those home health aides from the worker cooperative organization (who have an ownership stake in the business and who are more involved in organizational decision making) will indicate greater job satisfaction than workers affiliated with the conventional for-profit organization or with the nonprofit organization.

METHODS AND DATA

The purpose of this exploratory research is to examine whether and how the structure of the organization matters to the job satisfaction of the home health aides. To examine differences in the three types of organizations, I began by conducting interviews with home health aides and agency staff, and engaging in participant observation at the agencies. I then followed up with a survey. The survey instrument was based on one used by Kruse et al. (2010) in their employee ownership and productivity-related shared capitalism research project. For the current project, the survey language was changed to better apply to the home care industry, and the survey was shortened and translated into Spanish because a large proportion of the workforce are native speakers of Spanish. It included over 50 Likert-scale items related to the degree of participation that home health aides have in making decisions about their work, how they feel about their companies and their jobs, and their level of participation in decisions about their work. It also contained questions on demographics, one open-ended structured question, and one unstructured question soliciting elaboration about topics from the survey on which the caregivers wanted to elaborate. Bilingual home health aides and administrators assisted in the validation of the survey.

Demographic data were collected on

1. caregiver age ranges (18–24, 25–30, 31–39, 40–49, 50–59, 60–69, 70 +);
2. years with the company (less than 2, 2-4, 5-10, more than 10);
3. sex (female or male); and
4. race, ethnicity, and native language.[3]

Age ranges and years at the company were used as control variables in the data analyses. Nearly all of the participants were female. Since different race and ethnicity data were collected, I did not perform cross-organizational analysis of race and ethnicity of the caregivers.

Job Satisfaction

I used a job satisfaction construct to evaluate home health aides' feelings toward their workplaces. As with other organizational phenomena, effects and causes are often reciprocal. A number of studies of the direct care industry (some focused on nursing homes) identify various factors that are important (Friedman, Daub, Cresci, & Keyser, 1999; Parsons, Simmons, Penn, & Furlough, 2003). Items related to pay (e.g., "I am paid fairly for what I do here" and "pay and benefits are important to my ability to do my job")[4] were distinct from other job satisfaction-related items so are not included. The job satisfaction dependent variable is constructed from five items from the survey identified using confirmatory factor analysis. The coefficient alpha statistic for this construct is 0.77. The survey items are:

1. I like the type of work that I do,
2. I am satisfied with my job,
3. I see my current job as part of a long-term career,
4. In the past year, my supervisor gave me helpful opinions about my work, and
5. Promotions are handled fairly here.

Participation in Decision Making

I began with 10 survey items related to the home health aides' participation in decision making at their firms; confirmatory factor analysis yielded two components. The 10 items were:

1. Home health aides are expected to make decisions and solve problems here,
2. I feel my ideas count on the job,
3. Someone asks for my advice on how to deal with problems or issues at work often,
4. My company's culture encourages me to share ideas about improving the company,
5. I get the information I need to do my job,
6. We are kept informed of important issues,
7. I am told about changes that affect my work,
8. I am involved in setting goals or planning with my care team,
9. I have the flexibility to provide specific services in the order that would best support my client, and
10. I am satisfied with the influence I have in decisions that affect my work.

The first seven items constituted one variable that is related to home health aide perceptions of their knowledge about decisions made in the organization that affect their work and their feelings about whether they are included and valued in the decision making processes. The coefficient alpha statistic for this variable is 0.80. The latter three items comprise the second variable reflecting home health aide perceptions that they actually have a say in the day-to-day performance of their jobs and their satisfaction with this level of influence. The coefficient alpha statistic for this variable is 0.71. These two variables are referred to in this study as the two dimensions of participation – informed participation and influence participation.

RESULTS

Agency Priorities

All three organizations claim a focus on quality care for clients and emphasize the training and skills of their home care workers. The CFP emphasizes a cooperative effort between the agency and the client that seeks client autonomy and recognizes a client's desire to manage his or her own care to the best of the client's ability. Therefore, clients are included in decisions made about their treatment. This organization also draws attention to the rights of clients that include concerned, personalized, skilled care and services provided with dignity, respect, and confidentiality. The NPO's mission statement is directed toward clients and stresses services enabling clients to remain in their homes with skilled care and whatever level of support the client needs. Like the CFP, the NPO stresses that the client, along with his or her family and medical professionals, has input into the plan of care. Although not emphasized to the general public in their marketing materials, at least some of the administrators at both the CFP and the NPO care about the working conditions of the home health aides. At the WCO, the mission and goals include quality care for clients *and* quality jobs for caregivers. They emphasize providing the highest possible salaries and benefits, providing workers opportunities to learn and grow as members of a health care team, and providing reliable, high-quality home health care services to clients. In addition, the WCO worked actively to ensure that everyone had access to at least a 30-hour work week to protect their access to certain benefits.

Caregiver Thoughts about Their Jobs, Participation in Decision making, and Pay

From interviews, open-ended survey responses, and participant observation, themes of needing better pay or benefits (such as paid sick days) and the difficulty of the work were echoed among the home health aides across all three agencies. Common comments at the for-profit, nonprofit, and worker cooperative firms were: “Taking care of patients is a hard job. I believe we should make $10 an hour for the work we have to do in patients’ homes. We aides go through a lot with these patients,” “We need a salary increase,” “Please, we need a good salary increase,” “They need to raise the pay,” “I’ve worked here 3 years and haven’t received any more pay,” “This (work) pays very little,” and “We are underpaid and no one seems to care about us home health aides …”. A similar but important comment on the relationship between caregivers and their first line supervisors was that home health aides needed “a pay increase and coordinators who listen to home health aides.” Getting enough hours without too much travel (with associated uncompensated time and travel costs) was mentioned by caregivers at all three agencies. They sometimes mentioned remaining in a bad environment to prevent a reduction in income. To a question of whether they are paid fairly, responses from the WCO were significantly more positive than at the other two organizations even though the pay ranges provided by their agencies were not much different.

I was not able to collect individual pay data in this study, but ranges for home health aide jobs were provided by the agencies. While the ranges overlap, the top of the NPO range was slightly higher, with the WCO and the CFP respectively being slightly lower. Home health aides were unionized at all three of the agencies and they had similar medical and other benefits. However, these benefits were limited and caregivers were encouraged to take advantage of government and union-sponsored services. In addition, at the WCO, the union was an active participant in some workgroup meetings and agency efforts to improve home care aides’ jobs, and their access to education and health care.

Relationships between caregivers and coordinators were contentious at both the nonprofit and the conventional for-profit organizations. In part at least, the daily process of negotiating access and leaving a client’s home with all the associated rules can be a feat in itself. There are requirements and rules concerning exact timekeeping, when work can start or end, and what to do if no one answers when the aide has arrived to work or someone answers and sends the aide away. The interactions that occur often involve the caregiver and a coordinator who is remotely advising an aide on a problem situation at a client’s home. The relationships are often fraught with misunderstanding.

In contrast, such was not usually the case at the worker cooperative. Coordinators were sometimes promoted from positions as caregivers and ongoing teamwork helped to foster a collaborative work environment in which each could understand the job of the other. An example of the different approach to problem solving in the area of caregiver – coordinator relations came up during the implementation of an electronic caregiver monitoring system. Two of the three organizations were having substantial problems with operational kinks in the system and getting the caregivers to learn to use the monitoring devices despite recurring problems. At a minimum, the aides reported malfunctions, difficulty with use, and too many rigid requirements for check in and out. At the worker cooperative, part of a work group meeting that I attended was allocated to discuss why and how to resolve problems with the phone's use and how to encourage caregivers to use the system. An administrator involved in processing and reporting data for paychecks and for contract providers fielded questions and complaints about the system. He tried to convey the value to all involved of proper use of the monitoring system. The effort was directed toward gaining agreement by home health aides to use the system and to disseminate information to others about it. By contrast, at the nonprofit organization, an administrator attended training classes to discuss the necessity of overcoming difficulties with the system so that aides would be paid. "It's ridiculous to not use the system … If you're having problems, you should be calling your coordinators. It's your responsibility and if you don't do it, if you miss the deadlines, you lose." This example is representative of the difference between the atmosphere at the WCO and that at the NPO and the CFP; at the worker cooperative, there was a feeling of being in good company relative to others in the industry who worked for other agencies. Among other quotes from the cooperative were: "The cooperative is a great place to work," "I feel satisfied here. It feels like family," "The cooperative feels like family," "I am pleased with how this company works," "Well, I love working for CHCA … Yes, the pay isn't great but I love my job and caring for people in general … the cooperative changed my life for the better and I'm very appreciative …," and "I am thankful for the concern that is shown for each one of us."

These comments are consistent with results from the survey data, to which we now turn.

Job Satisfaction Based on Organization Type and Participation

Table 1 presents mean scores by organization type for the variables used in the regression analyses. With the exception of the control variables (years

Table 1. Variable Means.

	Conventional For-Profit			Nonprofit			Worker Cooperative		
	n	Mean	Std. dev.	*n*	Mean	Std. dev.	*n*	Mean	Std. dev.
Years at company[a]	163	2.45	1.078	196	2.62	1.034	249	2.27	1.007
Age range[b]	156	3.86	1.257	191	4.30	1.248	248	4.1	1.256
Informed[c]	165	2.87	1.063	194	3.00	1.095	248	4.54	.856
Influence[c]	164	3.22	1.057	194	3.92	.922	236	4.59	.778
Job satisfaction	166	3.11	1.129	195	3.38	1.054	252	4.49	.853

[a]1: less than 2; 2: 2–4; 3: 5–10; 4: more than 10.

[b]1: 18–24; 2: 25–30; 3: 31–39; 4: 40–49; 5: 50–59; 6: 60–69; 7: 70 +.

[c]The participation and job satisfaction variables are the result of an SPSS principal components analysis factor score process. The values shown here are reverse calculated from *z* scores produced as a result of the factor analysis.

at company and age range), the variable means become progressively more positive from the CFP to the NPO to the WCO. Job tenure is highest at the NPO and lowest at the WCO but is not a significant factor in the results of the regression analyses presented later in this section. (One reason for lower tenure at the WCO may be the growth that the agency has experienced.) The average age is highest at the NPO and lowest at the CFP. In most cases, age range is a significant factor in the regression analyses. The averages for the informed, influence, and job satisfaction variables are all significantly higher at the WCO than at the CFP or NPO.

Table 2 contains descriptive statistics and correlations for variables used in the regression analyses.

The following are regression analyses based on the proposition that job satisfaction is higher at the worker cooperative organization. The analyses are based on self-reported data from caregivers. The proposition was that workers at the worker cooperative would indicate higher levels of job satisfaction than workers at the other agencies. Results from two sets of regressions (dependent and independent variable combinations) are shown. The first examines the effect of the organization type on the two dimensions of the participation variable. Next job satisfaction is regressed on the organization type alone, and then on the organization type and the two dimensions of participation.

I use a hierarchical technique, beginning with control variables and adding predictors successively. In the first regressions (Tables 3a and 3b), Model 1 includes the control variables, age, and years at company.

Table 2. Variable Descriptive Statistics and Correlations.

	Mean	Std. dev.	1	2	3	4
Years at company[a]	2.43	1.04	1			
Age range[b]	4.12	1.26	.345**	1		
Informed[c]	3.66	1.06	.056	.066	1	
Influence[c]	4.04	.94	.006	.091*	.458**	1
Job satisfaction	3.81	1.04	.016	.146**	.629**	.494**

[a]1: less than 2; 2: 2–4; 3: 5–10; 4: more than 10.
[b]1: 18–24; 2: 25–30; 3: 31–39; 4: 40–49; 5: 50–59; 6: 60–69; 7: 70+.
[c]The participation and job satisfaction variables are the result of an SPSS principal components analysis factor score process. The values shown here are reverse calculated from z scores produced as a result of the factor analysis.
**Correlation is significant at the 0.01 level (2 tailed).
*Correlation is significant at the 0.05 level (2 tailed).

Model 2 includes the control variables and dummy variables representing the conventional for-profit and nonprofit organizations. A significant dummy variable regression coefficient for an organization type indicates that the level of the dependent variable for this organization type differs significantly from the level for the reference category. The worker cooperative organization is the reference category; therefore, regression coefficients for the nonprofit and conventional for-profit variables are in relation to the worker cooperative. Not shown is a third regression in which the nonprofit organization is the reference category. This provides the missing comparison between the nonprofit and the conventional for-profit organizations.

Informed Participation and Influence Participation by Organization Type
Model 2 in Tables 3a and 3b shows that when the participation variables are regressed on organization type, the organization type variables contribute significantly (approximately 21% and 11%, respectively) to variance in the models. The dummy variable coefficients indicate that CFP and NPO variables are negative in relation to the WCO.

Job Satisfaction by Organization Type
In Table 4a, Model 2 shows that when job satisfaction is regressed on organization type, the organization type variables contribute significantly (approximately 13%) to variance in the models. The dummy variable coefficients indicate that CFP and NPO variables are negative in relation to the WCO.

Table 3a. Regression Model: Informed Participation on Organization Type.

	Model 1	Model 2
Predictors		
Constant	–.096 (.154)	.417 (.145)**
Control variables		
Years at company	–.063 (.045)	–.012 (.040)
Age range	.066 (.036)	.042 (.032)
Independent variables		
CFP		–.951 (.096)***
NPO		–.914 (.091)***
WCO		–
R^2	.008	.221
ΔR^2	.008	.214
ΔF statistic	2.027	70.758***
n	520	520

Standard errors in parentheses. CFP, conventional for-profit; NPO, nonprofit; WCO, worker cooperative.
*$p \leq .05$; **$p \leq .01$; ***$p \leq .001$.

Table 3b. Regression Model: Influence Participation on Organization Type.

	Model 1	Model 2
Predictors		
Constant	–.225 (.150)	.160 (.150)
Control variables		
Years at company	–.022 (.043)	.007 (.041)
Age range	.074 (.035)*	.050 (.033)
Independent variables		
CFP		–.769 (.100)***
NPO		–.468 (.093)***
WCO		–
R^2	.009	.115
ΔR^2	.009	.107
n	534	534
ΔF statistic	2.300	31.916***

Standard errors in parentheses. CFP, conventional for-profit; NPO, nonprofit; WCO, worker cooperative.
*$p \leq .05$; **$p \leq .01$; ***$p \leq .001$.

Table 4a. Regression Model: Job Satisfaction on Organization Type.

	Model 1	Model 2
Predictors		
Constant	−.448 (.153)**	−.063 (.151)
Control variables		
Years at company	−.010 (.045)	.029 (.042)
Age Range	.119 (.036)***	.104 (.034)**
Independent variables		
CFP		−.750 (.100)***
NPO		−.683 (.095)***
WCO		–
R^2	.022	.147
ΔR^2	.022	.125
ΔF statistic	5.970**	38.225***
n	528	528

Standard errors in parentheses. CFP, conventional for-profit; NPO, nonprofit; WCO, worker cooperative.
*$p \leq .05$; **$p \leq .01$; ***$p \leq .001$.

Job Satisfaction by Organization Type and Informed Participation

Model 2 in Table 4b shows that when job satisfaction is regressed on organization type and the information participation variable, the organization type and the participation variables contribute significantly (approximately 38%) to variance in the models. The dummy variable coefficients indicate that both NPO and CFP variables are negative in relation to the WCO, although the CFP coefficient is not strong enough to be significant at the 95% level after controlling for this participation variable.

Job Satisfaction by Organization Type and Influence Participation

In the last regression, Model 2 shows that when job satisfaction is regressed on organization type and the influence participation variable, the organization type and participation variables contribute significantly (approximately 26%) to variance in the models. As before, the dummy variable coefficients indicate that CFP and NPO variables are negative in relation to the WCO.

Not shown in Tables 4a, 4b, and 4c are the results of the regression in which the nonprofit organization is the reference category for organization type. These tests indicate that job satisfaction is not significantly different in the CFP relative to the NPO. Also not shown in Table 4b and 4c are results for a model including the interaction terms created from each dimension of

Table 4b. Regression Model: Job Satisfaction on Organization Type and Informed Participation.

	Model 1	Model 2
Predictors		
Constant	−.491 (.159)**	−.325 (.133)*
Control variables		
Years at company	−.006 (.047)	.043 (.037)
Age range	.123 (.037)***	.078 (.030)**
Independent variables		
CFP		−.186 (.097)
NPO		−.197 (.092)*
WCO		–
Informed[a]		.575 (.041)***
R^2	.025	.400
ΔR^2	.025	.376
ΔF statistic	6.118**	100.458***
n	486	486

Standard errors in parentheses. CFP, conventional for-profit; NPO, nonprofit; WCO, worker cooperative.
[a]Informed participation variable.
$*p \leq .05$; $**p \leq .01$; $***p \leq .001$.

participation and the two dummy variables for organization type. The interaction terms also did not contribute to variance in any of the models.

DISCUSSION AND CONCLUSION

In previous research, when findings that job satisfaction-related attitudes differed in organizations with different structural characteristics, the differences were often attributed to different human resource, motivation, or high performance work-related processes and practices within the organizations (Benz, 2005; Borzaga & Tortia, 2006; Friedman et al., 1999; Mirvis & Hackett, 1983). The external environment in the home care industry, including the federal government payer, constrains and directs many internal processes within the three organizations – at a minimum, those related to monitoring, reporting, training, and wages for caregivers. However, the findings of the current study indicate that caregivers who work at the worker cooperative provided notably different responses to most of the

Table 4c. Regression Model: Job Satisfaction on Organization Type and Influence Participation.

	Model 1	Model 2
Predictors		
Constant	−.437(.158)**	−.128 (.143)
Control variables		
Years at company	−.007(.046)	.019 (.040)
Age Range	.111(.037)**	.083 (.032)*
Independent variables		
CFP		−.410 (.101)***
NPO		−480 (.093)***
WCO		–
Influence[a]		.403 (.042)***
R^2	.020	.282
ΔR^2	.020	.262
ΔF statistic	4.985**	59.803***
n	496	496

Standard errors in parentheses. CFP, conventional for-profit; NPO, nonprofit; WCO, worker cooperative.
[a]Influence participation variable.
*$p \leq .05$; **$p \leq .01$; ***$p \leq .001$.

survey items and all of those related to their satisfaction with their jobs relative to those caregivers affiliated with the other organizations. Job satisfaction is higher at the worker cooperative (Table 4a) as is participation (Tables 3a and 3b). Job satisfaction remains higher even when controlling for participation (Table 4a–4c). Therefore, there are other aspects of the work at the worker cooperative that contribute to this better outcome. While workers at all of the agencies in this study indicated that extremely low compensation is a meaningful problem for their overall well-being, I was not able to perform an in-depth pay satisfaction analysis and those survey items broadly related to pay were not linked to satisfaction. The results in this study may reflect that this work is "caring labor" for which neither the commonly understood economic theory of the person motivated entirely by self-interest (see Folbre & Nelson, 2000) nor study results from workers in other industries is a good fit. This does not affect the moral imperative to pay home health care workers fairly.

The findings of this research are limited by the omission of the government-owned organization type. In the United States, for-profit, nonprofit, and government-owned are the three most common types of home health care agency found with government type being the third largest. In New York where the data were collected, government-owned home health care agencies are the second largest type. Selection bias may be a factor in these findings in that the organizations that granted research access have generally positive reputations in the local home care community as organizations that care about not only quality of care to clients, but also the quality of working conditions for caregivers. To the extent that this bias exists, however, it should lead to smaller differences among the organization types, so the comparisons done here can be seen as conservative ones. The survey is also the primary source of data from the majority of home health aides. As with surveys, social desirability may affect some of the survey responses and there may be common method variance in the results. However, data gathered via participant observation and interviews are helpful in ameliorating this possibility. Finally, this study involved respondents from just three organizations (one of each type of business), and including more organizations would allow more focus on the effects of the structural characteristics of the organizations.

Findings related to the employee-owned organization in comparison to other ownership types provide new information on how ownership and participatory programs can be important, particularly in an environment with multiple structural and process constraints, and generally adverse working environments. A key contribution of this research is that it highlights positive outcomes from the worker cooperative organizational form in this industry in comparison to the nonprofit and conventional for-profit organizations. The growing shortage of home health aide workers, combined with the low wages and poor prospects in this occupation, do not bode well for an aging society. Besides being a growth industry, the direct care industry is a large employer of poor, historically disenfranchised women in the United States who will likely provide home health care services to many U.S. families. On behalf of caregivers and those for whom they provide care, the conditions of the work need improvement. If participative democratic workplaces (e.g., worker cooperatives) provide better outcomes, they should receive more attention from lawmakers, the business community, and researchers.

NOTES

1. A group that includes home health aides, nursing assistants, and personal assistants.

2. Paraprofessional Healthcare Institute (PHI) is a research, policy, and training organization that works toward improving the quality of eldercare and disability services by improving the jobs of direct care workers (http://phinational.org/).

3. One agency limited the race, ethnicity, and language data that I was able to collect.

4. Pay-related items from the survey did not factor with any of the organization outcomes examined nor with each other.

REFERENCES

Banijamali, S., Hagopian, A., & Jacoby, D. (2012). *Why they leave: Turnover among Washington's home care workers*. Retrieved from http://seiu775.org/files/2012/02/Why-They-Leave-Report1.pdf. Accessed on April 1, 2013.

Barbarotta, L. (2010). *Direct care worker retention: Strategies for success*. Institute for the Future of Again Services and the American Association of Homes and Services for the Aging. Retrieved from http://www.leadingage.org/uploadedFiles/Content/About/Center_for_Applied_Research/Publications_and_Products/Direct%20Care%20Workers%20Report%20%20FINAL%20%282%29.pdf. Accessed on June 3, 2013.

Benz, M. (2005). Not for the profit, but for the satisfaction? Evidence on worker well-being in nonprofit firms. *Kyklos*, *58*(2), 155–176.

Bishop, C., Weinberg, D., Leutz, W., Dossa, A., Pfefferle, S., & Zincavage, R. (2008). Nursing assistants' job commitment: Effect of nursing home organizational factors and impact on resident well-being. *The Gerontologist*, *48*(1), 36–45.

Black, J. S., & Gregersen, H. B. (1997). Participative decision-making: An integration of multiple dimensions. *Human Relations*, *50*(7), 859–878.

Boris, E., & Honey, M. (1988). Gender, race and the policies of the labor department. *Monthly Labor Review*, *111*(2), 26.

Boris, E., & Klein, J. (2012). *Caring for America: Home health workers in the shadow of the welfare state*. New York, NY: Oxford University Press.

Borzaga, C., & Tortia, E. (2006). Worker motivations, job satisfaction, and loyalty in public and nonprofit social services. *Nonprofit and Voluntary Sector Quarterly*, *35*(2), 225–248.

Bureau of Labor Statistics (BLS). (2012). *Home health personal care aides. Bureau of Labor Statistics Occupational Outlook Handbook, 2012–13 Edition*. Retrieved from http://www.bls.gov/ooh/Healthcare/Home-health-and-personal-care-aides.htm. Accessed on April 1, 2013.

Castle, N. G., Engberg, J., Anderson, R., & Men, A. (2007). Job satisfaction of nurse aides in nursing homes: Intent to leave and turnover. *Gerontologist*, *47*, 193–204.

Centers for Medicare and Medicaid Services (CMS). (2009). The official United States site for medicare, download database page, *Home Health Compare Data*, March 5, 2009. Retrieved from http://www.medicare.gov/Download/DownloadDB.asp. Accessed on April 20, 2011.

Cohen, M. A., & Tumlinson, A. (1997). Understanding the state variation in Medicare home health care: The impact of Medicaid program characteristics, state policy, and provider Attributes. *Medical Care*, *35*(6), 618–633.

Collopy, B., Dubler, N., Zuckerman, C., Crigger, B., & Campbell, C. S. (1990). Special supplement: The ethics of home care: Autonomy and accommodation. *The Hastings Center Report*, *20*(2), 1–16.

Department of Labor (DOL). (2008). *Fact Sheet #25: The home health care industry under the Fair Labor Standards Act (FLSA).* Retrieved from http://www.dol.gov/whd/regs/compliance/whdfs25.pdf. Accessed on March 18, 2010.

Driscoll, J. W. (1978). Trust and participation in organizational decision making as predictors of satisfaction. *Academy of Management Journal, 21*(1), 44–56.

Folbre, N., & Nelson, J. A. (2000). For love or money-or both? *Journal of Economic Perspectives, 14*(4), 123–140.

Friedman, S. M., Daub, C., Cresci, K., & Keyser, R. (1999). A comparison of job satisfaction among nursing assistants in nursing homes and the Program of All-Inclusive Care for the Elderly (PACE). *The Gerontologist, 39*(4), 434–439.

Institute for the Future of Aging Services (IFAS). (2007). The long-term care workforce: Can the crisis be fixed? Prepared for *National Commission for Quality Long-Term Care*. Retrieved from http://www.leadingage.org/uploadedFiles/Content/About/Center_for_Applied_Research/Center_for_Applied_Research_Initiatives/LTC_Workforce_Commission_Report.pdf. Accessed on April 1, 2013.

Kahana, E. F., Kiyak, H. A., & Namazi, K. H. (1997). Job commitment and turnover among women working in facilities serving older persons. *Research on Aging, 19*(2), 223–246.

Karsh, B., Booske, B., & Sanford, F. (2005). Job and organizational determinants of nursing home employee commitment, job satisfaction and intent to turnover. *Ergonomics, 48*(10), 1260–1281.

Kinsella, K., & He, W. (2009). *An aging world: 2008*. United States Census Bureau, International Population Reports, P95/09–1. Washington, DC: United States Government Printing Office.

Kruse, D. L., Freeman, R. B., & Blasi, J. R. (Eds.). (2010). *Shared capitalism at work: Employee ownership, profit and gain sharing, and broad-based stock options*. Chicago, IL: University of Chicago Press.

Lund, M. (2012). Opportunities and challenges for the expansion of worker-owned home care cooperatives serving rural Wisconsin: A report to the cooperative development foundation. *Co-opera Company*. Retrieved from http://www.cdf.coop/wp/wp-content/uploads/2013/03/Att-I-Opps-and-Challenges-Coop-Care-Expansion-report.pdf. Accessed on June 3, 2013.

Mirvis, P. H., & Hackett, E. J. (1983). Work and work force characteristics in the nonprofit sector. *Monthly Labor Review, 106*(4), 3–12.

Parsons, S. K., Simmons, W. P., Penn, K., & Furlough, M. (2003). Determinants of satisfaction and turnover among nursing assistants: The results of a statewide survey. *Journal of Gerontological Nursing, 29*(3), 51–58.

PHI National. (2012). *Care Gap: U.S. facing shortage of direct care workers*. Retrieved from http://phinational.org/charts/care-gap-us-facing-shortage-direct-care-workers. Accessed on April 1, 2013.

PHI National. (2013). *Value the care!: Minimum wage and overtime for home care aides*. Retrieved from http://phinational.org/sites/phinational.org/files/policy/wp-content/uploads/phi-value-the-care-04.pdf. Accessed on April 1, 2013.

Scott-Ladd, B., Travaglione, A., & Marshall, V. (2006). Causal inferences between participation in decision making, task attributes, work effort, rewards, job satisfaction and commitment. *Leadership & Organization Development Journal, 27*(5), 399–414.

Seavey, D. (2004). The cost of frontline turnover in long-term care. Prepared for *Better Jobs Better Care* (www.bjbc.org). Retrieved from http://phinational.org/sites/phinational.org/files/clearinghouse/TOCostReport.pdf

Seavey, D. (2007). *Written statement of Dorie Seavey, PhD. PHI Director of policy research before the subcommittee on workforce protections, committee on educations and labor*. United States House of Representatives. Hearing on "H.R. 3582: The fair home health care act." New York, NY: PHI National.

Summer, L., Friedland, R., Mack, K., & Mathieu, S. (2004). *Measuring the years: State aging trends and indicators data book*. Center on an Aging Society Health Policy Institute, Georgetown University for the National Governors Association Center or Best Practices. Retrieved from http://phinational.org/sites/phinational.org/files/clearinghouse/NGA%20Booklet.pdf. Accessed on April 1, 2013.

Swan, J. H., & Estes, C. L. (1990). Changes in aged populations served by home health agencies. *Journal of Aging and Health*, *2*(3), 373–394.

Witt, L. A., Andrews, M. C., & Kacmar, K. M. (2000). The role of participation in decision-making in the organizational politics-job satisfaction relationship. *Human Relations*, *53*(3), 341–358.

CHAPTER 2

CAN GROUP-INCENTIVES WITHOUT PARTICIPATION SURVIVE THE FREE-RIDER PROBLEM? A VIEW FROM THE LAB

Philip Mellizo

ABSTRACT

Purpose – *Group incentive schemes have been shown to be positively* associated *with firm performance but it remains an open question whether this association can be explained by the motivating characteristics of the group-incentive scheme itself, or if this is due to factors that tend to accompany group-incentive schemes. We use a controlled experiment to directly test if group-incentive schemes can motivate sustained individual effort in the absence of rules, norms, and institutions that are known to mitigate free-riding behavior.*

Design/methodology/approach – *We use a controlled lab experiment that randomly assigns subjects to one of three compensation contracts used to incentivize an onerous effort task. Two of the compensation contracts are group-incentive schemes where subjects have an incentive to*

Sharing Ownership, Profits, and Decision-making in the 21st Century
Advances in the Economic Analysis of Participatory & Labor-Managed Firms, Volume 14, 27–59

ISSN: 0885-3339/doi:10.1108/S0885-3339(2013)0000014003

free-ride on the efforts of their coworkers, and the third (control) is a flat-wage contract.

Findings – *We find that both group-incentive schemes resulted in sustained, higher performance relative to the flat-wage compensation contract. Further, we do not find evidence of free-riding behavior under the two group-incentive schemes.*

Research limitations/implications – *Although we do find sustained cooperation/performance over the three work periods of our experiment under the group-incentive schemes, further testing would be required to evaluate whether group-incentive schemes can sustain cooperation over a longer time horizon without complementary norms, policies, or institutions that mitigate free-riding.*

Originality/value – *By unambiguously showing that group-incentive schemes can, by themselves, motivate workers to provide sustained levels of effort, this suggests that the "1/*n *problem" may be, in part, an artifact of the rational-actor modeling conventions.*

Keywords: Group-incentives; experimental methods; free-riding behavior

JEL classifications: M52; C91; D03

INTRODUCTION

Group incentives schemes such as gain sharing, profit sharing, and share ownership are ubiquitous in the U.S. economy and have been shown to be, on average, *positively* associated with firm performance (e.g., Freeman & Dube, 2000; Kruse, 2002; Kruse & Blasi, 1997; Weizman & Kruse, 1990). It remains an open question, however, whether any of this positive association can be explained by the motivating characteristics of the group-incentive scheme itself, or if group-incentive schemes are correlated with "other reasons" that do explain firm performance differences. Indeed, the task of econometrically identifying whether any such causal relationship exists using conventional data is an extremely difficult one, and there are several reasons why this is the case.

First, and at the most fundamental level is what Alchien and Demsetz label in their 1972 paper as "the metering problem" – or the extreme difficulty of measuring the individual contribution of a given worker to firm output from period to period (particularly so in white-collar employments). Furthermore, the well functioning of any workplace relies on the willingness for workers to engage in other activities that may not reflect their own private contribution to firm output, such as providing mentorship to new employees, helping other workers with their own work tasks, or providing important information and feedback to management in meetings. Not every human input can be evaluated which can make it difficult to evaluate how incentive contracts affect individual output and effort across firms.

Second, there exist many complex factors that determine the size of the private return of the group-incentive scheme that may muddy the sense of causation that workers may (or may not) experience when linking their decision to provide more effort in response to the incentive scheme. That is, there are other factors that will determine the size of total output aside from worker effort including: (1) the firm's production methods and access to capital technologies, (2) its investment strategy, (3) its market position, (4) consumer demand for the service or product, (5) the human capital hired into the firm, (6) the social capital that exists among labor, (7) the firm's access to government subsidies or protections, and (8) the market conditions facing the firm. In other words, it is difficult to untangle successful firms that happen to use group-incentive schemes from firms that are successful *because* they use group-incentive schemes.

Third, there are many firm-specific factors that could contribute to increases in worker motivation in firms that use group-level incentives that *could* be independent from the material incentives. For example, the literature suggests that firms that provide group financial incentives also tend to employ progressive management practices that encourage workers to become more involved in both firm-level and shopfloor decision-making and planning (e.g., Conyon & Freeman, 2004; Freeman & Dube, 2000). It has been argued that the combination of group incentives along with participatory management policies may help create a "cooperative culture" that supports mutual monitoring, information sharing, and commitment that all offset free-riding behavior (e.g., Kruse et al., 2004).

In an effort to mitigate many of the above listed confounds that complicate identification, the methodological strategy used in this paper employs an experimental laboratory study in order to directly examine whether two uncertain group-incentive schemes motivate individuals differently than a certain, flat-wage compensation contract. We collected data from a real-effort experiment to compare changes in the performance of research participants randomly assigned to one of three compensation contracts labeled Control, Treatment 1, and Treatment 2.

In the Control treatment subjects were paid a flat-wage of 40 Experimental Monetary Units (10 EMUs = $1.00) for each of three, 6-minute work periods. In Treatment 1 subjects were paid a flat-wage of 30 EMUs and the monetary value of 1 out of 9 total equity shares in each of three, 6-minute work periods. And in Treatment 2 subjects were paid a flat-wage of 10 EMUs and the monetary value of 3 out of 9 total equity shares in each of three, 6-minute work periods. The value of an equity share was determined by the sum total of efforts multiplied by a random value between 1 and 2 (a stochastic marginal revenue per capita return). Extensive piloting of the addition task with unpaid volunteers revealed that we could expect about 20 correct answers to be produced in the absence of extrinsic motivators. We then used this figure and an expected multiplier of 1.5 to calibrate the expected value of a single share in the group-incentive schemes to be 33% of base pay.[1] In Treatment 1 where subjects had just one share, the value of this therefore 33% of pay and in Treatment 2 where subjects owned three shares the total share value was 100% of pay. We find these numbers to be relatively consistent with many share-to-pay ratios observed in the field. For example, Kruse, Blasi, and Park (2010) report data from the *2002–2006 General Social Survey* showing that the *mean* value of employer stock was 81.7% of pay.

The data collected in our experiment limit our investigation to an examination of observed behavioral differences that arise under three incentive schemes. Further, a between-subjects design was used in order to have an apples-to-apples comparison of performance under these three randomly assigned compensation schemes.

There are three innovative characteristics in our experimental design. First, we believe ours to be the first real-effort voluntary contribution mechanism (VCM) setting where the private payoff is partly determined by a stochastic marginal per capita return.[2] This decision was made in order to create uncertainty over the link between one's effort contribution and expected private return. Second, all subjects in Treatments 1 and 2 were paid a flat-wage in each round in addition to the value of their ownership share. We included this in the design since workers are hardly (if ever) paid exclusively via a group-incentive contract. The existing experimental literature on profit-sharing abstracts from guaranteed wages to better make the free-riding incentive more salient to subjects (e.g., Nalbantian & Schotter, 1997). Our third design innovation was to pay workers on the basis of ratio of shares owned rather than simply by a factor of $1/n$. We believe this design feature to be more consistent with many firm-wide group incentives that pay out proportional to equity shares rather than by following strict egalitarian distribution norms.

The findings reported herein provide evidence that uncertain group-incentive schemes can result in higher performance among workers relative to certain flat-wage compensation with equivalent expected earnings. Further, no evidence of free-riding behavior under the two group-incentive schemes is found in the data.

USING THE LAB TO STUDY THE ECONOMICS OF PERSONNEL: A NOTE ON METHODOLOGY

Most existing theoretical work within modern *Agency Theory* that investigates the motivational properties of different incentive structures typically assumes rationality and self-interest. Although there are many circumstances when human behavior looks *as if* it is reasonably approximated by the very specific psychology of the rational actor, contributions from the behavioral economics, experimental economics, and related social science literatures have illuminated a number of complexities when it comes to understanding *motivation* that are not accounted for by conventional theory. For example, we have learned that (1) tournament compensation schemes can induce at least as much effort as theoretically equivalent piece-rate schemes, but at the cost of much wider variance (e.g., Bull, Schotter, & Weigelt, 1987; Shearer, 2004; Van Dijk, Sonnemans, & Van Winden, 2001), (2) workers tend to reciprocate of "gift-wages" with higher effort even in cases when effort cannot be contracted for (e.g., Charness & Haruvy, 2002; Fehr, Kirchsteiger, & Riedl, 1998; Gächter & Falk, 2001; Maximiano, Sloof, & Sonnemans, 2007), and (3) there are many scenarios when pay-for-performance contracts can actually *decrease* worker motivation by crowding out intrinsic motivation (e.g., Gneezy & Rustichini, 2000; Fehr et al., 1998; Titmuss, 1971).[3]

Furthermore, a large body of research from experimental economics shows that the "*1/n problem*" can be successfully "managed" in the provided sufficient levels of other-regarding preferences (e.g., Bolton & Ockenfels, 2000; Charness & Rabin, 2002; Fehr & Schmidt, 1999; Pech, 2008), communication is allowed (e.g., Cooper, DeJong, Forsythe, & Ross, 1992; Croson, Boles, & Murnighan, 2003; Duffy & Feltovich, 2002; Frohlich & Oppenheimer, 1998; Ledyard, 1995; Sally, 1995; Suetens, 2005), at least a fraction of individuals display a willingness to enforce cooperation at a monetary and/or social cost (Anderson & Stafford, 2003; Andreoni, Harbaugh, & Vesterlund, 2003; Carpenter & Seki, 2005; Cinyabuguma, Page, & Putterman, 2005; Dickinson, 2001; Fehr & Gächter, 2000), or subjects have developed some type of group identity (Charness & Jackson, 2007; Cox, Lobel, & McLeod, 1991; Eckel & Grossman, 2005; McLeish & Oxoby, 2007). Furthermore, Ostrom (1999) identifies up to 27 different rules used by communities to enforce the sustainable management of common property resources. It is therefore not much of a stretch to imagine that similar informal rules and institutions likely do develop to sustain mutual cooperation under firm-level, group-incentive schemes.

Indeed, disentangling and *identifying* the (causal) role that group-incentive schemes play in worker motivation is an extremely difficult task using conventional data. And while it is nearly impossible to control for all potential sources of endogeneity and/or selection bias in any empirical study, controlled experimentation does mitigate some potential sources that may otherwise call the attention of the "identification police" when using conventional firm data to study the motivational effect of group-incentives on workers including

(1) the plethora of, and variation in, group incentive plans across employed across firms (i.e., different definitions of "profit" in profit-sharing plans, differences in the execution of pay cash payments vs. deferred payments, the fraction of profit share that is discretionary, etc.),
(2) the difficulty in suitably measuring, categorizing, and controlling for the influence of firm unobservable heterogeneity such as the precise production task, monitoring arrangement, the sense of community and solidarity among coworkers, the presence of explicit worker empowerment initiatives, or the quality of the firm management, that are bundled with the group incentive,
(3) the selection of highly (un)productive workers into firms that use group-incentive schemes due to their own preference to work within teams (or to free-ride on others) or for reasons that are correlated with unobservable characteristics that affect performance,
(4) external market and industrial conditions facing the firm, the firm's clientele, and the firm's suppliers face.

Of course, the cold and impersonal environment of the lab that allows a way to "cleanly" study very specific theoretical hypotheses simultaneously creates obvious concern over the generalizability of lab findings to the field. For instance, a typical lab experiment in economics uses random assignment of participants (almost always a convenience sample of college students) that may be unfamiliar with the experimental settings, unfamiliar with each other, and are evaluated in contexts where the monetary incentives are relatively weak. By contrast, in "real" firms there is familiarity among coworkers, the financial stakes are large, and workers are self-selected by role, expertise, and work task. One way that may help bridge the gap between the lab and naturally occurring field data is through replication of the experimental protocol both within the lab and outside of it through field experiments.

Though still quite new to economics in general, field experiments replicate lab protocols with either (a) a nonrandom set of subjects that share some "common experience" (e.g., all subjects work at the same firm, have the same occupation, etc.), and/or (b) random subjects in a contextually rich settings (i.e., a church, beach, firm, etc.). While field experiments that take place in real-world setting may help mitigate concerns over the external validity of an experiment, much like case studies, they do little to address concerns over generalizability when simply analyzed in isolation. That is, findings from a specific field experiment may not necessarily predict what would happen in another context for precisely the same reasons that raise concerns of generalizability in lab studies. Further, there is also a loss of control in the nature of the data collected in field experiments when compared to lab experiments.

Lab experiments therefore offer a new way of understanding the behavioral responses to firm organization that complement the contextually rich field and case studies traditionally used to study theoretical propositions and predictions made of participatory organizations. It is insufficient to rely solely on experiments to refute, confirm, or explore existing formal and/or discursive theories of the workplace, but taken in combination with other empirical methods a more complete picture is likely to emerge.

PROTOCOL SUMMARY AND EXPERIMENTAL DESIGN

Throughout the 2011–2012 academic year, we recruited members of the UMass-Amherst and UMass-Boston communities via table-tents, fliers, and brief announcements given in lecture halls and sessions at each of the different institutions. The participants in our study were not informed about the precise nature of the experiment before arrival. In our recruitment, we promised a $5.00 show-up fee, plus the chance to earn additional money in the experiment. Our recruitment procedure allowed subjects to select a time-slot that was convenient for their own schedule, and we confirmed their participation by e-mail. Upon arriving at the experiment, a subject's experience in all treatments was the following.

First all subjects signed a consent form for their participation and were seated at a computer terminal where they found a sheet introducing the study to them and a copy of experiment instructions. After all subjects were seated, the lab assistant made it clear that communication was not allowed for the duration of the experiment. The lab assistant then read the instructions aloud along with the subjects. In the instructions (as given in the appendix) the participants learned that they were going to be randomly assigned to a group of three total subjects through the computer network. They also learned that these groups of three would not change throughout the duration of the experiment, and that all subjects would be engaging in the same work task for three, 6-minute work periods.

The Work Task

For the work task used in the experiment, subjects added sets of three two-digit numbers that appeared on their computer screen. Participants were not allowed to use a calculator, but could use scratch paper and a pencil that were provided to them. After solving a problem, a subject would submit his or her answer and would be presented with a new problem to solve. The numbers to be added together were randomly generated, but all subjects in a given treatment were presented with the same set of math problems, given in the same order. We chose to use this specific real-effort because (1) we would expect adding sets of numbers together to yield a low intrinsic reward, (2) it requires little skill, (3) a typical college aged subject is familiar with simple arithmetic, and most importantly, (4) previous studies have found that this same real-effort task did not result in biased performance in any systematic manner (Mellizo, Carpenter, & Matthews, 2011; Niederle & Vesterlund, 2007). It also allows the collection of measures of both *effort* (trying hard measured with the total number of questions attempted) and *effective effort* (quality of work measured by the number of correct responses).

Treatments and Subject Earnings

From the experiment instructions each subject knew that for each 6-minute period of work (solving simple addition problems) they would be paid a flat-wage. This was common for all treatments. In the control treatment, this payment for their effort was the only source of their earnings (aside from the show-up fee). In Treatment 1 and Treatment 2, subjects knew that they would be paid a flat-wage in addition to the value of the firm stock that they held. The difference between Treatment 1 and Treatment 2 is in the number of stock shares that each subject holds relative to the total number of firm shares. In Treatment 1 each of the three subjects in each group was allocated one equity share out of a total of nine firm shares, and in Treatment 2, each of the three subjects in each group was allocated three equity shares out of a total of nine firm shares.

Asset Price Determination

In publicly traded ESOPs the value of the share is partially reflective of the productivity of its work force, but it is also a function of the various factors that fall outside of the control of the workforce including the investment decisions of its shareholders, the health of its CEO, the presence of market speculators, exogenous forces that influence the demand for the firm's services, and so on. The value of a firm share is therefore a function of both the combined effort of its workforce and a vector of uncertainty (a similar argument could be made for a profit-sharing arrangement). In this experimental protocol the value of the firm's stock is the sum of the output provided by all three subjects measured by the number of correct answers provided in their work task multiplied by a mean reverting stochastic process (r) that falls between 1.0 and 2.0. The product is then divided by the total number of shares (9) to determine the value of each share (Table 1).[4]

EXPECTATIONS

From a Behavioral Economic perspective, however, it would not be surprising for a worker to "irrationally" demonstrate a higher level of motivation and thus offer higher levels of effort to try to influence the share value by providing high levels of effort, even when the share value is only *very* marginally influenced by any single employee (especially with a stochastic MRPC). Similar in many ways to the "paradox of voting" (Downs, 1957), we suspect that workers might provide higher effort under share ownership since they potentially: (1) feel morally obliged to work hard under such a system, (2) are not solely motivated by their own material payoff but their social preferences (e.g., Charness & Rabin, 2002; Fehr & Schmidt, 1999), (3) are attempting to give structure with higher effort to an otherwise

Table 1. Treatment Summary.

Treatment	Control Treatment	Treatment 1 (Small-Scale)	Treatment 2 (Full)
Description	Flat-wage of 40 EMUs paid with certainty at the end of each round (zero pay variability)	Flat-Wage of 30 EMUs paid with certainty at the end of each round plus "small-share" ownership where each team member owns 1 of 9 total firm shares and is compensated according to the share value at the end of each work period (moderate pay variability)	Flat-Wage of 10 EMUs paid with certainty at the end of each round plus "full-ownership" where each team member owns 3 of 9 total firm shares and is compensated according the share value at the end of each work period (high pay variability)

unpredictable situation (e.g., Glass & Singer, 1972; Whitson & Galinsky, 2008), (4) receive a "warm glow" by acting in the collective interest (Andreoni, 1990), or perhaps (5) are responding to a "minimax regret" criterion by selecting an action (high effort) that yields minimal regret in a worse-case scenario (e.g., Ferejohn & Fiorina, 1974).

Although all of the above potential explanations could be used to inform the design of the current study, we instead chose to anchor the experimental design to rational predictions that would fall from a "straw-man" principal-agent model that predicts zero differences in labor supply between the three different contracts since the incentive to free-ride would make mutual defection a Nash equilibrium in Treatments 1 and 2. Further, the flat-wage paid in all treatments is independent from firm performance so a rational worker would consider the flat-wage to be a sunk benefit, and thus offer zero effort.

FINDINGS

Can Group-Incentive Schemes Increase Effort in the Absence of Any Institutional or Cultural Controls?

The subsequent analysis centers on both *effective effort*, measured using the number of correct answers provided, and *effort*, measured as the total number of attempted questions. Table 2 provides subgroup summary statistics of total attempted questions and correct answers across periods and

Table 2. Descriptive Statistics.

Treatment	Statistic	Correct Answers			Total Attempted		
		Period 1	Period 2	Period 3	Period 1	Period 2	Period 3
Control (40 EMU flat-wage)	Mean	23.444	22.666	19.66667	26.22222	25.33333	21.44444
	Max.	32	30	27	33	32	31
	Min.	17	16	15	18	18	16
	Std. Dev.	5.3176	4.974	4.242641	5.238745	5.361903	5.150512
Small (flat-wage + (1/9 shares)	Mean	26.266	27.066	26.73333	29.06667	30.66667	30.73333
	Max.	40	41	40	45	45	45
	Min.	15	15	17	17	20	20
	Std. Dev.	6.5733	7.411	6.123336	6.573395	7.286648	6.638273
Full (flat-wage + (3/9 shares)	Mean	24.666	23.25	26.08333	27	26.33333	28.08333
	Max.	35	32	34	38	37	38
	Min.	14	16	18	16	18	19
	Std. Dev.	5.8672	5.479	5.853644	6.281285	6.065301	6.200562

Table 3. Kruskal–Wallis Rank Tests and One-Way ANOVA *F*-Tests.

Kruskal–Wallis Equality-of-Populations Rank Test by Treatment			One-Way ANOVA *F*-Tests		
	Correct Prob > χ^2	Total Prob > χ^2		Correct Prob > F	Total Prob > F
Overall	0.0094	0.0022	Overall	0.0054	0.0008
Period 1	0.5470	0.5085	Period 1	0.5321	0.5030
Period 2	0.2519	0.1576	Period 2	0.1712	0.1030
Period 3	0.0132	0.0080	Period 3	0.0133	0.0043
Null hypothesis: Populations from which the samples originate have the same median in the overall sample (by compensation treatment)			Null hypothesis: Equivalent means in effort and effective effort across compensation schemes		

treatments. Table 3 provides full Kruskal–Wallis rank tests and one-way ANOVA *F*-tests.

Are there Differences in Effort Across Treatments Over All Three Periods?

From Table 3, Kruskal–Wallis rank tests reject the null that the populations from which the samples originate have the same median in the overall sample (summing correct answers and total attempts across all three periods respectively) when measuring both the number of correct answers provided (Prob > $\chi^2 = 0.0094$) and total number of problems attempted (Prob > $\chi^2 = 0.0022$) suggesting that the compensation schemes generated different levels of performance. *F*-tests evaluating equivalence of mean performance across compensation schemes reinforce the nonparametric findings by rejecting the null hypothesis with ($p = 0.005$) and ($p = 0.001$) for number of correct answers and total attempted respectively.

Kruskal–Wallis and *F*-test from Table 3 suggest that the differences in both effort and effective effort according to treatment are concentrated on differences that arise in Period 3. Treatment differences are not apparent in either Period 1 (Prob > $\chi^2 = .547$ and *p*-value = 0.532 for correct answers; Prob > $\chi^2 = .509$, and *p*-value = .503 for total attempted), or Period 2 (Prob > $\chi^2 = .252$ and *p*-value = .171 for correct answers; Prob > $\chi^2 = .157$ and *p*-value = .103 for total attempted). On the basis of these simple tests, it would appear that the bulk of the treatment differences in the overall sample arise from Period 3 behavior (Prob > $\chi^2 = .013$ and *p*-value = .013 for correct answers; Prob > $\chi^2 = .008$, and *p*-value = .004 for total attempted).

Table 4A. Least Squares Regression: Dependent Variable Correct Answers.

	Overall (1)	Period 1 (2)	Period 2 (3)	Period 3 (4)
Small	4.762***	2.822	4.400*	7.067***
	(1.367)	(2.445)	(2.528)	(2.117)
Full	2.740**	1.222	.5833	6.417***
	(1.342)	(2.432)	(2.273)	(2.189)
Constant	21.925***	23.444***	22.666***	19.667***
	(.9501)	(1.745)	(1.632)	(1.392)
N	108	36	36	36
R^2	0.0946	0.0375	0.1014	0.2303

Notes: Robust standard errors in parentheses. Significance of asterisks: *10%, **5%, ***1%.

WHICH COMPENSATION SCHEMES ARE DRIVING THE DIFFERENCES IN PERFORMANCE?

The analysis in the previous section reveals that there are differences in performance behavior across the different treatments. We now turn to analyzing which compensations schemes drive performance differences by analyzing the OLS regressions in Tables 4A and 4B.[5]

Tables 4A and 4B show OLS regressions that evaluate the effect of the compensation schemes on the number of correct answers (effective effort) and on the number of total questions attempted (effort) respectively. Regression 1 evaluates the overall effect of the compensation schemes across all three periods, while regressions 2, 3, and 4 evaluate the compensation effects in Period 1, Period 2, and Period 3 respectively. The reference category is the Control (flat-wage compensation). On average, a subject randomly assigned to the small-scale ownership treatment answered 4.762 more correct answers (p-value = 0.001) throughout the duration of the experiment relative to the Control and also attempted 5.822 more questions compared to the Control (p-value = 0.001). Similarly, subjects randomly assigned to the "Full" (100% employee owned) treatment (where each subject paid the value of three firm shares) answered an average of 2.74 more questions correctly relative to the Control (p-value = 0.044) while attempting 2.805 (p-value = 0.056) more questions.

Looking at column two in both Tables 4A and 4B we again notice that there are no statistically significant performance differences under the three compensation schemes in Period 1 though the signs on both the small- and full-share ownership treatments were positive. In Period 2, subjects in the small-ownership treatment answered an average of 4.40 more questions correctly than subjects in the flat-wage treatment (p-value = 0.091), while attempting an average of 5.33 more questions than in the Control (p-value = 0.047).

The regression specification in column 4 in both Tables 4A and 4B evaluating Period 3 performance, however, suggest a sharp diversion between the flat-wage contract and the two group-incentive contracts. Subjects that were paid a flat-wage in Period 3 were solving, on average 19.33 problems correctly while mean total attempts were 21.44. In the small-share ownership treatment subjects solved an average of 7.067 more answers correctly than under the flat-wage contract (p-value = 0.002) and attempted 9.288 more questions (p-value = 0.001) relative to the flat-wage contract. Similarly, under the full ownership compensation contract subject solved an average of 6.417 more problems correctly than in the flat-wage contract (p-value = 0.006) and attempted an average of 6.638 more problems (p-value = 0.011).

Finally, we do not find statistical differences in the number of correct answers offered when comparing the two group-incentive schemes under any of the regression specifications in Table 4A. We do note, however, statistical differences in overall total questions attempted (from specification 1 in Table 4B). On average, subjects assigned to the small-ownership treatment attempted 3.02 questions more than those assigned to the full-ownership treatment throughout the duration of the study (p-value = 0.037). We

Table 4B. Least Squares Regression: Dependent Variable Total Attempted.

	Overall (1)	Period 1 (2)	Period 2 (3)	Period 3 (4)
Small	5.822***	2.844	5.333**	9.288***
	(1.452)	(2.426)	(2.588)	(2.418)
Full	2.805*	.7778	1.000	6.638**
	(1.453)	(2.498)	(2.482)	(2.462)
Constant	24.333***	26.222***	25.333***	21.444***
	(1.047)	(1.719)	(1.76)	(1.695)
N	108	36	36	36
R^2	0.1269	0.0408	0.1287	0.2816

Notes: Robust standard errors in parentheses. Significance of asterisks: *10%, **5%, ***1%.

do not find statistical differences in total attempts, however, between small and full ownership in any single period.

DOES SUBJECT ABILITY EXPLAIN THE DIVERGENCE IN PERIOD 3 PERFORMANCE?

A principle hurdle for encountered in research aimed to measure performance is in controlling for employee ability. In "traditional" data, self-reports, attitudinal surveys, IQ tests, years of education, quality of education, resume quality, years of job experience, and managerial evaluations are among some of the variables used to serve as a proxy for unobservable worker characteristics like skill level of intrinsic motivation. A notable advantage of using an experiment is in collecting observations on a simple, specific, and well-defined effort task at the individual level. We use Period 1 and Period 2 essentially as baseline estimates of one's ability recalling that from the previous section no performance differences arose in Period 1, and only marginal performance differences arose in Period 2 across treatment.

Regressions (4) and (8) in Table 5 regress the compensation schemes controlling for Period 1 and Period 2 performance on Period 3 correct answers (left panel) and Period 3 total attempted (right panel) respectively. The inclusion of these controls does not diminish the treatment effects describing performance differences in Period 3. Both small-share and full-share treatments are positive and highly significant at the .01 level in explaining the number of correct answers and the number of total questions attempted. Further, subjects in full-ownership contract solved 1.99 more problems correctly than those in the small-share contract (p-value = 0.051).

Finally, in Table 6 we report regressions where the dependent variable is the difference in performance in Period 3, and Period 1 is our within sample control. The reported coefficients describe the average differences in differences between Period 3 and Period 1 performance as explained by the compensation scheme.

Notice that in the flat-wage treatment (the reference category), there was an average decrease in performance between Period 1 and Period 3 of 3.778 correct answers (p-value = 0.028) and 4.778 total questions attempted (p-value = 0.007). The coefficients for small- and full-share ownership compensation schemes measure the difference in the performance differences

Table 5. Period 3 Performance Controlling for Period 1 and Period 2 Performance.

	Dependent Variable: Correct Answers					Dependent Var: Total Attempted			
	(1)	(2)	(3)	(4)		(5)	(6)	(7)	(8)
Small	7.067***	5.021***	3.668**	3.806***	Small	9.289***	6.913***	4.768***	5.209***
	(−2.118)	(−1.716)	(−1.363)	(−1.308)		(−2.419)	(−1.748)	(−1.608)	(−1.362)
Full	6.417***	5.531***	5.966***	5.795***	Full	6.639***	5.989***	5.791***	5.800***
	(−2.19)	(−1.769)	(−1.305)	(−1.362)		(−2.462)	(−1.849)	(−1.597)	(−1.553)
Corr1		0.725***		0.223	Total1		0.835***		0.304
		(−0.104)		(−0.162)			(−0.092)		(−0.200)
Corr2			0.772***	0.598***	Total2			0.848***	0.603***
			(−0.069)	(−0.138)				(−0.055)	(−0.160)
Con.	19.67***	2.677	2.158	0.885	Con.	21.44***	−0.462	−0.028	−1.792
	(1.393)	(−2.26)	(−1.66)	(−1.503)		(−1.691)	(−2.675)	(−1.942)	(−1.532)
n	36	36	36	36	n	36	36	36	36
R^2	0.23	0.698	0.800	0.815	R^2	0.282	0.786	0.850	0.869

Notes: Robust standard errors in parentheses. Significance of asterisks: *10%, **5%, ***1%.

Table 6. Controlling for Within Sample Differences in Period 3–Period 1.

Dependent Variable: Correct Answers	Coefficient (Std. Err.)	Dependent Variable: Total Attempted	Coefficient (Std. Err.)
Small	4.244**	Small	6.444***
	(1.858)		(1.777)
Full	5.1944**	Full	5.861***
	(1.945)		(1.934)
Constant	−3.778**	Constant	−4.778***
	(1.639)		(1.671)
N	36	*N*	36
R^2	0.235	R^2	0.3898

Notes: Robust standard errors in parentheses. Significance of asterisks: *10%, **5%, ***1%.

between Period 3 and Period 1 relative to the control treatment. These differences are positive and highly significant for the number of correct answers (left panel in Table 6) and total answers attempted (right panel in Table 6). Taking the regression results in Table 5 and 6 in mutual consideration the flat-wage 40 EMU compensation scheme does not keep subjects as motivated as either the 30 EMU flat-wage + 1/9 shares compensation scheme or the 10 EMU flat-wage + 3/9 shares compensation scheme over three 6-minute work periods.

CONCLUSION

Agency theory predicts that group incentive-schemes are doomed to fail since rational workers would follow their private incentive to shirk. Indeed, in "baseline" experiments (no communication and full anonymity among participants) where free-riding is a dominant strategy for subjects, we typically observe moderate free-riding in early periods that steadily intensifies throughout the duration of the study (see Camerer, 2003). Importantly, when added layers of "realism" are introduced into the experiment and compared to the "baseline" (such as the opportunity for subjects to mutually monitor the output of their peers) we see that the "free-rider problem" does not appear to be much of a problem at all (e.g., Fehr & Gächter, 2000).

In this paper, we add to the growing line of research that highlights conditions when free-riding does not arise. The provocative finding from the present study is that we fail to find evidence of free-riding in an environment absent of known rules and norms known to mitigate free-riding. The experiment reported herein is different from standard "baseline" experimental studies used to study free-riding in three important ways. First, we asked subjects to perform a real-effort task as opposed to having subjects make non-effort decisions over their contribution to a common account. Second, in our study, subjects were informed that combined value of their effort only partially contributed to the total value of output (the other being an exogenous stochastic component), as opposed to having the whole value of output exclusively determined by effort contributions. And third, the total compensation of subjects in our study was partially via a group-incentive scheme and partially via a flat-wage that was independent of output. Under these conditions, we not only found an absence of free-riding, we further found that the two different group-incentive compensation schemes significantly out-performed the control treatment where subjects were paid a flat-wage payment scheme without group-incentives.

Although we did find sustained cooperation over the three periods of our experiment under the group-incentive schemes, we recognize that this is still a relatively short period of time. Further testing would be required to evaluate whether group-incentive schemes can sustain cooperation in the long run without norms, policies, or institutions such as communication and mutual monitoring that control free-riding. It very well could be that team identity could be built by introducing a group-incentive scheme – especially if it is proven to be successful in early periods, putting the group in a "good equilibrium" where cooperation becomes the norm. We can, however, imagine scenarios where cooperation may start to break down if, say, one group member is working hard but has an off period which sends a signal of shirking that threatens the confidence of other group members. Or, if a group experiences a poor run of exogenous factors (modeled in our study as a stochastic MPCR) that results in poor returns, despite the strong effort given by the group, we might see effort dwindling from discouragement. Without a mechanism to communicate with other team members we speculate that the "good equilibrium" we find in this study could possibly slide toward the Pareto inferior Nash equilibrium that might be very difficult to break.

That said, if the survey findings reported in Freeman, Kruse, and Blasi (2010) generally apply, an experimental study on the long-run effects of group incentives in a social vacuum may prove interesting, but an ultimately moot endeavor. Specifically, they find that workers in firms that use some form of group-incentive scheme are more willing to engage in mutual monitoring than in workplaces that do not have group-incentive schemes because they (1) are guarding against having their own job negatively affected by the shirking behavior, (2) want to keep work standards high, (3) perceive poor performance by their coworkers as having financial cost that will affect all in the group, (4) like to help others, and (5) may receive help from their coworkers in the future. In other words, we speculate that the "good equilibrium" that we observe in the cold social environment used in the present study is likely to be sustained in common social environments.

Finally, it is important to note that the payment structures used in this study may actually bias our results downward for at least two reasons. First, in our design we differentiated compensation schemes by *substituting* base pay with uncertain group-incentive pay in order to keep expected returns constant. As documented by Kruse, Freeman, and Blasi (2010), a comprehensive literature shows that firms that employ group-incentive schemes in the form of ESOPs, ESPPs, and profit sharing typically *do not* substitute base pay in exchange for asset ownership, stock, or profit share. In fact, group-incentive schemes tend to be associated with base pay and benefit schemes that are above market. Second, we used a between-subjects design to control for selection effects by randomly assigning participants into treatment that without telling subjects that (a) there were other treatments, or (b) any information regarding the nature of those treatments. Indeed, a crucial piece to the emergence of a gift-exchange in labor contracts is the knowledge that one is actually receiving an *intentional* gift from someone (e.g., Gächter & Thöni, 2010). A simple extension of the present study could accommodate both of these considerations by comparing the efficacy of two compensation structures with common base pay, but where one includes an additional group-incentive component. Further, these compensation schemes could then be evaluated with treatments that allow for the analysis of the knowledge set of subjects (i.e., whether they "know" about the other possible compensation schemes they could have received), as well as the *timing* that this knowledge is obtained by subjects (e.g., before random assignment into treatment or after random assignment into treatment), which has been shown to have an affect perceptions and attitudes (Kahneman & Thaler, 2006).

NOTES

1. The return for each correct answer contributed to share value that yielded a return $(s/9)m\sum_i e_i$ where $s = 1$ in Treatment 1 (base pay = 30) and $s = 3$ in Treatment 2 (base pay = 10).

Share value was calibrated assuming $m = 1.5$ and $e_i = 20$. Notice that the marginal revenue per share return of a correct answer is $sm/9$ and always <1 making non-contribution (free-riding) a dominant strategy for a self-interested worker with any non-negative cost of effort function. Further, because $sm > 1$ player contributions are Pareto-improving.

2. A VCM public goods setting arises when the dominant strategy for an individual is to (voluntarily) contribute nothing but full contribution from all parties results in Pareto improving outcomes.

3. Many theories from social psychology (e.g., Deci, 1971; Deci & Ryan, 1985, 2000) and also from economics (e.g., Bowles & Hwang, 2008; Frey & Jegen, 2001; Huck, Kübler, & Weibull, 2012; Rob & Zemsky, 2001) have all been developed in to capture these empirical regularities.

4. Notice that the expected earnings under both group-incentive contracts would be 40 EMUs provided the group produced an average of 60 correct answers in 6 minutes. Several pilot sessions conducted at the College of Wooster prior to live data collection revealed that, on average, a single subject would solve 20 problems in 6 minutes. We calibrated payoffs accordingly.

5. All OLS regressions reported herein are *robust to Negative Binomial and Poisson regression* routines with robust standard errors that are typically fit to non-negative count data. For ease of exposition and interpretation we simply report the OLS regression results.

ACKNOWLEDGMENTS

This research was supported by the Louis O. Kelso Fellowship program and the Foundation for Enterprise Development. I would like to thank Joseph Blasi, Douglas Kruse, Eric Olsen, Fidan Kurtulus, Richard Freeman, Jeffrey Carpenter, Peter Hans Matthews, Jim Warner, John Spraggon, Mike Carr, John Lanz, the anonymous referee and the participants at the 2011 Midyear Fellows Workshop at Rutgers University, the 2011 Summer Beyster Fellowship Symposium, and the 2011 ICAPE conference at UMass-Amherst for their many helpful comments received on previous drafts. Any and all errors in the chapter are mine.

REFERENCES

Andreoni, J. (1990). Impure altruism and donations to public goods: A theory of warm-glow giving. *The Economic Journal*, *100*(401), 464–477.

Anderson, L. R., & Stafford, S. L. (2003). Punishment in a regulatory setting: Experimental evidence from the VCM. *Journal of Regulatory Economics*, *24*, 91–110.

Andreoni, J., Harbaugh, W., & Vesterlund, L. (2003). The carrot or the stick: Rewards, punishments, and cooperation. *American Economic Review*, *93*, 893–902.

Bolton, G., & Ockenfels, A. (2000). ERC: A theory of equity, reciprocity, and competition. *American Economic Review*, *90*, 166–193.

Bowles, S., & Hwang, S. (2008). Social preferences and public economics: Mechanism design when social preferences depend on incentives. *Journal of Public Economics*, *92*, 1811–1820.

Bull, C., Schotter, A., & Weigelt, K. (1987). Tournaments and piece rates: An experimental study. *The Journal of Political Economy*, *95*, 1–33.

Camerer, C. (2003). *Behavioral game theory: Experiments in strategic interaction*. Princeton, NJ: Princeton University Press.

Carpenter, J. P., & Seki, E. (2005). Do social preferences increase productivity? Field experimental evidence from fisherman in Toyama Bay. Economic Inquiry. *Western Economic Association International*, *49*, 612–630.

Charness, G., & Rabin, M. (2002). Understanding social preferences with simple tests. *Quarterly Journal of Economics*, *116*, 817–869.

Charness, G., & Haruvy, E. (2002). Altruism, equity, and reciprocity in a gift- exchange experiment: An encompassing approach. *Games and Economic Behavior*, *40*, 203–31.

Charness, G., & Jackson, M. (2007). Group play in games and the role of consent in network formation. *Journal of Economic Theory*, *136*, 417–445.

Cinyabuguma, M., Page, T., & Putterman, L. (2005). Cooperation under the threat of expulsion in a public goods experiment. *Journal of Public Economics*, *89*(8), 1421–1435.

Conyon, M., & Freeman, R. B. (2004). Shared modes of compensation and firm performance: UK evidence. In *Seeking a premier economy: The economic effects of British economic reforms, 1980–2000* (pp. 109–146). Chicago, IL: University of Chicago Press.

Cooper, R., DeJong, D., Forsythe, R., & Ross, T. (1992). Communication in coordination games. *Quarterly Journal of Economics*, *107*, 739–771.

Cox, T. H., Lobel, S. A., & McLeod, P. L. (1991). Effects of ethnic group cultural differences on cooperative and competitive behavior on a group task. *The Academy of Management Journal*, *34*, 827–847.

Croson, R., Boles, T., & Murnighan, J. (2003). Cheap talk in bargaining experiments: Lying and threats in ultimatum games. *Journal of Economic Behavior and Organization*, *51*, 143–59.

Deci, E. L. (1971). Effects of externally mediated rewards on intrinsic motivation. *Journal of Personality and Social Psychology*, *18*, 105–115.

Deci, E. L., & Ryan, R. M. (1985). *Intrinsic motivation and self-determination in human behavior*. New York, NY: Plenum.

Deci, E. L., & Ryan, R. M. (2000). The "what" and "why" of goal pursuits: Human needs and the self-determination of behavior. *Psychological Inquiry*, *11*, 227–268.

Dickinson, D. L. (2001). The carrot versus the stick in work team motivation. *Experimental Economics*, *4*, 107–124.

Downs, A. (1957). An economic theory of political action in a democracy. *The Journal of Political Economy*, *65*(2), 135–150.

Duffy, J., & Feltovich, N. (2002). Do actions speak louder than words? An experimental comparison of observation and cheap talk. *Games and Economic Behavior*, *39*, 1–27.

Eckel, C., & Grossman, P. (2005). Managing diversity by creating team identity. *Journal of Economic Behavior and Organization*, *58*, 371–392.

Fehr, E., & Gächter, S. (2000). Cooperation and punishment in public goods experiments. *The American Economic Review*, *90*(4), 980–994.

Fehr, E., Kirchsteiger, G., & Riedl, A. (1998). Gift exchange and reciprocity in experimental markets. *European Economic Review*, *42*, 1–34.

Fehr, E., & Schmidt, K. M. (1999). A theory of fairness, competition and cooperation. *Quarterly Journal of Economics, 114*, 817–868.

Ferejohn, J. A., & Fiorina, M. P. (1974). The paradox of not voting: A decision theoretic analysis. *The American Political Science Review, 68*(2), 525–536.

Freeman, R., & Dube, A. (2000). *Shared compensation systems and decision making in the U.S. job market*. Draft, Harvard University Department of Economics.

Freeman, R., Kruse, D., & Blasi, J. (2010). Worker responses to shirking under shared capitalism. In D. Kruse, R. Freeman, & J. Blasi (Eds.), *Shared capitalism at work: Employee ownership, profit and gain sharing, and broad-based stock options* (pp. 77–103). Chicago, IL: University of Chicago Press.

Frey, B. S., & Jegen, R. (2001). Motivation crowding theory. *Journal of Economic Surveys, 15*(5), 589–611.

Frohlich, N., & Oppenheimer, J. (1998). Some consequences of e-mail vs. face-to-face communication in experiment. *Journal of Economic Behavior & Organization, 35*(3), 389–403.

Gächter, S., & Falk, A. (2001). *Reputation or reciprocity? An experimental investigation*. CESifo Working Paper Series No. 496.

Gächter, S., & Thöni, C. (2010). Social comparison and performance: Experimental evidence on the fair wage-effort hypothesis. *Journal of Economic Behavior & Organization, 76*(3), 531–543.

Glass, D., & Singer, J. (1972). *Urban stress: Experiments on noise and social stressors*. New York, NY: Academy Press.

Gneezy, U., & Rustichini, A. (2000). Pay enough or don't pay at all. *Quarterly Journal of Economics, 115*, 791–810.

Huck, S., Kübler, D., & Weibull, J. (2012). Social norms and economic incentives in firms. *Journal of Economic Behavior & Organization, 83*(2), 173–185.

Kahneman, D., & Thaler, R. (2006). Anomalies: Utility maximization and experience utility. *Journal of Economic Perspectives, 20*, 221–234.

Kruse, D. (2002). Research evidence on prevalence and effects of employee ownership. *Journal of Employee Ownership Law and Finance, 14*(4), 65–90.

Kruse, D., & Blasi, J. (1997). Employee ownership, employee attitudes, and firm performance: A review of the evidence. In D. Lewin, D. J. B. Mitchell, & M. A. Zaidi (Eds.), *Human resources management handbook*. Greenwich, CT: JAI Press.

Kruse, D. L., Blasi, J. R., & Park, R. (2010). Shared capitalism in the US economy: Prevalence, characteristics and employee views of financial participation in enterprises. In D. Kruse, R. Freeman, & J. Blasi (Eds.), *Shared capitalism at work: Employee ownership, profit and gain sharing, and broad-based stock options* (pp. 41–76). Chicago, IL: University of Chicago Press. Chapter 1.

Kruse, D., Freeman, R., & Blasi, J. (2010). Do workers gain by sharing? Employee outcomes under employee ownership, profit sharing, and broad based stock options. In D. Kruse, R. Freeman, & J. Blasi (Eds.), *Shared capitalism at work: Employee ownership, profit and gain sharing, and broad-based stock options* (pp. 257–289). Chicago, IL: University of Chicago Press.

Kruse, D., Freeman, R., Blasi, J., Buchele, R., Scharf, A., Rodgers, L., & Mackin, C. (2004). *Motivating employee-owners in ESOP firms: Human resource policies and company performance* (Vol. 8, pp. 101–127). Bingley, UK: Emerald Group Publishing Limited.

Ledyard, J. O. (1995). Public goods: A survey of experimental research. In A. Roth & J. Kagel (Eds.), *The handbook of experimental economics*. Princeton, NJ: Princeton University Press.

Maximiano, S., Sloof, R., & Sonnemans, J. (2007). Gift exchange in a multi-worker firm. *Economic Journal, 117*, 1025–1050.

McLeish, K., & Oxoby, R. (2007). Identity, cooperation, and punishment. IZA Discussion Paper No. 2572.

Mellizo, P., Carpenter, J., & Matthews, P. H. (2011). *Workplace democracy in the lab*. IZA Working Paper No. 5460.

Nalbantian, H. R., & Schotter, A. (1997). Productivity under group incentives: An experimental study. *The American Economic Review*, 314–341.

Niederle, M., & Vesterlund, L. (2007). Do women shy away from competition? Do men compete too much? *Quarterly Journal of Economics, 122*, 1067–1101.

Ostrom, E. (1999). Coping with tragedies of the commons. *American Review of Political Science, 2*, 493–535.

Pech, W. J. (2008). Essays on behavioral economics. *Electronic doctoral dissertations for UMass Amherst. Paper AAI3*, 336936.

Rob, R., & Zemsky, P. (2001). Social capital, corporate culture, and incentive intensity. *RAND Journal of Economics, 33*, 243–257.

Sally, D. (1995). Conversation and cooperation in social dilemmas: A meta-analysis of experiments from 1958 to 1992. *Rationality and Society, 7*, 58–92.

Suetens, S. (2005). Cooperative and noncooperative R&D in experimental duopoly markets. *International Journal of Industrial Organization, 23*, 63–82.

Shearer, B. (2004). Piece rates, fixed wages and incentives: Evidence from a field experiment. *Review of Economic Studies, 71*, 513–534.

Titmuss, R. M. (1971). *The gift relationship: From human blood to social policy*. New York, NY: Random House.

Van Dijk, F., Sonnemans, J., & Van Winden, F. (2001). Incentive systems in a real effort experiment. *European Economic Review, 45*, 187–214.

Weizman, M., & Kruse, D. (1990). Profit-sharing and productivity. In A. S. Blinder (Ed.), *Paying for productivity: A look at the evidence*. Washington, DC: Brookings Institution.

Whitson, J. A., & Galinsky, A. D. (2008). Lacking control increases illusory pattern perception. *Science, 322*, 115–117.

APPENDIX

Experiment Instructions

Thank you for participating in our study today. You will earn $5.00 just for showing up on time and during the experiment, you will have the opportunity to earn more money. The monetary unit that is used throughout the duration of this experiment is an "experimental monetary unit" (EMU). At the conclusion of the experiment, all EMUs that you have accumulated will be converted into dollars at the rate of 10 EMUs = $1.00. At the conclusion of the experiment, the payments that you have accumulated will be paid to you in cash. This research is sponsored by the Federation for Enterprise Development Beyster Fellowship Program.

Please note that any and all actions and decisions that you make in the exercises or responses you provide are strictly confidential and anonymous. We intend to use the data collected from our study for academic work as it relates to firm organization and industrial relations.

A lab assistant will read all subsequent instructions aloud to you. Please read along with the lab assistant as s/he reads them to you. If you have any questions while these instructions are being read, please raise your hand and we will attempt to answer them. ***You are not allowed to communicate with other participants during the experiment, even to clarify instructions***. Again, if you have any questions, please raise your hand and a lab assistant will assist you. At the end of the experiment session, we will call you individually by your ID number distributed to you to give you your earnings in cash.

Instructions

You have been randomly put into a group with 2 other people (3 total). You are connected through the computer network in this room and your respective identities will remain anonymous throughout the experiment.

In this experiment you will be completing a production task that consists of adding up sets of 2-digit numbers. The use of a calculator is prohibited, but you may use scratch paper and pencil provided to you on your desk. The numbers that you will be adding together are randomly drawn and each problem is presented in the following way:

Example: Screen Shot

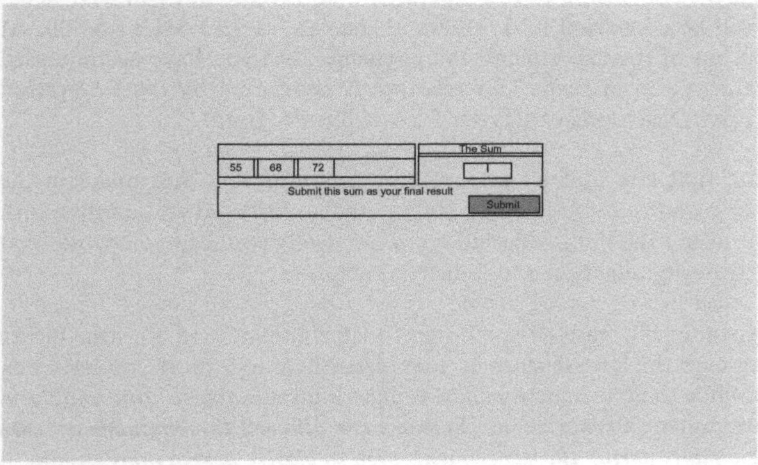

After you submit an answer ***on the computer***, you will be given a new problem to solve. The production task of solving addition problems in each Period will last for 6 minutes.

At the end of 6 minutes you will be presented with a summary of

(1) how many problems you correctly solved as well as your payment for the period
(2) the sum of all correct answers submitted by your group of 3 people
(3) a reminder of how much you were compensated for solving problems in the period. You will be compensated a **fixed payment = 40.00 EMU per period**.

There will be 3 work periods.

"Small-Share Treatment"

Experiment Instructions

Thank you for participating in our study today. You will earn $5.00 just for showing up on time and during the experiment, you will have the opportunity to earn more money. The monetary unit that is used throughout the duration of this experiment is an "experimental monetary unit" (EMU). At the conclusion of the experiment, all EMUs that you have accumulated will be converted into dollars at the rate of 10 EMUs = $1.00. At the conclusion of the experiment, the payments that you have accumulated will be paid to you in cash. This research is sponsored by the Federation for Enterprise Development Beyster Fellowship Program.

Please note that any and all actions and decisions that you make in the exercises or responses you provide are strictly confidential and anonymous. We intend to use the data collected from our study for academic work as it relates to firm organization and industrial relations.

A lab assistant will read all subsequent instructions aloud to you. Please read along with the lab assistant as s/he reads them to you. If you have any questions while these instructions are being read, please raise your hand and we will attempt to answer them. ***You are not allowed to communicate with other participants during the experiment, even to clarify instructions***. Again, if you have any questions, please raise your hand and a lab assistant will assist you. At the end of the experiment session, we will call you individually by your ID number distributed to you to give you your earnings in cash.

Experiment Instructions: The Work Task

You have been randomly put into a group with 2 other people (3 total). You are connected through the computer network in this room and your respective identities will remain anonymous throughout the experiment.

In this experiment you will be completing a production task that consists of adding up sets of 2-digit numbers. The use of a calculator is prohibited, but you may use scratch paper and pencil provided to you on your desk. The numbers that you will be adding together are randomly drawn and each problem is presented in the following way:

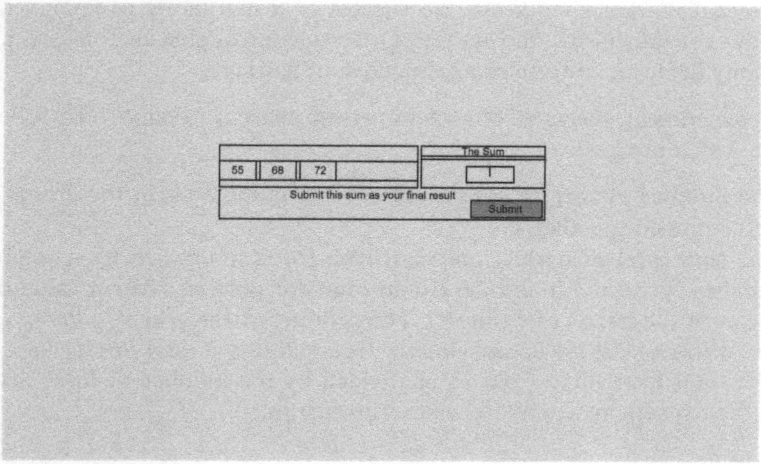

After you submit an answer ***on the computer***, you will be given a new problem to solve. The production task of solving addition problems in each Period will last for 6 minutes.

Part 2 of Instructions – Compensation

In addition to being compensated a **fixed wage of 30.00 EMU** for the 6- minute period, you will also earn dividends corresponding to the value of your ***ownership share***.

What is an ownership share and how are dividends issued?
All three individuals in your group have been allocated **ONE** ownership share of the firm that you belong to. In this experiment, there are **9 total ownership shares** in the firm. Because each individual in your group has the same number of shares (1), and there are 9 total shares, all of the workers in your firm own (1 + 1 + 1)/9 = one-third (1/3rd) of the total shares in the firm.

Determination of the value of a share
The value of a share in any firm is determined by both

(1) the performance of the workers that belong to the firm (worker productivity) and
(2) a number of factors that fall outside of the direct control of workers such as the investment decisions of other shareholders, the presence traders that are speculating on the performance of the firm, changes in

external market conditions, the success of a marketing campaign that draw consumers in, and so on. These uncontrollable factors are randomly determined from the perspective of workers.

In this experiment, the value of each ownership share is calculated by following the 3-step process:

(1) The number of correct answers from all 3 individuals in the group are first summed together.
(2) The sum total of correct answers from (1) is multiplied by a random number between 1.0 and 2.0 (to account for portion of firm value that is out of the hands of workers). The product of the *group's total of correct answers* and *the random number* is equal to the *total firm value.*
(3) The total firm value from (2) is divided by the number of total shares in the firm (there are 9 total shares in each firm).

Example 1:
Let us assume that Subject 1 solves 12 addition problems correctly, Subject 2 solves 18 correctly, and Subject 3 solves 24 correctly. Let us further assume that the randomly determined number between 1.0 and 2.0 is = 1.64

Step 1 of 3:
Subject 1: 12 correct answers
Subject 2: 18 correct answers
Subject 3: 24 correct answers
12 + 18 + 24 = 54 total correct answers

Step 2 of 3:

$$(54 \text{ total correct answers}) \times 1.64 \text{ (randomly determined value)}$$
$$= 88.56 \text{ (total group value)}$$

Step 3 of 3:

$$\frac{88.56 \text{ (Total Group Value)}}{9 \text{ shares}} = 9.84 \text{ EMU}$$

The value of a single ownership = 9.84 EMU
Because you have 3 shares, your ***dividends*** are

$$\mathbf{(1\ shares) \times (9.84) = 9.84}$$

Recall that earnings for all subjects in each Period is = *fixed wage + dividends,* so in this example,

Payoff = 30.00 EMU (fixed wage) + 9.84 (dividends) = **39.84 EMU**

At the end of each 6-minute work period you will be presented with a summary of

(1) how many problems you correctly solved as well as your payment for the period
(2) the sum of all correct answers submitted by your group of 3 people
(3) firm value attributable to factors beyond the control of the effort of workers (the randomly determined value)
(4) the overall value of the firm (product of line (2) and line (3))
(5) the overall value of each individual firm share (line (4) divided by 9 total firm shares)
(6) a statement of your dividends (equal to the value of an ownership share)
(7) your wage for the period (30.00 EMU)
(8) your payment for the pay period (line (7) + line (8))

There will be 3 work periods. At the end of the 3rd period there will be a short survey and we will compile your earnings from all 3 work periods.

"Full Ownership"

Experiment Instructions

Thank you for participating in our study today. You will earn $5.00 just for showing up on time and during the experiment, you will have the opportunity to earn more money. The monetary unit that is used throughout the duration of this experiment is an "experimental monetary unit" (EMU). At the conclusion of the experiment, all EMUs that you have accumulated will be converted into dollars at the rate of 10 EMUs = $1.00. You will be paid in cash today, at the end of the experiment. At the conclusion of the experiment, the payments that you have accumulated will be paid to you in cash. This research is sponsored by the Federation for Enterprise Development Beyster Fellowship Program.

Please note that any and all actions and decisions that you make in the exercises or responses you provide are strictly confidential and anonymous. We intend to use the data collected from our study for academic work as it relates to firm organization and industrial relations.

A lab assistant will read all subsequent instructions aloud to you. Please read along with the lab assistant as s/he reads them to you. If you have any questions while these instructions are being read, please raise your hand and we will attempt to answer them. ***You are not allowed to communicate with other participants during the experiment*, *even to clarify instructions*.** Again, if you have any questions, please raise your hand and a lab assistant will assist you. At the end of the experiment session, we will call you individually by your ID number distributed to you to give you your earnings in cash.

Experiment Instructions: The Work Task

You have been randomly put into a group with 2 other people (3 total). You are connected through the computer network in this room and your respective identities will remain anonymous throughout the experiment.

In this experiment you will be completing a production task that consists of adding up sets of 2-digit numbers. The use of a calculator is prohibited, but you may use scratch paper and pencil provided to you on your desk. The numbers that you will be adding together are randomly drawn and each problem is presented in the following way:

After you submit an answer ***on the computer***, you will be given a new problem to solve. The production task of solving addition problems in each period will last for 6 minutes.

Part 2 of Instructions – Compensation

In addition to being compensated a **fixed wage of 10 EMU** for the 6-minute period, you will also earn dividends corresponding to the value of your ***ownership share***.

What is an ownership share and how are dividends issued?
All three individuals in your group have been allocated **THREE** ownership shares of the firm that you belong to. In this experiment, there are **9 total ownership shares** (all shares owned by you and fellow workers) in the firm. Because each individual in your group has the same number of shares (3), and there are 9 total shares, all of the workers in your firm own (3 + 3 + 3)/9 = 100% of the total shares in the firm.

Determination of the value of a share
The value of a share in any firm is determined by both

(1) the performance of the workers that belong to the firm (worker productivity) and
(2) a number of factors that fall outside of the direct control of workers such as the investment decisions of other shareholders, the presence of traders that are speculating on the performance of the firm, changes in external market conditions, the success of a marketing campaign that draws consumers in, and so on. These uncontrollable factors are randomly determined from the perspective of workers.

In this experiment, the value of each ownership share is calculated by following the 3-step process:

(1) The number of correct answers from all 3 individuals in the group are first summed together.
(2) The sum total of correct answers from (1) is multiplied by a random number between 1.0 and 2.0 (to account for portion of firm value that is out of the hands of workers). The product of the *group's total of correct answers* and *the random number* is equal to the *total firm value.*
(3) The total firm value from (2) is divided by the number of total shares in the firm (there are 9 total shares in each firm).

Example 1:
Let us assume that Subject 1 solves 12 addition problems correctly, Subject 2 solves 18 correctly, and Subject 3 solves 24 correctly. Let us further assume that the randomly determined number between 1.0 and 2.0 is = 1.64

Step 1 of 3:
Subject 1: 12 correct answers
Subject 2: 18 correct answers
Subject 3: 24 correct answers
12 + 18 + 24 = 54 total correct answers

Step 2 of 3:

$$(54 \text{ total correct answers}) \times 1.64 \text{ (randomly determined value)}$$
$$= 88.56 \text{(total group value)}$$

Step 3 of 3:

$$\frac{88.56 \text{ (Total Group Value)}}{9 \text{ shares}} = 9.84 \text{ EMU}$$

The value of a single ownership = 9.84 EMU
Because you have 3 shares, your dividends are

$$\mathbf{(3\ shares) \times (9.84) = 29.52}$$

Recall that earnings for all subjects in each Period is = *fixed wage + dividends,* so in this example,

Payoff = 10 EMU (fixed wage) + 29.52 (dividends) = **39.52 EMU**

At the end of each 6-minute work period you will be presented with a summary of

(1) how many problems you correctly solved as well as your payment for the period
(2) the sum of all correct answers submitted by your group of 3 people
(3) firm value attributable to factors beyond the control of the effort of workers (the randomly determined value)
(4) the overall value of the firm (product of line (2) and line (3))

(5) the overall value of each individual firm share (line (4) divided by 9 total firm shares)
(6) a statement of your dividends (equal to the value of an ownership share)
(7) your wage for the period (10.00 EMU)
(8) your payment for the pay period (line (7) + line (8))

There will be 3 work periods. At the end of the 3rd period there will be a short survey and we will compile your earnings from all 3 work periods.

Before we have a work period, we will have a short 2-minute training period where you familiarize yourself with the work task of solving addition problems.

Are there any questions?

CHAPTER 3

INFORMATION TECHNOLOGY AND HIGH PERFORMANCE WORKPLACE PRACTICES: EVIDENCE ON THEIR INCIDENCE FROM UPSTATE NEW YORK ESTABLISHMENTS

Derek C. Jones and Jeffrey Pliskin

ABSTRACT

Purpose – *To examine the nature and the determinants of the incidence and diffusion of a range of new technologies.*

Design/methodology/approach – *We collected new survey data in 2001 for medium sized establishments in upstate and central New York.*

Findings – *Our econometric findings suggest that the use of new technologies tends to be more extensive in firms in which greater use is made of flexible work practices and flexible compensation practices and when skill levels are high. We find that the use of IT, the intranet, and computer literacy training is greater when the average tenure of managers is*

Sharing Ownership, Profits, and Decision-making in the 21st Century
Advances in the Economic Analysis of Participatory & Labor-Managed Firms, Volume 14, 61–81

ISSN: 0885-3339/doi:10.1108/S0885-3339(2013)0000014004

low, which might reflect a greater comfort with new technologies by younger managers. Larger establishments tend to use the Internet more extensively, which may reflect the cost of setting up Internet billing and purchasing systems, and an intranet communication system. Managerial tenure does not affect the use of the Internet in general perhaps because these might be operations that are less central to the activities of more senior managers. Also, we find mixed evidence for our digital divide hypothesis that predicts that the use of new technologies would be greatest in metropolitan areas and least in rural locations.

Research limitations/implications – *We recognize it is potentially risky to draw inferences from a relatively small survey.*

Originality/value – *Some findings mesh with those contained in earlier studies (e.g., Black & Lynch, 2004) though, importantly, now finding emerge when a broader range of new technologies is being considered.*

Keywords: High performance workplace practices; information technology; New York State

JEL classifications: JO; M50

INTRODUCTION

Some economists argued that the unanticipated acceleration of U.S. aggregate productivity growth in the 1990s was partly attributable to investments in a variety of new information technologies.[1] The term, "The New Economy" was coined because these investments transformed the ways many firms were organized and operated.[2] While macroeconomists were examining aggregate and industry-level data to identify the role of investments in information technology, applied micro-economists used data on individual firms and establishments (e.g., plants) to investigate the factors that explain (within industry) differences in productivity across firms and across plants, including international productivity differences.[3] One focus of some of these studies is the role that different rates of adoption of the new information and communication technologies played in these productivity differences. In addition to investments in information technologies, economists have also examined the productivity effects of adopting high performance workplace practices (HPWPs) (e.g., team production and group incentive pay[4]) as well as the interaction of information technologies and HPWPs.[5]

In this paper we use new survey data on upstate New York establishments to investigate the determinants of the use of information technologies, such as computers, intranets for communication with employees, or the Internet for purposes such as recruitment. Among the determinants we examine is the establishment's use of HPWPs.

Our data are unusual in several respects. In contrast to some previous work that has concentrated on larger establishments, our surveys emphasize medium-sized establishments (employing 100–500). In addition, whereas much previous work has focused on establishments located in metropolitan markets, to investigate hypotheses relating to the potential impact of location, survey data are generated so that many establishments are located in rural areas, which we expect would reduce the use of both information technologies and participatory workplace practices. In addition, the central and upstate New York region is interesting to study because growth was much slower over the decade preceding the collection of our data than in most other areas of the United States and, indeed, some parts (especially rural areas) were and still are often regarded as economically depressed.

But perhaps of most interest is that the range of technologies we investigate is broader than has often been examined in the literature, which has tended to focus on the use of personal computers by both managerial and nonmanagerial workers. Since the pace of technical change means that this "computer focus" does not adequately capture many relevant new technologies, our surveys were designed to also provide evidence on the nature and determinants of other and newer technologies, such as intranets, Internet billing, and web sites. Also, we note that previous work on the new economy has centered on profit sharing and the use of HPWPs, such as team production, Total Quality Management, and quality circles (e.g., Black & Lynch, 2001). In addition to these innovations in work organization and compensation, we also investigate potential relationships between compensation practices, such as employee ownership. In recent years employee ownership and other forms of "shared capitalism" (Kruse, Freeman, & Blasi, 2010) have become commonplace in the United States and we argue such practices may be associated with the incidence of new technologies. Hence, potentially our data enable us study more comprehensively than have others, associations between the existence of a range of information technologies and diverse flexible work practices and forms of flexible compensation.

The plan of this paper is as follows. In the next section, we briefly sketch out some of our key hypotheses about the use of information technologies.

In the third section, we describe our survey data and summarize the diffusion of new information technologies among our sample of establishments. Empirical findings on the determinants of diverse measures of IT use are reported in the fourth section. The final section contains conclusions.

THE USE OF INFORMATION TECHNOLOGIES

Our exploratory econometric work builds on the work of others in related areas and examines the role of factors including enterprise size and worker characteristics such as tenure, skill, and union membership. For example, it is hypothesized that larger establishments and establishments that are part of larger organizations will be better able to afford the initial investment costs associated with the introduction of new technologies.[6] Also, firms with more educated or skilled work forces[7] are likely to receive bigger benefits from IT investments (and meet less resistance to these changes from their workforces) and that highly unionized establishments are more apt to resist technical changes. Tenure of nonmanagerial workers may have an ambiguous effect on the use of IT. Increases in tenure will tend to lead to bigger payoffs because workers will remain at the establishment longer. On the other hand, high average tenure might indicate an older workforce that may experience difficulties adapting to new methods. Our work will enable us to see whether such factors appear to play similar roles for different technological innovations. For example, unions may see the development of intranets and online recruitment technologies as greater challenges to their traditional roles than the introduction of other new technologies such as Internet billing and Internet purchasing.

Another area we investigate in this broad area is whether or not innovations concerning new technologies tend to coexist with innovations in other areas, especially concerning work organization and new forms of compensation. In particular, many have argued (e.g., Milgrom & Roberts, 1995) that there are synergies to the introduction of *packages* of HPWPs.[8] Moreover some have argued that the individual, group, and organizational payoffs to participatory workplace practices tend to be higher when accompanied by flexible forms of compensation systems such as profit sharing and employee ownership (e.g., Ben-Ner & Jones, 1995). While there is an emerging empirical literature in this field, again we seek to examine incidence for larger sets of new technologies and for packages of HPWPs and flexible compensation that are broader than others typically have examined in the literature on the new economy, mainly by the inclusion of employee ownership in our study. That is, we investigate whether the roles played by participatory workplace practices and flexible compensation in influencing the adoption of new technologies might differ by the type of new technology. For example, the existence of self-managed teams is likely to yield bigger payoffs to the presence of an extensive intranet that will enable teams to access and use much more current information (e.g., order details and task schedules) than otherwise. However, such considerations are apt to be far less important for other new technologies such as online billing and recruitment. In addition, we are also interested in determining whether data generated for establishments located in a relatively slow-growing part of the United States provide evidence on the incidence of IT practices that resembles that obtained for larger firms and establishments located in more buoyant areas of the United States.

Moreover, we are interested in determining whether there is a "digital divide" among establishments by location. In other words, are these new technologies, as well as workplace practices that often accompany these technological innovations, to be found as frequently in firms that are located in rural regions as in firms that are found in metropolitan areas? We hypothesize that, for several reasons including geographical isolation,[9] it is harder for managers in nonmetropolitan establishments to innovate than for their metropolitan counterparts. Managers of establishments in nonmetropolitan areas, and especially those in rural areas, do not have easy access to local trade associations, active Chambers of Commerce, or even informal business associations. Since rural managers do not have these sorts of networks, they have much more difficulty than do urban managers in learning new practices from other managers or in being alerted to the potential of new technologies and innovative workplace practices from them.

Second, factors such as the size of the firm, the small size of towns, the depressed nature of local communities, and geographic isolation reduce the amount of new talent coming into firms. Especially in rural areas, establishments rarely get new managers coming from other firms where they might bring new ideas. And they seldom (or never) get new professionals (with MBAs or equivalent qualifications) who come with "the latest ideas."[10] Again, this diminishes the chances that managers will even be aware of or be thinking about new management practices or new technologies. Third, isolation means that managers do not have easy access to universities and other institutions that tend to facilitate the discussion of new ideas, for example, by arranging for one-day seminars. Fourth, rural firms tend to develop long-term relationships with managers and managers sometimes become complacent and lack an incentive to be "up on the latest techniques." They are not being pushed by others or even expected to be innovative.

A second theme in accounting for a possible digital divide based on firm location, is that workers in nonmetropolitan areas tend to have fewer employment options than their urban counterparts. In turn, this shapes labor relations and the ability and readiness of such workers to seek employment in and undertake training for jobs in firms employing new technologies and new forms of work organization. Especially in rural areas, for any given occupation, there is likely to be only one or two potential employers. Also, rural counties are geographically large and transportation costs for low-income workers are a major expense. Moreover, there are other important features of local nonmetro labor markets. On average, many workers in several industries have only a high school level of education and low skills. There is substantial regional immobility of labor, with most native-born workers remaining close to the areas in which they were born or, in the case of immigrants from overseas, remaining in the area in which they initially arrived. Labor market experience is limited and usually restricted to one line of activity. In addition, firms and establishments are predominantly small to medium size. Since these workers are less likely than their metro and urban counterparts both to have computers in the home and to have easy access to such facilities in community centers such as libraries and universities,[11] we expect that workers in rural settings are apt to be less prepared than their metropolitan and urban counterparts for jobs that involve new technologies or new methods of work organization.

A related argument concerns the comfort level of managers with the adoption of new technologies. We hypothesize that older managers are much less apt than their younger counterparts to introduce new technologies. In other words, an organizational culture that embraces widespread technological innovativeness is more likely to be associated with the presence of younger managers.

SURVEY DATA

Our survey data collection proceeded in two steps. First, surveys were mailed to all medium-sized for-profit establishments in four adjacent counties (Oneida, Herkimer, Onondaga, and Madison) and to 10–20% of randomly chosen medium-sized establishments in all other counties in upstate and central New York.[12] After several pilot surveys, two detailed surveys were distributed in the middle of the summer of 2001. In the survey whose findings are discussed in this paper, the focus was on new technologies and HR practices with many questions soliciting information on the diffusion of diverse new technologies (NT) and work innovations.[13] After a period of some weeks, nonrespondents[14] were contacted by phone. They were urged to either submit the information by mail or to arrange for a telephone survey. The net result is that we have about 125 responses for the NT-HR survey.[15] In fact essentially all of the responses were submitted during the period July 2001–September 2001. Indeed the initial response rate from adjacent counties was more than 20% and thus quite encouraging. However, subsequently the response rates dropped substantially, especially in the aftermath of September 11 (and with the onset of the business recession).

The basic picture that emerges from these data is reported in Table 1 and is most interesting. Parts A and B report information on the existence of individual new technologies in 2000 and 1998 respectively for all respondents. From this we see that by 2000 the presence of a web site had become quite commonplace: 85% of establishment either had their own web site or were part of a larger organization that had one. In 1998, the corresponding figure was only 49%, implying a fairly rapid rate of adoption. Intranet systems for communicating with employees had also become widely used by 2000, and this technology was also adopted relatively quickly over the previous two years. We also observe that the use of the Internet to advertise for job vacancies grew very rapidly between 1998 and 2000 and that nearly half of the establishments used the Internet for recruiting by 2000. In contrast, the use of the Internet for billing was essentially absent in upstate New York throughout the period. The use of Internet-based purchasing systems was virtually nil in 1998, but had been adopted by 10% of the establishments by 2000. On average, 55% of nonmanagerial workers used information technologies during a typical workday, a modest increase over the 44% figure for 1998. Formal training in computer literacy and other new technologies has increased modestly between 1998 and 2000, perhaps reflecting the increased use of IT by nonmanagerial workers and the greater use of the intranet.

We also examine the existence of new technologies by location. Firms are divided in to three groups – those that are located in four large metropolitan areas (e.g., close to or in Rochester, Buffalo, Albany, and Syracuse), close to or in urban areas (e.g., in Utica or Binghamton) and in

Table 1. Incidence of New Technologies Among New York Establishments.

	Web Site	Internet Billing	Internet Purchasing	Intranet	Technology Training	Internet Recruiting	Use of IT
Part A: Year = 2000							
All	85	5	10	75	28	48	55
Metro	85	8	15	79	36	58	62
Urban	93	2	7	78	26	56	60
Rural	93	3	7	79	17	34	37
FWP	91	6	12	75	37	58	61
No FWP	89	5	7	73	13	43	44
Part B: Year = 1998							
All	49	1	1	37	21	12	44
Metro	50	2	2	46	32	23	49
Urban	54	0	0	39	14	7	48
Rural	55	0	0	28	13	3	31
FWP	56	2	0	47	26	14	50
No FWP	52	0	0	31	10	14	34

	Percent of Establishments with the Number of Practices	
Number of Internet/Intranet Practices	1998	2000
Part C: An Index of Internet/Intranet Use		
0	38	8
1	32	12
2	24	40
3	6	33
4	1	6
5	0	2

Notes to Parts A and B:

1. Web Site: the percent of establishments with either their own web site or a company web site if part of a larger organization.
2. Internet Billing: the percent of establishments with an Internet-based billing system.
3. Internet Purchasing: the percent of establishments with an Internet-based purchasing system.
4. Intranet: the percent of establishments that have an intranet system to communicate with employees.
5. Technology Training: the average percent of nonmanagerial employees who receive formal training in computer literacy and other technologies that are new to the firm.
6. Internet Recruiting: percent of establishments that advertise job vacancies on the Internet.
7. Use of IT: the average percent of nonmanagerial employees who use information technologies sometime during a typical workday.
8. All: all establishments.
9. Metro: establishments located in metropolitan areas.
10. Urban: establishments located in urban areas.
11. Rural: establishments located in rural areas.
12. FWP: establishments that use at least one of the following flexible workplace practices for its nonmanagerial workers – self-directed work teams, Total Quality Management, and employee problem solving groups or quality circles.
13. No FWP: establishments that do not use any of the following flexible workplace practices for its nonmanagerial workers – self-directed work teams, Total Quality Management, and employee problem solving groups or quality circles.
14. The summary statistics for establishments with and without flexible workplace practices are based on fewer establishments than the other results because of missing data on the use of these practices.

Notes to Part C:

(1) Internet/intranet practices consist of an establishment or company web site; an Internet-based billing system; an Internet-based purchasing system; the use of the Internet to recruit new employees; and an intranet system to communicate with employees.
(2) Totals do not add to 100% because of rounding.

rural areas (not in or close to a town with more than 50,000). As expected we find that the use of IT by nonmanagerial employees, technology training, and Internet recruiting are lower in rural areas than in metropolitan and urban areas. Surprisingly, the presence of web sites and the use of the intranet to communicate with employees is at least as great in rural areas as in urban and metropolitan locations.

Comparing establishments that used one or more flexible workplace practices with those who had none, we find that in the former, there was greater use of IT by nonmanagerial employees and a higher proportion of these workers received technology training. In addition, establishments with flexible workplace practice tended to make greater use of the internet to recruit workers.

In Part C of Table 1 we construct a simple index of Internet/intranet use. This index equals the number of Internet/intranet practices used by an establishment, where these practices include: an establishment or company web site; an Internet-based billing system; an Internet-based purchasing system; the use of the Internet to recruit new employees; and an intranet system to communicate with employees. This index captures the increased use of these practices that is revealed in Parts A and B. For example, while 38% of the establishments used none of the five practices in 1998, this was the case in only 8% of the establishments in 2000. This part of Table 1 also shows that very few establishments were very wired in 2000 – only 2% had all five practices and an additional 6% had four out of the five practices. Also there is some indication that the rate of adoption of new technology slowed toward the end of the study period.

THE DETERMINANTS OF THE INCIDENCE OF NEW TECHNOLOGIES

In this section we report econometric results on the factors that are associated with the use of information technologies. Our analysis is cross-sectional and focuses on 2000, which is the year for which we have the most observations. We examine the following five indicators of the use of information technologies: the percentage of nonmanagerial workers who use information technologies on the job; a three-level index to measure the extent to which Internet/intranet technologies are used; the use of the intranet; the incidence of the use of the Internet to recruit new employees; and, finally, the proportion of nonmanagerial workers who received formal training in computer literacy and other technologies that are new to the establishment. For each measure, we include controls for unionization; the use of flexible workplace practices (self-directed work teams, Total Quality Management, and employee problem solving groups or quality circles), group incentive pay (gain-sharing or profit sharing), and employee ownership; establishment size, whether the establishment is part of a larger organization, tenure of both nonmanagerial employees and managers, the skill level of the establishment's average nonmanagerial employee's job, industry (manufacturing, finance, retail, and other industries), and location (metropolitan, urban, and rural).

Column 1 of Table 2 reports the coefficients from a two-limit tobit model for the percentage of nonmanagerial workers who use new technologies sometime during the typical workday. A two-limit tobit model is used to account for both establishments in which no nonmanagerial workers use IT (2 left-censored observations) and establishments in all nonmanagerial workers use IT (19 right-censored observations). Our preliminary findings indicate that use is greater for skilled workforces and in establishments located in urban or metropolitan locations. The average tenure of managers is associated with a smaller percentage of nonmanagerial workers using IT, which might reflect the greater familiarity of younger managers with new technologies. IT use is positively associated with financial participation by nonmanagerial workers. Workers in establishments that use group incentives or encourage employee ownership might cooperate with the adoption of new technologies insofar as they will benefit financially if these technologies improve business performance. IT use increases with the tenure of nonmanagerial workers, but the coefficient is not significant at conventional levels. IT use is not associated with unionization, establishment size (measured by the natural logarithm of establishment employment), being part of a larger organization, or the use of flexible workplace practices (Table 3).

We classified establishments into high, moderate, and low users of new technologies that involve the Internet or the intranet. The classification reflects the use of the following technologies: having a web site (either at the establishment level or firm level for those establishments that are part of a larger organization); the use of an Internet-based billing system; the use of an Internet-based purchasing system; the use of an intranet system for communicating with employees; and advertising external vacancies using the Internet. To be classified as a high user, the establishment must have had at least three of these five systems. Moderate users had two systems, while low users had only one system or none. Since the three

Table 2. Determinants of the Use of New Technologies.

	IT use (1)	IT Index (2)	Intranet Use (3)	Internet Recruiting (4)	Technology Training (5)	Any Training (6)
ln(labor)	−6.75 (1.45)	.46 (2.08)	3.78 (.51)	.70 (2.39)	2.8 (.53)	−.79 (.10)
Large	2.04 (.29)	.67 (2.20)	30.2 (2.60)	−.47 (1.34)	7.8 (.95)	11.88 (1.01)
ln(tenure)	10.6 (1.54)	.09 (.30)	33.6 (2.95)	−.70 (1.84)	17.65 (2.10)	38.22 (3.17)
ln(tenure of managers)	−39.1 (4.79)	.04 (.13)	−29.2 (2.33)	.57 (1.44)	−28.63 (3.13)	−50.61 (3.48)
High skill	30.1 (3.93)	.92 (2.80)	37.4 (3.10)	.94 (2.41)	18.5 (2.12)	22.83 (1.77)
Low skill	−2.38 (.24)	.85 (1.92)	10.1 (.63)	.05 (.10)	−7.1 (.61)	44.17 (2.69)
Unionization	6.22 (.75)	−.99 (2.82)	−33.8 (2.56)	−.40 (1.00)	−11.77 (1.21)	−21.20 (1.55)
Flexible workplace practices	.37 (.05)	.55 (1.90)	8.6 (.78)	.60 (1.75)	13.19 (1.58)	33.18 (2.75)
Employee ownership	13.9 (.65)	1.07 (2.65)	3.0 (.22)	1.12 (2.36)	−11.5 (1.22)	−15.30 (1.10)
Incentive pay	19.6 (2.79)	.20 (.69)	6.46 (.57)	.40 (1.17)	14.32 (1.69)	1.48 (.13)
Metropolitan	16.7 (1.99)	−.44 (1.20)	−.89 (.06)	.72 (1.60)	18.46 (1.82)	12.53 (.86)
Urban	23.2 (2.85)	.07 (.21)	11.56 (.88)	.62 (1.44)	17.56 (1.80)	29.80 (2.15)
No. of observations	91	95	92	95	90	90
No. of left-censored observations	2		20		14	2
No. of right-censored observations	19		17		12	29

Notes: (1) See Table 3 for variable definitions. (2) The results for IT Use, Intranet Use, Technology Training, and Any Training were obtained from two-limit tobit models with a lower threshold of 0 and an upper threshold of 100. (3) The results for IT Index were obtained from an ordered probit model. (4) The results for Internet Recruiting were obtained from a probit model. (5) All models include industry dummy variables. (6) Absolute value of asymptotic t statistics are in parentheses.

Table 3. Definitions of Variables.

Variable Name	Definition
IT use	Percent of nonmanagerial employees who use IT sometime during the workday.
IT index	A three-level index that denotes high, moderate, and low users of the Internet/intranet based on five features: web site, Internet billing system, Internet purchase system, intranet communication system, and advertising external vacancies on the Internet. High users have at least three features, moderate have two, and low users have no more than one.
Intranet use	Percent of employees who receive intranet communications.
Internet recruiting	A dummy variable that equals 1 if the establishment advertises external vacancies on the Internet.
Technology training	Percent of nonmanagerial employees who receive training in computer literacy or new technologies.
Any training	Percent of nonmanagerial employees who receive any type of training.
Labor	Total establishment employment.
Large	A dummy variable that equals 1 if the establishment is part of a larger organization.
Tenure	Average tenure of nonmanagerial employees (years).
Tenure of managers	Average tenure of managers (years).
High skill	A dummy variable that equals 1 if the skill level of the average nonmanagerial employee's job is very or extremely skilled.
Low skill	A dummy variable that equals 1 if the skill level of the average nonmanagerial employee's job is slightly skilled or not skilled.
Unionization	A dummy variable that equals 1 if some nonmanagerial employees are covered by a collective bargaining agreement.
Flexible workplace practices	A dummy variable that equals 1 if some nonmanagerial employees participate in one or more of the following practices: self-directed work teams, Total Quality Management, and employee problem solving groups or quality circles.
Employee ownership	A dummy variable that equals 1 if there is a plan that encourages some nonmanagerial employees to own shares of the company.
Incentive pay	A dummy variable that equals 1 if the compensation of some nonmanagerial employees includes a group incentive (e.g., gain-sharing or profit-sharing bonus).
Metropolitan	A dummy variable that equals 1 if the establishment is located in or near one of the four large cities in upstate New York.
Urban	A dummy variable that equals 1 if the establishment is located in or near one of the smaller cities in upstate New York.

categories are ordered, we estimated an ordered probit model to examine how the use of Internet/intranet practices varied with establishment characteristics. Our preliminary results, which are reported in column 2 of Table 2, show that these practices are more common in establishments that are larger as well as being part of a larger organization and in those that encourage employee ownership or use flexible workplace practices. Consistent with the argument that unions are unfavorably disposed toward new technologies, these practices are less common in unionized establishments. In addition, we find that these new technologies occur less often in firms in which the typical nonmanagerial worker's job is moderately skilled relative to either very/extremely skilled or slightly/not skilled. We are unable to explain this non-monotonic relationship with the skill level of the workforce. There is no association between the IT index and location in a metropolitan, urban, or rural area.

We report in column 3 of Table 2 the coefficients of a two-limit tobit model for the percentage of employees who receive intranet communications. A two-limit tobit model is used to account for both establishments in which no workers receive intranet communications (20 left-censored observations) and establishments in all workers receive intranet communications (17 right-censored observations). Consistent with a "union resistance to new technology" argument, the tobit results indicate that intranet use is lower in establishments that are unionized. In addition, intranet use is also found to be lower in establishments that have a shorter average tenure for managers, a finding that again might reflect the greater willingness of younger managers to embrace new technologies. In contrast, average tenure of nonmanagerial workers is positively associated with the extent of intranet use. Intranet use is also greater when the job of the average nonmanagerial is very or extremely skilled. This finding is consistent with the hypothesis that the payoff to intranet use is likely to be greater in firms in which skilled workers may be able to use new technologies for diverse applications, such as accessing online plans and diagrams. There is no strong evidence that intranet use is affected by establishment location or is associated with HPWPs, contrary to our hypothesis that firms with these practices are more likely to embrace and benefit from new technologies. Although establishment size does not matter, intranet use is greater when the establishment is part of a multiple establishment organization, perhaps reflecting the need to communicate among separate establishments.

The use of the Internet to advertise external job vacancies is examined by estimating a probit model (see column 4 of Table 2). We find that the use of the Internet for recruiting is greater in larger establishments, when establishments have flexible workplace practices, and in those in which the job of the average nonmanagerial is very or extremely skilled. Skilled workers might be more inclined to search for new positions using the Internet as well as conventional means. Establishments with some employee ownership are also more likely to advertise vacancies on the Internet. The probability of Internet recruiting declines as the average tenure of nonmanagerial workers increases, which might indicate that firms with a more stable workforce are less likely to adopt a new approach to recruiting. (This interpretation is also supported by unreported results in which we replaced the average tenure of workers with the natural logarithm of the estimated number of workers with less than 1 year of tenure with the firm. The coefficient of this variable was positive and highly significant.) Coefficients that are not quite statistically significant at conventional levels imply that this recruiting tool is more common when the average tenure of managers is high and when firms use profit sharing or gain sharing. However use of the Internet for recruitment is found to be negatively associated with unionization, being part of a larger organization, and being located in a rural area. Perhaps firms located in rural areas primarily recruit workers from the immediate areas and that these potential hires may not have access to the Internet and can rely on connections within their local communities to learn of job openings.

In the remaining columns of Table 2 we report findings concerning the determinants of the provision of training to nonmanagerial workers.[16] In column 5 we first report findings for the use of formal training in computer literacy and other new technologies that is provided to nonmanagerial workers. This is done by estimating a two-limit tobit model for the percentage of these workers who received such training. We use a two-limit tobit model to account for both establishments in which no nonmanagerial worker receives training (14 left-censored observations) and those in which all nonmanagerial workers receive training (12 right-censored observations). For this technology we find support for our digital divide hypothesis – more training is provided to workers when the establishment is located in a metropolitan or urban area rather than in a rural area. The following establishment characteristics are also associated with more workers receiving this sort of training: the job of the average nonmanagerial worker is very or extremely skilled; use of group incentives; the average tenure of managers is shorter; and the average tenure of nonmanagers is longer. In addition, the use of flexible workplace practices is also associated with more workers being trained in new technologies, but the coefficient is not quite significant at the 10% level. More nonmanagerial workers receive computer training in nonunionized establishments, but the coefficient on unionization is not significant at the 10% level even for a one-tailed test. In some cases, our training findings correspond to our results on the use of IT and the intranet. For example, establishments with short tenures for managers might use more computer literacy training because more of their nonmanagerial workers use IT and more workers receive intranet communications. A similar conclusion might explain why a greater proportion of the workforce might receive technology training when the average nonmanagerial job is very or extremely skilled. In contrast, we find that establishments with flexible workplace practices provide more computer literacy training (coefficient is nearly significant at the 10% level), but their nonmanagerial workers are not more likely to use IT or receive intranet communications.

To help gauge whether our results on computer literacy training are largely capturing differences across establishments in their training infrastructure, in column 6 of Table 2 we report the estimated two-limit tobit model for the use of formal training for any purpose (including computer literacy) that is provided to nonmanagerial workers. (Both training results are for the same establishments.) One notable difference between the results for the two training measures is that a higher percentage of workers receive formal training of any kind when the job of the average nonmanagerial is slightly skilled or not skilled relative to when the job is moderately skilled. This suggests that low skilled worker tend to receive general training but not training in computer literacy and other new technologies. Although establishments in metropolitan locations provide technology training to a greater fraction of its nonmanagerial workforce than establishments located in rural areas, there is no significant difference between these two locations in the proportion provided training in general.

In general, our findings, which are based on a modest number of establishments, suggest that as expected the use of new technologies is more extensive when the workforce of the establishment is highly skilled. Larger establishments tend to use the Internet more extensively, which may reflect the cost of setting up Internet billing and purchasing systems, and an intranet communication system. We find that the use of IT, the intranet, and computer literacy training is greater when the average tenure of managers is low, which we argued above might reflect a greater comfort with new technologies by younger managers. Managerial tenure does not affect the use of the Internet in general perhaps because these might be operations that are less central to the activities of more senior managers. We find weak evidence in support of our digital divide hypothesis which, reflecting differences in several factors including human capital and the costs of information, predicts that the use of new technologies would be greatest in metropolitan areas and least in rural locations. In addition, we also find some support for the hypothesis that use of new technologies will be more extensive when firms also use flexible work practices and have adopted flexible compensation systems such as profit sharing or employee ownership. As such these findings are consistent with those who hypothesize that the payoff to new technologies is apt to be greater when introduced in firms with innovative work organizations and flexible compensation systems. Finally, there is weak evidence that the presence of unions deters the introduction of new technologies.

CONCLUSIONS

Based on survey data for medium-sized establishments in upstate and central New York, we examine the nature and the determinants of the incidence and diffusion of a range of new technologies. While it is potentially risky to draw inferences from a relatively small survey, it is clear that some new technologies were already quite widespread in upstate New York at the start of the 21th century. Web sites at either the establishment or company level had become quite commonplace by 2001, even in establishments located in rural areas. Intranet communication had also been adopted by a large fraction of the establishments in our survey and there is no indication of a digital divide between rural and more urban locations. Over the few years immediately prior to our survey, the use of the Internet for recruitment grew quickly. In contrast to the use of web sites, intranet communication, and Internet recruiting, Internet-based billing and purchasing systems had been adopted by relatively few establishments.

Based on our survey data we investigated the determinants of adoption of different technologies. These econometric findings suggest that the use of new technologies tends to be more extensive in firms in which greater use is made of flexible work practices and flexible compensation practices and when skill levels are high. As such these findings mesh with those contained in earlier studies (e.g., Black & Lynch, 2004) though, importantly, now the finding emerges when a broader range of new technologies is being considered.[17] We find that the use of IT, the intranet, and computer literacy training is greater when the average tenure of managers is low, which we argued above might reflect a greater comfort with new technologies by younger managers. Larger establishments tend to use the Internet more extensively, which may reflect the cost of setting up Internet billing and purchasing systems, and an intranet communication system. Managerial tenure does not affect the use of the Internet in general perhaps because these might be operations that are less central to the activities of more senior managers. Also, we find mixed evidence for our digital divide hypothesis that predicts that the use of new technologies would be greatest in metropolitan areas and least in rural locations.

Since the survey was undertaken a raft of even newer technologies have appeared and diffused rapidly including mobile devices such as smartphones and tablets, powerful software such as SAP, and various forms of social media, notably Facebook. The literature that examines the ramifications of these new technologies for firm and worker outcomes, and their relationships with financial participation and innovative work practices continues to mushroom. In some areas there have been strong strides made in identifying key mechanisms (such as the role of mutual monitoring) that typically lead to enhanced outcomes for both firms and workers (e.g., Kruse et al., 2010). At the same time the literature that investigates issues surrounding incidence is much less developed. However, the stylized facts do seem clear – the evidence points to the continued growing importance of flexible forms of compensation, including forms of performance-related pay (e.g., Bryson, Freeman, Lucifora, Pellizzari, & Perotin, 2012) and other forms of shared capitalism, as well as innovative work practices such as teams and quality circles (e.g., Askenazy & Caroli, 2010). And these developments appear to have proceeded apace with the diffusion of new technologies. Thus if new technologies continue to appear we would expect to see a continuation of these mutually associated and reinforcing trends, and employee ownership and profit sharing would be expected to continue to spread. However some see dark clouds on the horizon. Thus Gordon (2012) expects the pace of technological innovation to slow; he is not confident that future innovations will result in the efficiency gains (including reductions in monitoring costs) that appear to have flown from new technologies in the past (Lazear, 2000.)

NOTES

1. For example, see Jorgenson, Ho, and Stiroh (2008), Oliner and Sichel (2000), and Oliner, Sichel, and Stiroh (2007) for assessments of the relative importance of information technology in explaining aggregate productivity growth and productivity growth outside the information technology-producing sectors.
2. See, for example, the discussions in Jones (2003).
3. See Syverson (2011) for a survey.
4. Blinder (1990, p. 1) argued that the productivity slowdown of the 1970s and 1980s might lead the United States "to slip into the second rank of nations in terms

of wealth and income." Although, he recognized technological innovations would promote faster growth, he was not optimistic such innovations were on the horizon. Thus, he proposed that new forms of labor compensation might be adopted to enhance labor productivity.

5. For example, see Batt (1999), Black and Lynch (2001, 2004), Brynjolfsson and Hitt (2000), Bresnahan, Brynjolfsson, and Hitt (2002), Bartel, Ichniowski, and Shaw (2007), on the role of investment in information technology. See Black and Lynch (2001, 2004) and Cappelli and Neumark (2001) on the role of adoption of high performance workplace practices. Askenazy and Caroli (2010) examined the effect of new work practices such as job rotation and quality norms and new information and communication technologies on work injuries and psychological stress.

6. This parallels the hypothesis that Osterman (1994) advanced about the greater ability of larger organizations (i.e., larger establishments and establishments that are part of a larger organization) to afford to invest in new flexible workplace practices such as self-managed teams, job rotation, quality circles, and Total Quality Management.

7. Gale, Wojan, and Olmsted (2002) examine how worker skill requirements vary with the number of production technologies, communication technologies, and work organization practices used in sample of U.S. manufacturing establishments. Bresnahan et al. (2002) examine the complementarity of information technology, workplace organization (e.g., self-managed teams and quality circles), and the skill level of workers.

8. For an early empirical study that investigated possible complementarities among various human resource management practices, see Ichniowski, Shaw, and Prennushi (2007).

9. Bartoloni and Baussola (2001) examine the role of information effects on technological diffusion using a sample of Italian manufacturing firms. Bloom and Van Reenen (2010) discuss the role of information in explaining the slow diffusion of new management practices, which they argue often "resemble" new process technologies.

10. Bloom and Van Reenen (2010) in their review of the diffusion of new management practices discuss the importance of prior experience with a new innovation as explaining its adoption.

11. The survey data were collected in 2001.

12. Lists of firms by size were obtained from a private vendor. These lists were checked for accuracy by comparing with lists of firms provided by other sources such as local development bodies and Chambers of Commerce.

13. The other survey attempted to collect business information, including expenditures by types of IT (including hardware, software, and communication technologies). Again the survey was ambitious and aimed to assemble panel data for years since 1996.

14. Almost 20% of surveys were returned as non-deliverable – addresses were inaccurate.

15. Our econometric work below is based on fewer observations because of missing data on some variables.

16. Bartel et al. (2007) found that establishments in the valve manufacturing industry were more likely to provide technical training when they adopted new production technologies.

17. In many ways our survey findings correspond to the experiences of the 10 establishments studied in depth by Jones, Kato, and Weinberg (2003).

ACKNOWLEDGMENTS

We are indebted to the Levitt Center at Hamilton College for financing the survey of upstate New York establishments. We are grateful for comments on earlier drafts from Ann Owen and participants at a Conference of the International Association for the Economics of Participation. In addition, we acknowledge research assistance from Michael Kaufman, Jiang Li, Farah Zakir, and Hedgecote Associates.

REFERENCES

Askenazy, P., & Caroli, E. (2010). Innovative work practices, information technologies, and working conditions: Evidence for France. *Industrial Relations*, *49*(4), 544–565.

Bartoloni, E., & Baussola, M. (2001). The determinants of technology adoption in Italian manufacturing industries. *Review of Industrial Organization*, *19*, 305–338.

Bartel, A., Ichniowski, C., & Shaw, K. (2007). How does information technology affect productivity? Plant level comparisons of product innovation, process improvement, and worker skills. *Quarterly Journal of Economics*, *122*(4), 1721–1758.

Batt, R. (1999). Work organization, technology, and performance in customer service and sales. *Industrial and Labor Relations Review*, *52*(4), 539–564.

Ben-Ner, A., & Jones, D. C. (1995). Employee participation, ownership, and productivity: A theoretical framework. *Industrial Relations*, *34*(4), 532–554.

Black, S. E., & Lynch, L. M. (2001). How to compete: The impact of workplace practices and information technology on productivity. *Review of Economics and Statistics*, *83*(3), 435–445.

Black, S. E., & Lynch, L. M. (2004). What's driving the new economy: The benefits of workplace innovation. *Economic Journal*, *114*(February), F97–116.

Blinder, A. S. (1990). Introduction. In A. S. Blinder (Ed.), *Paying for productivity*. Washington, DC: The Brookings Institution.

Bloom, N., & Van Reenen, J. (2010). Why do management practices differ across firms and countries. *Journal of Economic Perspectives*, *24*(1), 203–224.

Bresnahan, T., Brynjolfsson, E., & Hitt, L. M. (2002). Information technology, workplace organization, and the demand for skilled labor: Firm-level evidence. *Quarterly Journal of Economics*, *117*(1), 339–376.

Brynjolfsson, E., & Hitt, L. M. (2000). Beyond computation: Information technology, organizational transformation and business performance. *Journal of Economic Perspective*, *14*(4), 23–48.

Bryson, A., Freeman, R., Lucifora, C., Pellizzari, M., & Perotin, V. (2012). *Paying for performance: Incentive pay schemes and employees' financial participation*. Center for Economic Performance, Discussion Paper No. 1112, January.
Cappelli, P., & Carter, W. (2000). *Computers, work organization, and wage outcomes*. NBER Working Paper #7987.
Gale, H. F., Wojan, T. R., & Olmsted, J. (2002). Skills, flexible manufacturing technology and work organization. *Industrial Relations*, *41*(1), 48–79.
Gordon, R. J. (2012). *Is U.S. economic growth over? Faltering innovation confronts the six headwinds*. NBER Working Paper No. 18315, August.
Ichniowski, C., Shaw, K., & Prennushi, G. (2007). The effects of human resource management practices on productivity. *American Economic Review*, *87*(3), 291–313.
Jones, D. C. (Ed.). (2003). *New economy handbook*. Amsterdam: Academic Press.
Jones, D. C., Kato, T., & Weinberg, A. (2003). Managerial discretion, business strategy and the quality of jobs: Evidence from medium sized manufacturing establishments in Central New York. In E. Applebaum, A. Bernhard & R. Murnane (Eds.), *Low wage America* (pp. 479–525). New York, NY: Russell Sage.
Jorgenson, D. W., Ho, M. S., & Stiroh, K. J. (2008). A retrospective look at the U.S. productivity growth resurgence. *Journal of Economic Perspectives*, *22*(1), 3–24.
Kruse, D., Freeman, R., & Blasi, J. R. (2010). *Shared capitalism at work*. University of Chicago Press, Chicago, IL and NBER.
Lazear, E. P. (2000). Performance pay and productivity. *The American Economic Review*, *90*(5), 1346–1361.
Milgrom, P., & Roberts, J. (1995). Complementarities and fit: Strategy, Structure and organizational change in manufacturing. *Journal of Accounting and Economics*, *19*, 178–208.
Oliner, S. D., & Sichel, D. E. (2000). The resurgence of growth in the late 1990s: Is information technology the story? *Journal of Economic Perspective*, *14*(4), 3–22.
Oliner, S. D., Sichel, D. E., & Stiroh, K. J. (2007). Explaining a productive decade. *Brookings Papers on Economic Activity*, (1), 81–137.
Osterman, P. (1994). How common is workplace transformation and who adopts it? *Industrial and Labor Relations Review*, *47*(2), 173–188.
Syverson, C. (2011). What determines productivity. *Journal of Economic Literature*, *49*(2), 326–365.

CHAPTER 4

THE RELATIVE SURVIVAL OF WORKER COOPERATIVES AND BARRIERS TO THEIR CREATION

Erik K. Olsen

ABSTRACT

Purpose – *The purpose of this paper is to demonstrate that the conjecture that worker cooperatives (firms that practice participatory management and share profits broadly) suffer a competitive disadvantage relative to conventional firms is not supported by existing empirical research. It also considers alternative explanations for why such cooperatives are rare.*

Design/methodology/approach – *Historical analysis, literature survey, and survival analysis.*

Findings – *Studies of worker cooperatives in a variety of national settings indicate their failure rate is lower than conventional firms at least in the short and medium term. This contradicts the proposition that they are rare because they suffer a competitive disadvantage and focuses attention instead on their low formation rate.*

Sharing Ownership, Profits, and Decision-making in the 21st Century
Advances in the Economic Analysis of Participatory & Labor-Managed Firms, Volume 14, 83–107

ISSN: 0885-3339/doi:10.1108/S0885-3339(2013)0000014005

Research limitations – *The "liability of newness," wealth and credit constraints, entrepreneurial rents, and collective action problems are cited as important barriers for the creation of worker cooperatives de novo, but these factors should be greatly reduced for those created through the conversion of an existing firm. Paradoxically, the overwhelming majority of cooperatives are created from scratch, and hence this explanation remains incomplete.*

Practical implications – *Existing policies incentivizing the creation of worker cooperatives, and current initiatives to promote them, do not encourage the creation of inferior economic institutions.*

Originality/value – *This paper contradicts the widely held belief that the distinctive features of worker cooperatives (participatory management and broadly shared profit) place them at a competitive disadvantage in a market economy. It also provides insight into why cooperatives are rare by challenging explanations based in presumed inefficiencies and focusing attention instead on barriers to creation.*

Keywords: Worker cooperatives; producer cooperatives; survival analysis; cooperative formation

JEL Classifications: D02; J54; P51

Increasingly worker cooperatives (WCs) are proposed in the United States to achieve a range of objectives, including local economic development, reductions in income inequality, and an improved work experience because of participatory management (Alperovitz, 2013; Burczak, 2006; Gibson-Graham, 2006; United Steelworkers, 2012; Wolff, 2012). They have a long history in the United States, with the earliest ones predating the emergence of industrial capitalism, and almost 2,000 created since then. But a recent census (Deller, Hoyt, Hueth, & Sundaram-Stukel, 2009) found only 223 in existence, mostly clustered in retail and trade sectors. This historic failure rate of almost 90 percent could indicate that WCs are at a competitive disadvantage to conventionally owned firms (CFs), which, if true, would make them inferior institutions for achieving most objectives. Therefore, any discussion of the advantages of WCs must also consider their past performance and reasons for their relative scarcity.

The purpose of this paper is to demonstrate that the conjecture that WCs suffer a competitive disadvantage relative to CFs is not supported by existing research. Since the size of any population depends on how frequently new members are added, how frequently they drop out, and how long-lived the members of that population are, the question of why WCs are so rare involves their formation, failure, and survival. There is a growing literature on the survival of WCs, which indicates that while a significant percentage of them fail – especially during their early years – they do not fail at a rate that exceeds that of CFs. Instead, once created the expected survival of WCs meets or exceeds that of CFs. This finding complements decades of research on the productivity of WCs that finds they do not suffer a productivity disadvantage relative to CFs (Doucouliagos, 1995; Fakhfakh, Pérotin, & Gago, 2012; Pencavel, 2012). Taken together these results indicate that the answer to the question of why WCs are rare relative to CFs involves obstacles to their creation, not their survival, but it also indicates that when the risk of failure is considered, the creation of WCs is a more complicated issue than has previously been recognized.

To frame this last issue it should be recognized that there are two potential avenues for WC formation. They can either be created de novo or through the conversion of existing noncooperative firms. Both of these methods have been used in the United States (Berman, 1982; Lindenfeld, 1982; Ohio Employee Ownership Center, 2005), but overwhelmingly WCs in the United States are created from scratch. This presents a puzzle because survival analysis indicates that established firms fail less often and remain in operation longer than newly formed ones, and hence WCs created through the conversion of successful CFs could have a survival advantage over those created de novo. Furthermore, existing US federal policies give substantial incentives to business owners to sell to their employees, either through an employee stock ownership plan (ESOP) or the formation of a WC. Despite this very few WCs have been created this way.

This paper consists of two primary sections. The first addresses the creation of WCs historically in the United States and WC survival. It estimates of the number of WCs in the United States to establish an order-of-magnitude estimate of the number that have existed, their method of financing, and some basic information about how this population has changed over time. It also estimates the survival and hazard functions for all US CFs over the period 1992–2012, calculated on an establishment basis from the US Bureau of Labor Statistics *Business Employment Dynamics* (*BED*) series (Bureau of Labor Statistics, 2012a), as well as short and medium-term survival over the period 1977–2010, calculated on an enterprise basis from the US Census Bureau *Business Dynamics Statistics* (*BDS*) series (Census Bureau, 2012).[1] These findings are then compared with the survival and hazard reported for WCs by a number of studies. This characterization of the basic features and relative performance of WCs provides the basis for a new way of approaching the question of how they are created and insight into why they are so rare. These two issues are addressed in the second primary section of the paper. It is argued there that several of the reasons typically advanced for why WCs are rare relative to CFs are contradicted by the evidence of survival and failure and should be discounted.

For the purposes of this paper a WC is defined as an enterprise in which the worker-members have rights to both control of the firm and its profits. Membership in the cooperative should be broadly available to workers in the enterprise; as a group the worker-members should manage the affairs of the enterprise, ideally on the basis of one person-one vote; they own the equity of the firm either collectively or through individual capital accounts; and they divide the residual income of the firm in an equitable manner. This is a very broad definition that encompasses a range of firms from egalitarian collectives practicing direct democracy to democratic employee stock-ownership plan (ESOP) companies (as discussed below). A CF is defined as a firm in which control rights, ownership of capital, and claims on profit belong to an individual entrepreneur or a group of shareholders other than the employees of the firm.

CREATION, HAZARD, AND SURVIVAL OF WORKER COOPERATIVES

US Worker Cooperatives

Commons (1918, pp. 97, 127–130) documents the founding of WCs in the United States as early as 1791. Estimating how many have existed in the United States since that time, or reliably documenting the fate of those that were created, is constrained by the lack of reliable data. State and federal agencies have very rarely collected data on WCs, and until recently there was no national federation that might track them. Legislation allowing for incorporation as a WC (as distinct from a consumer, producer, or other type of cooperative[2]) was first adopted in Massachusetts in 1982 (Ellerman & Pitegoff, 1982–1983), and only a handful of states have done so since then, so public records are of limited use in identifying and documenting WCs.

Two studies use archival research to estimate the number of cooperatives historically in the United States, as well as some basic information about their industrial distribution. Aldrich and Stern (1983) identify 595 WCs established over the century 1835–1934, while Jones (1984) finds 414 over the 90-year period 1840–1930. The difference between these estimates is partially explained by Jones's stricter standards for inclusion. Jones defines a WC according to four criteria: "(a) many workers (or members) own stock, (b) ownership is widely distributed among the workers who own much of the voting stock, (c) working-members participate in the enterprise's management and control, and (d) they share in the distribution of the surplus, usually on the basis of work" (1984, p. 37). Aldrich and Stern give an "ideal" definition for a WC (p. 373), which is stricter than the one used by Jones, but do not describe the specific criteria used for inclusion in their dataset. Jones later drew from Aldrich and Stern's data to augment his own, but notes that he did not accept some of the firms identified in their data as valid WCs either because they failed to meet his criteria or there was insufficient information to verify that they did (Conte & Jones, 1985, p. 378).

Both studies find a sharp increase in the number of WCs established in the 1880s, most of which can be attributed to the efforts of the Knights of Labor. Jones estimates that 275 WCs were founded in the United States in the 1880s and attributes 200 – between one-third to one-half of all WCs created in the United States prior to the great depression – to the Knights of Labor. With the decline of the Knights of Labor the pace at which WCs were created in the United States fell off dramatically, falling to 55 per decade from 1895 to 1925. With few exceptions, all of the WCs identified by Aldrich and Stern or Jones created prior to the Great Depression were manufacturing enterprises, with notable industrial clusters in wood products (shingle, cooperage), metal products (foundries), and textiles.

A second wave in the United States came with the federally funded "self-help" WCs during the Great Depression. At their peak in 1935 these numbered an estimated 225–250 enterprises and employed over 12,000 worker-members (Jones, 1984; Jones & Schneider, 1984). Many of these enterprises grew out of earlier barter or scrip organizations, but those that did emerge as worker (rather than consumer) cooperatives also engaged almost exclusively in production activities, including agriculture, forestry, fisheries, mining, durable and nondurable manufacturing (Kerr, 1939, pp. 7–10). Government support of the self-help cooperatives ended in 1938, and the available information indicates that all had disappeared before the end of the Second World War. In the decades from the 1940s until the 1970s the founding of new WCs was limited to the well-known plywood cooperatives in the Pacific Northwest (30 firms) and a smaller number in refuse collection (12 firms) (Jones, 1984).

A third, and by far the largest, wave of new WCs in the United States occurred in the late 1970s. Jackall and Crain (1984, p. 88) estimate that in 1980 there were "at least 750–1,000" WCs in the United States. They define a WC simply as a worker-owned and managed business (p. 103), and note that almost all of these businesses were created in the previous decade. These third-wave cooperatives were of a distinctly different character than those earlier in US history. Rather than being aided by a national labor organization or government grants, this new group of WCs that emerged in the 1970s was primarily the product of small groups of committed workers using their own resources to start new enterprises. Jackall and Crane find that 70 percent of funding for US WCs operating in 1980 came from the members of the cooperative or loans from friends or family. The primary source of outside loaned funds came from other cooperatives. They note that "(a)ccess to normal capital markets is severely limited, either because banks or funding agencies will not lend to worker cooperatives or because they wish to impose controls unacceptable to cooperative groups" (p. 96). Another salient difference in this third wave is that rather than manufacturing or natural resource-based industries, which characterized almost all WCs in the United States prior to that time, these new firms operated primarily in trading activities and social services.[3]

One final study of US WCs should be commented on here. Deller et al. produced the first reasonably comprehensive census of all US WCs in 2009, and found 223 nationally with a total employment of 2,380 (2009, Table 2). They use a fairly complicated set of criteria to first identify cooperative businesses and then classify these businesses as worker, producer, purchasing, or consumer cooperatives. In this taxonomy WCs are identified as those in which the members of the cooperative are workers at the enterprise, control rights are not limited to a subset of worker-members but broadly distributed, and the residual income of the firm is returned to the worker-members as patronage dividends (p. 10). About 80 percent of the WCs identified by Deller et al. are classified as engaged in "Commercial Sales and Marketing."[4] This research contains no information about the length of operation for the firms it identifies, and there are no reliable estimates of the founding of WCs during the 1980s or 1990s, so it is not possible to speculate with any precision about how many of the third-wave WCs of the 1970s survived to be counted in Deller et al.'s census. But their findings do suggest that the third-wave WCs suffered considerable attrition in the intervening years. This research also confirms two characteristics of the modern population of US WCs initially identified by Jackall and Crain: the shift from production to trading activity and a small average firm size (both sources show an average of 10 employees).

Each of the individual studies discussed in this section are limited by the available data sources, but taken together they do provide a basis for a general characterization of the history of US WCs. Roughly 2,000 WCs have been created in the United States since the late eighteenth century, about one-quarter of which (200 Knights of Labor coops and 250 self-help cooperatives) were sponsored either by a labor organization or the state. The remaining three-quarters were the result of the independent initiative of groups of workers, with a large majority of these constituted by the third-wave of WCs of the late 1970s. Between the early and late twentieth century the industrial composition of US WCs changed from firms engaged almost exclusively in manufacturing to firms primarily engaged in trading activities. Since the 1970s US WCs have had an average firm size of 10 workers, which makes them characteristically very small businesses.

Survival and Hazard of Firms: Liability of Newness and Adolescence

Creating WCs and having them compete in markets with existing firms exposes them to risk of failure. This risk is a crucial aspect of the dynamics and viability of this organizational form. Perhaps the most important feature of the risk of failure is that it is not uniform; it is highest for young firms and decreases with age.

Fig. 1 shows the survival function for all new US business establishments with employees over the 1994–2012 period.[5] A survival function shows the cumulative proportion of firms surviving until the beginning of an annual interval, with adjustments made for those whose survival is not known because of censoring (Lee & Wang, 2003, p. 89). The survival function in Fig. 1 makes several things apparent. Seventy-nine percent of new US business establishments survive their first year of operation, 49 percent survive the fifth year, and 25 percent survive until at least the end of their seventeenth year. At the end of the eighteenth year, the limit of the *BED* data, 24 percent of establishments created at the beginning of the period are still in operation. Comparable survival figures for US enterprises from the *BDS* data (not shown in Fig. 1) are 78 percent survival at the end of year one, and 46 percent survival at the end of year five. Because the *BDS* reports annual results only for the first five years of the life of an enterprise, it is not possible to estimate survival beyond the fifth year. Both the *BED*

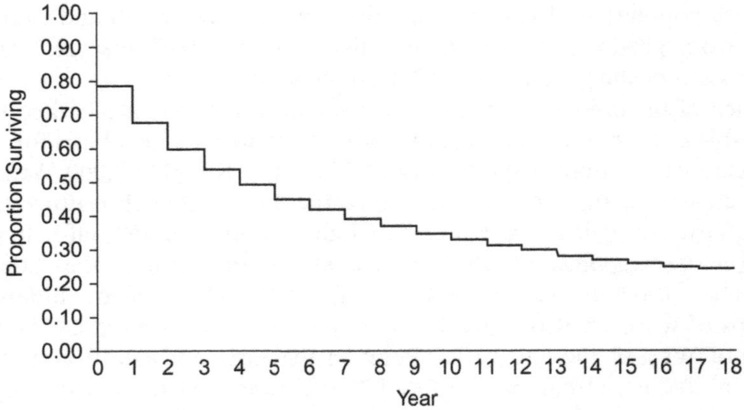

Fig. 1. Survival Function. All US Establishments (1944–2012). *Source*: BLS (2012a); author's calculations.

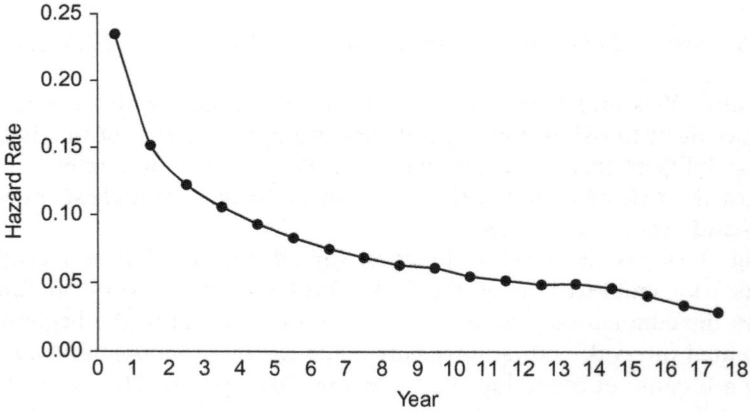

Fig. 2. Hazard Function. All US Establishments (1944–2012). *Source*: BLS (2012a); author's calculations.

and *BDS* data show that the survivors grow larger over time, employing larger numbers of workers.

Fig. 2 shows the hazard function for new establishments in the *BED* dataset. The hazard is defined as the probability of not surviving to the midpoint of an annual interval, given survival at the start of the interval.[6] Effectively the hazard is monotonically decreasing with age (there is a very small increase from year 13 to 14), with a maximum of .24 in the 1st year, declining to .11 in the 4th year, and .03 in the 18th year. For US enterprises in the *BDS* series (not shown in Fig. 2) the hazard peaks at .25 in the first year and then declines monotonically to .10 in the fifth year. The data are insufficient to calculate the annual hazard beyond that year.

Fig. 1 and 2, and the similar outcomes observed in the *BDS* data, illustrate the well-known empirical regularity that Stinchcombe (1965, p. 148) termed the "liability of newness." Numerous reasons are given for why this exists. Stinchcombe points to factors internal and external to the firm. Workers in new firms must discover how to effectively perform new roles rather than being taught by those who preceded them. They must also learn how to effectively relate to one another and develop sanctions and rewards. New firms also lack established relationships with potential suppliers, creditors, customers, and other parties external to the firm. This requires them to rely heavily on relationships with strangers whose behavior, reliability, and product quality may not be well-known to them. Stinchcombe's analysis is certainly an incomplete inventory of reasons potentially leading to a liability of newness – it does not, for example, recognize the issue of scale economies that new firms may have difficulty achieving – but the liability of newness phenomenon is a well-established empirical regularity. The relevant question for the purposes of this paper is whether or not WCs also exhibit high rates of attrition in their early years.

Unfortunately the data necessary to estimate the survival and hazard functions for US WCs do not exist.[7] But the hazard for WCs has been studied in the United Kingdom by Ben-Ner (1988a) and Thomas and Cornforth (1989), Canada by Staber (1989), Israel by Russell and Hanneman (1995a), France by Pérotin (2004), and Uruguay by Burdín (2012). Ben-Ner, Thomas and Cornforth, Russell and Hanneman, and Pérotin all have access to data from national cooperative associations and so in these studies a WC is defined according to the rules of these associations. Staber relies on archival research using government business registration records, cooperative directories, and newspaper or newsletter reports to gather data, and uses the criteria of "worker-owned and worker-directed" (p. 67) to identify a WC. Burdín is able to use Uruguayan social security administrative records, which identify firms registered as a WC, to track their creation and failure.

There are some important differences in the data and methodology of these studies that create a degree of heterogeneity among them. For example, because registered WCs in Uruguay often employ large numbers of nonmember employees, Burdín restricts his dataset to only those firms with a ratio of employees to members of less than 20 percent (p. 8). This contrasts with Russell and Hanneman who note that nonmember hired labor accounted for a large proportion of the workforce in Israeli WCs, usually exceeding 40 percent after 1950 and 50 percent after 1980 (1995b, Table 3.1), but they do not impose any restriction on their data as a result of this issue. Russell and Hanneman, Pérotin, and Burdín all discuss their treatment of censored cases (or employ methodologies where this is well known), while Ben-Ner, Staber, and Thomas and Cornforth do not. There are other issues that may also affect the comparability of the various estimates considered here – most obviously the potential heterogeneity of the economic institutions and conditions in the different national economies of these studies – but, to some degree, this is unavoidable in a survey of literature such as this. Caution is therefore required when drawing analogies between these various studies, and a great deal of effort is made not to draw conclusions beyond what can reasonably be supported.

Because of the range of methods used to estimate and present hazard in these studies it is not useful to compare them directly, but it is possible to draw some general conclusions from their results. Consistently these studies find that, unlike the hazard for US establishments shown in Fig. 2, WCs tend to suffer from a "liability of adolescence" rather than newness. Instead of peaking in year one the hazard for WCs peaks in years two or three and then declines.[8] Perhaps more importantly, this literature consistently finds hazard rates for WCs that are lower than for CFs in the same country or the United States.

Because the hazard is lower for WCs their cumulative survival is also higher. Most of the studies estimating the hazard for WCs do not estimate survival functions, but many do report either survival quartiles or sufficient information to calculate them. These quartiles provide point estimates of the survival function. Table 1 lists survival quartiles for 75, 50, and 25 percent survival ($t_{.75}$, $t_{.5}$, and $t_{.25}$) for WCs from the studies reporting them, with figures for CFs in the same country (if reported), and for US firms from both the *BED* and *BDS* data. All of these studies except Burdín use annual intervals, so in all cases the t_k quartile is found using linear interpolation to the nearest whole year.[9]

Burdín's data (2012, Fig. 3) covering the period 1997–2009 show that for WCs in Uruguay ($t_{.75}$, $t_{.5}$)=(2, 7), while for CFs ($t_{.75}$, $t_{.5}$)=(2, 5). Thus the early attrition of Uruguayan WCs and CFs is comparable, but the median lifespan of WCs exceeds that of CFs by two years. The early attrition of Uruguayan WCs is also lower, and median survival time longer, than that of US CFs observed in either the *BED* data ($t_{.75}$, $t_{.5}$, $t_{.25}$)=(1, 5, 17) or

Table 1. Survival Quartiles.

Source	Cohort	75% WC	75% CF	50% WC	50% CF	25% WC	25% CF
Thomas and Cornforth	1975–1981	3	1	≥5	4		
Thomas and Cornforth	1982–1983	1	1	3	4		
Thomas and Cornforth	1984	2	1				
Pérotin	1987	4					
Burdín	1997–2009	2	2	7	5		
Russell and Hanneman	1924–1992	2		4		10	
Staber	1940–1987	5		18		48[a]	
US BLS – *BED*	1994–2012		1		5		17
US Census – *BDS*	1977–2010		1		4		

[a]Staber reports 23% rather than 25% survival.

BDS data $(t_{.75}, t_{.5})$=(1, 4). Burdín also reports data (not shown in Table 1) for WCs through 12 years, and shows ≈38 percent still in existence at that age. This exceeds CFs in Uruguay (≈29 percent still operating) and the United States (31 percent of establishments still operating) and supports the conclusion that long-term WC survival exceeds that of CFs.

Russell and Hanneman report $(t_{.75}, t_{.5}, t_{.25})$=(2, 4, 10) for Israeli cooperatives formed during the period 1924–1992. They do not report survival quartiles for Israeli CFs, but their results indicate that while short-term survival of Israeli WCs is better than US CFs, and median survival equals US enterprises, the long-term survival is significantly worse than US establishments. Russell and Hanneman do not specify the percentage of failures of Israeli WCs in their data that occurred because of liquidation versus conversion into a CF (i.e., "degeneration" into a CF). But the high proportion of hired workers in Israeli WCs suggests that a tendency toward degeneration is also unusually high, and conversions into CFs could account for a significant proportion of failures. Thus while long-term longevity of Israeli WCs is likely to be lower than would be observed in other circumstances, this does not strongly indicate technological or competitive inferiority relative to CFs.

Staber's findings for Canadian WCs are remarkable because of the unusual longevity they exhibit. Not only is their early attrition lower than any of the other populations in Table 1, their median lifespan is more than four times longer than CF enterprises in the United States and more than two and one-half times longer than the next longest-lived cohort of WCs. Staber's observed $t_{.23}=48$ is nearly three times longer than $t_{.25}$ for CF establishments in the United States and close to five times longer than that reported for Israeli WCs.

Thomas and Cornforth's result for the 1982–1983 cohort of WCs is the only one observed in the United Kingdom whose median survival time, $t_{.5}=3$, is worse than that of CFs in the United Kingdom, $t_{.5}=4$ (1975–1979 cohort), as well as both CF enterprises and establishments in the United States. However, this seems anomalous in comparison with the result they report for the broader 1975–1981 cohort ($t_{.5}\geq 5$), which meets or exceeds the median lifespan for all firms and establishments in the United Kingdom and the United States. For all UK cohorts short-term survival, as measured by $t_{.75}$, equals or exceeds that of CFs in the United Kingdom or the United States.

Pérotin reports a single survival quartile for the 1987 cohort, which is the only one for which she has comparable survival data for conventional French firms. She finds $t_{.75}=3$ for WCs and notes that less than 60 percent of conventional French firms survived that long (p. 78).

Several specific conclusions can be drawn from these studies. All find that the early survival of WCs meets or exceeds that CFs in the same country or in the United States. But like CFs, WCs also suffer from elevated hazard in their early years, which peaks in the second or third year and then declines monotonically. Four of the five cohorts with median lifespan data show this to be at least as long or longer than CFs in the same country or CF enterprises in the United States. Russell and Hanneman and Staber reach contradictory conclusions about the long-term survival of WCs, but when Burdín's long-term results are included, along with the possibility of an increased tendency toward degeneration in the Israeli WCs studied by Russell and Hanneman, there is support for the proposition that the long-term survival of WCs meets or exceeds that of CFs. It should also be noted that the long-term survival shown in Table 1 for CFs is observed on an establishment rather than an enterprise basis. Since this includes establishments created as new locations of existing successful enterprises, it is likely to overestimate the true long-term survival of US enterprises (as it does for median survival time), and it is enterprise survival that is the relevant comparator. The overall impression of these studies is that WCs face a hazard that is lower than CFs, at least in the short term, and this gives them a median lifespan at least as long or longer. This advantage is small but is observed in a variety of national contexts. Their long-term survival also appears comparable to CFs, but this deserves more study before it can be assessed with a high degree of confidence. These studies do not, therefore, support the proposition that WCs, once created, are at a competitive disadvantage to CFs.

There are a number of reasons to explain why WCs may experience increased longevity relative to CFs. Most obviously is the literature on the productivity of WCs mentioned above that shows them to be at least as efficient as CFs at turning inputs into products, if not more so. Productivity advantages would certainly provide a survival advantage. WCs are also able to adjust their labor costs in response to changes in the economic environment in ways that CFs may not. Pencavel and Craig (1994) showed that in response to price changes WCs adjust wages while CFs adjust worker hours. This wage flexibility may provide WCs with a means to survive economic conditions that CFs could not. Pérotin (2004) also points to cooperative members' enthusiasm and commitment, which provides an initial psychological resource leading to an early "honeymoon" period during which workers in a WC may be less likely to close down than would be an individual entrepreneur faced with the same information.

THE CREATION OF WCs

Creating Worker Cooperatives

The analysis in the first part of this paper indicates two issues that are particularly relevant to understanding the formation of WCs in the United States. The first is that the high level of risk new firms face is likely to discourage the founding of WCs from scratch. If workers are required to make an initial capital investment the cost to them from firm failure includes both the loss of this investment and the cost associated with job loss. A worker facing the choice of whether or not to choose employment in a CF or join as a founding member of a WC must weigh the potential cost of failure against the potential profit shares received. The elevated hazard during the early years of a firm's existence makes this risk especially high for a new firm, and hence this is an obvious barrier to founding a WC as a new enterprise.

A very simple model can illustrate this point. If k is the total capital necessary to start the firm and n is number of workers forming the cooperative, then each worker in a self-funding WC must provide k/n initial capital (or equivalent collateral), which is assumed to be a non-tradable membership in the cooperative that is lost if the firm fails. The total profit shares received by a member of a cooperative are $t\pi/n$, where t is years in operation, and π is the firm's total annual profit. Ignoring for simplicity discounting and opportunity cost, a cooperator will recoup their initial investment when $t\pi/n \geq k/n$. Re-writing this inequality and substituting t_5 (the median or expected survival time for a new firm) for t_1, the following condition needs to be met in order for a founding cooperator to expect to recoup their initial investment

$$\frac{\pi}{k} \geq \frac{1}{t_{.5}} \qquad (1)$$

A worker who does not expect to at least recoup their initial investment would be better off choosing employment in a conventional firm rather than joining as a founder in the WC, and according to (1) a shorter expected life span for the firm (lower values of $t_{.5}$) requires a higher expected rate of profit in order for the worker-investor to expect to recoup their investment.[10] This implies that the shift from manufacturing to trading industries in US WCs may be a result of increasing capital requirements in manufacturing, relatively high profit margins in trading sectors, or both.

It is important to note, however, that both potential cooperators and individual entrepreneurs face this risk disincentive (n does not appear in condition 1), so this does not contribute to an explanation of why WCs are rare relative to CFs unless it can be said to affect them asymmetrically. But the disincentive posed by the risk of failure should impact the creation of WCs differently depending on whether they are created de novo or as the conversion of an existing firm because the risk faced by an existing firm is different from that faced by a new one. After the period during which a WC might suffer from a "liability of adolescence" the hazard is monotonically decreasing for all firms, both cooperative and conventionally owned, and hence each year a firm remains in operation its expected future lifespan, or median remaining lifetime at time i, $t_{mr}(i)$, increases. For example, according to the survival function in Fig. 1 over one-half of all newly created US establishments will close by the end of their fifth year ($t_{mr}(0)=5$), but for those surviving beyond the fifth year one-half will remain in operation for an additional 12 years ($t_{mr}(5)=12$). Thus, as long as the conversion does not significantly increase the hazard, the viability of creating WCs with worker funding increases with the age of the enterprise, and the conversion of an existing firm to a WC could be viable in an industry whose profit rate does not justify the entry of a new one. More generally, the creation of WCs through the conversion of existing firms deserves greater attention from advocates and potential cooperators than it has in the past.

The second issue raised by the analysis in the first part of this paper is that it supports the conclusion that when groups of workers take the initiative to create a WC de novo they are likely to be credit constrained. Bowles and Gintis emphasized the issue of credit rationing of WCs in a series of papers (1992, 1993, 1994, 1996) arguing that one reason conventional capitalist enterprises are common and WCs rare is that workers generally have little wealth and thus lack collateral. Credit market imperfections result in borrowers without collateral being denied access to credit, and so they refer to this as the "wealth inequality constraint" to worker-owned enterprises. Drèze (1993, pp. 261–262) also attributes the lack of WCs in developed countries to lack of access to capital and conjectures that this would result in them spreading more easily in low capital intensity industries. Since self-funded WCs have been numerous in the United States only in retail and other commercial industries, which have relatively low capital requirements, his conjecture was an empirical reality in the United States when he made it and remains so.[11] Indeed the most compelling explanations for the shift in US WCs from production to trading sectors involve issues related to the financing of cooperatives.

There is also negative feedback from the shift to trading activities that further inhibits the growth of WCs in the United States. The share of US employment in trading sectors (Wholesale and Retail) remains almost unchanged since the 1930s (BLS, 2012b), so these sectors have not offered especially favorable growth possibilities. The trading sectors also have very limited capacity to export outside of their local or regional area, which restricts their usefulness in local economic development strategies targeting either expansion of the export base or import substitution.

Perhaps a more important problem is associated with the nature of retail and wholesale trade itself. The expansion of existing establishments in these sectors is constrained by the market area they serve. Growth for these types of enterprises occurs by creating new establishments in new market areas. But this type of growth is problematic for a WC not only because it extends the collective action problems of self-management from one establishment to many, but also because it challenges the control of the original worker-members. Furubotn (1976) emphasizes that the growth of a WC faces a political constraint because introducing new members reduces the influence of the original majority of worker-members. He points out that "New workers coming into a labor-managed enterprise are not just factors of production but potential policy makers as well. Thus, the way is open for a transfer of power; voting patterns can be shifted because of the added workers, and new policy directions established for the firm that are contrary to the desires of the original majority" (pp. 106–107). Since presumably workers in a WC choose this employment at least in part because they value control over their workplace, they must view the reduction in control that they experience when new worker-members are added as consequential. This will be especially pronounced when growth must take the form of discrete new establishments rather than the incremental growth of an existing one, which requires adding groups of new workers rather than the gradual addition of new members.

Both of the issues discussed in this section – the effect of the liability of adolescence on the incentive to form new enterprises and wealth and credit constraints – are significant impediments to the creation of new WCs from scratch. But it is important to recognize that they are much less significant impediments to creating a WC through the conversion of an existing firm. For conversions the equity of the firm itself provides collateral that can be pledged to finance the purchase from an existing owner, and conversions reduce the risk associated with the liability of adolescence because they may occur after the period of elevated hazard. Why WCs in the United States are created almost exclusively de novo despite these advantages is not easily explained.

Why Are Worker Cooperatives So Rare?

The survival data surveyed above also provides insight into the issue of why so few WCs exist in industrial market economies. It is usually assumed that in a competitive economy if a type organization provides superior efficiency then firms organized in this way have a competitive advantage and become predominant. Alchian (1950) initially proposed this and Alchian and Demsetz (1972) later employed this logic to propose that the "classic capitalist firm," in which capital hires labor, emerged and predominates because of its superior efficiency. Similarly, the relative scarcity of WCs is typically taken as prima facie evidence that inefficiencies leave them at a competitive disadvantage. But survival analysis indicates that WCs actually perform at least as well as CFs, or perhaps marginally better. Several decades of research on productivity reaches the same conclusion. This implies that WCs are rare because they are created at a rate much lower than CFs, not because they are less efficient.

This has not been generally recognized. Dow and Putterman (2000, p. 333) critically survey the leading hypotheses for why WCs are rare and judge the following to be logically coherent and empirically plausible: (1) inefficiencies arising from monitoring and work incentives; (2) worker wealth and credit constraints; (3) disincentives to formation associated with portfolio diversification risk; (4) underinvestment as a result of the horizon problem; and (5) inefficiencies from collective decision making. (1), (4), and (5) are plausible as explanations for why so few WCs exist only if they are subject to these effects *and* this puts them at a competitive disadvantage relative to conventional firms. But the existing survival and productivity research indicates that they do not suffer a competitive disadvantage, and hence these factors should be discounted as explanations for the rarity of WCs. This reduces the number of coherent and plausible explanations for the rarity of WCs to (2) and (3), both of which are impediments or disincentives to formation, not performance.[12]

The issue of WC formation is very poorly understood and little researched. Conte and Jones (1985) survey the cooperative literature for theories of why WCs are formed and identify three: as a response to high unemployment, as a response to stagnation in average real income, and as a tactic in strikes. They find that, with the exception of the self-help WCs during the depression, none of these theories effectively explain the formation of WCs in the United States prior to 1969. Russell and Hanneman (1995a, pp. 79–85) also find that these theories are not useful in explaining the formation of WCs in Israel. These theories also fail to provide convincing explanations for the increase in the rate of founding of WCs in the United States in the late 1970s, which was a period of declining unemployment, historically low levels of income inequality, and saw no union-created WCs.

Dow (2003, pp. 210–212) considers barriers to WC formation other than credit constraints. He emphasizes a point that appears frequently in the WC literature: a CF allows for the individual appropriation of entrepreneurial rents, while a WC necessitates sharing them. This implies that even if WCs have superior productivity and a longer expected life, the incentive for an entrepreneur to try to exploit this for personal gain is greatly reduced. This leads Ben-Ner to conclude that "a self-interested entrepreneur will not choose to establish a worker-owned firm.........if the establishment of a capitalist firm is a viable alternative" (1988b, p. 290).

Dow also identifies a potentially significant collective action problem that arises when a WC is created from scratch (pp. 208–209). Creating a new WC involves assembling a group of willing and available workers with complementary skills, all of whom agree that a common project is viable and wish to participate on an equal footing with all other worker-members. The legal structure, bylaws, and working rules need to be negotiated in a collective setting and codified. Founding members must then provide the initial capital of the firm or engage in a search for a willing lender. The physical assets of the firm must be purchased and installed. This collective process involves significant costs and is subject to free-riding because once established the benefits of the WC accrue to all members while these start-up costs may be unevenly distributed. Conversely, a single wealthy entrepreneur can purchase the necessary assets, establish the structure, bylaws, and work rules by fiat, and then hire employees. Any entrepreneurial rents from this endeavor are then the property of this single entrepreneur.

This collective action problem helps explain why WCs created de novo are rare, but it is less convincing as an explanation for why so few are created as conversions. If an existing firm is successful then the current workforce need only expect that it will remain so after the conversion. The legal structure, by-laws, and working rules require modification, but they need not be created anew. The capital of the firm provides collateral to finance the conversion, and the physical assets of the firm are already in place. If the argument that WCs are rare because so few are created is correct, it remains to be explained why their creation occurs almost exclusively by starting from scratch.

CONCLUSIONS

Why WCs are rare relative to CFs is an important unresolved question. The existing theories for why this is so can be grouped into two broad classes. First are those that assume some inefficiency puts WCs at a competitive disadvantage, and market selection has led to the predominance of CFs. The rarity of WCs is itself often implicitly taken as evidence supporting these theories. But the survival and hazard analysis surveyed in this paper shows that WCs do not fail at rates that exceed CFs and consequently their survival time meets or exceeds that of CFs. These results compliment the research on the productivity of WCs, which does not find them to be at a disadvantage relative to CFs. The implication of this research is that theories explaining the rarity of WCs by assuming they must suffer from some inefficiency should be discounted.

A second set of theories for why WCs are rare points to impediments to their formation. This paper is broadly supportive of this type of explanation. Several impediments are considered here. Existing theoretical and empirical research points to financing constraints as a key limitation on the creation of WCs. The shift to less capital-intensive industries by US WCs also supports this conclusion. But the elevated early risk associated with new businesses also constitutes an important disincentive to founding WCs as new enterprises, especially in the presence of credit constraints that require workers to advance their own limited wealth to capitalize the firm. WCs in the United States are almost always created as new enterprises using funds from the worker-members themselves. The liability of adolescence experienced by new WCs makes this viable only where the initial capital requirements are low, the expected profit rate is high, or both. Except in circumstances like these workers are likely to choose conventional employment rather than the uncertain rewards of collective entrepreneurship. The elevated hazard of new business is a disincentive to the formation of both WCs and CFs, but wealth inequality, credit constraints, collective action problems, and the potential to capture entrepreneurial rents make CFs more likely to be created than WCs.

However, an important question is also raised but not answered by this paper. The factors tending to inhibit the formation of WCs are greatly reduced when the creation occurs through the conversion of an existing firm. Credit constraints are reduced because the equity of a successful existing firm provides collateral; the elevated hazard associated with new firms is greatly reduced because a WC created through a conversion is not a new firm; the collective action problem involved in the transition of an existing firm is lower than that associated with founding a new firm; and any entrepreneurial rents from the founding of the firm could be captured by a founding entrepreneur in the pricing of the firm itself. Portfolio diversification remains an issue, as does conjoining portfolio risk with the risk of job loss, but these seem insufficient to resolve this question.

This question becomes even more vexing when it is acknowledged that there are also significant incentives for the conversion of existing businesses into WCs in US law, and yet these incentives are almost never used to create WCs. Since 1974 the method of using the equity of a firm as collateral to finance a transition from conventional ownership to employee ownership has been successfully used in the creation of thousands of majority or wholly employee owned businesses in the United States, employing over 1 million workers (Olsen, 2011). These conversions did not, however, create WCs, but rather created companies that are majority employee-owned (MEO) through an employee stock ownership plan (ESOP). Unlike US WCs these existing MEO-ESOPs have a median firm size of 135 employees and are both industrially and geographically diverse (Olsen, 2011). Less than one-quarter of these firms are in Wholesale or Retail trade. MEO-ESOPs are perhaps the most tax-favored businesses under US law, including significant incentives to existing owners to sell to their employees, and these same incentives are available for WC conversions.

Residual claimancy and control rights, the two things that are combined in both the CF and the WC, need not be combined in an ESOP company. Control rights *may* belong to employee-shareholders via pass-through voting rights, but in practice this seems to be very rare (Logue & Yates, 2001, Chap. 3; The ESOP Association 2010, pp. 19, 34). ESOPs also differ from WCs in that the egalitarian aspects of WCs, notably the "one-person one-vote" principal and an equal distribution of shares, are usually absent. So in practice existing legislation has produced MEO-ESOPs rather than WCs, but this does not exhaust the possibilities of the law. There is no legislative prohibition against the creation of democratic ESOPs that pass on voting rights to workers according to the "one-person one-vote" principal, and distribute shares equally.[13] It remains an open question as to why most existing MEO-ESOPs do not incorporate these features. If they did they would be counted as a WC under even the narrowest of definitions.

It is also possible to use the equity of an existing conventional firm to finance a conversion to a WC that need not involve an ESOP at all. The primary financial incentive for the owners of existing enterprises to sell their equity to the workers in that company comes from subsection 1042 of Title 26 US Code (Federal tax code). It allows for an owner of a firm to defer capital gains taxes on the sale if they sell their equity to either an ESOP *or* an "eligible worker-owned cooperative." This "1042 rollover" provides a significant incentive for the seller to choose their own workers over an outside buyer, and it does not discriminate between ESOPs and WCs. There are a number of other benefits written into US law that incentivize the conversion of conventionally owned enterprises to MEO-ESOPs or WCs, but the 1042 rollover provision is perhaps the most significant. This existing provision has helped to create thousands of MEO-ESOPs but almost no WCs.

If the rarity of WCs is to be explained by the impediments to their creation, and these impediments are the risk of failure, credit constraints, and collective action problems, then this explanation remains incomplete because these can clearly be overcome through the conversion of existing successful firms – something that is heavily incentivized by existing legislation. Further research should aim to complete this explanation. But current advocates for using WCs to achieve desired outcomes should be reassured that the WC is not an inferior institution whose survival is suspect.

NOTES

1. The *BED* series is collected on an establishment rather than an enterprise basis, which makes it only a proxy for enterprise survival. *BDS* series reports survival data on an enterprise basis, but only releases annual data for the first five years for an annual cohort and then switches to aggregated five-year intervals. This makes it impossible to calculate a survival function or hazard after the first five years. But the information provided suggests that enterprise survival is similar to establishment survival.

2. This paper adopts the terminology given by Deller et al. (2009), which distinguishes between "worker," "producer," "purchasing," and "consumer" cooperatives.

3. Jackall and Crain use their own non-standard industrial classifications to characterize the activities of firms in their sample of WCs, so it is not possible to clearly identify whether firms engaged in trading activities or production, but it appears that trading activities were dominant.

4. Defined as "farm supply and marketing; biofuels; grocery and consumer goods retail; arts and crafts and entertainment" (p. 10).

5. This survival function is estimated using the life-table method (Lee & Wang, 2003, pp. 87–94) with annual cohorts pooled.

6. More formally, this is defined as

$$\hat{h}(t_{mi}) = \frac{2\hat{q}_i}{(1+\hat{p}_i)}$$

where, t_{mi} is the midpoint of interval i, $\hat{q}_i$ is the conditional probability of dying during interval i, and $\hat{p}_i$ is the conditional probability of surviving interval i.

7. Data is, however, available for publicly traded companies with employee ownership. Blair, Kruse, and Blasi (2000) study the survival of publicly traded companies in which at least 20 percent of the equity is held by employees through an ESOP or similar plan and Park, Kruse, and Sesil (2004) study the survival of companies with at least 5 percent of this type of employee ownership. Both find increased survival by employee-owned companies relative to comparable companies without employee ownership. See also Blasi, Kruse, and Weltmann in this volume.

8. An outlier among these studies is Staber (1989). He estimates hazard initially for three three-year intervals and finds that it peaks for Canadian WCs during the second interval rather than the first and then decreases until year 15 at which point it rises for two five-year intervals before falling again. He refers to this rise in years 15 through 25 as a "mid-life crisis" for WCs.

9. Let t_i be the time index for the survival function $\hat{S}(t_i)$. If $[t_i, t_{i+1})$ is the interval such that $\hat{S}(t_i) \geq \hat{S}(t_k)$ and $\hat{S}(t_{i+1}) < \hat{S}(t_k)$, where t_k is the survival time of the

kth percentile, then linear interpolation of the survival time of this percentile is defined as

$$t_k = t_i + \frac{[\hat{S}(t_i) - \hat{S}(t_k)]}{[[\hat{S}(t_i) - \hat{S}(t_{i+1})]}$$

10. It might be argued that condition (1) is too restrictive because (ignoring opportunity cost) in order to invest a worker must simply believe that π/k will be positive. But it is credible to assume that someone considering this investment recognizes that positive profits alone are not sufficient to compensate for risk because the expected profits are uncertain. Condition (1), the basic insight of which remains even under more complex specifications and less-restrictive assumptions, simply requires that workers expect that there will be positive profits *and* they will be sufficient to return their initial investment in the expected lifetime of the firm.

11. In 2011 the economy-wide capital/labor ratio in the United States was $262,102 per worker on average. This is calculated as the ratio of total private business fixed assets net of farm assets (34,728 trillion dollars) in 2011 from BEA (2012) and total nonfarm employment December 2011 (132,498 thousand) from BLS (2012b). For the Retail trade, Wholesale trade, and Manufacturing sectors this ratio was $79,671, $93,352, and $193,295, respectively.

12. Dow (2003) makes the same basic argument for why WCs are rare as Dow and Putterman (2000). He also acknowledges (p. 227) that WCs are rare is because so few are created, not because they fail at higher rates, but does not seriously consider the implications of this. Bonin, Jones, and Putterman (1993) give this explanation for why WCs are rare: "The weight of the theoretical reasoning and evidence surveyed convinces us that the explanation of the relative scarcity of PCs lies in the nexus between decision making and financial support" (p. 1316). For them portfolio diversification risk prevents workers from investing a large part of their wealth in a single firm, and external financers are likely to demand a premium to lend to WCs. Thus WCs will suffer from an inability to attract financing at competitive rates. To the degree that these are impediments to the creation of WCs, rather than performance, their explanation is similar to the argument of this paper. But they also note "we acknowledge the need for research to distinguish between this and competing explanations, such as those focusing on collective choice or incentive issues" (p. 1317). The survival analysis in this paper does not support the conclusion that these things contribute to an explanations for why WCs are rare.

13. See Ellerman (1985) for a discussion of how ESOPs can, and have been, structured in this way.

ACKNOWLEDGMENTS

Thanks go to Doug Kruse, Christopher Gunn, Virginie Pérotin, Al Campbell, and Robin Hahnel for insightful comments on drafts of this paper or helpful conversations about these issues. The paper has been greatly improved by their input. Any remaining errors are attributable to the author alone. This work was supported by the Joseph Cabral Distinguished Scholar and Fellow award from the Rutgers School of Management and Labor Relations.

REFERENCES

Alchian, A. A. (1950). Uncertainty, evolution, and economic theory. *Journal of Political Economy*, *58*(3), 211–221.

Alchian, A. A., & Demsetz, H. (1972). Production, information costs, and economic organization. *The American Economic Review*, *62*(5), 777–795.

Aldrich, H., & Stern, R. N. (1983). Resource mobilization and the creation of US producer's cooperatives, 1835–1935. *Economic and Industrial Democracy*, *4*(3), 371–406.

Alperovitz, G. (2013). *What then must we do? Straight talk about the next American revolution*. White River Junction, VT: Chelsea Green Publishing.

Ben-Ner, A. (1988a). Comparative empirical observations on worker-owned and capitalist firms. *International Journal of Industrial Organization*, *6*, 7–31.

Ben-Ner, A. (1988b). The life cycle of worker-owned firms in market economies: A theoretical analysis. *Journal of Economic Behavior and Organization*, *10*(3), 287–313.

Berman, K. (1982). The worker-owned plywood cooperatives. In F. Lindenfeld & J. Rothschild-Whitt (Eds.), *Workplace democracy and social change* (pp. 161–175): Boston, MA: Porter Sargent Publishers, Inc.

Blair, M., Kruse, D., & Blasi, J. (2000). Is employee ownership an unstable form? Or a stabilizing force? In T. Kochan & M. Blair (Eds.), *The new relationship: Human capital in the American corporation* (pp. 241–298). Washington, DC: The Brookings Institution.

Bonin, J. P., Jones, D. C., & Putterman, L. (1993). Theoretical and empirical studies of producer cooperatives: Will ever the twain meet? *Journal of Economic Literature*, *31*(3), 1290–1320.

Bowles, S., & Gintis, H. (1992). Power and wealth in a competitive capitalist economy. *Philosophy and Public Affairs*, *21*(4), 324–353.

Bowles, S., & Gintis, H. (1993). A political and economic case for the democratic enterprise. *Economics and Philosophy*, *9*(1), 75–100.

Bowles, S., & Gintis, H. (1994). Credit market imperfections and the incidence of worker-owned Firms. *Metroeconomica*, *45*(3), 209–223.

Bowles, S., & Gintis, H. (1996). The distribution of wealth and the viability of the democratic firm. In U. Pagano & R. Rowthorn (Eds.), *Democracy and efficiency in the economic enterprise* (pp. 64–81). New York, NY: Routledge.

Burczak, T. A. (2006). *Socialism after Hayek*. Ann Arbor, MI: University of Michigan Press.

Burdín, G. (2012). *Does workers' control affect firm survival? Evidence from Uruguay*. University of Siena, Department of Economics Working Paper No. 641. Retrieved from http://www.econ-pol.unisi.it/dipartimento/en/node/1651. Accessed on December 11, 2012. Forthcoming in *ILRReview*.

Commons, J. R. (1918). *History of labor in the United States*. New York, NY: Macmillan Company.

Conte, M. A., & Jones, D. (1985). In search of a theory of formation for U.S. producer cooperatives: Tests of alternative hypotheses. In B. D. Davis (Ed.), *Proceedings of the thirty seventh annual meeting*. Industrial Relations Research Association Series, December 28–30, 1984, Dallas. Madison, WI: IRRA.

Deller, S., Hoyt, A., Hueth, B., & Sundaram-Stukel, R. (2009). *Research on the economic impact of cooperatives*. Madison, WI: University of Wisconsin Center for Cooperatives. Retrieved from http://reic.uwcc.wisc.edu/downloads/. Accessed on February 22, 2013.

Doucouliagos, C. (1995). Worker participation and productivity in labor-managed and participatory capitalist firms: A meta-analysis. *Industrial and Labor Relations Review*, *49*(1), 58–77.

Dow, G. K. (2003). *Governing the firm: Workers' control in theory and practice*. New York, NY: Cambridge University Press.

Dow, G. K., & Putterman, L. (2000). Why capital suppliers (usually) hire workers: What we know and what we need to know. *Journal of Economic Behavior and Organization*, *43*(3), 319–336.

Drèze, J. H. (1993). Self-management and economic theory: Efficiency, funding and employment. In P. K. Bardhan & J. E. Roemer (Eds.), *Market socialism*. New York, NY: Oxford University Press.

Ellerman, D. (1985). ESOPs & CO-OPs: Worker capitalism & worker democracy. *Labor Research Review*, *1*(6), 55–69.

Ellerman, D., & Pitegoff, P. (1982–1983). The democratic corporation: The new worker cooperative statute in Massachusetts. *Review of Law and Social Change*, *11*(3), 440–472.

Fakhfakh, F., Pérotin, V., & Gago, M. (2012). Productivity, capital, and labor in labor-managed and conventional firms: An investigation on French data, *ILRReview*, *65*(4), 847–879.

Furubotn, E. G. (1976). The long-run analysis of the labor-managed firm: An alternative interpretation. *The American Economic Review*, *66*(1), 104–123.

Gibson-Graham, J. K. (2006). *A postcapitalist politics*. Minneapolis, MN: University of Minnesota Press.

Jackall, R., & Crain, J. (1984). The shape of the small worker cooperative movement. In R. Jackall & H. M. Levin (Eds.), *Worker cooperatives in America* (pp. 88–108). Berkeley, CA: University of California Press.

Jones, D. C. (1984). American producer cooperatives and employee-owned firms: A Historical perspective. In R. Jackall & H. M. Levin (Eds.), *Worker cooperatives in America* (pp. 37–56). Berkeley, CA: University of California Press.

Jones, D. C., & Schneider, D. J. (1984). Self-help production cooperatives: Government-administered cooperatives during the depression. In R. Jackall & H. M. Levin (Eds.), *Worker cooperatives in America* (pp. 57–84). Berkeley, CA: University of California Press.

Kerr, C. (1939). *Productive enterprises of the unemployed, 1931–1938*. Unpublished doctoral dissertation, University of California, Berkeley, CA.

Lee, E. T., & Wang, J. W. (2003). *Statistical methods for survival data analysis*. Hoboken, NJ: Wiley.

Lindenfeld, F. (1982). Workers' cooperatives: remedy for plant closings? In F. Lindenfeld & J. Rothschild-Whitt (Eds.), *Workplace democracy and social change* (pp. 337–352). Boston, MA: Porter Sargent Publishers, Inc..

Logue, J., & Yates, J. (2001). *The real world of employee ownership*. Ithaca, NY: ILR Press.

Ohio Employee Ownership Center. (2005). *Select machine – A worker co-op (press release)*. Retrieved from http://www.oeockent.org/for-business-owners/cooperatives/108. Accessed on April 28, 2012.

Olsen, E. (2011). Majority employee owned enterprises in the U.S.: A profile. Paper presented at Mid-Year Fellows Workshop in Honor of Louis O. Kelso, Rutgers University, February 24–25. Retrieved from http://smlr.rutgers.edu/midyearfellowsworkshop. Accessed on January 1, 2012.

Park, R., Kruse, D., & Sesil, J. (2004). Does employee ownership enhance firm survival? In D. Jones, V. Pérotin, & A. Robinson (Eds.), *Advances in the economic analysis of participatory and labor-managed firms* (*Vol. 8*, pp. 3–33). Boston, MA: Elsevier.

Pencavel, J. (2012). *Worker cooperatives and democratic governance*. Stanford Institute for Economic Policy Research Discussion Paper No. 12-003. Retrieved from http://siepr.stanford.edu/?q=/system/files/shared/pubs/papers/12-003.pdf. Accessed on December 11, 2012.

Pencavel, J., & Craig, B. (1994). The empirical performance of orthodox models of the firm: Conventional firms and worker cooperatives. *Journal of Political Economy*, *102*(4), 718–744.

Pérotin, V. (2004). Early cooperative survival: The liability of adolescence. In D. Jones, V. Pérotin, & A. Robinson (Eds.), *Advances in the economic analysis of participatory and labor-managed firms* (*Vol. 8*, pp. 67–86). Boston, MA: Elsevier.

Russell, R., & Hanneman, R. (1995a). The formation and dissolution of worker cooperatives in Israel, 1924–1992. In R. Russell (Ed.), *Utopia in Zion: The Israeli experience with worker collectives* (pp. 57–95). Albany, NY: The State University of New York Press.

Russell, R., & Hanneman, R. (1995b). The use of hired labor in Israeli worker cooperatives, 1933–1989. In R. Russell (Ed.), *Utopia in Zion: The Israeli experience with worker collectives* (pp. 96–128). Albany, NY: The State University of New York Press.

Staber, U. (1989). Age-dependence and historical effects on the failure rates of worker cooperatives: An event-history analysis. *Economic and Industrial Democracy*, *10*, 59–80.

Stinchcombe, A. (1965). Social structure and organizations. In J. G. March (Ed.), *Handbook of organizations* (pp. 142–193). Chicago, IL: Rand McNally & Company.

The ESOP Association. (2010). *2010 ESOP company survey*. Washington, DC: The ESOP Association.

Thomas, A., & Cornforth, C. (1989). The survival and growth of worker co-operatives: A comparison with small business. *The International Small Business Journal*, *8*(1), 34–50.

United Steelworkers of America. (2012). *Worker ownership for the 99%*. Retrieved from http://www.usw.org/media_center/releases_advisories?id=0523. Accessed on December 11, 2012.

US Department of Commerce, Bureau of Economic Analysis. (2012). *Table 3.1ES. Current-cost net stock of private fixed assets by industry*. Retrieved from http://bea.gov/iTable/iTable.cfm?ReqID=10&step=1. Accessed on December 10, 2012.

US Department of Commerce, Census Bureau. (2012). *Business dynamics statistics*. Retrieved from http://www.census.gov/ces/dataproducts/bds/data_firm.html. Accessed on December 29, 2012.

US Department of Labor, Bureau of Labor Statistics. (2012a). *Table 7. Survival of private sector establishments by opening year*. Business Employment Dynamics. Retrieved from http://www.bls.gov/bdm/us_age_naics_00_table7.txt. Accessed on December 15, 2012.

US Department of Labor, Bureau of Labor Statistics. (2012b). Current employment statistics. Retrieved from http://bls.gov/data/. Accessed on November 10, 2012.

Wolff, R. D. (2012). *Democracy at work: A cure for capitalism* .Chicago, IL: Haymarket Books.

CHAPTER 5

FIRM SURVIVAL AND PERFORMANCE IN PRIVATELY HELD ESOP COMPANIES

Joseph Blasi, Douglas Kruse and Dan Weltmann

ABSTRACT

Purpose – *Using a population study, we provide evidence on the important but understudied issue of company survival under employee ownership, as well as on the performance effects of employee ownership and the issue of whether employee ownership substitutes for other pension benefits.*

Design/methodology/approach – *Company survival and pension benefits are assessed using a unique dataset from Dun & Bradstreet of privately held Employee Stock Ownership Plan (ESOP) companies over the 1988–1999 period, matched to non-ESOP companies in the same industry. Performance is assessed using pre/post-comparisons of ESOP adopters in the 1988–1994 period.*

Findings – *Privately held ESOP companies in 1988 were only half as likely as non-ESOP firms to go bankrupt or close over the 1988–1999 period, and only three-fifths as likely to disappear for any reason. The ESOP companies had significantly higher post-adoption annual*

Sharing Ownership, Profits, and Decision-making in the 21st Century
Advances in the Economic Analysis of Participatory & Labor-Managed Firms, Volume 14, 109–124

ISSN: 0885-3339/doi:10.1108/S0885-3339(2013)0000014006

employment and sales growth, along with higher sales per employee. ESOP companies are four times more likely than their non-ESOP pairs to have defined benefit pension plan and other forms of defined contribution plans.

Research implications – *The greater survival was not explained by higher productivity, or by greater compensation flexibility. The higher survival may instead be tied to complementary policies adopted along with ESOPs to create a more committed and engaged workforce that contributes ideas to enhance survival and is more flexible when economic difficulties arise. The pension results are consistent with other studies on compensation under employee ownership, suggesting that employee ownership is generally used as a form of efficiency wage to provide above-market compensation.*

Social implications – *Higher survival among ESOP companies could result in lower job loss and unemployment, potentially providing a public policy rationale for support of employee ownership.*

Originality/value – *The chapter provides the first examination of company survival in privately held ESOP companies, and one of the few examinations of how ESOPs relate to other pension benefits.*

Keywords: Employee ownership; ESOPs; survival analysis; economic performance; pension benefits

JEL classifications: J33; L25; J54

INTRODUCTION

Most research on the relationship between company performance and employee ownership has been conducted on publicly held firms, due to the easy availability of data on such firms. In this study we use a unique sample of privately held Employee Stock Ownership Plan (ESOP) companies in the 1988–1998 period to shed light on the relationship of employee ownership to firm survival, performance, and pension benefits.

Firm survival is an understudied outcome in the employee ownership field. Longer survival is generally a mark of success for a company, with obvious benefits for employees through reducing the risk of job loss and uncertainty over future employment. Lower rates of job loss are also likely to have wider benefits for the economy, by reducing unemployment with its economic and social costs. Employee ownership may enhance company survival in several related ways, by: (1) increasing productivity through greater cooperation, information-sharing, and commitment; (2) reducing dysfunctional workplace conflict that can contribute to firm failure; (3) increasing employee investments in valuable firm-specific skills; and (4) creating a workplace culture that instills a sense of ownership, with a corresponding commitment to preserve employee jobs whenever possible. Employee ownership may also lead to lower rates of company survival if it contributes to increased employee conflict (Hansmann, 1996), or if firms face extra difficulties in attracting high-quality workers or access to capital financing. See Park, Kruse, and Sesil (2004) for further discussion of the alternative views. Prior evidence from U.S. studies shows that firms with employee ownership have higher survival rates: public companies with substantial employee ownership stakes in 1983 were 20% more likely than closely matched industry pairs to survive through 1995 (Blair, Kruse, & Blasi, 2000), and those with substantial employee ownership stakes in 1988 were 21% more likely to survive through 2001 (Park et al., 2004). Also, Welbourne and Cyr (1999) found that among companies with initial public offerings in 1988, those with broad-based employee ownership had higher survival rates. Six studies of worker cooperatives outside the United States have found high survival rates compared to conventional firms (reviewed by Olsen in this volume).

Productivity is much more commonly studied in the employee ownership literature. Contrary to negative predictions based on the free rider problem, studies have generally found that employee ownership is linked to higher performance. Two reviews concluded that "Two thirds of 129 studies [including both performance and attitude studies] on employee ownership and its consequences found favorable effects relating to employee ownership, while one tenth found negative effects" (Kaarsemaker, 2006), and "research on ESOPs and employee ownership is overwhelmingly positive and largely credible" (Freeman, 2007). Formal meta-analyses that combined the results of studies have found evidence of a positive association between employee ownership and performance (Doucouliagos, 1995; Kruse & Blasi, 1997). To address selection effects based on unobservable variables, many of the studies have used longitudinal data, comparing performance before and after the adoption of a plan, or examining other time-series variation (e.g., percent covered or size of stake), or using other selection corrections. There has been substantial dispersion of outcomes in the performance studies, which recent research on employee attitudes and behaviors suggests may be due to complementarities between group incentives, closeness of supervision, pay levels, and high-performance HR policies (Kruse, Freeman, & Blasi, 2010).

We also contribute new evidence on pension benefits under employee ownership. The economic theory of compensating differentials predicts that employees will give up some pay or other benefits in exchange for employee ownership, and the substitution of variable pay is unattractive to risk-averse employees. There were some examples of explicit wage or benefit concessions in the 1980s (Blasi & Kruse, 1991), but apart from these few concessionary situations, there is no evidence of generally lower fixed pay or benefits in exchange for employee ownership and profit sharing. A comprehensive study that combined longitudinal Census Bureau establishment data with all ESOP adoptions over the 1980–2001 period found that employee wages (excluding ESOP contributions) either increased (for small ESOPs) or stayed constant (for large ESOPs) after adoption, controlling for state-level and industry-level wage changes and other company characteristics (Kim & Ouimet, 2014). Consistent with this, comparisons of matched ESOP and non-ESOP firms find similar levels of pay and other benefits in the two types of firms, so that ESOPs appear to come on top of other worker pay and benefits (Kardas, Scharf, & Keogh, 1998; Scharf & Mackin, 2000). Other forms of employee ownership are associated with higher average compensation levels (Blasi, Conte, & Kruse, 1996), pension assets (Kroumova, 2000), wage growth (Renaud, St-Onge, & Magnan, 2004), and overall worker wealth (Buchele, Rodgers, & Scharf, 2010). This indicates that employee ownership may operate in the same manner as an above-market efficiency wage (discussed in Kruse et al., 2010, pp. 378–382).

In this study we provide new evidence on firm survival, finding that privately held ESOP companies (which have not been studied in prior research) were more likely than closely matched pairs to survive over the 1988–1999 period. We also examine economic performance by doing pre-/post-comparisons of employment, sales, and productivity growth in ESOP adopters, finding that these outcomes tend to improve after adoption but only the sales growth difference is strong enough to be statistically significant. Apart from survival and performance, we shed light on two additional important outcomes, showing that: (1) ESOPs do not appear to substitute for other pension benefits, given that ESOP companies are more likely than their pairs to have both defined benefit and other defined contribution pension plans, and (2) ESOP companies tend to have more stable employment.

DATA

We constructed the dataset by merging all of the ESOP information from the Form 5500 with the Dun and Bradstreet data on privately held companies over the 1988–1999 period. As a result, this was a population study. All ESOPs must be reported on the Form 5500 filed with the U.S. Department of Labor. In the 1988–1994 period all large ESOPs (more than 100 participants) were required to file each year, while small ESOPs were required to file at least once every 3 years. Using this information we constructed two groups of firms: all ESOPs existing in 1988 and all ESOPs adopted over the 1988–1994 period. The ESOPs were matched to Dun and Bradstreet companies using company name, city, and state, resulting in a match for 1,176 companies in 1988 and 343 companies adopting companies over the 1988–1994 period. To construct matched non-ESOP pairs, we used information on employment and industry (four-digit SIC) for 3 million Dun and Bradstreet companies. For each ESOP company we picked the closest non-ESOP company in employment size (as of 1988 for the first sample or the adoption year for the second sample) in the same industry. We then obtained full Dun and Bradstreet information for all ESOP companies and their pairs, and matched the data to the 1988–1999 Form 5500 datasets to obtain data on all pension plans maintained by these companies over that period.[1] A limitation of the study is that all of the variables necessary to compute a Cobb–Douglas production function were not available, so the study uses total sales divided by the number of employees as a productivity measure.

Table 1 contains descriptive statistics for the population of 1988 ESOPs and their pairs. There it can be seen that an average of 85% of employees were ESOP participants in the ESOP companies, with an average of $15,026 stock per participant. The average employment was close to 500 in the ESOP companies and their pairs (naturally close since matching was done on employment), while total sales averaged just over $80 million in the ESOP companies and $89 million in the non-ESOP companies. Average sales per employee were, however, higher in the ESOP companies. Approximately one-third of the companies were in manufacturing, and one-fifth in finance, insurance, and real estate.

Table 2 contains descriptive statistics for the second group of firms, comprising companies that adopted ESOPs over the 1988–1994 period and their pairs. Relative to the 1988 ESOP companies, the adopters had a smaller percent of employees as ESOP participants (40.2%) but slightly larger average employer stock per participant ($18,023). Average employment was 389 for the ESOP adopters and 464 for their pairs, and both average

Table 1. Descriptive Statistics on 1988 ESOP Companies and Pairs.

	ESOP cos. (1)	Non-ESOP Pairs (2)	Diff. (3)
Number of companies	1176	1176	
ESOP characteristics			
Year adopted			
Pre-1980	44.3%		
1980–1984	23.1%		
1985–1988	32.6%		
Participants as pct. of employment	84.9%		
Employer stock per participant			
Mean	$15,026		
Median	$8,698		
Company characteristics in 1988			
Total employment			
Mean	503.1	485	18.1
Median	154	155	−1
Total sales			
Mean	$80,684,000	$89,395,000	-$8,711,000
Median	$18,550,000	$16,100,000	$2,450,000
Sales/employee			
Mean	$286,305	$164,256	$122,049
Median	$104,167	$94,980	$9,187
Industry			
Mining, construction	8.9%	8.9%	
Manufacturing	32.8%	32.8%	
Trans., comms., utilities	2.2%	2.2%	
Wholesale trade	17.9%	17.9%	
Retail trade	9.0%	9.0%	
Finance, insur., real estate	19.6%	19.6%	
Services	9.5%	9.5%	

sales and sales per employee were also lower in the ESOP adopters. Just over one-fourth of the companies were in manufacturing, and one-fourth in finance, insurance, and real estate.

FIRM SURVIVAL

A first look at firm survival is provided in Fig. 1, which displays the survival rate by year for the 1988 ESOP companies and their pairs. There it can be seen that the ESOP companies were more likely to remain in existence

Table 2. Descriptive Statistics on 1988–1994 ESOP Adopters and Pairs.

	ESOP cos. (1)	Non-ESOP Pairs (2)	Diff. (3)
Number of companies	343	343	
ESOP characteristics			
Year of ESOP adoption			
1988	25.4%		
1989	21.0%		
1990	18.7%		
1991	9.3%		
1992	11.1%		
1993	8.5%		
1994	6.1%		
Participants as pct. of employment	40.2%		
Employer stock per participant			
Mean	\$18,023		
Median	\$10,016		
Company characteristics in adoption year			
Total employment			
Mean	388.9	464.1	−75.2
Median	155	137	18
Total sales			
Mean	\$64,558,000	\$126,250,000	−\$61,692,000
Median	\$20,000,000	\$19,950,000	\$50,000
Sales/employee			
Mean	\$171,969	\$199,149	−\$27,180
Median	\$109,191	\$103,896	\$5,295
Industry			
Mining, construction	6.4%	6.4%	
Manufacturing	28.9%	28.9%	
Trans., comms., utilities	2.0%	2.0%	
Wholesale trade	14.6%	14.6%	
Retail trade	8.5%	8.5%	
Finance, insur., real estate	25.4%	25.4%	
Services	14.3%	14.3%	

Statistically significant difference at $^{*}p < .05$; $^{**}p < .01$.

in each year over the 1988–1999 period. At the end in 1999, 69.6% of the ESOP firms remained as distinct companies, compared to 54.8% of their non-ESOP pairs. This indicates a relative hazard ratio of 0.79, meaning that the risk of disappearance for ESOP companies is only 79% of the risk

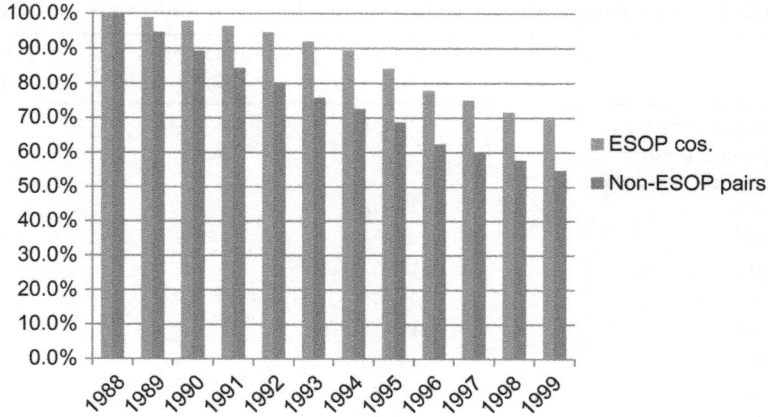

Fig. 1. Survival of 1988 ESOP Companies.

for non-ESOP companies (alternatively, the survival ratio is 1.27 meaning a 27% higher chance of survival among ESOP companies).

Companies may disappear as independent entities either because they fail and close, or because they merge or are acquired by another company. This latter outcome can be a mark of success in some cases, as other firms want to acquire or merge with successful companies. The Dun and Bradstreet database contains notes from their investigators on the reason for disappearance for most but not all of the companies (in some cases the company disappeared and the investigator could not determine why). Table 3 shows that ESOP companies were about half as likely as their pairs to disappear due to a clearly identified bankruptcy or closing (5.9% compared to 11.7%), while their likelihoods of being merged or acquired were similar (11.1% and 12.1%). The ESOP companies were less likely to disappear for other or unknown reasons (13.5% compared to 21.4%).

The comparisons of survival can be misleading if companies do not maintain their ESOP status over the sample period. The large majority of companies, however, did maintain their ESOP status. Table 3 shows that over four-fifths (82.5%) of the 1988 ESOP companies maintained their ESOP over the sample period (as long as the company remained in existence), while 5.2% of their non-ESOP pairs had adopted an ESOP by the end of the period.

The employment behavior of the non-ESOP pairs is consistent with their lower rate of survival. Table 3 shows that their average annual employment

Table 3. Outcomes for 1988 ESOP Companies and Pairs.

	ESOP cos. (1)	Non-ESOP Pairs (2)
Number of companies	1176	1176
Disposition of company by 1999		
Survived	69.6%	54.8%**
Bankrupt or closed	5.9%	11.7%**
Merged or acquired	11.1%	12.1%
Other/unknown	13.5%	21.4%**
ESOP maintained through period	82.5%	
ESOP added in period		5.4%
Average annual post-1988 growth in:		
Employment	0.7%	−3.3%**
Sales	2.7%	0.6%*
Sales/employment	2.2%	3.8%
Employment variability post-1988:		
S.d. of ln(employment)	0.259	0.308**
S.d. of annual change in ln(employment)	0.182	0.235**

Statistically significant difference at $^{*}p < .05$; $^{**}p < .01$.

change was −3.3% compared to 0.7% for the ESOP companies, indicating strong employment declines for many of the non-surviving paired companies. Similarly, the non-ESOP companies had significantly higher employment variability, measured both as the simple standard deviation of the logarithm of employment and as the standard deviation of the annual change in the logarithm of employment (measuring variability around a growth trend so that average growth or decline does not contribute to variability).

Firm survival is assessed more rigorously in Table 4, which uses Cox proportional-hazards models to predict the likelihood of firm failure or disappearance.[2] Columns 1–3 treat failure only as a bankruptcy or closing as noted by Dun and Bradstreet investigators, so that other outcomes represent simple censoring of the survival path, while columns 4–6 treat any disappearance as a failure.

The higher survival of ESOP companies holds when controlling for the presence of other pension plans. Columns 1 and 4 indicate relative hazard ratios of .46 and .586, indicating that ESOP companies were only 46.0% or 58.6% as likely as otherwise-similar non-ESOP companies to fail over this period (depending on the measure of failure). Since prior research indicates that company size and productivity are positive predictors of survival (Geroski, Mata, & Portugal, 2010; Santarelli & Vivarelli, 2007), we add

Table 4. Predicting Company Survival (Based on Cox Proportional Hazard Models Predicting Survival Over 1988–1999 Period. Figures Represent Hazard Ratios).

	Failure = Bankrupt or Closed			Failure = Disappeared for any Reason		
	(1)	(2)	(3)	(4)	(5)	(6)
Values in 1988						
ESOP	0.460**	0.480**	0.563**	0.586**	0.632**	0.670**
	(4.78)	(4.38)	(3.33)	(7.09)	(5.93)	(4.98)
Defined benefit plan	0.625	0.746	0.666	0.848	0.899	0.864
	(1.64)	(1.02)	(1.35)	(1.41)	(0.89)	(1.18)
401(k) plan	0.814	0.808	0.848	0.972	1.015	1.002
	(0.82)	(0.82)	(0.61)	(0.25)	(0.13)	(0.02)
Deferred profit sharing plan	0.965	1.025	1.038	1.000	1.022	1.057
	(0.15)	(0.10)	0.15	(0.00)	(0.20)	(0.51)
Other defined contribution plan	1.339	1.315	1.228	−0.550	1.076	1.111
	(1.06)	(0.97)	(0.71)		(0.55)	(0.78)
Ln (employment)		0.865**	0.938		0.938*	0.953
		(2.65)	(1.19)		(2.36)	(1.70)
Ln(sales/employee)		0.705**	0.718**		0.809**	0.820**
		(4.40)	(4.09)		(5.15)	(4.66)
Post-1988 employment variability[a]			2.877**			1.357*
			(5.81)			(2.41)
Number of companies	2352	2272	2216	2352	2272	2216
Number of failures	207	192	180	890	828	772
Time at risk	22996	22558	22501	22996	22558	22501
Log likelihood	−1545.1**	−1417.7**	−1316.3**	−6700.1**	−6204.2**	−5776.5**

[a]S.d. of annual change in ln(employment).

*$p < .05$; **$p < .01$ (Z-statistics in parentheses).

these variables as controls in columns 2 and 5.[3] The relative hazard ratios rise only slightly – to 48.0% and 63.2% – when controlling for total employment and sales per employee. This latter result indicates that the higher survival is not explained by higher productivity, consistent with the findings on public companies in Park et al. (2004). Columns 3 and 6 add post-1988 employment variability as a predictor – this may be inappropriate as a predictor to the extent that it is endogenous to the survival process (e.g., companies facing difficulties may have strong swings in employment), but it is appropriate to the extent that it reflects a company strategy of preserving employment security that can create greater employee commitment and willingness to adapt to circumstances threatening the company (as discussed in Park et al., 2004). Table 4 shows that employment variability is a strong positive predictor of failure, and its inclusion modestly raises the hazard ratio for ESOP companies

PERFORMANCE CHANGES

For companies that adopted ESOPs in the 1988–1994 period, Table 5 provides a comparison between the ESOP and non-ESOP companies of the change in employment, sales, and sales/employee growth in the 3 years prior to adoption and the 3 years after adoption. Such a comparison automatically controls for industry and year effects, along with adoption-year employment levels since that was used for matching.

For both ESOP adopters and their pairs, columns 1 and 2 show that average sales and employment growth were faster before than after adoption, while sales/employee growth was similar pre- and post-adoption for

Table 5. Pre/post-Adoption Comparisons (ESOP Sample = Companies Adopting ESOP in 1988–1994 Period).

	ESOP cos. (1)	Non-ESOP Pairs (2)	Diff. (3)
Average annual growth			
Employment			
3 years pre-adoption	8.3%	6.2%	2.1%
3 years post-adoption	2.6%	−1.9%	4.5%**
Change	−5.7%	−8.1%	2.4%
n		254	234
Sales			
3 years pre-adoption	11.8%	10.1%	1.7%
3 years post-adoption	5.3%	1.4%	3.9%*
Change	−6.5%	−8.8%	2.3%
n		138	77
Sales/employee			
3 years pre-adoption	3.3%	6.0%	−2.7%
3 years post-adoption	3.2%	3.6%	−0.4%
Change	−0.1%	−2.4%	2.3%
n		115	65

*$p < .10$; **$p < .05$.

ESOP companies but slowed down for their non-ESOP pairs. The net difference is shown in column 3, where it can be seen that the ESOP companies had significantly higher post-adoption annual employment growth (4.5%) and sales growth (3.9%), while the difference in sales/employee growth was close to zero and not statistically significant (–0.4%). The difference in the pre/post change was 2.4% for employment growth, 2.3% for sales growth, and 2.3% for sales/employee growth. While the results are not statistically significant for sales/employee growth, they do indicate that the raw data from a population study of ESOP adoption shows ESOPs to be associated with higher sales/employee growth and generally better performance, consistent with other studies.

PENSION BENEFITS

Finally, the data show that ESOP companies were more likely than their pairs to have other types of pensions. Table 6 shows that ESOP companies were 4 times more likely than non-ESOP companies to have a defined benefit pension in 1988 (20.1% compared to 4.9%), and likewise at least 4 times more likely to have 401(k) plans, deferred profit sharing plans, or other

Table 6. Presence of Non-ESOP Pension Plans.

	ESOP cos. (1)	Non-ESOP Pairs (2)	Diff. (3)
ESOP companies in 1988			
Presence of plan in 1988			
Defined benefit	20.1%	4.9%	15.2%**
401(k)	33.3%	6.2%	27.1%**
Profit sharing non-401(k)	35.7%	8.0%	27.7%**
Other defined con.	14.7%	2.3%	12.4%**
Number of companies	1176	1176	
ESOP adopters in 1988–1994			
Presence of plan in adoption year			
Defined benefit	21.0%	6.4%	14.6%**
401(k)	52.4%	7.9%	44.5%**
Profit sharing non-401(k)	51.2%	8.8%	42.4%**
Other defined con.	14.2%	2.3%	11.9%**
Number of companies	343	343	

Statistically significant difference at $^{*}p < .05$; $^{**}p < .01$.

types of defined contribution pension plans. Similarly, ESOP adopters in 1988–1994 were 3 times more likely than their non-ESOP pairs to have defined benefit pensions (21.0% compared to 6.4%), and at least 5 times more likely to have the other types of pension plans. These results go against the idea that ESOPs are substituting for other types of pensions, and point toward ESOPs typically adding to rather than substituting for other forms of compensation. This is consistent with other evidence that ESOPs may act as a form of efficiency wage, particularly the gift-exchange version (Kruse et al., 2010, pp. 378–380).

DISCUSSION AND CONCLUSION

Our main result of interest is that ESOP companies have longer survival rates than non-ESOP companies. They are less likely to disappear, whether disappearance is measured as bankruptcy or closure, or more broadly to include mergers, acquisitions, or other reasons. Mere survival is of course not necessarily an indicator of success, since poorly performing companies may continue due to management entrenchment, and the economy may be better off if the resources were allocated elsewhere. Both prior evidence and findings from this study, however, indicate that employee ownership is associated with better performance on average, so entrenchment is unlikely to explain the longer survival.

We find that higher productivity is linked to higher survival, unlike in Park et al. (2004) where the relationship in public companies was very tenuous. Our stronger results in this study might be explained by the much tighter controls for industry membership (using four-digit SIC rather than two-digit SIC, which better controls for difference in technology and product markets among industries). As in Park et al., however, we find that higher productivity does not explain the higher survival of employee ownership firms. The relationship between employee ownership and survival is partly mediated by employment stability. As noted by Park et al. (2004, p. 30):

> The apparent effect of employment stability is complicated, and may involve more mechanisms. Company policies designed to increase commitment of employees will help make employment more stable. These policies may affect identification of the employee with the company, which may increase productivity and the willingness of workers to be flexible and make adjustments during economic difficulties. It is very possible that employment stability is related to a culture that emphasizes employee participation in decisions.

Apart from employment stability, the longer survival of employee ownership firms could reflect greater compensation flexibility and/or lower compensation levels that allow firms to overcome economic difficulties. Both of these explanations, however, are very unlikely. For the compensation flexibility argument to work, total compensation in ESOP firms would have to be able to fall below non-ESOP levels. The evidence from prior studies – including the pre/post comparison of wage levels before and after all ESOP adoptions in the 1980–2001 period for publicly traded corporation ESOPs (Kim & Ouimet, 2014) and a series of studies on closely held company ESOPs comparable to this population of firms (Blasi, Freeman, & Kruse, 2013, pp. 181–182; 263n26-29) – strongly indicates that ESOPs tend to come on top of other compensation, so that any flexibility in ESOP contributions will not lower total compensation below what it would have been in the absence of the ESOP. Here we also provide evidence that other types of pensions are more likely in ESOP than in non-ESOP firms, so ESOP companies are not saving on labor costs through lower pension coverage.

Therefore, the greater survival exhibited by employee ownership companies remains not fully explained. There has been substantial progress in explaining the higher productivity that often accompanies employee ownership; in particular, high-performance policies such as employee involvement, training, and job security complement employee ownership in affecting employee attitudes and behaviors that contribute to better performance (Kruse et al., 2010). Such policies appear to be part of an "ownership culture" that may improve not only short-term performance, but also employee commitment, flexibility, and ideas for innovations (Harden, Kruse, & Blasi, 2010) that contribute to long-term survival. It would be valuable to analyze such information in a firm-based longitudinal dataset than can track company survival.

There could be a large payoff to further research on this topic. If the greater survival is in fact linked to employee ownership, this would not only make employee ownership companies generally attractive to employees, but also provide a public policy rationale for support of employee ownership, given the broad economic and social costs of unemployment resulting from firm closings.

NOTES

1. To ensure accurate matching, keywords from each Dun and Bradstreet company name were used to search all Form 5500 company names, and matches were individually determined based on company name, city, and state.

2. Specifications with other survival techniques produced similar results.

3. Prior literature also indicates that survival is increased by human capital and decreased by financial constraints (Geroski et al., 2010; Mossman, Bell, Swartz, & Turtle, 1998; Musso & Schiavo, 2008; Santarelli & Vivarelli, 2007). We did not employ these measures in our dataset, although Park et al. (2004) found that results for employee ownership were not substantially changed when financial strength measures were included.

REFERENCES

Blair, M., Kruse, D., & Blasi, J. (2000). Is employee ownership an unstable form? Or a stabilizing force? In M. Blair & T. Kochan (Eds.), *The new relationship: Human capital in the American corporation* (pp. 241–298). Washington, DC: Brookings Institution.

Blasi, J., Conte, M., & Kruse, D. (1996). Employee ownership and corporate performance among public corporations. *Industrial and Labor Relations Review*, *50*(1), 60–79.

Blasi, J., Freeman, R., & Kruse, D. (2013). *The citizen's share: Putting ownership back into democracy*. New Haven, CT: Yale University Press.

Blasi, J., & Kruse, D. (1991). *The new owners the mass emergence of employee ownership in public companies and what it means to American business*. New York, NY: HarperCollins.

Buchele, D. K., Rodgers, L., & Scharf, A. (2010). Show me the money: Does shared capitalism share the wealth? In D. Kruse, R. Freeman, & J. Blasi (Eds.), *Shared capitalism at work: Employee ownership, profit sharing, gain sharing, and broad-based stock options* (pp. 351–376). Chicago, IL: University of Chicago Press.

Doucouliagos, C. (1995). Worker participation and productivity in labor-managed and participatory capitalist firms: A meta-analysis. *Industrial and Labor Relations Review*, *49*(1), 58–77.

Freeman, S. F. (2007). *Effects of ESOP adoption and employee ownership: Thirty years of research and experience*. Working Paper No. 07-01. Organizational Dynamics Programs, University of Pennsylvania, Philadelphia, PA.

Geroski, P. A., Mata, J., & Portugal, P. (2010). Founding conditions and the survival of new firms. *Strategic Management Journal*, *31*(5), 510–529.

Hansmann, H. (1996). *The ownership of enterprise*. London: The Belknap Press.

Harden, E., Kruse, D., & Blasi, J. (2010). Who has a better idea? Innovation, shared capitalism, and HR policies. In D. Kruse, R. Freeman, & J. Blasi (Eds.), *Shared capitalism at work: Employee ownership, profit and gain sharing, and broad-based stock options* (pp. 225–256). Chicago, IL: University of Chicago Press.

Kaarsemaker, E. (2006). *Employee ownership and its consequences: Synthesis-generated evidence for the effects of employee ownership and gaps in the research literature*. York, UK: University of York.

Kardas, P., Scharf, A., & Keogh, J. (1998). Wealth and income consequences of ESOPs and employee ownership: A comparative study from Washington state. *Journal of Employee Ownership Law and Finance*, *10*(4), 3–52.

Kim, E. H., & Ouimet, P. (forthcoming). Broad-based employee stock ownership: Motives and outcomes. *Journal of Finance*.

Kroumova, M. (2000). *Investment in employer stock through 401(k) plans: Is there reason for concern?* Ph.D. dissertation, Rutgers University, New Brunswick, NJ.

Kruse, D., & Blasi, J. (1997). Employee ownership, employee attitudes, and firm performance: A review of the evidence. In D. Lewin, D. J. B. Mitchell, & M. A. Zaidi (Eds.), *Human resources management handbook, part 1* (pp. 113–151). Greenwich, CT: JAI Press.

Kruse, D., Freeman, R., & Blasi, J. (Eds.). (2010). *Shared capitalism at work: Employee ownership, profit sharing, gain sharing, and broad-based stock options*. Chicago, IL: University of Chicago Press.

Mossman, C. E., Bell, G. G., Swartz, L. M., & Turtle, H. (1998). An employment comparison of bankruptcy models. *The Financial Review*, *33*, 35–54.

Musso, P., & Schiavo, S. (2008). The impact of financial constraints on firm survival and growth. *Journal of Evolutionary Economics*, *18*(2), 135–149.

Park, R., Kruse, D., & Sesil, J. (2004). Does employee ownership enhance firm survival? In V. Perotin & A. Robinson (Eds.), *Advances in the economic analysis of participatory and self-managed firms* (Vol. 8, pp. 3–34). 113–151. Greenwich, CT: JAI Press.

Renaud, S., St-Onge, S., & Magnan, M. (2004). The impact of stock purchase plan participation on workers' individual cash compensation. *Industrial Relations*, *43*(1), 120–147.

Santarelli, E., & Vivarelli, M. (2007). Entrepreneurship and the process of firms' entry, survival and growth. *Industrial and Corporate Change*, *16*(3), 455–488.

Scharf, A., & Mackin, C. (2000). *Census of Massachusetts companies with employee stock ownership plans (ESOPs)*. Boston, MA: Commonwealth Corporation.

Welbourne, T. M., & Cyr, L. A. (1999). Using ownership as an incentive: Does the "Too many Chiefs" rule apply in entrepreneurial firms? *Group and Organization Management*, *24*(4), 438–460.

PART II
COMPARATIVE SYSTEMS OF OWNERSHIP AND PARTICIPATION

CHAPTER 6

WHAT DOES MONDRAGON TEACH US ABOUT WORKPLACE DEMOCRACY?

Tom Malleson

ABSTRACT

Purpose – *The Mondragon cooperatives are the most thoroughly studied and well-known example of worker cooperatives in the world. Yet while there has been much discussion and wide recognition of the empirical growth of the Mondragon co-ops, there is substantial confusion about the lessons we can draw from this case in thinking about workplace democracy more broadly.*

Design/methodology/approach – *The normative and empirical literature on Mondragon is carefully analyzed to draw out the main implications from this case study for the broader issue of workplace democracy.*

Findings – *I contend that Mondragon teaches us two main lessons. First, that workplace democracy can indeed operate in a way that is economically sustainable and socially superior to conventional firms. Second, Mondragon sheds light on the question of whether co-ops are doomed to degenerate.*

Sharing Ownership, Profits, and Decision-making in the 21st Century
Advances in the Economic Analysis of Participatory & Labor-Managed Firms, Volume 14, 127–157

ISSN: 0885-3339/doi:10.1108/S0885-3339(2013)0000014007

Research limitations/implications – *This paper advances our understanding and conceptualization of workplace democracy.*

Practical implications – *This paper provides practitioners with an up-to-date and comprehensive analysis of the world's most successful cooperative network.*

Social implications – *This paper provides insight into the practical feasibility and normative desirability of alternative organizations of workplaces in the form of worker cooperatives.*

Originality/value – *This paper will be of particular interest to scholars and activists interested in democratic alternatives to conventional hierarchical firms by illustrating the strengths and weaknesses of the Mondragon cooperatives and drawing out the lessons that this specific yet influential example has for issues of workplace democracy more broadly.*

Keywords: Workplace democracy; worker cooperatives; Mondragon; social economy

JEL Classification: J54; B52; D70; L10; L20; N34; P51

INTRODUCTION

Without a doubt the Mondragon cooperatives are the most thoroughly studied and well-known example of worker cooperatives in the world.[1] For advocates, Mondragon is a stunning success story, the world's outstanding example of the feasibility of building a cooperative economic system within the context of the capitalist system, even a vivid illustration of seeds of a new world within the womb of the old (Gibson-Graham, 2003; Morrison, 1997; Whyte & Whyte, 1988). For critics, the successes of Mondragon appear much less generalizable than the shortcomings – serving as yet another reminder of the undesirability if not impossibility of workplace democracy.[2]

In particular, while there has been wide recognition of the empirical growth and "success" of the Mondragon co-ops, there is substantial *confusion* about the lessons we can draw from this case in thinking about the practicality of workplace democracy more broadly.[3] The aim of this paper is to sort through this confusion in order to provide some analytical clarity about the main lessons of the Mondragon experiment. The point is neither to condemn nor to deify Mondragon, but to clarify the lessons that this particular experiment in the Basque region of northern Spain holds for those activists and scholars across the globe interested in the possibilities of workplace democracy.

I contend that Mondragon teaches us two main lessons. First, that workplace democracy can indeed operate in a way that is economically sustainable and socially superior to conventional firms – provided it makes use of appropriate structures and practices. Second, Mondragon sheds light on the question of whether co-ops are doomed to degenerate. This paper offers two main analytical clarifications regarding degeneration. The first is in terms of the degree of perfectionism with which worker cooperatives are conceptualized. The second is in terms of the nature of the market pressures that cooperatives face. These clarifications help us to think clearly about what a co-op really is, and allow us to see that degeneration is not a feature inherent to co-ops *per se* but a result of the broader market system within which they operate. I argue that while Mondragon *has* partially degenerated, such degeneration is not inevitable for worker co-ops: Mondragon itself may well regenerate, and, more broadly speaking, degeneration can be countered by restructuring market systems in various ways.

In order to evaluate the empirical performance of the Mondragon co-ops it's useful to divide the analysis into two periods, corresponding to the original Mondragon Group (from the 1950s to 1980s) and the global Mondragon Corporation (from the 1990s to the present). In the following sections we explore the historical development of Mondragon in each era, and then discuss the main lessons that can be derived from this experience.

HISTORY OF THE ORIGINAL MONDRAGON GROUP

The Mondragon cooperatives (often referred to simply as "Mondragon") started when five young workers graduated from a technical training school run by a catholic priest José María Arizendiarrieta in the small town of Mondragon, in the Basque country of Northern Spain. In 1956, with minimal resources, they managed to scrape together enough money from friends and acquaintances to buy a small bankrupt factory in order to start producing stoves as a small worker co-op.

After a few years, demand for the products was sufficient for the co-op to expand into several, though they soon found themselves with limited access to finance as local banks were skeptical about the long-term viability of co-ops and were hostile to worker ownership (Morrison, 1997). A decisive breakthrough came in 1959 when a small handful of co-ops affiliated together to create a co-operative bank – the *Caja Laboral* (CL) to pool the co-ops' resources and attract local savings in order to finance their development. The CL was set up as a second-degree cooperative, meaning that it was structured as a co-op of co-ops, managed by a mix of its own workers as well as representatives from the co-ops that were its principal clients. The CL was designed to perform two basic functions: to provide *finance* at below market rates and, through its *Empresarial* division, to provide business and managerial advice to help set up new cooperatives and assist those in economic trouble.[4] The CL was (and still is) organized like a credit union, which allows it to attract the savings of the local population, as well as to hold the deposits of the associated co-ops. In this way the CL acts to recycle the community's capital *through* the democratic workplaces. Its significance can hardly be overstated: as Morrison (1997) points out, it effectively freed Mondragon from dependence on capitalist financiers.

The co-ops operate according to ten guiding principles (Morrison, 1997). (I) *Open admission* – no one can be denied entry based on gender, ethnicity, etc. (II) *Democratic organization* – one-member one-vote.[5] (III) *Sovereignty of labor* – meaning that members control the co-op and distribute its surplus. (IV) *Instrumental character of capital* – so that the co-ops pay a just but limited return on invested capital, and ensure that owning capital does not give any additional rights of governance beyond membership. (V) *Participation in management* – to ensure member participation and the ongoing development of skills necessary to manage. (VI) *Pay solidarity* – to limit the differential between highest and lowest paid.[6] (VII) *Intercooperation* – cooperation among the co-ops. (VIII) *Social transformation.* (IX) *Universality* – emphasizing solidarity with all workers. (X) *Education* – which is ongoing in terms of both cooperative values and technical skills.

New members are required to pay a substantial investment fee (that goes into their personal internal capital account).[7] This fee acts to screen out workers who are not committed to staying, is psychologically important in making workers feel like co-owners, and is important for providing an internal source of financing. Of a co-op's surplus, 10% is mandated by law toward charities and nonprofit organizations, 45% goes into the firm's collective reserve fund, and the remaining 45% goes into members' individual capital accounts (the bulk of which cannot be withdrawn until retirement (Freundlich, Grellier, & Altuna, 2009)). In other words, this structure effectively means that up to 90% of profits are saved internally to help refinance the whole system.

The ultimate authority in each co-op has always been the General Assembly, which meets at least once per year. It elects the Governing Council which is the highest governing body of the co-op – representing the Assembly between meetings, overseeing the execution of assembly decisions, and monitoring senior management (Lafuente & Freundlich, 2012). The Governing Council also appoints the CEO and approves his or her choice of senior managers; the CEO and senior managers form the management council which runs the day-to-day affairs of the co-op. There is also a Social Council, elected by members in various departments to help with personnel issues (e.g., health benefits, safety). Although it officially has only advisory power, its purpose, while somewhat vague, is generally seen as a kind of internal union. It does not engage in collective bargaining but serves to strengthen communication, represents shop- or office-floor perspectives, and allows rank-and-file members' more direct engagement with management. Whyte and Whyte argue that whereas the Governing Council represents the members as *owners*, the Social Council represents them as *workers* – playing the essential role of guiding education, discussion and decision-making (1988, p. 148). Finally, an Audit Committee audits the books.

Since 1987, the Mondragon co-ops as a whole have been collectively represented in a Cooperative Congress, which acts like a mini-parliament, comprising elected representatives from every co-op (in rough proportion to their size) to consider issues of broad concern to the whole system. It is important to note that while each co-op is independent (i.e., under the direct democratic control of its members), it is also embedded in a larger network of supporting structures that provide financial, business, technical, educational, and social support (Lafuente & Freundlich, 2012; MacLeod & Reed, 2009).

LESSONS FROM THE ORIGINAL MONDRAGON GROUP

When we review the evidence from the first thirty years of its existence, the overarching message is that Mondragon demonstrates that workplace democracy can be just as economically successful as conventional firms, while being socially superior in certain respects. However, such success is not inevitable, but is due to a set of well-designed structures and practices.

If we consider first the economic dimension, it is undeniable that Mondragon has been a remarkable success. Starting from five workers with basically no assets, by the late 1980s it had grown to 166 co-ops, employing 21,000, with $1.6 billion in sales (Morrison, 1997). In their economic analysis of Mondragon, Thomas and Logan (1982) found that co-op efficiency actually *exceeded* that of the largest conventional firms in Spain by 7.5% and medium and small enterprises by 40%. Levin (1983) confirms that Mondragon had higher labor productivity than the largest Spanish firms. Likewise, Bradley and Gelb report that more than half the members considered themselves to be working "significantly harder" than they would for conventional firms (1981, p. 224). According to Whyte and Whyte, "all economists who have studied Mondragon's financial history report that the cooperatives have far outpaced private Spanish firms" (1988, p. 131). Indeed, I am not aware of any studies finding Mondragon to be *less* efficient than comparable conventional firms, though it is fair to say that the comparative emprical literature is not large.[8]

Since the publication of Ward's (1958) famous theoretical paper, neoclassical economists have often predicted that co-ops will react perversely to changes in the market – firing when demand increases and expanding during downturns.[9] There is, however, no evidence for this here (Bradley & Gelb, 1985). Nor have the co-ops suffered from underinvestment (as was predicted by Furubotn & Pejovich, 1970); indeed, between 1971 and 1989 gross capital formation in Mondragon co-ops occurred at an annual rate of 9%, compared to the national equivalent of only 4% (Moye, 1993, p. 261). This pattern has not noticeably changed over the years. For instance, Arando, Freundlich, Gago, Jones, and Kato (2010, p. 15) show that from 1996 to 2006, Mondragon's industrial group's investment more than quadrupled, whereas the investment of conventional firms in similar industries only doubled. So, overall it is clear that Mondragon's system of mandating large levels of internal reinvestment has been very effective at ensuring growth.

Critics of cooperatives often worry that their economic success is simply due to state subsidy. While it is true that the co-ops have been supported in various ways, such as by having reduced corporate tax rates, and by being provided a portion of start-up capital (Ammirato, 1996, p. 29), they receive far less institutional support than conventional firms get from banks, stock markets, and the whole political–legal apparatus which has been designed with standard firms in mind. Indeed, the reason that Mondragon had to form itself into a network in the first place was, at least in part, to emulate the institutional support that capitalist firms get as a matter of course from the state and society at large. Moreover, regardless of the support the co-ops receive, there is no evidence that the co-ops' survival has been *dependent* on state subsidy, or that the funds they receive have been economically wasted – the opposite in fact seems to be true, in terms of the large number of jobs and the immense wealth the co-ops have generated. Perhaps the strongest evidence for this is that during the formative first twenty years, Mondragon operated under Franco's regime that, with important exceptions, was generally hostile toward cooperatives – for instance in 1959 the government suspended medical and retirement care to Mondragon members on the grounds that they were owners not workers (Azevedo & Gitahy, 2010) – yet they continued to flourish nevertheless.[10] More recently, the Spanish state has become more supportive of co-ops, but in an environment that remains overwhelmingly geared toward the success of traditional capitalist firms.

Taking a step back, we can see that Mondragon provides invaluable guidance as to the prerequisites for economic success. We can highlight three essential structures that have been instrumental in this regard. First, it is well known that in many cases the central if not fundamental constraint to co-op formation is that workers simply lack the wealth and financial support to start their own co-op (Dow, 2003; Drèze, 1993). The CL thus represented a crucial innovation in this regard: not only did it provide financial help to existing co-ops in the early decades, but the Empresarial division was vital in helping to set up new co-ops in the first place. For new co-ops to be set up, a group of workers approached the CL with their idea. Provided the workers' vision was of a cooperative firm with appropriately rigorous democratic structures, the CL helped to carry out an in-depth feasibility study, which could take one or two years. If the project proved feasible, the CL would bring in engineers to start planning construction of the new workplace, as well as providing the bulk of the initial financing. According to Campbell et al., the co-op members were expected to put up roughly 20% of the initial start-up capital (without which it was thought that projects might fail from lack of commitment). A further 20% was available from a state loan at 3% interest, while the remainder was supplied by the CL (Campbell, Keen, Norman, & Oakeshott, 1977, p. 44). Beyond this, the CL provided management skills, seminars in cooperativist ideals, and even covered the new firm's losses for the first couple of years (which were expected to be paid back once the firm became profitable). The CL thus illustrates the importance of some kind of co-op bank for facilitating co-op formation.

Second, Mondragon has hit upon a durable structural form based on collective ownership combined with individual internal capital accounts (Ellerman, 1984, 1990). To see the importance of this, consider for a moment the Plywood co-ops of the northwestern United States, which were structured like normal corporations on the basis of individual-owned shares (the difference being that no shares were owned by outsiders) (Bellas, 1972; Berman, 1967). This meant that each member owned a share which gave him or her membership rights (to elect the management of the firm) *as well as* traditional property rights (as owners of the firm's assets). The problem is that when these co-ops were successful, the value of the shares rose hugely. And since the firms were structured so that the shares gave both membership *and* traditional property rights, expensive shares meant that membership itself became very exclusive. In this case, shares of the plywood co-ops went as high as $95,000 (often requiring $20,000 down-payment) (Ellerman, 1990). This meant that retiring workers could not find new members who could afford to purchase the shares, thus shares were sold to outsider speculators (in which case the firm degenerated quickly), or were not sold at all, and new employees were hired as nonmembers (in which case the firm degenerated slowly). This is why Vanek calls firms of this structure "mules" – they are hybrids of capitalistic individual-style ownership with cooperative practices, which due to their structure are unable to reproduce another generation (quoted in Ellerman, 1984, p. 258).

By contrast, Mondragon is collectively owned but with individual capital accounts instead of shares. Each year a portion of the firm's profits goes into the individual internal accounts, which receive interest. Members are permitted to withdraw the interest but not the bulk of the principal, until they leave the firm. When an individual member leaves, she has a claim on the accumulated profit share in her internal capital account, but not on a portion of the value of the firm as traditional stockholders do. This assures both the avoidance of "mules" and a large and vital source of internal finance (since, as mentioned above, up to 90% of co-op profits are reinvested internally), which ensures growth and sustainability. Since new members simply open new internal accounts, membership (with the corresponding governance rights) is importantly distinct from traditional property rights.[11] If a co-op does well, members get more money in their individual accounts, but membership itself (and governance rights) does not become more expensive since individuals do not have claims on "shares" of the firm, only on a portion of its accumulated earnings. In this way the co-ops avoid the structural problems that led many co-ops in the United States and elsewhere to degenerate.

Third, Mondragon illustrates the importance of *networking* for co-op survival. As Smith (2001) says, co-ops often face the stark choice of "blooming together or wilting alone." Mondragon's network provides numerous economic benefits: it allows for the sharing of technical knowledge and business strategy; for relocating members from co-ops facing problems to co-ops doing well; it allows for opportunities for intra-cooperation and the development of economies of scale. Moreover, networking allows co-ops to share risk through cross-investment, meaning that members don't have to have all their "eggs" (their job and their invested savings) in one basket. Networking makes co-op practices more familiar externally, to regional workers, managers, bankers and politicians, as well as serving as a positive model for other workers to emulate. Additionally, networking helps to promote a spirit of solidarity and common purpose necessary to combat feelings of isolation that co-op members can easily feel in an overwhelmingly capitalist world. Clustering together in a network or league can provide a self-sustaining burst of energy as positive externalities reinforce each other, knowledge acquired in one place transfers over, and practices from one co-op are emulated in another.

While many authors have commented on the usefulness of cooperative networking (Menzani & Zamagni, 2010; Smith, 2001), it is less often recognized that, conceptually, what networks represent is an attempt by co-ops to envelop themselves within a web of supportive institutional structures – a kind of miniature *cooperative market system*, to protect themselves from the biases inherent in the fact that the dominant market system is a corporate one. In other words, Mondragon's extensive networking teaches us to shift our inquiry from asking about what kind of firms are able to survive in *the* market, to asking about the complementarities, or tensions, that exist *between* specific firms and specific market environments.

THE SOCIAL SUCCESS OF THE ORIGINAL MONDRAGON

One of the most striking social achievements of the Mondragon co-ops is that their wage structure is much more egalitarian than conventional firms. In the early years the largest permissible difference between the highest and lowest paid was 3:1. In the 1980s this was relaxed to 6:1, which is the level it has basically remained ever since (Arando et al., 2010).[12] This is of course much greater equality than capitalist firms. For instance, in the social democratic countries, an average CEO makes 15 times more than an average worker (and substantially more than that vis-à-vis the lowest paid), and the average American CEO makes an incredible 300 times the average wage (*The Economist*, 2006). The general picture at Mondragon today is that the lowest earners tend to earn more than in comparable capitalist firms, the middle earners the same, and managers and the highly skilled earning up to 30% less (Arando et al., 2011). Managers stay for a variety of other reasons and moral incentives, such as their ethical commitment to the co-ops; indeed the fact that the co-ops can attract such loyalty (so that managers decline leaving even though it could substantially increase their salary) strongly suggests that the co-ops *are* socially different kinds of firms, and deeply rewarding in their own way – why else would managers stay?

A second important success of Mondragon is the virtual elimination of job loss and the minimization of business failure. For instance, Morrison claims that during Mondragon's first thirty years of operation over 160 co-ops were formed yet *only three closed* (1997, p. 174). Likewise, Moye reports that even during the Basque recession from the mid-1970s to 1984, when the region saw the loss of 100,000 jobs and a 20% unemployment rate, *not a single* Mondragon member lost his or her job (1993, p. 253). Such stable employment in a capitalist context is practically unheard of. Moreover, it's important to note that although changes in market demand are reacted to in the normal manner (rising demand leading to growth, slow times leading to declines), the *kind* of changes that take place are often more humane than in capitalist firms. During the Basque recession, capitalist businesses tended to react to the downturn by disinvesting, often permanently closing their doors or moving to new sites where unions were weaker or taxes lower. The co-ops, however, reacted quite differently. The co-ops tended to treat labor as a constant cost, achieving flexibility in other ways. So recession was dealt with in the short term by transfers between co-ops, cutting prices, and producing for inventory, while in the long term, wages and hours were cut (in ways that were collectively chosen to be fair across the board), and large-scale reinvestment occurred. Lay-offs, at least of members (non-members is a different story which we discuss below), practically never happened, and only as a last resort. Indeed, this pattern of humane response to recession has repeated itself in the 2008 recession (Arando et al., 2010).

Moreover, even though in certain respects shop floor conditions have not been noticeably different than in capitalist firms (Dow, 2003), it is nevertheless apparent that members have far preferred working in a co-op than the alternative. Mondragon members have reported being much less likely to be willing to transfer jobs to a capitalist firm (even for monetary increases of up to 50%) than the other way around – 27% compared to 54% (Bradley & Gelb, 1981, p. 220).

There is, however, a puzzle about job satisfaction. While Mondragon members have consistently reported higher job satisfaction than in conventional firms over the years (Cheney, 1999; Moye, 1993), there is also contradictory evidence that co-ops can actually be *more stressful* work environments than capitalist firms (Arando et al., 2011). What explains this discrepancy? While there is no consensus in the literature about why this is so, I would offer the following speculation: this conundrum can be understood as a manifestation of the multifaceted nature of work "freedom." Co-ops tend to provide workers with more freedom in the sense of control or self-determination. And while on the one hand this control and empowerment can be liberating, it can also bring with it heavy responsibility. If I become equal and a co-owner, the responsibility of the firm's success becomes *my* responsibility too – this breeds stress. In contrast, workers in conventional firms, though not free in most senses, do have the freedom to abdicate significant responsibility in saying to themselves, "this is the boss's firm, so as long as I get paid I don't care what happens." Co-op job satisfaction reports may be ambiguous because the freedom of sharing control in a cooperative workplace is at the same time both hard and rewarding, both stressful and empowering. Freedom need not be easy for it to be valuable.[13]

A further social strength of Mondragon during this period was the connection with the community. One of its 10 principles of course is "social transformation." This principle is given some tangibility by the practice (mandated by Basque law) of directing 10% of annual profits toward charities and community projects. Beyond this, the community clearly benefits from the long-term stable employment, and the fact that the revenues of the firms largely stay in the community through the CL. Both of these factors have brought decades of positive externalities to the community. In this light, the deep roots that the Mondragon co-ops have laid in the region belie the traditional Marxist objection that co-ops are simply group-capitalists, interested only in profit-maximization.

Considering these social attributes together it is reasonable to conclude with Morrison that Mondragon's operation as a whole can be characterized by "the assertion of economic rationality with a human face" (1997, p. 188).

So while original Mondragon has had a number of social successes, for our purposes the most important question is what Mondragon's experience can teach us in terms of building democracy at work.

The first thing to point out is that maintaining healthy democracy, where the average worker really does feel empowered, of equal status, and free to participate in collective decision-making is very difficult (Holmstrom, 1989). Self-management is both a science and an art, and one that is rarely achieved to everyone's satisfaction.

Mondragon, during its first period, was a fundamentally different type of business than the typical capitalist firm. Strictly speaking, conventional firms are hierarchies in the sense that they embody formally institutionalized inequality whereby the power and authority of those at the top is unaccountable to those at the bottom. Mondragon, in this strict sense, was not a hierarchy but a democracy. This does not mean that there was complete equality or that everyone participated in every decision; large and complex organizations (be they businesses or states) require a division of labor, management, and expertise, which means that some individuals will have more decision-making power than others. The difference with hierarchical firms is that in Mondragon (and worker co-ops more generally) every member was (and, indeed, still is) formally equal, and all those who exercised power and authority at the top were accountable to the General Assembly at the bottom. Indeed, the General Assemblies (through their Governing Council) had the power to fire the top management, and have occasionally done so (Smith, 2001, p. 32).

That said, Mondragon should not be interpreted as any kind of democratic paradise. A number of authors have pointed to the shortcomings of democratic participation. For instance, one study found that 13% of co-op members felt that they directly "participated in important decisions," and 20% indirectly through representatives, compared to only 4% and 3%, respectively, in comparable capitalist firms. Inversely, 30% of co-op members felt that they did not participate in firm governance, compared to 80% in capitalist firms (Bradley & Gelb, 1981, p. 222). This points to considerably more participation in the co-ops, but clearly not any kind of universal engagement (at least during the time of this study). Moreover, Cheney (1999) has argued that democratic participation started to ossify and become routinized throughout the 1990s. He reports that in some of the co-ops the Assemblies have become "as predictable as Catholic Masses" with the same people in charge year after year; likewise Bakaikoa, Errasti, and Begiristain (2004, p. 80) point to the fact that attendance at the Assemblies often does not exceed 30% of the members. However, while these critiques are important, it is not clear that the routine nature and low attendance at Assemblies are necessarily a sign of democratic decay.[14] It *may* be the case that people aren't attending because they are disillusioned and think participation is meaningless; but it may also be the case that the *real* participation happens elsewhere, in regular, smaller meetings leading up to the Assemblies. After all, an occasional, large Assembly is hardly the place for sustained deliberation; for large workplaces, it would be impossible for such Assemblies to be anything much more than routine and symbolic. The crux of the issue is the quality of participation *surrounding* the Assemblies: whether there are meaningful opportunities for rank-and-file members to learn about the issues, for different positions to be heard, evaluated, deliberated, *and then* voted on.

Mondragon's experience is useful in highlighting two main obstacles to workplace democracy, as well as pointing to two main requirements for maintaining healthy democracy.

The main obstacles are the classic albatrosses of democratic practice: size and complexity.[15] The larger the co-op, the more that specialization is required, so the harder it becomes to have broad deliberation, and the more important it becomes to have managers to oversee and coordinate. Likewise, the more that organizations become technically complicated, the more that experts are required, which again produces barriers to widespread deliberation. It's likely that both of these factors have exerted increasing pressure on Mondragon over the years as the organization has grown in both size and complexity. In both cases, size and complexity naturally tend to remove decision-making from ordinary workers; and without opportunities for actual face-to-face decision-making, members are not likely to feel the freedom of self-determination that gives democracy its essential energy and vitality.

Yet while these obstacles are consistent constraints on democratic practice, they can be largely mitigated, if not completely overcome, through sufficient dedication and the appropriate practices. Mondragon's experience points to two necessary things in this regard. First, workplace democracy requires solid *parliamentary structures*, by which I mean the establishment of a democratic constitution, regular General Assemblies, decision-making transparency, and availability of information. While these structures are clearly important, by themselves they constitute simply the shell or skeleton of a democratic body. For the workplace to be a living, breathing democracy, requires that the skeleton be fed with the oxygen and nutrition of participation. So, second, healthy workplace democracy requires rigorous *practices of participation*.

These practices in turn require at least two things. (i) *The means for members to acquire the necessary skills and knowledge required to participate*. To this end Mondragon has engaged in regular training of its members in both technical skills and the theory and practice of cooperativism so that shopfloor members can become knowledgeable and confident enough to begin holding managers and experts to account. It is sometimes questioned whether the democratic practices of Mondragon are a result of a specific Basque culture prone to democratic participation (Whyte & Whyte, 1988). While there may be an element of truth in this, what stands out at Mondragon is not any kind of natural or spontaneous drive to participate among the people, but rather an intense effort to foster and *build* a democratic culture.[16] Not only is education a foundational value at Mondragon, but the co-ops actually grew out of schools set up by Arizmendiarrieta, who even went so far as to characterize cooperativsm as "an educational movement that uses economic action" (quoted in Morrison, 1997, p. 15). This emphasis became a defining mark of Mondragon. To give one example, Fagor (the largest co-op group) in 1987 had 30% of its 6,602-person workforce involved in technical or professional training courses, in addition to the $730,000 spent on more general education for members.[17] In addition, one of Mondragon's main groups is the Knowledge group (focusing on research and development), and Mondragon has also created a university.

The second practice of participation required for healthy workplace democracy is *the opportunity for regular participation.* In large co-ops this requires open channels of communication as well as efforts to decentralize where possible in order to have semi-autonomous teams or working groups where direct participation can take place. Such opportunities have been fostered at Mondragon in a couple of ways. The Social Councils have provided important channels for rank-and-file members to challenge management, which is important since without ways of mobilizing dissent there is likely to be little accountability. Unfortunately, some Social Councils have been accused of simply rubber-stamping management decisions (Cheney, 1999; Kasmir, 1996); nevertheless, the model of having a kind of internal organization like a Social Council – with teeth – that could serve to foster a "loyal opposition" is very useful for democratic vibrancy. Also, attempts are made to decentralize and experiment with flat structures of decision-making (Mondragon, 2012, pp. 39–44). For example, Irizar (a bus manufacturing co-op of Mondragon) has developed a flat organizational structure based on work teams, with no bosses but with "shared leadership." Not only is this participation good from a democratic perspective, it has also proven to be important from an economic perspective as it increases innovation, the transfer of ideas, and overall productivity (MacLeod & Reed, 2009).[18]

In sum, Mondragon provides two important lessons in terms of maintaining healthy democracy at work. First, the constraints of size and complexity are best overcome with rigorous parliamentary structures, within which practices of participation are encouraged (by fostering both the knowledge and the opportunities necessary for direct participation). Second, a lasting lesson of Mondragon is that it is better to think of democracy not as a *goal* that can be reached once and for all, but as a *process*: a continual attempt to enhance participatory structures and train more democratically engaged people.

HISTORY OF THE GLOBAL MONDRAGON CORPORATION

Mondragon underwent massive, some would say fundamental, changes in the 1980s and 1990s, due to substantial pressures from globalization. Members widely believed that they would have to adapt to the global competition if they were to survive. To get a sense of the global pressures they faced, consider the dilemma of Irizar – one of the most successful co-ops associated with Mondragon. In the 1990s Irizar was able to manufacture a bus at home at a cost of €180,000, whereas the same vehicle could be produced by competitors in China for only €12,000 (MacLeod & Reed, 2009, p. 137). Pressures like these led Mondragon to undertake significant restructuring in the 1990s so as to be better able to compete internationally. The system changed its name from the "Mondragon Cooperative Group" to the "Mondragon Cooperative Corporation"[19]; since 2007 the corporation has simply been referred to as "Mondragon." The co-ops that had previously been organized into geographical groups were reorganized into four business groups: a financial group, a retail group (dominated by the Eroski supermarket chain), an industrial group (itself divided into several divisions), and a knowledge (research/training) group – thus allowing for greater inter-firm cooperation and synergy, as well as economies of scale (MacLeod & Reed, 2009, p. 120).

Probably the most significant change of this period is the composition of its workforce. Mondragon has witnessed a massive expansion of nonmember workers through two avenues. First, the 1990s saw a sharp increase in the number of temporary nonmember workers in the co-ops (reaching a high of 29.8% in 2000 (Arando et al., 2010)). Second, and more significantly, there has been a dramatic increase in the number of nonmember workers working in Mondragon-owned subsidiaries and affiliates that are not co-ops. This happened primarily through the expansion of the large

Eroski supermarket chain outside of the Basque region into other parts of Spain and France (Arando et al., 2011). It also happened from Mondragon becoming multinational, and like others multinationals, increasingly establishing foreign subsidiaries in places with low-cost labor such as China, Brazil, Mexico, Poland, and the Czech Republic. It's important to note that these firms outside of the Basque region, in Spain and overseas, are structured as conventional capitalist firms; the employees are *not* members of Mondragon.[20] While Smith (2001) points out that there is no evidence that Mondragon has refused any requests for foreign subsidiaries to be transformed into co-ops, it is nevertheless clear that the priority is in maintaining the co-ops "at home" as opposed to democratizing the affiliates (Luzarraga & Irizar, 2012). The official rationale for not having democratized any of the foreign subsidiaries is the legal barriers that exist in certain countries to setting up worker co-ops; the fact that some of the subsidiaries are joint ventures with conventional investors; and the supposed lack of interest in cooperatives among many of the foreign workers (Azevedo & Gitahy, 2010).[21]

HAS MONDRAGON DEGENERATED?

Critics of co-ops have long argued that they are doomed to degenerate (Luxemburg, 1900 [1986]; Mandel, 1975; Marx, 1933 [1867]; Webb & Webb, 1907). This "degeneration thesis" is commonly attributed to Beatrice and Sidney Webb (1907) who argued that worker co-ops would inevitably be strangled by capitalist competition, which would either force them under, due to the uncompetitiveness of their democratic structure, or force the workers to abandon such a structure, in which case the firms may succeed, but no longer as co-ops (cf. Gibson-Graham, 2003; Jones, 1975).[22]

Is such analysis apposite to the case of Mondragon? It's true that globalization has deeply altered the composition of Mondragon.[23] While the base of Mondragon in the Basque country has remained staunchly cooperative, Mondragon as a whole has not. The fundamental fact is that, according to José María Ormaechea (a past president of the General Council[24]), by 2006 *only 38% of workers in Mondragon were co-op members* compared to 80% in 1990. In addition, four joint-stock companies were being established for every one co-op (cited in MacLeod & Reed, 2009, p. 134). The fact that fewer than 40% of the personnel are actual co-op members means that members now represent only a minority of total workers in the business as a whole.[25] The members have, in effect, become privileged quasi-capitalist employers of a larger body of nonmember workers.

Throughout the 1990s and 2000s Mondragon managed to substantially increase its economic growth (Errasti, Heras, Bakaikoa, & Elgoibar, 2003). By 2011 Mondragon as a whole had grown to encompass 254 firms (111 co-ops and 143 noncooperative subsidiaries, of which 94 were abroad), employing about 83,000 people, with assets of a tremendous €32 billion (Mondragon, 2011). While this growth is impressive, and shows that Mondragon has been successful at sustaining its jobs at home in substantial part through expansion abroad, the fact that this growth has been achieved by a workforce of whom the majority are conventional, disenfranchised, non-co-op members, means that the success is not entirely different from that of other multinationals.[26] Members in the Basque region, many of whom are deeply committed to workplace democracy, have found themselves in a paradoxical situation where they are also shareholders profiting off the cheaper labor of disenfranchised workers in the rest of Spain and the Global South.

Throughout the contemporary period Mondragon has been able to maintain its record of virtual guaranteed employment, although again this fact is less impressive when it's recalled that global Mondragon is able to assure work for its members by firing its nonmembers when necessary. For example, in the midst of the recession of 2008–2009, the number of members rose by 6.1% whereas the overall numbers of employment fell by 8.3%, meaning that the security of the members was achieved, at least in part, through the disposability of the nonmembers (Flecha & Cruz, 2011, p. 160).

So has Mondragon degenerated? There is much confusion in the literature about this. On the one hand, some authors, like Errasti et al., are firm in their diagnosis that the existence of a majority of nonmembers in Mondragon does "re-affirm the predictions" of degeneration (2003, p. 562). Some, like Erik Olin Wright (2010), avoid the degeneration label, preferring to refer to Mondragon's composition in terms of "hybridity" in a less critical way. On the other hand, others are much more celebratory of Mondragon, emphasizing its phenomenal global growth as a "democratic" and "cooperative" success (Flecha & Cruz, 2011; Forcadell, 2005). Indeed, Gibson–Graham go so far as to praise Mondragon for being the "most successful cooperativist regional economy in the world" (2003, p. 154).

How can we make sense of this conflicting mess of interpretations? I suggest that the confusion can be largely clarified by recognizing an underlying pattern: that these different positions represent a spectrum of opinion between two basic poles, which we can label "better-than-nothing" and "perfectionist."

The "better-than-nothing" (or anti-perfectionist) perspective focuses on the concrete advantages that Mondragon has over standard firms, and highlights the ways in which real-world examples are more complex than ideals. It also tends to be laudatory of Mondragon's success and downplaying, if not outright vague, about any essential characteristics of democracy (cf. Flecha & Cruz, 2011; Forcadell, 2005). In this vein Blasi and Kruse encourage people " 'giving up' on a certain unrealistic perfectionism about institutional designs .... [And so asking] the question, 'Would you rather have a business world that looked meaningfully different ... or would you rather hold out for some distant less-likely to achieve utopia where all differences of power, prestige and rewards are theoretically eliminated?' " (2012, p. 59).

The perfectionist pole, on the other hand, insists on having clear standards of what exactly a democratic firm means. The standard idea is that a co-op is only genuinely a co-op if it fills two basic criteria. The significant majority of the workers must be full members (perhaps 75% or more), and the nonmembers must be able to *become* members should they wish to do so (after a reasonable probationary period and a not prohibitively-high investment stake). By this measure, workplaces with fewer than, say, 50% members are not genuine co-ops;[27] they either have degenerated or were never true cooperatives to begin with – in either case they are more accurately seen as "capitalist partnerships." According to this perspective Mondragon as a whole can no longer be viewed as a co-operative system.

The major advantage of the "better-than-nothing" perspective is that it allows us to see the complexity and hybridity of real-life institutions. It induces us to study and work within real, concrete, existing institutions, and so to keep our feet firmly planted on solid ground. The major weakness is that it risks sacrificing conviction on the altar of expediency and becoming a cheerleader for normative mediocrity. We risk severe normative slippage when we join authors such as Logue (2006) who unhesitatingly call firms (like the Cooperativa Ceramiche d'Imola) "worker cooperatives" even though only 13% of its workers (172 out of 1,350) are members. Likewise, the careless celebration of Mondragon as a *cooperative* success story is problematic if we let the growth of assets – the billions of euros of wealth under Mondragon's control dazzle us from the disheartening reality of the dilution of democratic membership, that has accompanied such growth. All that glitters is not gold.

On the other hand, the major advantage of perfectionism is that it provides a strong and clear normative ideal of a co-op for advocates to strive for. Without the criterion of high percntage membership, and the ability for the majority of non-members to become members, there is no meaningful sovereignty of labor. By this line of thinking, a business that doesn't meet these standards is not a genuine worker co-op. It is not a *democratic* organization since the majority of affected workers are barred from participating in the decision-making. Nor is it an *egalitarian* organization since the profits, which are created by all, are not shared by all; instead there is a stark structural divide between a marginalized majority from whom profits are appropriated and a privileged minority who benefit off the labor of others. Consider, for example, a typical law firm. The partners of the firm may well make decisions collectively and may all share in the firm's profits. But given that all the other staff – the junior lawyers, paralegals, and administrative staff – are disenfranchised from this decision making, and barred from sharing in the profits which they have helped to create, we cannot call such a partnership a "cooperative" without doing serious violence to the idea of workplace democracy.

The major weakness of perfectionism is that it tends to impose a rigid ideal of what counts as success, and so is quick to denounce deviations from the ideal. Moreover, the label of "degeneration" is, of course, extremely pejorative. And while in some sense the *point* of the perfectionist perspective is to be critical, it could well be argued that calling Mondragon "degenerated" is overly harsh to the efforts of the generations of members who have achieved major cooperative victories in the face of extremely difficult circumstances. Especially since it may well be that the majority of Mondragon remains deeply committed to the ideals of workplace democracy, and is doing all that is possible in adverse market conditions to sustain it (indeed, I am sympathetic to such a perspective.) The problem with perfectionism, in other words, is that it risks downplaying or trivializing the importance of concrete improvement.

Recognizing this spectrum gives some underlying order to the disparate positions in the literature. And while both poles have their rationale it seems to me that we should conclude that the right position is, as Aristotle might say, the middle one. We should adopt a soft perfectionism – that is, a perfectionism that is not dismissive of reformism nor insensitive to empirical realities. Such a perspective allows us to be honest enough to recognize that Mondragon has in some sense degenerated, because it's important to retain a perfectionist ideal of what a co-op is, since this gives us a target to strive for. That said, having a goal should in no way blind us from the importance of real life attempts to improve things, or distract us from the messiness and hybridity that inevitably characterizes practical experience (such as the experience of large cooperatives competing in international markets). Ultimately, there is no contradiction between wanting to work from where we are, for example, by analyzing and emulating the complex benefits that Mondragon has over normal firms, while still holding out an ideal to strive for.

IS WORKPLACE DEMOCRACY DOOMED TO DEGENERATE?

The partial degeneration of the world's most famous worker cooperative network naturally raises questions as to the feasibility of workplace democracy more broadly. Are worker co-ops doomed to degenerate? Should activists and scholars interested in social justice abandon their interest in workplace democracy? Do we need to reevaluate our positive evaluation of the original Mondragon in light of the history of global Mondragon? To all of these questions I think the answer is a solid "no." In what follows I want to make two general points: (i) degeneration is not inevitable even within the current market system, and (ii) degeneration itself should be recognized as a symptom of a particular *market system* just as much as it is as symptom of firms, and so can always be alleviated by shifting the way the market system works.

Even in the context of the current global market system, degeneration is not inevitable. The success of the original Mondragon group is still very relevant as a model for other co-ops to emulate today because major (and increasing) parts of economies in the North are largely isolated from the odious competition that comes from the race-to-the-bottom. For instance, in the United States, manufacturing – which is the area that tends to face the most severe competitive pressures from global trade – accounts for a continually decreasing part of the economy, only 11% of employment as of 2003. Simultaneously, northern economies are becoming more and more service-oriented – and services are much less dependent on global trade (only 5–7% of U.S. services are exported). Indeed, it has been estimated that locally oriented economic activity now represents about 60% of all economic activity (Alperovitz, 2005, pp. 125–126). In Krugman's words, "although we talk a lot these days about globalization, about a world grown small, when you look at the economies of modern cities what you see is a process of localization: A steadily rising share of the work force produces services that are sold only within that same metropolitan area" (quoted in Alperovitz, 2005,

p. 126). This means that the contemporary world is, in certain ways, becoming *more* hospitable to co-ops. In other words, in large sections of the economy – up to 60% by this reckoning – co-ops would not face odious competition from firms benefitting off cheap and disenfranchised labor in the Global South, and so, if they are designed in robust and sustainable ways (like the original Mondragon), they may well flourish.

An additional reason to be wary of the claim of inevitable degeneration due to today's global competition is that Mondragon itself may well *regenerate*. It is clear that the existence of so many nonmember workers in Mondragon has been a source of much soul-searching and debate within the organization, and is something that many members wish to change. The bulk of Mondragon's nonmembers emerged from the expansion of the supermarket chain Eroski during the 1990s. To combat this, by the late 1990s a partial employee-ownership structure was established, and starting in 2011, Eroski has approved a multi-year initiative to cooperativize its operations to be completed by 2014–2016; this is expected to bring the ratio of members to workers back up to 70–75% for Mondragon as a whole (Arando et al., 2010, pp. 20–21). If this is successful it will represent a profound re-democratization of Mondragon. Beyond this, it's not inconceivable that the foreign subsidiaries will be slowly democratized, perhaps by being transformed into full member co-ops where local conditions allow, or at least acquiring increased rights to participation and profit sharing. Moreover, it's important to remember that a fundamental reason that a re-democratization of Mondragon is possible is that, as many commentators have pointed out, its democratic culture is key to its competitive advantage (Cheney, 1999; Forcadell, 2005; MacLeod & Reed, 2009). Its economic edge comes, at least in part, from the participation, motivation, loyalty, commitment, and constant training that flows from a democratically empowered workforce. This implies that even in a neoliberal global market environment, Mondragon may well be able to emerge as a model of democratic multinational business.

The second, and more fundamental, reason to be skeptical about claims of inherent degeneration is that lack of competitiveness is always relative to the prevailing market system.

The literature on Mondragon exhibits significant confusion about the nature of the market pressure that co-ops face. Many authors attribute the changes in Mondragon's composition to fundamental market pressures. For example, Bakaikoa et al. argue that "the [Mondragon] cooperatives are undergoing deep internal and external transformations due to *market pressures*" and "market imperatives" (2004, pp. 82, 84, my emphasis).

Likewise, Gunn argues that although markets can be regulated they will always contain "anti-social properties" which limit democratic firms (2000, p. 458). Kasmir (1996) concurs. On the other hand, a number of authors have pointed to the ability of co-ops to survive in institutionally appropriate environments (Dow, 2003; Jones, 1975). Smith (2001) highlights the importance of cooperative networks for softening competitive markets. More generally, Ammirato (1996) and Zamagni and Zamagni (2010) emphasize the malleability of market systems in terms of providing institutional support for co-ops.

How can we clarify this second mess of contradictory interpretations? An analytical clarification may be helpful. As above, I suggest we make sense of these divergent perspectives by recognizing them as points on a spectrum – in this case between the poles of "market essentialism" and "institutionalism."

The market essentialist perspective posits the existence of inherent market pressures, forces, or imperatives that flow from the logic of a competitive market system, which serves to undermine co-op survival. While such a perspective is commonplace on the right (e.g., Alchian & Demsetz, 1972), it is also surprisingly common on the left, particularly in the Fabian and orthodox Marxian traditions (Luxemburg, 1900 [1986]; Mandel, 1975; Marx, 1933 [1867]; Webb & Webb, 1907).

At the other end of the spectrum, the institutionalist perspective regards any claim of "market pressure" or "market forces" in the abstract as essentially nonsensical. Of course no institutionalist would deny that Mondragon (and other co-ops) currently face very real market pressures in the historically-specific markets of Spain, the EU, and globally. However, they would insist that such pressures, though very real, are never unalterable, nor at root anything more than the outcome of historically contingent political and legal institutions that produce them. Since Polanyi's (2001 [1944]) groundbreaking work it has become increasingly clear that there is nothing at all natural about "the market"; nor indeed is there any such thing as a truly "free market" – *all* markets are built, shaped, and continually upheld by a range of legal–political institutions (property laws, bankruptcy courts, business subsidies, police forces, treasuries, central banks, union rules, tax regimes, welfare systems, etc.)

It is now commonly recognized that shaping the market system in different ways leads to very different economies (Albert, 1993; Baker, 2006; Hall & Soskice, 2001; Pontusson, 2005). Different market environments promote a competitive advantage of certain firms over others. In general, co-ops find themselves operating in market systems that are inhospitable and shaped in ways to promote their corporate competitors. Current market systems are built to make it as easy as possible for corporations to form and grow. Corporations are granted limited liability status (which allows them to grow massively by giving outside investors a legally protected opportunity for unlimited gain but only limited loss)[28] and they benefit from the entire financial structure of large banks and stock markets to finance their operations; co-ops on the other hand are left to fend for themselves; very few institutional mechanisms have yet been created to allow them to easily raise finance without threatening their democratic structure (such as co-op banks or co-op bonds).

If we think of firms as cars in a race, the market system is the kind of road (its shape, surface material, etc.), and the management is the driver. So if there are different kinds of cars competing, the kind of car that will win the race is, of course, partly determined by the driver and partly determined by which car is better suited for the particular road. We are not surprised that a (capitalistic) tank beats a (cooperative) electric car on an off-road race, but, equally, no one should disagree with the proposition that the road could be changed (flattened, paved over, etc.) so that the electric car would win.

To reiterate, the main institutionalist point is that the way the market system is structured determines the kind of competition that takes place, and therefore the kind of degeneration that will transpire. Over the last hundred years there have been many examples of different kinds of economic activity that have been uncompetitive, but for various reasons it has been thought important to shape and regulate the market system so that they survive. For instance, most agree that the fact that pregnant women aren't as competitive as men does not justify their being paid less – it means that the market should be regulated (e.g., by mandating pay equity); the fact that child labor is very cheap and ultra competitive does not mean that we should simply let nonchild labor firms degenerate – we should prevent, and indeed historically have prevented, this kind of degeneration by regulating the market differently (in this case by simply outlawing the practice). Progressives have long recognized, implicitly at least, that there is a crucial difference between competition that is socially useful and odious competition that is socially harmful. The impetus behind market regulation is simply the promotion of the former over the latter.

Were the market system to be shaped and regulated differently there is every reason to think that co-ops could outcompete their corporate competition.[29] This is not the place to go into detail about what exactly a cooperative market system would look like, but we can get glimpses of such a system by considering the economic environment created by successful co-op networks such as Mondragon in Spain and La Lega in Italy.[30] In general, the basic tool for protecting desirable firms from odious international competition is the implementation of tariffs.[31] An additional extremely powerful tool is the tax system: raising corporate taxes or lowering co-op taxes would have a very powerful effect on their relative competitive position. For example, the use of tax breaks allowed co-ops in Venezuela to grow from 800 in 1998 to a reported number of over 100,000 in 2006, with 1.5 million members (Hahnel, 2007).[32] The bottom line is that degeneration is not a feature of firms *per se* but flows from the ways in which they are fostered or hindered by the market system in which they operate. If socially decent types of business, like the original Mondragon Group, cannot survive in a harsh global market environment, this is a condemnation not of the co-ops, but of the market environment itself.

CONCLUSION

Overall, what lessons can we draw from the experience of Mondragon in terms of the prospects for workplace democracy? How generalizable are Mondragon's successes and failures?

While we should always be cautious about generalizing from single examples, I think we can conclude that the original Mondragon group shows that workplace democracy is entirely feasible. We have seen that worker cooperatives can be economically efficient and socially superior to normal firms. The proviso, of course, is that the success of worker co-ops is no more inevitable than their failure; success depends on the maintenance of profitable businesses as well as rigorous implementation of the sustainable structures and democratic practices examined here.

The second section sought to untangle the confusion around degeneration. In particular two analytical clarifications were offered. The point of the first distinction is to clarify when a firm genuinely counts as a worker cooperative. It was argued that a middle-path between perfectionism and a "better-than-nothing" approach is desirable. The second clarification was in terms of the nature of the market pressures that cooperatives face. Here the experience of Mondragon teaches us the institutionalist lesson that the kind of firms that will succeed in a certain context is largely dependent on the structure of the specific market system.

In the years that come it may well be that the global market will face little regulation, or, more accurately, will *be regulated* in such a way as to foster harsh corporate-led and profit-driven competition in a race-to-the-bottom. In this case, all kinds of progressive firms – from unionized firms, to those with environmental protocols, to worker co-ops – may struggle to compete. But reflecting on the experience of Mondragon reminds us that nothing about this kind of degeneration is inevitable. To the extent that co-ops are forced under by odious competition (such as exploited, disenfranchised labor in the developing world) this should motivate us not to turn away from co-ops, but to push forward in reforming the market systems themselves so that decent business structures can thrive. That is not an easy task. But ultimately the specter of degeneration is only as inevitable as our incapacity to challenge a corporate market system which rewards firms for engaging in odious competitive practices.

NOTES

1. This paper is part of a larger work on economic democracy, *After Occupy: Economic Democracy for the 21st Century*, (Malleson, 2014). I am indebted to the anonymous reviewer for helpful feedback and clarifications.

2. Probably the most well-known critical account of Mondragon is Kasmir (1996) who makes a classical Marxist argument to the effect that Mondragon fosters middle-class values and undermines the working-class union movement without fundamentally challenging the worker–manager class divide.

3. Throughout this paper I assume that authentic workplace democracy requires a worker cooperative, whereby worker-owners, collectively, are the sole decision-makers. I, therefore, leave to the side the examples of partial democratization such as firms with German-style co-determination, or American employee shared ownership plans (ESOPs).

4. For example, in 1985 the CL was offering loans to its member co-ops at a maximum rate of 13%, 8% for special sectors, and free of interest for very special cases, compared to the prevailing market rate of 18% (Ammirato, 1996, p. 48). From the 1990s, the CL's Empresarial division was moved to other institutional locations in Mondragon, and the focus on creating new co-ops shifted to sustaining existing ones (Freundlich, 1998).

5. Originally, 10% of workers were allowed to be non-members in order to ensure flexibility for things such as seasonal work, though, as we will see, this changed radically in later years.

6. For thirty years the ratio between the highest and lowest-paid workers could not exceed 3:1. This has loosened in recent years to 6:1 (and 9:1 in a very few cases) (Flecha & Cruz, 2011).

7. In the early years this investment was equivalent to roughly double the members' annual earnings (Dow, 2003, p. 59). Today it is roughly one year's earnings at

the co-op's lowest pay rate, approximately 14,000 euros. Efforts are made to ensure that the membership fee is never an insurmountable barrier to membership. For instance, new members can often pay make this investment through wage deductions spread out over a period of five years (Arando, Gago, Jones, & Kato, 2011, p. 7).

8. One note of caution in this regard is Morris (1992, p. 53) who claims that the co-ops may have been less efficient than some of their *international*, particularly Japanese, competitors. The most recent comparative empirical account, Arando et al. (2011), finds certain Mondragon co-ops to be more efficient than comparable conventional firms, and others to not be significantly different.

9. Ward (1958) expected this behavior due to the fact that workers in a co-op strive (he claimed) to maximize net income per worker. The intuitive idea here is that the more people employed means the more people that get a slice of the pie – so co-op members will have an incentive to shrink their membership to get a bigger slice of the pie for themselves. However, others, such as Jaroslav Vanek and Joan Robinson were quick to point out that even theoretically this argument makes little sense, as it would require co-operatives, which are organizations based on solidarity, to self-mutilate in order to make more money (see Bonin & Putterman, 1987).

10. Mondragon responded to this situation by setting up an internal Social Security Service, which in 1967 was transformed into an independent co-op called Lagun-Aro (Azevedo & Gitahy, 2010).

11. So in a Mondragon co-op, members have two analytically distinct sets of rights: membership rights (to governance) and property rights which do not give individuals a claim to a portion of the assets (as in conventional firms), but give individuals a claim to a share of the post-tax profits. Should a co-op dissolve, the proceeds from the sale of its assets *cannot* go to co-op members but, according to Basque cooperative law, must stay in the regional co-op federation.

12. Currently the top salary for Mondragon managers is 6:1, although a few CEOs do earn up to 9:1. In the industrial group, which is the largest group in Mondragon, 67% of workers earn between the lowest rate and double that rate, while 30% earn up to 3.5 times the lowest rate, and only 3% earn between 3.5 and 6 times that rate (Flecha & Cruz, 2011).

13. An additional issue is that work satisfaction is related not just to the objective conditions of the workplace but also to expectations of what work will be like. So it's entirely possible for a co-op workplace to be have *somewhat* better working conditions than conventional firms, but if there are also *much* higher expectations of what cooperative work should be like, overall job satisfaction might actually be lower.

14. Since the co-ops are largely autonomous it's hard to generalize about the levels of democratic participation *overall*, since this likely varies quite substantially from co-op to co-op.

15. For example, see the classic work of Michels (1962 [1911]).

16. Thus in Arizmendiarreta's words, "people do not normally become co-operators spontaneously, they have to be taught – the soil may be fertile but it has to be cultivated" (quoted in Morris, 1992, p. 9).

17. This focus on education has continued throughout the years. For instance, in recent years it has been reported that investment in continuous training in Mondragon represents 2.7% of the wage bill (compared with averages of 1.2% for Spanish firms and 1.6% in EU companies) (Arando et al., 2010, p. 36).

18. According to the Economist Intelligence Unit, Irizar is "probably now the most efficient coach builder in the world" (Forcadell, 2005).

19. This may be more than merely a semantic change. For instance, Cheney documents evidence of members saying things like this: "this place *feels* a lot more like a corporation and a lot less like a cooperative than it used to" (1999, p. 75). Of course, this is somewhat speculative since there is very little data (beyond the memories of present members) of what members thought of their workplaces during the 1960s and 1970s.

20. The bulk of Mondragon's nonmembers (about 30,000 of them) are in Spain working for the Eroski retail chain. There are also about 12,000 nonmembers working in foreign affiliates, largely in the Global South (Arando et al., 2010).

21. An additional obstacle is the financial difficulty that many foreign workers face in making investments at anywhere near the same level that Basque members can make given the massive differences in relative purchasing power. (Thanks to the anonymous reviewer for pointing this out).

22. This is the classic idea of degeneration of a cooperative constitution by capitalist competition. There is, however, at least one other kind of degeneration, that of organizational deformity – which refers to the erosion of meaningful participatory democracy and the rise of oligarchy – due to a growth in scale and technocratic values that affect all kinds of democratic organizations, co-ops included (Michels, 1962 [1911]). Here we focus on the first kind.

23. Luzarraga and Irizar (2012) have argued that Mondragon's response to globalization has not been delocalization (i.e., the normal response of multinationals moving to cheaper places, usually in the Global South) but *multilocalization*, whereby foreign subsidiaries are set up as a defensive mechanism to *protect* the democratic jobs at home. Hence, the new management slogan at Mondragon of "How many new jobs do we need to create abroad to maintain one job at home?"

24. The General Council is the executive management of the entire Mondragon Corporation. It is elected by the Standing Committee, itself elected from the Governing Councils of the Groups and Divisions, which, in turn, have been elected by Governing Councils of individual cooperatives (Freundlich et al., 2009).

25. However, as discussed below, this is starting to change with the attempt to cooperativize Eroski.

26. That said, while the foreign subsidiaries are not co-ops, there is some evidence that Mondragon is a more humane employer than other multinationals, in terms of offering better wages, working conditions, and management practices than the local competition (Luzarraga & Irizar, 2012; MacLeod & Reed, 2009).

27. Co-ops with 50–75% members are in a gray area. It seems to me that these can be considered genuine co-ops only if the nonmembers can become members should they wish to do so.

28. The fact that the state grants limited liability protection is a massive boon to conventional firms. In 2005, for example, American companies paid $278 billion in corporate income taxes – which shows how much they desire the benefits of limited liability, since these companies are free to organize themselves as private partnerships instead (foregoing limited liability) and thereby foregoing this tax. The fact that they choose to pay the tax is evidence of the immense and ongoing value that legal incorporation has (Baker, 2006).

29. For the evidence of this, as well as a compilation of the empirical record comparing the performance of conventional and cooperative firms, see Malleson (2014).

30. Consider, for instance, the region of Emilia Romagna in Northern Italy, where 8,000 co-ops (of all kinds, worker, consumer, etc.) account for about 40% of the region's GDP, and 24% of the population works in, or is a member of, a cooperative. Worker co-ops alone constitute 12.75% of GDP, and dominate in many industries, including construction, agriculture, food processing, wine making, transport, retail, machine production (Ammirato, 1996; Restakis, 2010).

31. For a discussion of the feasibility of tariffs see Chang (2002). For a discussion of ways to protect co-ops in the North without harming poorer workers in the South, see Schweickart (2002).

32. These numbers should probably be taken with a grain of salt. For instance, there are reports of enterprises claiming to be co-ops in order to avoid paying taxes without actually transferring power to the workers (Harnecker, 2005). Regardless, it appears that the growth of co-ops due to tax breaks has been profound.

REFERENCES

Albert, M. (1993). *Capitalism against capitalism* (P. Haviland, Trans.). London: Whurr Publishers.

Alchian, A., & Demsetz, H. (1972). Production, information costs, and economic organization. *The American Economic Review*, *62*(5), 777–795.

Alperovitz, G. (2005). *America beyond capitalism: Reclaiming our wealth, our liberty, and our democracy*. Hoboken, NJ: Wiley.

Ammirato, P. (1996). *La Lega: The making of a successful cooperative network*. Aldershot: Dartmouth.

Arando, S., Freundlich, F., Gago, M., Jones, D. C., & Kato, T. (2010). Assessing Mondragon: Stability and managed change in the face of globalization. *William Davidson Institute Working Paper* (1003), 1–47.

Arando, S., Gago, M., Jones, D., & Kato, T. (2011). *Efficiency in employee-owned enterprises: An econometric case study of Mondragon*. IZA Discussion Paper No. 5711. Institute for the Study of Labor, Bonn, Germany.

Azevedo, A., & Gitahy, L. (2010). The cooperative movement, self-management and competitiveness: The case of Mondragón Corporación Cooperativa. *WorkingUSA: The Journal of Labor and Society*, *13*(1), 5–29.

Bakaikoa, B., Errasti, A., & Begiristain, A. (2004). Governance of the Mondragon Corporacion Cooperativa. *Annals of Public and Cooperative Economics*, *75*(1), 61–87.

Baker, D. (2006). *The conservative nanny state*. Washington, DC: Center for Economic and Policy Research.

Bellas, C. (1972). *Industrial democracy and the worker-owned firm: A study of twenty-one plywood companies in the Pacific Northwest*. New York, NY: Praeger Publishers.

Berman, K. (1967). *Worker-owned plywood companies: An economic analysis*. Washington, DC: Washington State University Press Pullman.

Blasi, J. R., & Kruse, D. L. (2012). Broad-based worker ownership and profit sharing: Can these ideas work in the entire economy? Paper presented at the International Association for the Economics of Participation. Rutgers University, NJ.

Bonin, J. P., & Putterman, L. (1987). *Economics of cooperation and the labor-managed economy*. Chur, Switzerland: Harwood Academic Publishers.

Bradley, K., & Gelb, A. (1981). Motivation and control in the Mondragon experiment. *British Journal of Industrial Relations*, *19*(2), 211–231.

Bradley, K., & Gelb, A. (1985). *Mixed economy "versus" cooperative adjustment: Mondragon's experience through Spain's recession*. Development Research Department, Economics and Research Staff, World Bank, Washington, DC.

Campbell, A., Keen, C., Norman, G., & Oakeshott, R. (1977). *Worker-owners: The Mondragon achievement*. London: Anglo-German Foundation for the Study of Industrial Society.

Chang, H.-J. (2002). *Kicking away the ladder: Development strategy in historical perspective*. London: Anthem.

Cheney, G. (1999). *Values at work: employee participation meets market pressure at Mondragón*. Ithaca, NY: ILR.

Dow, G. (2003). *Governing the firm: Workers' control in theory and practice*. Cambridge: Cambridge University Press.

Drèze, J. (1993). Self-management and economic theory: Efficiency, funding, and employment. In P. Bardhan & J. Roemer (Eds.), *Market socialism: The current debate* (pp. 253–265). New York, NY: Oxford University Press.

Economist. (2006). The rich, the poor and the growing gap between them – Inequality in America. *The Economist*, June 17.

Ellerman, D. (1984). Workers' cooperatives: The question of legal structure. In R. Jackall & H. M. Levin (Eds.), *Worker cooperatives in America* (pp. 257–274). Berkeley, CA: University of California Press.

Ellerman, D. (1990). *The democratic worker-owned firm: A new model for the east and west*. London: Unwin Hyman.

Errasti, A. M., Heras, I., Bakaikoa, B., & Elgoibar, P. (2003). The internationalisation of cooperatives: The case of the Mondragon Cooperative Corporation. *Annals of Public and Cooperative Economics*, *74*(4), 553–584.

Flecha, R., & Cruz, I. S. (2011). Cooperation for economic success: The Mondragon case. *Analyse & Kritik*, *01*, 157–170.

Forcadell, F. J. (2005). Democracy, cooperation and business success: The case of Mondragon Corporacion Cooperativa. *Journal of Business Ethics*, *56*(3), 255–274.

Freundlich, F. (1998). The Mondragon Cooperative Corporation (MCC): An introduction. Retrieved from http://www.ownershipassociates.com/mcc-intro.shtm. Accessed on March 13, 2013.

Freundlich, F., Grellier, H., & Altuna, R. (2009). Mondragon: Notes on history, scope and structure. *International Journal of Technology Management & Sustainable Development*, *8*(1), 3–12.

Furubotn, E., & Pejovich, S. (1970). Property rights and the behavior of the firm in a socialist state: The example of Yugoslavia. *Journal of Economics*, *30*(3), 431–454.

Gibson-Graham, J. K. (2003). Enabling ethical economies: Cooperativism and class. *Critical Sociology*, *29*(2), 123–161.

Gunn, C. (2000). Markets against economic democracy. *Review of Radical Political Economics*, *32*(3), 448.

Hahnel, R. (2007). Venezuela: Not what you think. Retrieved from http://www.zmag.org/content/showarticle.cfm?ItemID = 14438. Accessed on March 4, 2008.

Hall, P. A., & Soskice, D. (Eds.). (2001). *Varieties of capitalism: The institutional foundations of comparative advantage*. Oxford: Oxford University Press.

Harnecker, C. P. (2005). The new cooperative movement in Venezuela's Bolivarian process. Retrieved from http://www.venezuelanalysis.com/analysis/1531. Acceseed in March 14.

Holmstrom, M. (1989). *Industrial democracy in Italy*. Aldershot: Avebury.

Jones, D. (1975). British producer cooperatives and the views of the webbs on participation and ability to survive. *Annals of Public and Cooperative Economics*, *46*(1), 23–44.

Kasmir, S. (1996). *The myth of Mondragon: Cooperatives, politics, and working-class life in a Basque town*. Albany, NY: State University of New York Press.

Lafuente, J. L., & Freundlich, F. (2012). The Mondragon Cooperative experience: Humanity at Work. Retrieved from http://www.managementexchange.com/story/mondragon-cooperative-experience-humanity-work. Accessed on March 13, 2013.

Levin, H. M. (1983). Raising employment and productivity with producer co-operatives. In P. Streeten & H. Maier (Eds.), *Human resources, employment and development* (Vol. 2, pp. 310–328). Concepts, Measurement and Long-Run Perspective. London: Macmillan.

Logue, J. (2006). Economics, cooperation, and employee ownership: The Emilia Romagna model – in more detail. Community Wealth, Ohio Employee Ownership Centre, Kent, OH.

Luxemburg, R. (1900 [1986]). *Reform or revolution*. London: Militant Publications.

Luzarraga, J. M., & Irizar, I. (2012). La Estrategia de Multilocalización Internacional de la Corporación Mondragon. *Ekonomiaz: Revista vasca de economía* (79), 114–145.

MacLeod, G., & Reed, D. (2009). Mondragon's response to the challenges of globalization: A multi-localization strategy. In D. Reed & J. J. McMurtry (Eds.), *Co-operatives in a global economy: The challenges of co-operation across borders* (pp. 111–140). Newcastle upon Tyne: Cambridge Scholars Publishing.

Malleson, T. (2014). *After Occupy: Economic Democracy for the 21st Century*. New York, NY: Oxford University Press.

Mandel, E. (1975). Self-management: Dangers and possibilities, *International*, *2*(3), 3–9.

Marx, K. (1933 [1867]). *Capital* (E. a. C. Paul, Trans.). London: Dent.

Menzani, T., & Zamagni, V. (2010). Cooperative networks in the Italian economy. *Enterprise and Society*, *11*(1), 98.

Michels, R. (1962 [1911]). *Political parties: A sociological study of the oligarchical tendencies of modern democracy* (E. a. C. Paul, Trans.). New York, NY: Free Press.

Mondragon. (2011). *2011 Annual report*. Spain: Mondragon.

Mondragon. (2012). *Corporate management model*. Spain: Mondragon.

Morris, D. (1992). *The Mondragon system: Cooperation at work*. Washington, DC: Institute for Local Self-Reliance.

Morrison, R. (1997). *We build the road as we travel*. Warner: Essential Book Publishers.

Moye, A. M. (1993). Mondragon: Adapting co-operative structures to meet the demands of a changing environment. *Economic and Industrial Democracy*, *14*(2), 251–276.

Polanyi, K. (2001 [1994]). *The great transformation*. Boston, MA: Beacon Press.

Pontusson, J. (2005). *Inequality and prosperity: Social Europe vs. liberal America*. Ithaca, NY: Cornell University Press.

Restakis, J. (2010). *Humanizing the economy: Co-operatives in the age of capital*. Gabriola Island: New Society Publishers.

Schweickart, D. (2002). *After capitalism*. Lanham, MD: Rowman & Littlefield.

Smith, S. (2001). *Blooming together or wilting alone? Network externalities and Mondragon and La Lega co-operative networks*. World Institute for Development Economics Research, Helsinki.

Thomas, H., & Logan, C. (1982). *Mondragon: An economic analysis*. London: G. Allen & Unwin.

Ward, B. (1958). The firm in Illyria: Market syndicalism. *American Economic Review*, *48*, 566–589.

Webb, S., & Webb, B. (1907). *The history of trade unionism*. London: Longmans, Green and Co.

Whyte, W. F., & Whyte, K. K. (1988). *Making Mondragon: The growth and dynamics of the worker cooperative complex*. Ithaca, NY: ILR Press.

Wright, E. O. (2010). *Envisioning real utopias*. London: Verso.

Zamagni, S., & Zamagni, V. (2010). *Cooperative enterprise: Facing the challenges of globalization*. Cheltenham: Edward Elgar.

CHAPTER 7

EMPLOYEE OWNERSHIP IN RUSSIA: EVOLUTION AND CURRENT STATUS

Tatiana Kachalina (Ershova)

ABSTRACT

Purpose – *The purpose of this article is to analyze the present state of employee ownership in Russia and reasons for its decline due to the drawbacks of economic reforms on the country.*

Design/methodology/approach – *The design of the article includes the analysis of the Russian model of ESOP and its differences from the U.S. analog. The author also describes the practical experience of the Russian people's enterprises and the drawbacks in the legal foundations of their work.*

Findings – *The key finding of this work is that the correction of these drawbacks would lead to broader development of employee owned companies in Russia.*

Social implications – *The author's ideas of changing focus of the market reforms in Russia and facilitating the development of economic democracy in the country constitute the major social implication of her research.*

Sharing Ownership, Profits, and Decision-making in the 21st Century
Advances in the Economic Analysis of Participatory & Labor-Managed Firms, Volume 14, 159–185

ISSN: 0885-3339/doi:10.1108/S0885-3339(2013)0000014008

Practical implications – *It may have practical implications both for developed market economies and economies in transition.*

Originality/value – *The originality of the paper is determined by drawing a logical link between the development of employee ownership and overall market reform in Russia, as well as by presenting a comparative analysis of the U.S. and Russian models of ESOP.*

Keywords: Employee ownership; market reform in Russia; economies in transition; economic democracy; people's enterprises; employee owned companies

JEL classifications: J5; P1; P2; P3; P5

EMPLOYEE OWNERSHIP AND MARKET REFORM IN RUSSIA

The issue of creation of the free market and an open private property system is crucial for all market-oriented countries, including transition economies. One of the tremendous results of the 20th century was a transition of socialist countries to the market economy. It was painful for all of these countries, though it yielded generally positive results. For Russia, the establishment of the market relationships was not only very painful but it brought about the results that were not expected by the majority of society. "The jump in the market" in Russia meant abrupt and almost revolutionary transition from a centralized economy with a complete absence of private ownership to a market-oriented economy that required an absolutely different institutional environment that was not created in Russia in the course of privatization of former government property in the country. The idea that the introduction of the institution of private ownership and the reduction of the role of the state would trigger the effective market mechanism in the economy was imposed on the Russian society. This mechanism was supposed to solve all of the nation's social and economic problems automatically and convert the country into a developed market economy in 5–10 years. However, the weakness of statehood and absence of market institutions became the background for the 10 years of negative dynamics that we observed and a subsequent decrease of employee ownership in the Russian transition economy. In a qualitative sense the present day Russian economy has arrived to a critical status that necessitates a precise appraisal of what was reached in the result of social and economic reforms and determine a direction of further movement.

The Russian economy has entered the 21st century with a "heritage" resulting from its 70 years history of the Soviet period and 10 years of market reforms. Indeed, at present in the Russian economy there is an undisputable presence of principally new features that were completely absent under the communist regime. First of all, the most important of these features are the development of the institution of the private ownership, the change in the role of government in the economic life of the country, and the development of competition, etc. These institutional characteristics provide clear evidence of the country's movement to the market economy. The traces of socialism become less and less traceable now: the centralized planning and equal payment system with fixed wages, government regulation of prices, and many other features disappeared.

However, we must ask, can the economy of the contemporary Russia be called a market and democratic one in the Western understanding of the term? This question can hardly have a single straightforward answer. In order to answer this question, it is necessary to give a brief summary of the results of market development of Russia in the post-Soviet period.

The mass privatization at the beginning of 1990s has not created the so called "effective owner" that induced hopes for forming a middle class in Russia. The privatization program resulted in the emergence of the Russian "economic elite" or oligarch groups that captured the main part of the nation's wealth and that opposes the overwhelming majority of population that is being more and more separated from ownership and economic power in the country. The absence of the efficient owner in the Russian economy is one of the main reasons for the decline of national production and low living standards of the majority of population, etc. The main reason for the absence of the efficient owner in Russia as well as the considerable reduction of employee's ownership in modern Russian enterprises is the economic strategy of reformers, which was aimed at the overwhelming concentration of ownership in the hands of oligarch groups controlling the main industries of Russian economy and appropriating the main share of the country's national wealth. It did not correspond to economic democracy and violated rights of human beings for private ownership and a decent life. It inevitably led to social tensions rather than to cooperation and social partnership.

Such terms as "economy of participation" and its main component the employee's ownership that are indispensable parts of the developed market economies in the modern world were devaluated in the years of the reforms. The will of the reform ideologists to conduct rapid privatization and the necessary support from the broad categories of working people needed for it resulted into passing enterprises to employees. Based on the law on privatization the employees of privatized enterprises got shares or could purchase them for vouchers they were provided with at the beginning of the reforms in Russia. At the moment of finishing privatization in the beginning of 1990s 50% of all shares of privatized companies in Russia were in the hands of their employees. It was the one of the world's highest indicator of shares in the hands of employees in the world that caused hope for the development of the Russian economy in the most democratic way. In 1995 the book by Joseph R. Blasi and Douglas L. Kruse *The New Owners: The Mass Emergence of Employee Ownership in Public Companies and What It Means to American Business* was published in Russian. The authors emphasized at "striking semblance" between 1990s' Russia and the United States in terms of development of employee ownership. Joseph R. Blasi and Douglas L. Kruse pointed out that "both economic systems were approximating from different sides to the same type of shareholding characterized by numerous companies where a significant part (but not the majority) of shares belonged to employees. For this reason the experience of one country was considered as useful for another one. There is no doubt that at present in the Russian Federation the employees still possess more shares that everywhere else in the world, including the USA" (Blasi & Kruse, 1995).

The reform ideologists were opposing this development of the reforms but they had to accept it as a temporary measure. They considered the employees' ownership of privatized companies as a possibility of coming back to socialism and an "unavoidable evil," that should be overcome in the time being. It is absolutely evident now that the democratization of ownership by the means of the development of employee ownership that constitutes a corner stone of the economy of participation was not a strategic goal of the reformers. By promoting the idea of the free market the ideologists of the reforms and their "clients" in fact were seeking the economic system that can allow them to appropriate the majority of the welfare of the country solely in their self-interests. The employee ownership concept did not fit in this context of the reforms. It was a not needed part and, therefore, its fate was predetermined.

The extremely complicated economic situation of Russia in the reform period "lessened" the task of the reformers. Unprecedented inflation rates and a cash crisis, predatory taxes, and hiding profits by the owners and top management led to a situation when the employee ownership of the privatized companies did not contribute to solving the economic problems of the employees and became economically inexpedient for them. As a result the share of employee ownership started to decline persistently. The dynamics of the share of employee ownership in Russia in the 10 post-privatization years were negative. At present, not more than 20% (and according to some estimates less than 15%) of the shares of the privatized companies remain in the hands of employees (see Ershova, 2000a). What are the reasons of that drastic decrease in employee ownership in privatized Russian companies?

- The employees were *de facto* separated from ownership of capital assets and from production management and consequently from real participation in the results of the company performance. Now in Russia there are practically no laws and bylaws regulating rights of employees to participate in enterprise management in the majority of joint stock[1] companies. The common shareholders are deprived not only of real management authority, but also of the control over activities of corporate boards of directors.
- Many Russian joint stock companies are still dominated by the authoritarian management style of the executive management administration that violates the rights of rank and file shareholders. In total, 75% of so called "red directors" preserved their positions after privatization and with that, their previous management style. Naturally, the interest of workers in increasing production and labor productivity started to go down. It led to social tensions rather than to partnership between social groups with different economic interests.
- The lack of openness and transparency of information about the real state of affairs in joint stock companies enables top managers to privatize the profits of the enterprises while passing the losses to employees. The employee owners practically have no confidence and top managers as a rule pursue their self-interests of enrichment and preserving power over production.
- Inequality of rights of shareholders is still preserved in the majority of Russian joint stock companies. The rule "one shareholder – one vote" was not observed in the course of privatization and the administration initially had additional benefits compared with common shareholders.
- The shareholders had a right to sell their stocks freely while the retired employees had a right to keep the stocks of companies they no longer worked for. Apart from that in crisis years many employees had to sell

their stocks due to long delays in wage payments, little or no dividends at all. As a result the recent years provided evidence of drastic decrease of employee shares in capital stock.

- In the reform years not only is it the case that an efficient owner was not created but the entire definition of private ownership was devaluated. Most of the employees of the privatized companies lost the incentive to increase ownership by acquiring or receiving their company's shares because employee ownership frequently had an illusive character and yielded no economic benefit in Russia. For its part the government did not facilitate the creation and maintenance of employee ownership. Without a proper institutional environment and the economic support that was needed, "the feeling of being an owner" gradually became a junk definition.
- Recently the employee's shares started to be used as an instrument of the redistribution of ownership in Russia and certain interest groups or "shadow" entities started to buy and use them for getting controlling stakes of companies. It led to a paradoxical and ironic situation in the country when the employee ownership started to be used for the purposes directly opposing to economic democracy.

This last stroke completed the general picture of Russian economic reforms that resulted in the new social and economic phenomenon of "the Russian style of democratization." This Russian style of democratization led to the creation of a specific kind of social organization in Russia defined as "Kremlin capitalism" in the monograph that had the same title (Blasi, Kroumova, & Kruse, 1997). It is obvious now that the direction of the present day development of the Russian economy did not match with the progressive world trends. The unlimited power of top managers and large private owners over production forms grounds for the "old type" economy based on authoritarian organization of production management and it leaves no preconditions for the development of economic democracy in the society. All this leaves no motivation to employees, and no room to tap the production efficiency of labor, etc. that is so necessary for the free market economy. It is not possible to create a genuine democratic society without an effective owner – the worker shareholder of the privatized company – because its most important component, i.e., economic democracy, is missing.

Do these negative trends raise concerns of the Russian reformers? At present we can be absolutely certain that they do not. Moreover, the Russian establishment obviously opposes the development of the employee ownership in the country because it can prevent the acquisition of companies by larger holdings controlled by oligarchs.

As a result, the modern Russian economy is characterized by the obvious concentration of ownership in the hands of a limited number of people. Reforms are being continued but no turn the economic democracy can be observed. In general the currently existing economic system in Russia can be characterized as closed market economy with prevailing oligarchic trends (see Ershova, 2002).

THE RUSSIAN MODEL OF ESOP

Despite of these unfavorable developments and due to active efforts of progressive forces at the end of 1990s a unique system for the creation and development of employee ownership was established in Russia. This model was used by a number of the Russian enterprises called "people's enterprises" that are now the real routes of the economic democracy. Economically these people's enterprises are most close to the U.S. ESOPs, but they differ from them in some respects. So I would call them the "Russian model of the ESOP."

The major differences between the Russian and the American ESOPs are as follows:

1. In Russia ESOPs are used only by closed type joint stock companies with a limited number of personnel.
2. There are no tax benefits for them provided by the state.
3. There is no trustee fund in these enterprises.
4. There is no system for crediting the acquisition of company shares by employees
5. Shares are not retained in the trustee fund until full servicing of the credit and dividends are paid annually.
6. There is a different system of voting by the shareholders.

The activities of the people's enterprises are regulated by a special law "On the specifics of legal status of joint stock companies of employees (people's enterprises)," that was adopted in 1998 (http://www.flexa.ru/law/zak/zak073.shtml). This law legally solved the problem of creation and functioning of companies where most of the shares belong to employees.

People's enterprises represent the most promising form of the development of the economic democracy in Russia today and the only practical experience of enlarging employee share ownership in modern Russia. These enterprises are different from others because employees are their real masters. It provides them with tangible competitive advantages.[2] The Russian model of the ESOP is unique for former Soviet Republics and former socialist countries of Eastern Europe. Therefore, the business experience of the people's enterprises, i.e., the Russian model of ESOP, may present a certain theoretical and practical interest for transitory and developed market economies.

I will focus on more details on the analysis of functioning of the so called "people's enterprises" in Russia, since they represent most promising form of the development of the economic democracy in Russia today.

The law "On the specifics of legal status of joint stock companies of employees (people's enterprises)" legally solved the problem of the creation and functioning of joint stock companies where all or the most of the stock belong to employees. This law introduced the new organizational and legal form of enterprise in Russia – the employee joint stock company (people's enterprise). This law ensures the rights and interests of the employees of people's enterprises.

The joint stock companies in Russia are divided into two types: open and closed joint stock companies. The main difference in open and closed joint stock companies is that the shares of the later can be distributed between its founders or other predefined circles of people. The closed joint stock company does not have a right to make an open subscription for the shares issued or suggest the company for acquisition to unlimited circle of persons. The shareholders of a closed joint stock company have a priority right for acquiring shares sold by other shareholders of the company within their limited circle. Thus, from the existing types of joint stock companies closed joint stock companies "approximate" people's enterprises most closely.

The people's enterprise is a closed joint stock company having its certain characteristics unique only for people's enterprises which distinguish it from a common closed joint stock company. These characteristics are determined by the law on people's enterprises. It implies that the legal status of the people's enterprise is determined not only by the law on people's enterprises but by the law "on joint stock companies" as well in its provisions pertaining to closed joint stock companies if otherwise the issue is not provided for by the law on people's enterprises.

So, what are the rules of functioning of people's enterprises? The economic essence of the people's enterprise is as follows:

1. According to the law the people's enterprise can be created only by means of a transformation of another type of business institution,[3] except for state and municipal unitary enterprises.[4] An open joint stock

company with less than 49% of its stocks belonging to its employees also cannot become a people's enterprise. Meanwhile, a commercial enterprise with more than 75% of stocks belonging to the employees can become a people's enterprise. It provides for full employee control and the firm is protected from external influences by the control of employees over its financial flows.

2. The employees of people's enterprises become owners of more than 75% of its authorized stock (they should possess at least 75% of shares plus one vote) while other persons can have less than 25% of shares. The upper limit of the shares belonging to the employees is not established. It can imply that the founders of the people's enterprise can state in its Articles of Association that even all 100% of its shares can belong to the employees. The law provides for a possibility for gradual increase of the employees' share in the authorized stock of a company to the level of 75% and more. However, the law also stipulates a maximum time period for obtaining this share by the employees. This period depends on the original share of the employees in the authorized stock of the company. For companies with the employees' original share of 55–65% a period of up to five years is established. For companies with the original employees' share of less than 55% this period can be maximum of 10 years. If the company employees fail to increase their share in the authorized stock to 75% in the prescribed period the company should be legally restructured into ordinary corporation with no status of the people's enterprise in one year.
3. The law establishes the terms within which 75% of the company shares should be transferred to its employees after the creation of the enterprise. These terms are established subject to the part of the authorized stock of the people's enterprise belonging to persons who are not the employees. In case that 45% of the authorized stock of the people's enterprise belongs to persons (who are not its employees) the employees of the people's enterprise must become the owners of 75% of its authorized stock not later than the year end of the 10th financial year after the creation of the people's enterprise. In case from 35% to 45% of the authorized stock of the people's enterprise belongs to persons (who are not the employees) the employees of the people's enterprise must become owners of more than 75% of its authorized stock not later than at the year-end of the fifth financial year after the creation of the people's enterprise. In case 75% of the authorized stock will not belong to the employees in the prescribed terms it should be converted into a commercial institution of another form or liquidated. This is a key principle

of regulation and it distinguishes the people's enterprise from a common join stock company where employees cannot have relationship to ownership over capital assets of the company they work for.

4. In the people's enterprise the maximum degree of concentration of shares in the hands of a single shareholder is also established. The maximum number of shares of the employee that he can be provided to him/her upon the creation of the people's enterprise should be equal to the share of his/her wages in total wages of the company employees for the preceding 12 months. The employee can acquire the shares of the people's enterprise in another way as well: if the future employee of the people's enterprise was formerly an employee of the commercial enterprise he or she can convert the commercial enterprises shares into people's enterprise's shares.
5. In the people's enterprise there is a limitation not only regarding the amount of shares in the hands of one employee but regarding the salary of its director general that cannot exceed the average salary in the company by more than 10 times. Apart from that sale of shares retained on the enterprise's balance sheet to its CEO, deputy CEOs and assistants, members of supervisory board or members of the board of directors is not allowed. Employees leaving the enterprise cannot sell their shares to these persons, as well. These limitations are intended to prevent the concentration of a large numbers of shares in the hands of the company administration and the top management and ensure more or less proportional distribution of shares among all employees of the people's enterprises. That is why this provision is directly related to guaranteeing the principle of social justice and industrial democracy in people's enterprises. If some employee has an excessive number of shares, the people's enterprise must buyout the shares from such employee while the employee must sell it (in the amount of the excess over 5% of all equity). The buyout is made in three months from the occurrence of such an excess.
6. From the positions of creation of "new owners" the process of providing the employees with shares presents special issues. The people's enterprise does not have a mechanism of synchronic financing using outside loans to buy shares on behalf of the employees (like the U.S. ESOP) increasing the share ownership of employees but it does have a system of yearly bonuses of employees who are presented with the company's shares proportionally to the amounts of their wages for the past financial year. The law allows the people's enterprise to increase its authorized stock by an additional emission of shares every year for

the amount not less than net earnings actually used for accumulation for the reporting financial year. Therefore, the employees of people's enterprises have a possibility to become the owners of the capital assets of the enterprise without spending their own money for it. It increases their own incomes and eventually the solvent demand in the society in general. Thus procedure of increasing authorized stock is provided for people's enterprises only and it differs substantially from the procedure of increasing authorized stock of common joint stock companies. In the common joint stock company, the controlling stake is in the hands of persons who as a rule do not take part in the production process. But these people take decisions influencing the directions of the company's activities and appropriate a part of its profits that they use at their discretion.

7. In the people's enterprise, all after-tax profits remain at its disposal and fully allocated to the development of production and the direct motivation of employees. This provision induces the people's enterprise to issue additional shares secured with the actual deposits of part of net earnings in its production and financial assets. The growth of the real assets facilitates strengthening the economic position of the people's enterprise, and increases its sustainability and competitiveness. At the same time, the shares of the people's enterprise are secured with material assets and are not subjected to devaluation. This process goes in parallel with the huge increase of ownership of the employees of the people's enterprise. These shares together with the shares repurchased from the retired employees are distributed between all the entitled employees proportional to their wages for the reporting financial year.[5] The more efficient the people's enterprise is, the higher the price of these shares and, thus, the bigger the amount the employee gets. This approach removes the contradiction between labor and capital and directly motivates the employee to increase the quantity and quality of his/her labor and links the increase of his/her ownership and income with his/her labor contribution. This introduces a drastic change in the economic interests of the employee owner, his/her psychology and consequently his/her economic behavior. It also precludes separation of the hired employee from the capital assets of the company he/she works for.
8. One of the characteristics of the people's enterprise is a permanently maintained ratio between its employee and non-employee owners. The law provides for a regulation preventing separation of the means of production from the employees: the share of employees not possessing

the shares cannot be more than 10% of their total number of employees. This limitation is introduced in order to provide equal social and economic conditions for most of the employees of the people's enterprise based on implementation of their rights as owners of capital assets of the enterprise. That is why the number of the shareholders who are not the employees of the people's enterprise should be strictly limited. If this limitation does not exist, the people's enterprise will become a common joint stock company with power concentrated in the hands of narrow circle of persons, i.e., big owners directing the company's activity based on their personal self-interest motives and taking no care of the interests of the employees. That is why the people's enterprise is responsible for providing newly hired employees with shares. The newly hired employees become its shareholders after three months or maximum one year work on people's enterprise.

9. As far as the procedure of determining the amounts received by the employees as salaries and providing them with people's enterprise shares this procedure is determined by the general meeting of the shareholders. The decision is made based on the principle of "one shareholder – one vote." Providing the people's enterprise with a right to increase their authorized stocks by issuing additional shares, the law on people's enterprise retains this right only for the general meeting of the shareholders. The decision on this issue is also made by the general meeting basing on the principle of "one shareholder – one vote." Thus, the people's enterprise has a somewhat different procedure of voting for employee owners than in common joint stock companies. The regular procedure in common joint stock companies provides for the «one share – one vote» rule, i.e., the more ownership, the more rights. In the people's enterprise, most of decisions are made based on the principle "one shareholder – one vote." In fact, 11 of the 15 questions that are mandatory to be resolved by the shareholders' meeting are decided in this way, excluding these 4 only: establishing remuneration for the members of supervisory board, approval of the repurchase price of shares, approval of yearly balance sheet and income statement and approval of priority directions of the people's enterprise's activities. Voting based on the principle "one share – one vote" contributes to the atmosphere of trust between the managers and employees and establishes the principle of social justice in the company. The right to vote on this and other questions in the general meeting of the shareholders on the principle of "one shareholder – one vote" is a substantial advantage for the employees of the people's enterprises compared

with the employees of other traditional types of joint stock companies. Thus the employees of people's enterprises have the possibility to influence decision making on principal issues of company activities based on their own economic interests.

10. The circulation of shares is strictly regulated by law. While working in the people's enterprise the employee has a right to sell his/her shares. But it is preconditioned by a number of limitations preventing the transfer of shares from employees to «third persons». The shareholders have right to sell their shares only to the shareholders of the people's enterprise or the company itself. In case of their refusal the employee can sell them to employees of people's enterprise who are not its shareholders. The number of shares allowed for sale by a single shareholder cannot exceed 20% of the people's enterprise shares belonging to him/her for the end of the financial year.
11. The dismissed employee owners are bound to sell to the people's enterprise all of its shares that they have while the latter should buy the shares. These stocks would be further distributed among those working in the company. The repurchase price of a share cannot be less than 30% of the company's net assets and as a rule should correspond to their market value.[6] This mechanism safeguards the people's enterprise from being captured by external investors and that is quite common phenomenon under the conditions of consolidation of ownership in the hands of limited number of people in modern Russia.
12. The average number of people's enterprise's employees cannot be less than 51 people and the number of its shareholders cannot exceed 5,000.

Summing up it should be emphasized that the people's enterprise represents a unique form of joint stock companies in Russia. The people's enterprises improve the quality of work and motivate the employees to reduce of unproductive expenses. As it follows from the experience of most of the people's enterprises in Russia, their character creates a positive influence on enterprise performance and on the financial position of the company in general and on its separate employees as well. People's enterprises show good results in productivity, they are efficient and generally have a very low rate of employees' leaving the company. It is also necessary to mention that keeping the controlling stake in the hands of employees enables them to invest more funds in the development of the company without fearing a hostile takeover and, therefore, plan more efficient activity of such enterprises (see Kreychman, 2004).

PRACTICAL EXPERIENCE OF PEOPLE'S ENTERPRISES

There is practically no information on the people's enterprises in the Russian media. Meanwhile, most of them are quite sustainable and feel comfortable under the market conditions thus strengthening the regional and national economy by their successful work and socially responsible behavior. In February–March 2010 the group of the Russian economists together with the Analytical Center of the "Economy and Life" newspaper made a pooling of information on a series of the Russian people's enterprises (http://uomk.narod2.ru/vas2/ent/narsbor1.doc). The survey included such companies as Naberezhnye Chelny Paper Pland (Republic of Tatarstan), Tourinsk Paper Plant and "Soukhalozhskasbestcement" Plant (Sverdlovsk Region), "Iskozhs" (City of Yoshkar-Ola), "Konfil" Factory (City of Volgograd), "Astrakhan' Khleb," "Krasnaya Zvezda" (Republic of Udmurtia), "Zhukov mezhraigas" (Kaluga Region). These companies were engaged in such industries as paper production, light industry, food industry, fuel production, machine building, timber processing, and construction. The survey helped to reveal the following data:

1. On average gross annual output in large companies with the number of employees from 1,000 to 2,000 reaches 1.5–3 billion rubles per company and in the companies with less than 500 employees it was about 100–500 million rubles per company.
2. In the last decade, the output of the surveyed people's enterprises increased from three to eight times and that is not typical for many other Russian enterprises. Labor productivity and wages also increased by several times.
3. The depreciation of production equipment in these companies does not exceed 40–50% (in one exceptional case it was 60%). In one half of the surveyed companies, 40–70% of the equipment is not older than five years.
4. The company incomes are not wasted but reinvested. By the decision of employees up to 50% of profits are annually allocated for renovation of production equipment and technological modernization that as a rule covers 100% of their investment requirements.
5. The production and financial indicators (production output, sales, average monthly wages, and profitability) are generally matching or exceeding the industry averages.
6. 75–100% of output is sold domestically, 5–25% is sold abroad.

7. The companies intensively develop their social infrastructure (they have their own housing for employees, kindergartens polyclinics, recreation facilities and utilities). More than 30% of profits are allocated for social needs annually.
8. Mandatory repurchasing of shares from the retired employees guarantee them a substantial surplus for their pension that amounts to tens and in some cases hundreds of thousand rubles.

Tables 1–4 present the results of business activities of the number of the Russian people's enterprises for the years since their establishment.

As it follows from Table 1 all of the people's enterprises included in the table except "Archangelskkhleb" manifested a spectacular growth in production output varying from 2.08% (Tourinsk) to 37.17% (Cheliabinsk) per year on average for the period of 2000–2009 with Rospechat, Krasnaya Zvezda, Iskozh Factory and Konfil Factory scoring respectively 22.84%, 18.55%, 14.82%, and 6.27% of average annual growth in production output.

The growth (expressed in percentage) of the sales revenues of the companies (Table 2) generally corresponded to that of the production output (see Table 1), although it could be influenced by price fluctuations on the respective sectors the companies operate in.

Table 3 provides evidence of growth of the employee-owners' capital of the companies expressed as a percentage to the previous year most likely resulting from their successful performance in the market displayed in Tables 1 and 2.

As it has been shown in Table 4, the growth in the employee wages generally corresponded to that in the production output and sales revenues of

Table 1. Growth in Production Output of People's Enterprises (% to previous year).

People's Enterprise	2000	2001	2002	2003	2004	2005	2006	2007	2008	2009
«Rospeshat»	28	38.8	34.5	25.7	17.6	23.5	19.1	11.7	25.3	9.4
«Archangelskkhleb»						−1.8	−3.3	−2.4	−8.9	−1.6
«Cheliabinsk radio management»	40.2	16.7	94.1	44.4	19.8	42.3	9.6	17.8	14.7	75.1
«Iskozh Factory»	41.5	0.2	16.8	15.7	18.0	9.8	15.9	23.5	7.8	25.7
«Tourinsk Paper and Pulp Plant»	7.6	−0.4	2.0	5.1	−1.6	0.7	−0.6	6.0	1.4	3.2
«Krasnaya Zvezda»			11.5	39.0	31.6	15.8	31.0	18.1	19.4	0.6
«Konfil Factory»	1.1	3.7	12.0	−8.3	−1.5	19.2	−2.4	7.8	12.3	13.7

Table 2. Sales Revenue of People's Enterprises (% to previous year).

People's Enterprise	2000	2001	2002	2003	2004	2005	2006	2007	2008	2009
«Rospeshat»	−1	117.6	165.4	−1.0	148.1	205.0	56.7	−9.0	12.5	38.0
«Archangelskkhleb»						115.7	17.9	−6.9	21.5	7.5
«Cheliabinsk radio management»	125.3	10.7	8.0	3.7	19.5	6.6	2.7	28.3	−6.7	
«Iskozh Factory»	104.0	42.3	−30.4	−20.5	43.4	−17.1	−0.7	41.1	17.6	12.9
«Tourinsk Paper and Pulp Plant»	1.7	−47.3	−2.8	52.1	48.0	−34.5	63.3	15.2	31.1	72.0
«Krasnaya Zvezda»			−37.9	210.4	−25.9	66.7	22.7	20.7	27.7	43.0
«Konfil Factory»	22.3	4.6	25.0	−6.1	24.5	17.3	8.0	21.4	21.1	−0.8

Table 3. Net Assets of People's Enterprises (% to previous year).

People's Enterprise	2000	2001	2002	2003	2004	2005	2006	2007	2008	2009
«Rospeshat»	3.8	40.2	46.5	−2.7	5.0	87.3	92.2	20.7	26.8	13.0
«Archangelskkhleb»						50.2	41.4	31.1	22.2	63.8
«Cheliabinsk radio management»	14.5	12.8	15.4	25.6	19.8	19.9	15.6	18.9	13.9	−4.0
«Iskozh Factory»	10.6	26.3	−0.7	−6.8	10.8	15.1	5.7	16.7	14.1	12.2
«Tourinsk Paper and Pulp Plant»	89.9	−6.4	4.9	3.5	14.1	20.5	20.2	1.5	−0.4	3.4
«Krasnaya Zvezda»			20.6	50.9	13.8	31.0	32.6	27.2	10.5	20.7
«Konfil Factory»	34.8	34.3	4.5	33.1	30.1	21.8	17.9	17.0	17.9	88.5

Table 4. Average Wages of People's Enterprises (% to previous year).

People's Enterprise	2000	2001	2002	2003	2004	2005	2006	2007	2008	2009
«Cheliabinsk radio management»	32.7	39.0	22.3	34.5	25.6	29.6	17.7	19.5	9.0	4.2
«Iskozh Factory»	33.4	28.7	36.6	31.2	11.2	20.7	25.9	29.9	14.5	−6.4
«Konfil Factory»	29.8	25.6	31.7	27.7	16.2	36.8	11.1	22.7	33.9	22.4

the observed companies although the latter indicator is available for only three of them. An interesting observation in this respect that the growth in wages correlated with the company performance expressed in production output and sales revenues and not with some other exogenous factors like trade unions pressure or government policy.

The amount of the employees' average monthly wages substantially varies among companies and sectors of economy, as well as among the regions of Russia. However, the people's enterprises claim that this amount exceeds wages in similar companies with no employee ownership by about 25–30%. This amount is added by the dividends received by the employee owners annually and social benefits they are entitled to by their companies. About 30% of the companies' annual profits are allocated for social needs, including housing allowances, kindergartens, medical services, recreation facilities owned by the people's enterprises. These benefits are added by the substantial retirement bonuses described below.

At the initial stages of the development of the Russian people's enterprises, their possibilities to increase the production output were reduced by the wearing out of their production equipment, lack of investments, low product competitiveness and changes in the structure of demand. Therefore, they paid special attention to the modernization of production (technical reequipment and introduction of new technologies). Putting in operation of new production facilities and technologies resulted into considerable growth in output and sales revenues (see Tables 1 and 2). It is important that the funding from shareholders (shares and retained earnings) is the main source of financing of people's enterprises. The financing decisions are made by the employees who are the co-owners of the companies. On average 60% of the companies' capital investment needs are financed from their own sources, while the external sources (long- and short-term loans) account for about 30%. In some companies such as Naberezhnye Chelny paper plant capital investments are financed entirely from the company own sources. This policy substantially contributed to the increase of the net assets (owners capital), reduction of losses and achievement of indicators providing evidence of a successful and fast growing business (Tables 1 and 3). The possession of the controlling stake by the employees helps to eliminate the contradiction between the capitalized part of earnings and wages. The employees increase the value of stocks belonging to each of them by increasing their company's net worth and developing their enterprise.

The global economic crisis was a challenge for the people's enterprises that showed their economic sustainability during these crisis conditions, as well. Most of the people's enterprises' managers assessed their companies' economic position in the crisis years as good or satisfactory. The negative impact of the crisis was reduced to a minimum. On average, the company's sales remained at the pre-crisis level, while some of them managed to increase by 20%.[7] The rationalization of production helped to partially compensate the losses from the crisis. The people's enterprises generally managed to avoid personnel lay-offs in the crisis years. Only a few companies reported temporary lay-offs not exceeding 10% of the staff members. As a rule, wages did not decrease in the crisis years and in some companies it even increased (Table 4).[8] This helped to preserve a normal moral and psychological atmosphere in people's enterprises. Most of the companies continued production modernization in 2009 and in 2010, all of them proceeded to developing it.

In recent years, a kind of the mechanism of accumulation of savings in the individual accounts of the employee owners developed in the Russian people's enterprises. The employees can accumulate their wealth in two ways: by allocating a part of the company's profit to retained earnings and investments and by annual dividend distributions to the employees' individual accounts. Obviously, the longer an employee participates in the people's enterprises the greater his/her savings. The survey of the Ural group of the people's enterprises showed that the average amount allocated by such enterprises to their retiring employees varies from 2 to 7 million rubles. Depending on the years worked in the company, the amount of savings accumulated by the retiring employees may comprise from 20 to 300 thousand rubles that makes a substantial addition to the income of the retired person in Russia.

This seems to be a unique feature of the people's enterprises: for the company it is mandatory to buy the retiring employee's shares according to the law. The purchasing value of the shares (that grows annually proportionally to the number of years served and wage level) is proportionate to the net worth of the company. This purchasing value can be considered as a kind of accumulated nongovernment pension. And this is a very important development given the social problems encountered by the pension system of the Russian Federation.

Another competitive advantage of the people's enterprises is that their employees participate not only in the company modernization but in its management on different levels, as well. At the enterprise level, it takes form of the inclusion of the representatives of the employees in the company supervisory board and the appointment of "worker directors." At the shop floor level, the employees take part in production commissions, production team councils, and a council of employees. At the workplace level, employees are engaged in rationalization of the workplace, optimization of the workplace and the updating of its technological operations, etc. The survey of these enterprises showed the stable flow of rationalization suggestions protected by patents and copyrights. The rationalization suggestions by the employees mainly relate to energy saving, reduction of production waste, introduction of new products, automation of hand labor, etc.

The development of employee participation in management and partnership relations is strengthened by the training system involving employees of all levels, including workers, engineers, technicians, and managers.

THE LEGAL BARRIERS TO THE DEVELOPING OF PEOPLE'S ENTERPRISES AND WAYS OF OVERCOMING THEM

Regardless of these and other obvious advantages of the people's enterprises, their number in the Russian economy is not high and the establishment of such enterprises encounters serious problems. Let's explore the reasons for this.

According to official statistics there were 140 officially registered closed type joint stock companies of employees (the people's enterprises) operating in various industries and in the agricultural sector in many regions of the Russian Federation. These companies work in such industries as pulp and paper production, machine building, light, food and fuel industry, timber processing, and construction. All of them were established shortly after the adoption of the above mentioned legislation. However, the process of the creation and the ongoing functioning of people's enterprises in Russia encounters a number of difficulties caused by both imperfections in the legal basis of this type of firm (first of all, the law on people's enterprises) and the social contradictions between large owners and oligarch groups and these who lobby their interests in the Russian Federation government and Parliament. Let's analyze some of these difficulties.

First, in the past years the experience of legal practice helped to reveal a number of drawbacks in the law on people's enterprises that has an impact on their work. Particularly, according to the law, any commercial organization in Russia with a number of employees not less than 51 can be converted into people's enterprise, except state and municipal enterprises, as I mentioned earlier. The necessary condition for it is that the share ownership of employees should be not less than 49% of the authorized stock. Also an important condition for the creation and functioning of a people's enterprise is that the number of its shareholders must not exceed 5,000. In case this number is exceeded, the people's enterprise is bound to reduce it to the prescribed limit or convert itself into a commercial organization of another form.

These provisions of the law on people's enterprises provide the major obstacles to the development of the people's enterprises for the following reasons:

- That percentage (49%) of employee ownership can be met rather rarely under currently prevailing conditions of consolidation of property in the Russian enterprises.
- The requirement to limit the number of shareholders to 5,000 employees puts constraints on the possibility of the growth of the company. As it was mentioned above, all employees entering the people's enterprise are provided with a certain amount of stock after some period of working. Therefore, the number of employee owners will grow to the extent there is an increase in the overall number of employees. As a result, under certain circumstances the possibilities for the economic and social development of some growing people's enterprises related to the growth in number of their employees will be constrained.
- In the same way, a commercial organization cannot be converted into a people's enterprise if the number of its employees willing to become shareholders exceeds 5,000. A number of existing commercial organizations willing to be converted into people's enterprises inevitably face the problem of the reduction of the number of employees in order to preserve an existing people's enterprise or in order to create a new people's enterprise. Consequently, labor unions and part of the employees face the problem of defending their rights to employee ownership in case the decision for a reduction of personnel is taken. An unsolvable contradiction occurs: the choice is either to create a people's enterprise and provide social justice to employees and economic efficiency to the enterprise or not to create (not to preserve) the people's enterprise in order to save jobs and facilitate the growth of production and personnel.
- According to the current Russian legislation, the employees of the state and municipal enterprises cannot convert them into people's enterprises in case of their privatization. This rule actually limits the sphere of proliferation of the employee ownership in the economy.

All this together with the generally undemocratic direction of Russian market reform explain, in my opinion, why there are a very small number of people's enterprises existing in Russia for the moment. It should be emphasized that the law on people's enterprises itself needs improvement and requires the introduction of substantial adjustments aimed to increase the possibility of development of employee's ownership in Russia. According to most of the Russian experts examining issues of the establishment and development of employee ownership and people's enterprises it is necessary to eliminate the following wording from the law saying that other types of enterprises can be converted to the people's enterprises with the exception state unitary enterprises, municipal unitary enterprises and open-type joint stock companies which employees less that 49% of their authorized stock.

This legal change could be crucial for the development of employee ownership as a means to insure social justice and bridging the gap between workers and capital assets; thus it would lead to fair distribution of the production output and national wealth.

In addition to that, the currently discussed new version of the Civil Code of the Russian Federation provides that if the number of company shareholders exceeds 500 the legal form for such a company should be the so called "public" (or open type) joint stock company that is regulated by absolutely different legal documents and previsions. Thus, a substantial part of the people's enterprises with the number of employee exceeding this amount should then have to cancel their existence as closed type joint stock company of employees even though employees possess more that 75% of the company shares that are not sold in the open securities market. The concept of improvement of the Civil Code endorsed by the former President Dmitry Medvedev provides for the change in legal form of the joint stock companies by abolishing their division into open and closed type joint stock companies. The joint stock companies are supposed to be converted into "public" and "not public" while the people's enterprises would fall under the category of "economic society." This possibility can perhaps involve the danger of abolishing the law on people's enterprises. This idea was met by vigorous criticism from public representatives, including experts and scientists supporting idea of development of people's enterprises in Russia, staff members and directors of people's enterprises. This criticism took the form of seminars and round tables, media publications, and official requests to the Government of the Russian Federation and the President. The official responses by the State Legal Department of the President, the Presidential Council on Codification and Improvement of the Civil Code and the Ministry of Economic Development stated that the legal practice and experience of people's enterprises will be taken into account in the new laws on joint stock companies and economic societies. Particularly, the future law on economic societies will include a special chapter dedicated to the economic societies of employees (people's enterprises) based on the provisions of the recent law. However, actions by certain official bodies and statements by some officials cause doubts with regards of these assurances. Moreover, in the past decade all the attempts to make changes reflecting the legal and economic experience of the people's enterprises (from separate changes and additions to the preparation of the new version of the federal law of people's enterprises) have utterly failed.[9]

RUSSIA HAS A CHANCE TO BECOME A REALLY DEMOCRATIC SOCIETY

The Russian society and political establishment must recognize a necessity for a drastic change in the direction of development of market reforms. In its development, Russia should aim at insuring a good living for the majority of its members and not to the limited group of oligarchs only. Companies with employee participation that have been demonstrating their superior economic and social efficiency in many countries of the world should play the major role in the development of the democratization of Russian reforms. They represent the domestic producers economically and they are also politically interested in the development of the Russian economy in the direction of socially oriented reforms.

The movement for supporting people's enterprises and their successful functioning needs representation of its interests in the bodies of legislative and executive power from municipal to national level. This support should be provided by various social forces: the progressive scientific community, political parties and public institutions, people deputies, the mass media, etc.

A special role should be played by trade unions that are bound to represent and defend the interests of employees. The advocacy work in the employee's collectives of commercial organizations displaying the essence of people's enterprises and their advantages for employees compared with other forms of joint stock companies must become one of the major trade unions' activities.

Beside the explanatory work the trade unions should focus their efforts on organizational and practical support in the course of conversion of commercial organizations to people's enterprises since as yet there are no consulting companies in Russia servicing the process of the creation and functioning of companies with employee ownership.

Meanwhile, in representing the interests of employees of the people's enterprises, trade unions must not ignore the question of the improvement of labor legislation related to the emergence of a new form of ownership, i.e., employee ownership with relevant changes in the rights of employees. Being co-owners of the people's enterprise, employee shareholders cannot efficiently defend their rights by only participating in the general meeting of the shareholders or delegating their representative to the supervisory council. This issue mainly relates to the right to remain the employee of the people's enterprise and not to be fired without serious reasons.

Legal initiatives aimed at extending the possibilities of the creation and functioning of the people's enterprises, pursuing favorable credit and taxation policies with regards to these enterprises should become one of the main directions of the work of trade unions together with scientific community as both engage in sharing the ideas of economic democracy. However, the development of people's enterprises is not sufficient and exhaustive of what needs to be accomplished. In reality, all persons involved in production should have access to capital.

In the modern market economies, labor participation in the production process alone is not sufficient for meeting the growing demands of consumers. The production becomes more and more capital intensive and less labor intensive. The labor income does not grow to the same extent as production and it cannot insure the necessary level of solvent demand in the society, therefore. The way to solve the problem of solvent demand and providing most of the citizens with economic independence is to provide them with access to capital markets and possibility of acquisition of capital (see Ashford & Shakespeare, 1999). It would make them not only "workers of labor" but "workers of capital," as well, and facilitate considerable growth of their incomes (see Kelso & Kelso, 2001). It would result in the diminishing necessity of the vast redistribution of incomes in the society and related tax burden on producers. People would cease to need state assistance and get new motives for raising quality and competitiveness of their company products. They would start to "work with capital" and gradually become its owners or co-owners. Obviously, it is a way to forming the effective owner the Russian economy needs so much.

The main role in the democratization of ownership is played by institutional structures that created the legal and economic environment for ESOP functioning and other models of employee's financial participation. The absence of an adequate institutional environment for the reforms in Russia was the main reason for their failure. The institutional infrastructure is the main factor that determines the conditions of the environment of functioning of the markets. Social market institutions are much more important for the successful transformation of the economy than the degree and the path of liberalization of the reforms. The Russian economy still faces the problem of forming market institutions able to create an adequate environment for democratization of social and economic reforms in Russia. Undoubtedly, the main role in creating the institutional environment necessary for the democratization of property should be played by the state.

For more than 200 years, the role of the state in the market economy remains a subject of thorough research and endless disputes. This question is especially important for the countries with a transitional economy. At present most of researchers of the market transformation in Russia arrive at the conclusion that the stability and efficiency of the vertical structure of power is extremely important in any situation but in the periods of deep social political and economic changes the role of the state increases even more (Shakhmalov, 2005). However, I believe that the mere statement of this fact is not sufficient. It is necessary to determine what instruments and methods the Russian state should use and what democratic goals will be achieved as a result.

While analyzing the activities of the Russian government for the last several years it is necessary to note the clear increase of the impact of the state on the economy. Administrative and force-oriented methods prevail over institutional and economic ones. The government tries to address the consequences of behavior of separate oligarchs but it fails to eliminate oligarchy as a system by creating transparent rules favoring development of economic democracy. Under the conditions of certain positive changes of general economic environment, the serious transition of an institutional environment is not really to be observed. The participants in production permanently meet with the lack of legally fixed market institutions that would guarantee generally accepted norms and "rules of the game." One of the main principles of the market economy, i.e., separation of property and political power has not been implemented in its fullest extent. Moreover, the close relations of certain persons and groups with power structures and their self-interested exploitation became factors facilitating distribution and redistribution of ownership in Russia. The peculiar symbiosis of bureaucracy and big capital has occurred in Russia. The power and capital either were not separated from the very beginning or merged on new grounds.

In order to overcome these negative trends in the society and create the market economy of a more democratic type, it is necessary to use both the traditional methods of increasing of solvent demand of the population (creating new jobs, state orders, various investment programs) and the non-traditional ways and approaches developed by the proponents the so called "third way" (The Third Way: Does It Exist for Russia, 2004).

In the 21st century Russia needs radical turn of the economic reforms of the "third way" toward the democratization of ownership, forming efficient owners, employee ownership and the destruction of overwhelming power of oligarchs. Otherwise, the outcome for Russian reforms is predetermined. Under these conditions, the search for practical ways of setting up and developing the democratization of economic activities and a system of economic democracy becomes crucially important for Russia.

I would like to finish this article with the citation of my foreword to the Russian edition of the Louis and Patricia Kelso's book *Democracy and Economic Power*. The foreword was titled "Kelso time has come for Russia." In the foreword I wrote that in case the negative trends in the Russian economy prevail it will inevitably result into "returning to a totalitarian and antidemocratic regime in various forms starting from the military dictatorship and ending with "Gulag system" controlled by mafia and criminals. To leave such a dreadful scenario in the past we should admit that the time for the economic democracy has come in Russia! In the new century, a new time will come – "the time of Kelso" – and these who will not correct their watch are risking staying away from the mainstream of world history (Ershova, 2000b).

NOTES

1. The term "joint stock company" (JSC) is equivalent to the term "corporation" in its internationally accepted understanding. The Russian corporate law distinguishes between "open" and "closed" JSCs. The main difference between them is that the former can sell their shares in the open financial market while the latter can issue its shares only to a limited number of its shareholders specified in its Articles of Association (Incorporation) – see the Russian Law on Joint Stock Companies available in Russian at http://base.consultant.ru/cons/cgi/online.cgi?req = doc; base = LAW;n = 140364. The people's enterprises are closed JSCs with at least 75% of its employees being the shareholders.
2. While visiting one of such enterprises making confectionery products in Volgograd I noticed a huge stone board at the entrance. It said: "We work better than others because we work for ourselves."
3. According to the Civil Code of the RF a commercial organization is an organization pursuing receiving of profit as a main goal of its activity.
4. The legal status of unitary enterprises in Russia is defined in Federal Law No. 161-FZ "On State and Municipal Unitary Enterprises," which was approved by

the State Duma on October 11, 2002 and signed by President Putin on November 14, 2002.

A state and municipal unitary enterprise is a commercial enterprise that does not have a property title for assets assigned to it. The property of the unitary enterprise is undividable and cannot be distributed by parts among the employees of the enterprise. This property belongs to such an enterprise by virtue of the right for economic disposal and operational management. The assets of unitary enterprises belong to the federal government, a Russian region, or a municipality. A unitary enterprise holds assets under economic management (for both state and municipal unitary enterprises) or operative management (for state unitary enterprises only), and such assets may not be distributed among the participants, nor otherwise divided. A unitary enterprise is independent in economic issues and obliged only to give its profits to the state. Unitary enterprises have no right to set up subsidiaries, but, with the owner's consent, can open branches and representation offices. See http://en.wikipedia.org/wiki/Unitary_enterprise.

5. This provision is not applicable to the shareholders who are not the employees of this enterprise.

6. In practice the repurchase price of the stocks of the people's enterprise may not coincide with their market value because only a small portion of its stakes can be outstanding in the market that would necessarily obscure their real value. The stocks of most people's enterprise have no turnover in the security market because the newly issues shares of the enterprise are distributed among its employees.

7. Only one company traditionally supplying its products to the automotive industry affected by the crisis reported the decrease of its sales revenues from 20% to 30%.

8. Only one of the surveyed companies reported a temporary decrease in its employee's wages reaching 6% due to deep recession in the Russian automotive industry that was a traditional market for its products.

9. In the period from 1998 till 2009, the Russian Parliament approved 2,700 laws. About 80% of these introduced changes in the existing laws. However, no changes were made in the not so well-known and ignored law on people's enterprises.

REFERENCES

Ashford, R., & Shakespeare, R. (1999). *Binary economics: The new paradigm*. New York, NY: University Press of America.

Blasi, J. R., Kroumova, M., & Kruse, D. L. (1997). *Kremlin capitalism: The privatization of the Russian economy*. Ithaca and London: ILR Press, Cornell University Press.

Blasi, J. R., & Kruse, D. L. (1995). *The new owners. The hired worker – the mass owners of the joint stock companies*. Academy of national economy in the Government of the Russian Federation, Moscow, Delo Ltd., pp. 10–11. (Translated back from Russian into English by the author.)

Ershova, T. V. (2000a). *The necessity of democratization of ownership in Russia*. Professionals for cooperation, 4, Moscow, ROO "Kennan," pp. 247–256.

Ershova, T. V. (2000b). The time of Kelso has come to Russia. Foreword to the Russian edition. In L. O. Kelso & P. H. Kelso (Eds.), *Democracy and economic power* (p. 17). Rostov-on-Don: Phoenix.

Ershova, T. V. (2002). *Forming a free market in Russia: The binary perspective of development of neo-economy*. Economic theory at the threshold of XXI century – 6, Moscow, Urist, pp. 565–574.

Kelso, L. O., & Kelso, P. H. (2001). *Democracy and economic power*. Rostov-on-Don: Phoenix.

Kreychman, F. S. (2004). *Efficient company management based on democratization of ownership*. Moscow. Finance and statistics.

Shakhmalov, F. I. (2005). *State and economy. Power and business*. Moscow: ZAO Economics.

The Third Way: Does It Exist for Russia. On the History of the Russian Economic Thought. (2004), Moscow, Sovremennik.

CHAPTER 8

DETERMINANTS OF FINANCIAL PARTICIPATION IN THE EU: EMPLOYERS' AND EMPLOYEES' PERSPECTIVES

Iraj Hashi and Alban Hashani

ABSTRACT

Purpose – *The purpose of this paper is to investigate the incidence of employee financial participation (EFP) schemes in Europe and examine the factors that influence the likelihood of (i) a company offering EFP schemes and (ii) employees taking up EFP schemes.*

Design/methodology/approach – *Using a combination of descriptive and econometric techniques, the paper provides information on the incidence of EFP schemes in the EU and profiles a typical company and a typical employee that, respectively, offers and takes up EFP schemes. The empirical investigation is based on two models employing probabilistic techniques. Data used for this analysis include the European Company Survey (ECS) conducted in 2009 and three rounds of the European Working Conditions Survey (EWCS) conducted in 2000, 2005, and 2009.*

Sharing Ownership, Profits, and Decision-making in the 21st Century
Advances in the Economic Analysis of Participatory & Labor-Managed Firms, Volume 14, 187–215

ISSN: 0885-3339/doi:10.1108/S0885-3339(2013)0000014009

Findings – *Results display a significant rise in EFP in the EU-27 in the last decade. In addition, results seem to suggest that the employees' and companies' characteristics, as well as sector and region of operation explain some of the variation in likelihoods of companies and employees, respectively, offering and taking up EFP schemes.*

Research limitations/implications – *Due to data limitation, our analysis lacks a dynamic assessment of the relationship between parameters. Studies that exploit longitudinal data are suggested to follow this paper.*

Originality/value – *This paper contributes to the existing empirical literature by examining jointly the determinants of financial participation from both employers' and employees' perspective.*

Keywords: Employee financial participation; employee share ownership; profit sharing; EWCS; ECS

JEL classification: J33; M52; M54

INTRODUCTION

Employee financial participation (EFP) in the form of profit sharing (PS) and employee share ownership (ESO) have become increasingly popular amongst European companies. EFP schemes are considered as a possible solution to different agency problems. The concept of EFP involves employees being given the opportunity to participate in the financial results of their companies. It is argued that employees who participate in the financial results and ownership of a firm will become more committed to the goals of the firm, leading to improvements in individual and organizational performance. At macro level, EFP may be seen as a tool for redistribution of income and wealth and may have potential benefits on the level of employment and economic growth.

There is now a large literature on the incidence and impact of EFP schemes. So far, the empirical research has mainly been focused on the impact of EFP on company performance and the particular mechanisms through which EFP affects performance. Only a small number of studies focus on the determinants of financial participation. Especially, the analysis of determinants of employees taking up the EFP schemes is scarce.

This paper contributes to the existing literature by examining the incidence and determinants of financial participation from both companies' and employees' perspectives. Using a combination of descriptive and econometric techniques, it provides information on the incidence of EFP schemes in the EU and profiles a typical company and a typical employee that, respectively, offers and takes up EFP schemes. The empirical investigation is based on two models employing probabilistic techniques. Data used for this analysis include European Company Survey (ECS) conducted in 2009 and three rounds of European Working Conditions Survey (EWCS) conducted in 2000, 2005, and 2009. In the first model, using ECS data, the focus is on the factors that influence the likelihood of company offering an EFP scheme. A broad range of characteristics is investigated including companies' characteristics (size, region, sector of operation, HRM practices) and employees' characteristics (proportion of high-skilled workers, proportion of female employees and employee representation). In the second model, employing EWCS data, the focus is on the factors that influence the decision of individuals to take up an EFP scheme. Similarly, it explores a broad range of companies' characteristics (size, region, sector of operation, HRM practices) and employees' characteristics (gender, age, years at the company, type of contract, occupation) including dummies to control for years.

The rest of the paper is organized as follows. The next section provides a theoretical background of EFP followed by a section on the methodology. Then the descriptive results are presented. This is followed by discussion on determinants of financial participation followed by a presentation of empirical results. The last section concludes.

THEORETICAL BACKGROUND

The main argument in favor of introducing EFP schemes is that these improve workers' incentives and pose a solution to different agency problems (McNabb & Whitfield, 1998). The expectation of the theoretical literature is that the adoption of EFP schemes improves performance and creates incentives for workers to be more involved in, and to identify with, companies. EFP schemes give employees the right to share profits, to access information on company finances and operations, and right to participate in the management of the company (Rousseau & Shperling, 2003). Giving workers a stake in the success of the firm will motivate higher levels of effort, generate more positive attitude, and more co-operative behavior, and also help realign employee interests with those of the firm (Poutsma &

Huijgen, 1999). This in turn leads to increased labor productivity, efficiency, and competitiveness (Ben-Ner & Jones, 1995; Bryson & Freeman, 2007; Jones, Kalmi, & Kato, 2010; Kruse, Blasi, & Freeman, 2010; Oxera, 2007a, 2007b; Poutsma & Bramm, 2011 among others).[1]

Apart from productivity-related motives to adopt EFP schemes, they may as well be adopted in order to increase compensation flexibility (Kruse, 1996). By design, EFP schemes do not create a fixed obligation for the employer hence a part of the profit volatility risk is transferred to employees. EFP schemes may also be adopted because of tax concessions and other incentives that firms can enjoy (Pendleton, Poutsma, Brewster, & Van Ommeren, 2001). In addition, the adoption of EFP schemes can facilitate access to capital as the money spent in shares and deferred profit sharing arrangements can be invested. Besides, EFP schemes also discourage unionization of the employees. At macro level, EFP may be seen as a tool for redistribution of income and wealth and may have potential benefits on the level of employment and economic growth.

Despite the expected gains, the adoption of EFP schemes is associated with different theoretical objections ranging from risk-aversion of the employees for taking up EFP schemes to free rider problem arising with the increase of company's size (Kruse, Blasi, & Park, 2008). Risk aversion is considered as an important aspect in most theoretical models related to variable payment. The variability of rewards is a significant cost for risk-averse employees and is found to reduce the preference of adopting these schemes (Cadsby, Song, & Francis, 2007; Holmstrom, 1979). It is often argued that EFP schemes expose employees to the risk of ownership and participation without proportional gain attached to it (d'Art, 1992). So, if the company is to offer variable reward schemes, it has to pay higher remunerations to offset the incremental increase in risk. On the other hand, in presence of information asymmetries, the principal-agent problem might arise and the former has to elicit the necessary information to ensure performance. This can be achieved through incentive mechanisms based on group efforts; however, the relationship with the size of the company is expected to be non-linear.[2] As the group size increases, the free rider problem is expected to rise, which lowers the incentives of adopting the EFP schemes.

But, despite these problems related to the EFP schemes, still they are increasingly widespread and popular. They are found to be especially effective when combined with other forms of employee participation in the decision-making processes of firms (Bryson & Freeman, 2010; Klein, 1987; Pierce, Rubenfeld, & Morgan, 1991; Robinson & Wilson, 2006).

In particular, where employees have a small stake, high employee participation rates are necessary for the plan to be effective (Pendleton & Robinson, 2010). High employee participation rates combined with horizontal monitoring among peers are expected to mitigate the free rider problem as the threat of peer sanctions ensures that each agent contributes its share of effort (Weitzman & Kruse, 1990). Furthermore, the job stability that EFP schemes entail pose a good source of compensation for additional risk undertaken by employees.

While there is a vast empirical literature investigating the impact of EFP on company performance and the particular mechanisms through which EFP affects performance, there is limited number of studies investigating factors that influence the adoption EFP schemes. Moreover, the factors that influence the employees to take up EFP schemes are even less investigated in the empirical literature. Therefore, this paper aims at contributing to the existing literature by providing an analysis of factors that influence the likelihood of (i) a company offering EFP schemes and (ii) employees taking up EFP schemes. Specifically, it tries to answer the following questions: What kind of companies tend to adopt EFP schemes and whether location, sector of operation and composition of workforce explain some of the changes in likelihood of adopting these schemes? Similarly, the paper asks, whether individual and company characteristics explain the likelihood of employees taking up the schemes.

METHODOLOGY

This paper combines a descriptive analysis and an econometric multivariate estimation. The descriptive analysis profiles the incidence of EFP schemes in EU. It portrays the proportion of companies offering EFP schemes and the proportion of employees taking up EFP schemes. The econometric analysis, on the other hand, profiles a typical company and a worker that, respectively, offers and takes up EFP schemes. Data used for this analysis include a round of ECS and three rounds of EWCS.

The ECS is a large-scale company survey that was carried out in EU Member States and candidate countries. The unit of analysis in ECS is the establishment, the local unit in the case of multi-site enterprises. The sample is representative of establishments with 10 or more employees from all sectors of activity, except for agriculture and fisheries (NACE A and B, Rev. 1.1), activities of households and extraterritorial organizations

(NACE P and Q). The number of private establishments used for the analysis of profit sharing and share ownership was around 18,000. Portugal is excluded from the information on employee share ownership due to incompatibility of the process with other countries.

EWCS is a large-scale survey of working conditions across Europe undertaken by the European Foundation every four or five years to investigate a variety of factors influencing individuals' working and living conditions. One section of the questionnaire deals with remuneration and sources of income, asking the respondent whether they receive any income in the form of profit sharing or any income from the ownership of shares in the companies for which they work.[3] Given that individual subjects may be employed, unemployed, self-employed or retired, the present analysis is only concerned with the individuals who are in employment. The number of respondents used for analysis was around 40,000.

DESCRIPTIVE RESULTS

The following section summarizes the main findings of the data used in this paper. These cross-country surveys broadly confirm the empirical findings of previous reports, which noted that there was a significant rise in EFP in the EU-27 in the last decade.[4] This is true for both profit sharing and employee share ownership, although profit sharing is more widespread.

Since ECS was first conducted in 2009, it is not possible to observe the dynamics of EFP in EU companies over time using these data.[5] ECS finds that the average proportion of companies offering PS schemes stands at almost 19 percent whereas the proportion of companies offering ESO schemes stands at around 6.5 percent (Fig. 1). By design, this survey consists of predominantly small- and medium-sized firms, where EFP schemes are less prevalent and therefore the results are expected to be lower than that indicated by other surveys, which are concentrated on larger companies.

ECS data also allow a breakdown of the proportion of companies offering EFP schemes according to size and sector of operation. Fig. 2 shows the availability and extent of EFP schemes (ESO and PS) in companies of different size groups (large, medium, and small). As expected, the size of the company is closely associated with the incidence of EFP. It indicates

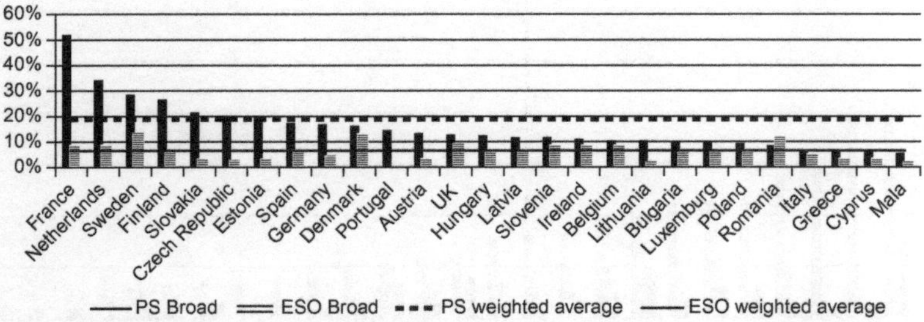

Fig. 1. Proportion of Companies Offering Broad Based PS and ESO Schemes. *Note*: For ESO schemes, Portugal is excluded from the data on employee share ownership schemes because the data on ESO is not compatible with that in other countries. Source: Authors' own calculations (based on ECS dataset, 2009).

that large companies almost always have higher levels of employee share ownership and profit-sharing schemes than medium and especially small companies. The distribution of EFP schemes shows an almost monotonic increase with the size of the firm.

Also a breakdown in the EFP incidence in different sectors of operation (according to NACE classification) maintains the relationship proposed in the following section. Companies operating in the Financial Intermediation sector have the highest levels of PS and ESO schemes. They are followed by companies operating in electricity, gas, and water supply sector and the real estate and business activities sector. The above sectors are followed by manufacturing, transport, and communication, wholesale trade and mining. Fig. 3 illustrates these findings graphically.

On the other hand, the proportion of employees participating in EFP schemes has been growing though in recent years growth has slowed (Fig. 4). The availability of the new EWCS 2010 makes it possible to compare the take-up of EFP schemes over the entire decade. The proportion of employees taking up profit-sharing schemes rose from 6.4 percent in 2000 to 9.1 percent in 2005 and then to 13.5 percent in 2010. Over the same period, the proportion of employees participating in employee ownership schemes increased from a weighted average of 1.4 percent in 1999/2000 to 2.3 in 2005 and 3.3 percent in 2010.[6]

The three rounds of EWCS clearly demonstrate that the proportion of employees participating in both ESO and PS schemes has grown in almost all countries. As far as PS schemes are concerned, these schemes are much more prevalent than ESO schemes (the weighted averages are about four times higher in each year).

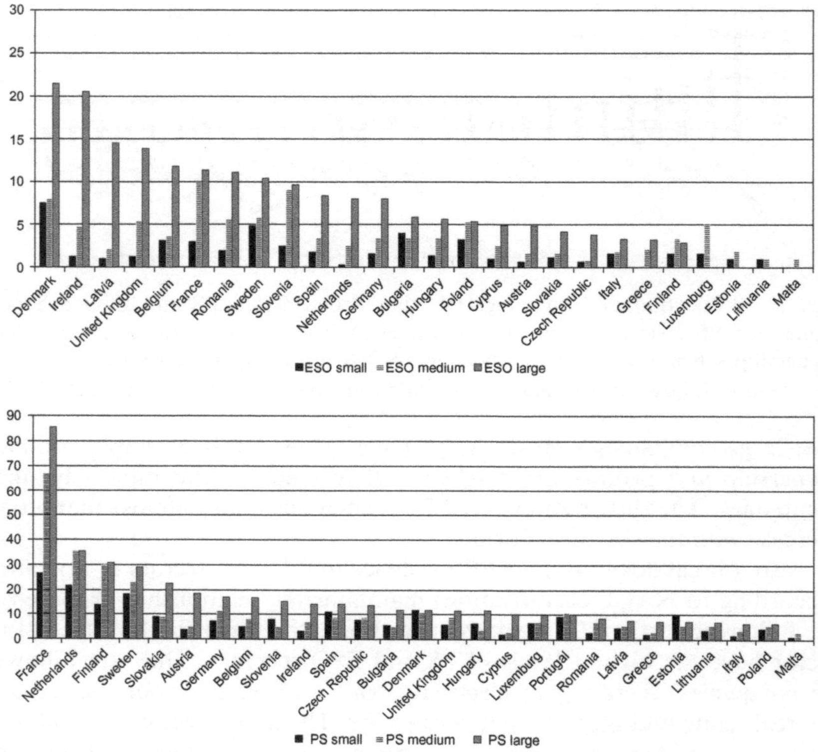

Fig. 2. Proportion of EU-27 Companies of Different Size Offering Employee Share Ownership (ESO) and Profit-Sharing (PS) Schemes to Their Employees, 2009 (in percent). *Note*: Portugal is excluded from the data on employee share ownership schemes because the Portuguese data on ESO is not compatible with that in other countries (European Foundation for the Improvement of Living and Working Conditions, 2010, p. 41). Source: Authors' own calculations (based on ECS dataset, 2009).

FACTORS THAT INFLUENCE FINANCIAL PARTICIPATION – DISCUSSION OF THE MODELS

As discussed, this paper examines the incidence and determinants of financial participation from both companies' and employees' perspective. In the first model, using ECS data, the focus is on the factors that may be deemed to predispose firms to introduce EFP schemes. A broad range of

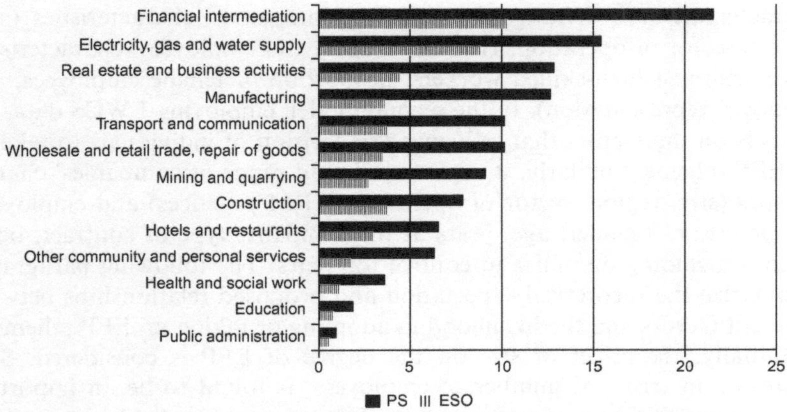

Fig. 3. Proportion of EU-27 Companies in Different Sectors Offering Broad-Based Employee Share Ownership (ESO) and Profit-Sharing (PS) Schemes 2009 (in percent). Source: Authors' own calculations (based on ECS dataset, 2009).

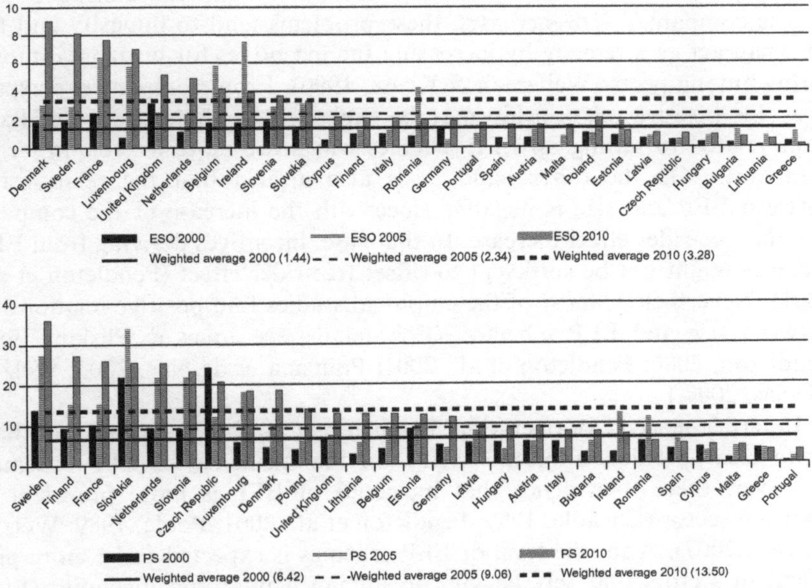

Fig. 4. Proportion of Employees Participating in Employee Share Ownership (ESO) and Profit Sharing (PS) Schemes in the EU Member States, 2000–2010 (in percent). Source: EWCS 2000, 2005, and 2010.

characteristics are investigated including companies' characteristics (size, region, sector of operation, HRM practices) and employees' characteristics (proportion of high-skilled workers, proportion of female employees, and employee representation). In the second model, employing EWCS data, the focus is on the factors that influence the decision of individuals to take up an EFP scheme. Similarly, it explores a broad range of companies' characteristics (size, region, sector of operation, HRM practices) and employees' characteristics (gender, age, years at the company, type of contract, occupation) including dummies to control for years. The following paragraphs summarize the theoretical expectation and proposed relationships between different factors and the likelihood in adopting or taking up EFP schemes.

Initially, the effect of size on the degree of EFP is considered. Size, expressed in terms of number of employees, is found to be an important determinant of financial participation. The arguments extend in two directions. On the one hand, it is expected that there is a positive relationship between size of the company and EFP schemes, as found by many studies (Festing, Groening, Kabst, & Weber, 1999). This positive relationship is mainly attributed to the information asymmetry and monitoring issues. As the companies' size increases, these problems tend to intensify and the EFP can act as a remedy by increasing the incentives for horizontal monitoring among peers (Weitzman & Kruse, 1990). From companies' perspective, this positive relationship may be explained by the existence of fixed costs related to setting up EFP schemes which are more feasible in larger companies. On the other hand, it is also argued that the relationship between EFP and size is negative since with the increase of the company size the free-rider effect increase. In that case, incentives deriving from EFP schemes might not be sufficient to offset free-rider effect (Pendleton et al., 2001). Nevertheless, most of the empirical studies find positive relationship between size and EFP schemes. (For details, see Jones & Pliskin, 1989; Pendleton, 2006; Pendleton et al., 2001; Poutsma & de Nijs, 2003; Welz & Macias, 2007.)

In terms of sector of operation, Pendleton et al. (2001) suggest that there is no clear prediction of the sector on the incidence of EFP schemes. However, there is evidence that incidence of EFP is more prevalent in financial sector (Cheadle, 1989; Pendleton et al., 2001; Poole, 1989; Welz & Macias, 2007). Also, the level of EFP schemes is expected to be more prevalent in sectors that rely heavily on human capital and ingenuity (Blasi et al., 2003). In manufacturing sector, due to high level of diversification and workforce composition, the level of EFP is expected to be limited. In cases when companies are highly diversified, EFP schemes might not be attractive as the performance of smaller establishments within the same company may vary widely, hence lowering the incentive for participation. The least prevalence of EFP schemes is expected in low value added sectors.

The composition of the company workforce has also been identified as an important factor in the adoption of the EFP schemes. Agency theory suggests that agency costs and agency problems may well be higher in some work environments than in others. It is often predicted that the productivity and output of managerial staff is harder to monitor and evaluate. Therefore it is expected that the extent of EFP schemes will be higher in companies with higher proportion of high-skilled workers. For the same reason, it is also predicted that the likelihood of offering EFP schemes is positively related to the increase of proportion of managerial employees. Similarly, workers in managerial position are expected to be more likely in taking up the EFP schemes due to increased incentives deriving from participation in the decision-making processes of firms (Klein, 1987; Pierce et al., 1991; Welz & Macias, 2007).

In terms of gender, usually a gap between men and women is observed in the incidence of EFP schemes. The gender gap tends to arise for at least two reasons. First, in cases where the EFP schemes are narrow (i.e. limited to particular group of employees) these schemes are usually offered to managerial positions in which females tend to be underrepresented. Secondly, the gender discrimination is also expected in cases where the scheme is broad based. This may be due to job segregation, that is, the different types of jobs that men and women hold and not necessarily the result of direct discrimination in the application of these schemes. Therefore it is predicted that an increase of proportion of female worker to be associated with lower probability of offering EFP schemes, similarly, female workers are more reluctant of taking up the scheme.

There is no well-defined prediction of the impact of employees' age in the likelihood of taking up EFP schemes. While on the one hand, older workers are more likely to remain with the company and so more likely to take up EFP schemes. On the other hand, due to career development effects younger workers are also likely to take up EFP schemes in order to signal commitment and identification with the company. Conversely, years spent at the company are expected to be positively related to the likelihood of employees taking up the scheme. More years spent at the company, signals more job security, which increases incentives from participation. This is closely related to the type of the contract the employees have. It is expected that EFP schemes will be more common among full-time employees with longer period contracts. They are usually core employees whose commitment and effort are important to workplace performance. Also, since their likelihood of being laid off is lower, they tend to have greater commitment and incentive to participate. This job stability poses a good source of compensation for additional risk undertaken by employees.

In a presence of well-developed HRM practices, greater levels of EFP schemes are expected. EFP schemes are often viewed as part of HRM system that aligns interest of principals and agents resulting in enhanced performance (Pendleton, 2001). In this framework, if the work is organized in teams, the likelihood of offering EFP schemes is expected to be higher as the level of horizontal monitoring increases, which in turn mitigates the free rider problem (Kaarsemaker, Pendleton, & Poutsma, 2009). Also, training may be another important determinant of taking up the EFP schemes. Workers who are offered employer-sponsored training opportunities are more likely to take up EFP schemes. Staying with one company and receiving trainings, the employees forego the possible opportunities from other companies. This investment, which can be opportunistically seized by the management and owners, is better protected in presence of EFP schemes. From the opposite perspective, companies that offer trainings are also more likely to offer EFP schemes as well. In similar way, investment incurred by providing trainings are better protected in presence of EFP schemes.

EFP schemes tend to discourage unionization of the employees (Ramsay, 1977). However, the relationship between EFP schemes and union representation is complex. This is also because the EFP schemes and union representations differ considerably among different states. In case of employee share ownership, the fundamental distinction between capital and labor, upon which unionization is based, gets blurred. Therefore the relationship between the two is expected to be negative. On the other hand, profit sharing can be complimentary with union representation. As profit sharing may be seen as a form of rent sharing, it is completely consistent with the usual objectives of union representation (Pendleton et al., 2001). Regardless of theoretical expectations, the empirical evidence of the relationship between EFP schemes and union representation is not conclusive (Pendleton, 1997).

In addition, the analysis is extended by the inclusion of the regional effects. Countries with reasonably similar characteristics were grouped so that they reflect these regulatory and institutional similarities. Also, in the EWCS model, due to data availability, year dummies were included to account for some dynamics of likelihood of taking-up schemes.

EMPIRICAL MODELS AND RESULTS

The paper focuses on two models and their extensions that examine: (1) the likelihood of companies offering EFP schemes and (2) the likelihood of employees taking up the EFP schemes. The baseline model used for assessing the likelihood of companies offering EFP schemes is as follows:

$$P(y=1|x)=\beta_0 + \beta_1 \text{ Proportion of female workers} + \beta_2 \text{ Proportion of high skilled workers} + \beta_3 \text{ Size} + \beta_4 \text{ Sector} + \beta_5 \text{ Region} + \varepsilon_i \quad (1)$$

where the dependent variable is the likelihood that the company will offer EFP schemes – either profit sharing (PS) or employee share ownership (ESO) schemes. Independent variables include proportion of female workers at the company, proportion of high-skilled workers, size of the company (Eurostat; SBS size class), sector of operation (NACE classification), and region. As an extension to the baseline model, other important determinants were included, namely employee representation and variables depicting human resource management (HRM) practices. Hence apart from variables from Eq. (1), other variables included control (i) whether companies have offered trainings during the last year, (ii) whether companies organizes the work in teams and (iii) whether there is any form of employee representation. Definition of variables is provided in Table 1. The summary statistics for all variables are provided in Appendix A. Most of our responses in the binary variables have sufficient variation, which is important for producing efficient results. For further details on the distribution of sample among differ sectors of operation, size groups and regions refer to summary statistics in Appendix A.

Two specifications were run (1.a) with PS as a dependent variable and (1.b) with ESO as a dependent variable. Also the extended versions of 1.a and 1.b were run to include additional variables (the extended specification of 1.a is labeled 1.aa and that of 1.b is labeled 1.bb). Diagnostic tests for all specifications indicate that the models and their extensions are performing well indicating good fit.[7] As results in Table 2 show, coefficients are mostly significant, and their magnitude and the direction of the effects are mostly as expected. Though there are few insignificant independent variables, jointly they are statistically significant in all specifications.[8] Columns A and C of Table 2 present the results of the baseline regression, whereas columns B and D present the results of the extended versions. Broadly,

Table 1. Description of Variables – Model 1 (Specifications 1.a; 1.aa; 1.b; 1.bb).

Name of the Variable	Description
Dependent Variable/s	
Employee share ownership schemes	Value of 1 if the employer offers share ownership schemes and 0 otherwise
Profit-sharing schemes	Value of 1 if the employer offers profit sharing schemes and 0 otherwise
Independent Variables	
Proportion of female employees*	Proportion of female employees expressed in percentage of total workforce.
Proportion of high-skilled workers*	Proportion of high-skilled workers expressed in percentage of total workforce.
Small (<50 employees)	1 if the company is small and 0 otherwise
Medium (50–250 employees)	1 if the company is medium and 0 otherwise
Large (>250) (Base category)	1 if the company is large and 0 otherwise
Sector	1 if the company operates in the particular sector and 0 otherwise
1. Manufacturing (Base category)	
2. Electricity	
3. Financial sector	
4. Wholesale and trade	
5. Construction	
6. Real estate and transport	
7. Other services	
Western Europe	1 if a company is from Western Europe and 0 otherwise (base category) (Austria, Belgium, France, Germany, Luxembourg, Netherlands, Ireland, UK)
Iberia region	1 if a company is from Iberian region and 0 otherwise (Spain and Portugal)
Nordic region	1 if a company is from Nordic region and 0 otherwise (Finland, Sweden, Denmark)
Central and Eastern Europe	1 if a company is from Central and Eastern Europe and 0 otherwise (Czech Republic, Hungary, Poland, Slovakia, Slovenia, Romania, Bulgaria)
Southern Europe	1 if a company is from Southern Europe and 0 otherwise (Cyprus, Greece, Italy, Malta)
Baltic region	1 if a company is from Baltic region and 0 otherwise (Estonia, Latvia, Lithuania)
Trainings last year	1 if a company has provided trainings for its employees during the last years and 0 otherwise
Teamwork	1 if a company organizes its work in teams and 0 otherwise
Employee representation	1 if a company has some form of employee representation and 0 otherwise

*Continuous variables.

results seem to suggest that the proportion of high-skilled workers, size of the company, region, and sector of operation seem to explain some of the variation in likelihoods of companies offering both PS and ESO schemes. Similarly, in the extended versions, the effect of representation and HRM practices seems to be highly significant.

Different scenarios were constructed to account for combined effect of different factors that influence the likelihood of a company offering EFP. These scenarios were interpreted in terms of predicted probabilities. A summary of predictions is presented in Table 3 (Panel A and B). In Panel A, the factors from baseline regression were analyzed, whereas in panel B, the other factors were included.[9]

Results for both PS and ESO schemes seem to display similar patterns. Table 3 shows that large companies in the financial sector are more likely to offer both PS and ESO schemes to their employees than small- or medium-sized firms or firms in other sectors of activity. Companies in Nordic countries are also more likely to offer their employees both kinds of EFP schemes. Again, companies in Southern Europe, all else equal, are least likely to offer EFP schemes. The gender ratio of the workforce does not seem to strongly affect the firm's decision to engage in EFP, but the proportion of high-skill employees has a positive effect on this decision. From the extended specification, companies that offer trainings and organize the work in teams display greater likelihood of adopting EFP schemes. Also, the existence of employee representation seems to positively influence the likelihood of introducing EFP schemes.

The second model investigates the likelihood of an employee taking up an EFP scheme. The basic specification of the participation model is as follows:

$$\begin{aligned} P(y=1|x) = \beta_0 &+ \beta_1 \text{ Gender} + \beta_2 \text{ Age} + \beta_3 \text{ Years at the company} \\ &+ \beta_4 \text{ Type of contract} + \beta_5 \text{ Occupation} + \beta_6 \text{ Training} \\ &+ \beta_7 \text{ Size} + \beta_8 \text{ Sector} + \beta_9 \text{ Region} + \beta_{10} \text{ Years} + \varepsilon_i \end{aligned} \tag{2}$$

where the dependent variable is the likelihood that an employee will take the participation schemes offered by the company – either profit sharing (PS) or employee share ownership (ESO) schemes. Independent variables include gender of an employee, age of an employee, years with the enterprise, type of the contract, occupation (ISCO-88), trainings attended by the employee, sector of the company where the respondent works (NACE classification), size of the company (Eurostat; SBS size class), region where the company is based and year dummies. Definition of variables is provided in

Table 2. Results from Model 1; Specification (1.a; 1.aa) Profit-Sharing Schemes and (1.b; 1.bb) Employee Share Ownership Schemes.

Variable	Profit Sharing				Employee Share Ownership			
	A Specification 1.a		B Specification 1.aa		C Specification 1.b		D Specification 1.bb	
	Coefficient	**Marginal effect**	**Coefficient**	**Marginal effect**	**Coefficient**	**Marginal effect**	**Coefficient**	**Marginal effect**
Proportion of female employees	−0.0006	−0.0001	−0.0003	−0.0001	0.0002	0.000	0.00035	0.00003
	(0.185)	(0.185)	(0.504)	(0.504)	(0.797)	(0.797)	(0.617)	(0.617)
Proportion of high-skilled workers	0.0051***	0.0012***	0.0051***	0.0012***	0.0073***	0.0007***	0.00724***	0.0007***
	(0.000)	(0.000)	(0.000)	(0.000)	(0.000)	(0.000)	(0.000)	(0.000)
Medium size	0.2943***	0.0744***	0.1988***	0.0489***	0.2851***	0.0324***	0.1879***	0.0199***
	(0.000)	(0.000)	(0.000)	(0.000)	(0.000)	(0.000)	(0.000)	(0.000)
Large size	0.5236***	0.1464***	0.3643***	0.0967***	0.6124***	0.0880***	0.4522***	0.0578***
	(0.000)	(0.000)	(0.000)	(0.000)	(0.000)	(0.000)	(0.000)	(0.000)
Southern Europe	−0.6824***	−0.1179***	−0.6024***	−0.1072***	−0.2973***	−0.0248***	−0.2156***	−0.0183***
	(0.000)	(0.000)	(0.000)	(0.000)	(0.000)	(0.000)	(0.003)	(0.003)
Baltic region	−0.1320**	−0.0295**	−0.0683	−0.0156	−0.2559**	−0.0217**	−0.1974*	−0.0168*
	(0.011)	(0.011)	(0.194)	(0.194)	(0.002)	(0.002)	(0.018)	(0.018)
Iberia region	−0.0955**	−0.0218**	−0.08117*	−0.0185*	−0.0987	−0.0094	−0.1362*	−0.0122*
	(0.012)	(0.012)	(0.034)	(0.034)	(0.146)	(0.146)	(0.046)	(0.046)
Nordic region	0.2075***	0.0531***	0.1616***	0.0404***	0.3733***	0.0479***	0.3331***	0.0404***
	(0.000)	(0.000)	(0.000)	(0.000)	(0.000)	(0.000)	(0.000)	(0.000)
CEE region	−0.2505***	−0.0549***	−0.2111***	−0.0465***	−0.0087	−0.0009	0.0266	0.0027
	(0.000)	(0.000)	(0.000)	(0.000)	(0.839)	(0.839)	(0.542)	(0.542)
Construction	−0.1167**	−0.0264**	−0.1023*	−0.0231*	0.0778	0.0083	0.0751	0.0078
	(0.004)	(0.004)	(0.012)	(0.012)	(0.167)	(0.167)	(0.188)	(0.188)
Electricity	0.1355	0.0343	0.0996	0.0246	0.3870**	0.0535**	0.3447*	0.0448*
	(0.240)	(0.240)	(0.387)	(0.387)	(0.004)	(0.004)	(0.012)	(0.012)
Financial sector	0.1245*	0.0313*	0.1153	0.0287	0.4338***	0.0615***	0.4288***	0.0588***
	(0.087)	(0.087)	(0.116)	(0.116)	(0.000)	(0.000)	(0.000)	(0.000)
Wholesale	0.0267	0.0064	0.046	0.011	0.058	0.0061	0.0737	0.0075
	(0.406)	(0.406)	(0.158)	(0.158)	(0.212)	(0.212)	(0.118)	(0.118)

p-values in parentheses – $^{*}p<0.05$, $^{**}p<0.01$, $^{***}p<0.001$.

Real estate	−0.0323	−0.0076	−0.0011	−0.0002	0.1277**	0.0140**	0.1529**	0.0164**
	(0.352)	(0.352)	(0.974)	(0.974)	(0.006)	(0.006)	(0.001)	(0.001)
Other services	−0.4989***	−0.0951***	−0.5166***	−0.0968***	−0.3734***	−0.0299***	−0.3973***	−0.0301***
	(0.000)	(0.000)	(0.000)	(0.000)	(0.000)	(0.000)	(0.000)	(0.000)
Trainings last year			0.0990***	0.0231***			0.1561***	0.0150***
			(0.000)	(0.000)			(0.000)	(0.000)
Teamwork			0.1293***	0.0291***			0.2216***	0.0193***
			(0.000)	(0.000)			(0.000)	(0.000)
Employee representation			0.25438***	0.0608***			0.2248***	0.0226***
			(0.000)	(0.000)			(0.000)	(0.000)
Constant term	−1.1066***		−1.3778***		−2.0011***		−2.3722***	
	(0.000)		(0.000)		(0.000)		(0.000)	
Pseudo R2			0.06	0.06	0.08	0.08	0.09	0.09
LR chi2			1024.41***	1024.41***	654.45***	654.45***	734.38***	734.38***
			(0.000)	(0.000)	(0.000)	(0.000)	(0.000)	(0.000)
Number of observations			17491	17491	16804	16804	16804	16804

p-values in parentheses – $*p<0.05$, $**p<0.01$, $***p<0.001$.

Table 3. Probability of a Company Offering an EFP Scheme to Its Employees.

Examples of Characteristics	PS	ESO
Panel A		
1. A large manufacturing company operating in Western Europe with the share of female employees of 37% (mean for the sample) and the share of high-skill employees[a] of 21% (mean for the sample) (Austria, Belgium, France, Germany, Luxembourg, Netherlands, Ireland, UK)	31%	11%
2. Same as 1 but in the financial and insurance sector	35%	21%
3. Same as 1 but in wholesale and trade sector	32%	12%
4. Same as 1 but in Nordic countries (Finland, Sweden, Denmark)	39%	20%
5. Same as 1 but in Central and Eastern Europe (Czech Republic, Hungary, Poland, Slovakia, Slovenia, Romania, Bulgaria)	23%	11%
6. Same as 1 but in the Baltic region (Estonia, Latvia, Lithuania)	26%	7%
7. Same as 1 but in the Iberian Peninsula (Portugal and Spain)	28%	9%[b]
8. Same as 1 but in Southern Europe (Cyprus, Greece, Italy, Malta)	12%	6%
9. Same as 1 but in a medium-sized company	23%	6%
10. Same as 1 but in a small company	15%	3%
11. Same as 1 but with share of female employees at 47% (instead of 31%)	31%	11%
12. Same as 1 but with share of high-skill[a] employees at 31% (instead of 21%)	33%	12%
Panel B		
13. A large manufacturing company operating in Western Europe with the share of female employees of 37% (mean for the sample) and the share of high-skill employees[a] of 21% (mean for the sample) and with the last three variables set to 0	18%	4%
14. Same as 13 but with work organized in teams	21%	6%
15. Same as 13 but has organized trainings during the last year	21%	6%
16. Same as 13 but has some form of employee representation	25%	6%
17. Same as 13 but with work organized in teams, had organized trainings during the last year and has some form of employee representation	33%	12%

Source: Authors' own calculations.
[a]High-skill employees are those with university and higher degrees or qualifications.
[b]This figure is for Spain only (Portugal is excluded from share ownership data in the ECS, 2009).

Table 4. Again two specifications were run (2.a) with PS as a dependent variable and (2.b) with ESO as a dependent variable. The summary statistics for all variables are provided in Appendix C. Most of our responses in the binary variables have sufficient variation, which is important for producing efficient results. For further details on the distribution of sample among differ sectors of operation, size groups, regions, and years refer to summary statistics in Appendix C.

Table 4. Description of Variables – Model 2 (Specifications 2.a and 2.b).

Name of the Variable	Description
Dependent Variable/s	
Employee share ownership schemes	Value of 1 if the employee participates in the employee share ownership schemes and 0 otherwise
Profit sharing schemes	Value of 1 if the employee participates in the profit sharing schemes and 0 otherwise
Independent Variables	
Gender	1 if the employee is male and 0 otherwise
Age[a]	Age of the employee
Years at the company[a]	Years at the company
Type of contract	1 if the employee has a permanent contract and 0 otherwise
Occupation[b]	1 if the employee has managerial position and 0 otherwise (other employees are the base category)
Training	1 if the employee attended a training paid for by the employer and 0 otherwise
Small (<50 employees)	1 if the company is small and 0 otherwise
Medium (50–250 employees)	1 if the company is medium and 0 otherwise
Large (>250)	1 if the company is large and 0 otherwise
Sector	1 if the employer of the responded operates in the particular sector and 0 otherwise
1. B+C	
2. D+E	
3. F	
4. G+I	
5. H	
6. J+L+M	
7. K	
8. N+O+S+T+U	
9. P+Q+R	
Western Europe	1 if a company is from Western Europe and 0 otherwise (base category) (Austria, Belgium, France, Germany, Luxembourg, Netherlands, Ireland, UK)
Iberia region	1 if a company is from Iberian region and 0 otherwise (Spain and Portugal)
Nordic region	1 if a company is from Nordic region and 0 otherwise (Finland, Sweden, Denmark)
Central and Eastern Europe	1 if a company is from Central and Eastern Europe and 0 otherwise (Czech Republic, Hungary, Poland, Slovakia, Slovenia, Romania, Bulgaria)
Southern Europe	1 if a company is from Southern Europe and 0 otherwise (Cyprus, Greece, Italy, Malta)
Baltic region	1 if a company is from Baltic region and 0 otherwise (Estonia, Latvia, Lithuania)
Years	Year dummies controlling for years 2000, 2005 and 2010 (2010 is the base year)

[a]Continuous variables.
[b]Employees whose occupation falls in any of the three major groups (1, 2, and 3 following ISCO-88) were classified as "managerial employees," whereas the rest were classified as "other employees."

Diagnostic tests for all specifications indicate that the models and their extensions are performing well indicating good fit.[10] As results in Table 5 show, coefficients are mostly significant, and their magnitude and the direction of the effects are mostly as expected. Though there are few insignificant independent variables, jointly they are statistically significant in all specifications.[11] Broadly, results based on three rounds of EWCS (2000,

Table 5. Results from Model 2; specification (2.a) profit sharing schemes and (2.b) employee share ownership schemes.

	Model 2.a: Profit-Sharing Schemes		**Model 2.b: Employee Share Ownership Schemes**	
Variable	**Coefficient**	**Marginal effect**	**Coefficient**	**Marginal effect**
Sex	0.2082***	0.0314***	0.2006***	0.0073***
	(0.000)	(0.000)	(0.000)	(0.000)
Age	−0.0032***	−0.0005***	−0.0005	(0.000)
	(0.001)	(0.001)	(0.779)	(0.779)
Years at the company	0.0080***	0.0012***	0.0125***	0.0005***
	(0.000)	(0.000)	(0.000)	(0.000)
Permanent contract	0.2562***	0.0351***	0.1594***	0.0053***
	(0.000)	(0.000)	(0.001)	(0.001)
Management	0.4488***	0.0794***	0.3923***	0.0181***
	(0.000)	(0.000)	(0.000)	(0.000)
B + C	0.2930***	0.0494***	0.2506***	0.0107***
	(0.000)	(0.000)	(0.001)	(0.001)
D + E	0.3672***	0.0706***	0.4597***	0.0276***
	(0.000)	(0.000)	(0.000)	(0.000)
F	0.1195**	0.0194**	0.1784***	0.0077***
	(0.017)	(0.017)	(0.000)	(0.000)
G + I	0.3466***	0.0585***	0.3420***	0.0150***
	(0.000)	(0.000)	(0.000)	(0.000)
H	0.1050*	0.0170*	0.1742*	0.0076*
	(0.063)	(0.063)	(0.072)	(0.072)
K	0.6617***	0.1465***	0.7395***	0.0566***
	(0.000)	(0.000)	(0.000)	(0.000)
J + L + M	0.4205***	0.0805***	0.3749***	0.0195***
	(0.000)	(0.000)	(0.000)	(0.000)
P + Q + R	−0.2838***	−0.0367***	−0.0970	−0.0033
	(0.000)	(0.000)	(0.298)	(0.298)
Small	−0.3502***	−0.0579***	−0.4253***	−0.0187***
	(0.000)	(0.000)	(0.000)	(0.000)
Medium	−0.2188***	−0.0304***	−0.2210***	−0.0071***
	(0.000)	(0.000)	(0.000)	(0.000)
Training	0.3603***	0.0611***	0.2294***	0.0095***

Table 5. (*Continued*)

Variable	Model 2.a: Profit-Sharing Schemes: Coefficient	Model 2.a: Profit-Sharing Schemes: Marginal effect	Model 2.b: Employee Share Ownership Schemes: Coefficient	Model 2.b: Employee Share Ownership Schemes: Marginal effect
	(0.000)	(0.000)	(0.000)	(0.000)
Year_2005	0.4442***	0.0771***	0.4200***	0.0192***
	(0.000)	(0.000)	(0.000)	(0.000)
Year_2010	0.5636***	0.0913***	0.4986***	0.0206***
	(0.000)	(0.000)	(0.000)	(0.000)
Southern Europe	−0.4771***	−0.0544***	−0.3889***	−0.0102***
	(0.000)	(0.000)	(0.000)	(0.000)
Baltic region	−0.0170	−0.0026	−0.4379***	−0.0108***
	(0.660)	(0.660)	(0.000)	(0.000)
Iberia	−0.4618***	−0.0539***	−0.3548***	−0.0097***
	(0.000)	(0.000)	(0.000)	(0.000)
Nordic	0.1906***	0.0319***	−0.0430	−0.0015
	(0.000)	(0.000)	(0.320)	(0.320)
CEE	0.1235***	0.0199***	−0.2689***	−0.0082***
	(0.000)	(0.000)	(0.000)	(0.000)
Constant term	−2.1487***		−2.7812***	
	(0.000)		(0.000)	
Pseudo R2	0.1431		0.1447	
LR chi2	3872.02***		1341.22***	
	(0.000)		(0.000)	
Number of observations	37920		37890	

p-values in parentheses – $^*p<0.05$, $^{**}p<0.01$, $^{***}p<0.001$.

2005, and 2010) seem to suggest that the parameterized factors (gender, qualifications of employees, the nature of their employment contract, size, location, and sector of activity of the enterprise) explain some of the differences in the likelihood of taking up EFP schemes.

Different scenarios were constructed to account for combined effect of different factors that influence the likelihood of an employee taking up EFP schemes. These scenarios were interpreted in terms of predicted probabilities. A summary of predictions is presented in Table 6. All predicted probabilities are statistically significant.

Results indicate that: male employees, employees of larger firms, those working in the financial sector and those that have managerial positions are more likely to participate in EFP schemes. Employees in Nordic countries and Eastern Europe are also more likely to take up EFP offers.

Table 6. Probability of Employees Taking up an EFP Scheme.

Examples of Characteristics	PS	ESO
1. A male employee of average age and experience, with a permanent contract, in a managerial/professional position in a large manufacturing enterprise in Western Europe (Austria, Belgium, France, Germany, Luxembourg, Netherlands, Ireland, United Kingdom)	33%	12%
2. Same as 1 but not in managerial/professional position	19%	6%
3. Same as 1 but a female employee	26%	8%
4. Same as 1 but in the financial and insurance sector	47%	24%
5. Same as 1 but in wholesale and trade sector	35%	13%
6. Same as 1 but in Nordic countries (Finland, Sweden, Denmark)	40%	10%
7. Same as 1 but in Central and Eastern Europe (Czech Republic, Hungary, Poland, Slovakia, Slovenia, Romania, Bulgaria)	38%	7%
8. Same as 1 but in the Baltic region (Estonia, Latvia, Lithuania)	32%	5%
9. Same as 1 but in Southern Europe (Cyprus, Greece, Italy, Malta)	18%	6%
10. Same as 1 but in Iberian Peninsula (Portugal and Spain)	18%	6%
11. Same as 1 but in a medium-sized company	26%	8%
12. Same as 1 but in a small company	21%	5%

Source: Authors' own calculations.

Employees in Southern European countries and the Iberian Peninsula are, all else equal, least likely to take up EFP schemes.

CONCLUSIONS

This paper has presented the incidence and determinants of EFP schemes in EU using a combination of descriptive and multivariate techniques. The distinguishing feature of this analysis is that it focused on both employers' and employees' determinants of offering and taking up EFP schemes, respectively. Descriptive results suggest that there was a significant rise in EFP in the EU-27 in the last decade. Both profit sharing and employee share ownership experienced continuous rise although profit sharing is more widespread. In terms of sector of operation, as predicted, companies in financial sector and in other high-value-added sectors display higher levels of EFP schemes compared to low-value-added sectors. Data suggest that the distribution of EFP schemes was an almost monotonic increase with size of the firm. The three rounds of EWCS clearly demonstrate that the proportion of employees participating in both ESO and PS schemes has grown in almost all countries. Due to data limitation, our analysis lacks a dynamic assessment of the relationship between parameters. Therefore, we are inclined to consider the results as indicative. However, the robustness of results is a strong indication of their reliability.

In terms of the likelihood of companies offering EFP schemes, empirical results show that large companies in the financial sector are more likely to offer EFP schemes to their employees than small- or medium-sized firms or firms in other sectors of activity. Companies in Nordic countries are also more likely to offer their employees both kinds of EFP schemes. Again, companies in Southern Europe, all else equal, are least likely to offer EFP schemes. The gender ratio of the workforce does not seem to strongly affect the firm's decision to engage in EFP, but the proportion of high-skill employees has a positive effect on this decision. Companies that offer trainings and organize the work in teams display greater likelihood of adopting EFP schemes. Also, the existence of employee representation seems to positively influence the likelihood of introducing EFP schemes.

In terms of likelihood of employees taking up EFP schemes, the estimation results, male employees, employees of larger firms, those working in the financial sector and those who have managerial positions are more likely to participate in EFP schemes. Employees in Nordic countries and Eastern Europe are also more likely to take up EFP offers. Employees in Southern European countries and the Iberian Peninsula are, all else equal, least likely to take up EFP schemes. In general, the relationships described in previous sections are maintained in both models and in all specifications.

NOTES

1. The bulk of the empirical evidence on EFP in a variety of countries and variety of settings have concluded that EFP has a positive influence on the performance of companies. For a review see (Blasi, Kruse, & Bernstein, 2003; Freeman, 2007; Kaarsemaker, 2006).

2. Some of these outcomes may of course be achieved through other incentive mechanisms based on individual effort, for example, piece rates (i.e., gain sharing, which is not discussed in this study). But, compared to EFP, these mechanisms are expensive. They require information on individual effort, impose central monitoring, which is difficult, especially in large firms, and do not encourage co-operation and innovation (Chen, 2009; Pendleton, 2006).

3. There are, however, problems of definition. Especially the definition of profit sharing in the EWCS questionnaire is too broad and does not correspond to the formal definition of genuine profit-sharing plans. In some countries, the EWCS

definition can include performance-related pay, bonuses, fringe benefits and even the 13th salary. Additionally, the distribution of these additional payments is often not linked to pre-defined criteria, so that it cannot be qualified as a plan. For that reason, the level of profit sharing according to EWCS is exceptionally high in almost all countries, but it does not reflect the actual situation.

4. For details see PEPPER IV report.

5. To some extent, this dynamics is reflected in the CRANET Surveys, which show that between 1999, 2005 and 2010, the proportion of employees to whom broad-based EFP schemes were offered has generally increased. For further details, see PEPPER IV report.

6. In calculating weighted averages, the population of each country is used as its weight.

7. See section B.1 ECS in Appendix B for goodness of fit tests for all specifications.

8. LR statistic for all specifications is presented at the bottom of Table 2.

9. Calculations of predicted probabilities are done using the **margins** command (introduced in STATA 11). All predicted probabilities are statistically significant.

10. See section B.2 EWCS in Appendix B for goodness of fit tests for all specifications.

11. LR statistic for all specifications is presented at the bottom of Table 5.

REFERENCES

Ben-Ner, A., & Jones, D. C. (1995). Employee participation, ownership and productivity: A theoretical framework. *Industrial Relations*, *34*(4), 532–555.

Blasi, J. R., Kruse, D. L., & Bernstein, A. (2003). *In the company of owners: The truth about stock options (And why every employee should have them)*. New York, NY: Basic Books.

Bryson, A., & Freeman, R. (2007). *Doing the right thing? Does fair share capitalism improve workplace performance?* Department of Trade and Industry Employment Relations Research Series, Number 81.

Bryson, A., & Freeman, R. (2010). How does shared capitalism affect economic performance in the UK?. In D. Kruse, R. Freeman, & J. Blasi (Eds.), *Shared capitalism at work: Employee ownership, profit and gain sharing, and broad-based stock options* (pp. 201–224). University of Chicago Press.

Cadsby, C. B., Song, F., & Francis, T. (2007). Sorting and incentive effects of pay for performance: An experimental investigation. *Academy of Management Journal*, *50*(2), 387–405.

Cheadle, A. (1989). Explaining patterns of profit-sharing activity. *Industrial Relations*, *28*, 398–400.

Chen, H. L. (2009). Investment opportunities and the relation between equity value and employees' bonus. *Journal of Business Finance and Accounting*, *30*, 941–973.

D'Art, D. (1992). *Economic democracy and financial participation: A comparative study*. London: Routledge.

Festing, M., Groening, Y., Kabst, R., & Weber, W. (1999). Financial participation in Europe: Determinants and outcomes. *Economic and Industrial Democracy*, *20*, 295–329.

Freeman, S. (2007). *Effects of ESOP adoption and employee ownership: Thirty years of research and experience*. Working Paper No. 7. Graduate Division, School of Arts and Sciences, Center for Organizational Dynamics, University of Pennsylvania.

Holmstrom, B. (1979). Moral hazard and observability. *Bell Journal of Economics*, *10*(1), 74–91.

Jones, D. C., Kalmi, P., & Kato, T. (2010). *HRM practices and firm performance: Evidence from finnish manufacturing*. Working Paper No. 485). Aalto University School of Economics.

Jones, D. C., & Pliskin, J. (1989). British evidence on the employee effects of profit sharing. *Industrial Relations*, *28*(2), 276–298.

Kaarsemaker, E. (2006). *Employee ownership and human resource management. A theoretical and empirical treatise with a digression on the Dutch context*. Doctoral Dissertation. Radboud University Nijmegen.

Kaarsemaker, E., Pendleton, A., & Poutsma, E. (2009). *Employee share ownership plans: A review*. (Working Paper). University of York, The York Management School.

Klein, K. J. (1987). Employee stock ownership and employee attitudes: A test of three models. *Journal of Applied Psychology*, *72*(2), 319–332.

Kruse, D. (1996). Why do firms adopt profit-sharing and employee ownership plans. *British Journal of Industrial Relations*, *34*(4), 515–538.

Kruse, D., Blasi, J. & Freeman, R., eds. (2010). *Shared capitalism at work: Employee ownership, profit and gain sharing, and broad-based stock options*. Chicago, IL: University of Chicago Press.

Kruse, D., Blasi, J., & Park, R. (2008). *Shared capitalism in the US economy: Prevalence, characteristics, and employee views of financial participation in enterprises*. Paper presented at NBER/ Russell Sage Foundation conference. October, New York.

McNabb, R., & Whitfield, K. (1998). The impact of financial participation and employee involvement on financial performance. *Scottish Journal of Political Economy*, *26*(1AQ: Please provide page no. in McNabb, R., & Whitfield, K. (1998).).

Oxera. (2007a). *Tax advantaged employee share schemes: Analysis of productivity effects Report 1: Productivity measured using turnover. HM Revenue and Customs Research Report 32.*

Oxera. (2007b). *Tax advantaged employee share schemes: Analysis of productivity effects Report 2: Productivity measured using gross value added*. HM Revenue and Customs Research Report 33.

Pendleton, A. (1997). Characteristics of workplaces with financial participation: Evidence from the workplace industrial relations survey. *Industrial Relations Journal*, *28*, 103–119.

Pendleton, A. (2001). *Employee ownership, participaton and governance. A study of ESOPs in the UK*. London: Routledge.

Pendleton, A. (2006). Incentives, monitoring, and employee stock ownership plans: New evidence and interpretations. *Industrial Relations*, *45*(4), 753–775.

Pendleton, A., Poutsma, E., Brewster, C., & Van Ommeren, J. (2001). *Employee share ownership and profit sharing in the European Union*. Dublin: European Foundation for the Improvement of Living and Working Conditions.

Pendleton, A., & Robinson, A. (2010). Employee stock ownership, involvement, and productivity: An interaction-based approach. *Industrial and Labor Relations Review*, *64*(1), 3–29.

Pierce, J., Rubenfeld, S. A., & Morgan, S. (1991). Employee ownership: A conceptual model of process and effects. *Academy of Management Review*, *16*, 121–144.

Poole, M. (1989). *The origins of economic democracy*. London: Routledge.

Poutsma, E., & Bramm, G. (2011). *Financial participation plans and company financial performance. Evidence from a Dutch longitudinal panel.* Paper for the 8th International Workshop on Human Resource Management 12–13 May 2011, Seville.

Poutsma, E., & de Nijs, W. (2003). Broad based employee financial participation in the EU. *International Journal of Human Resource Management*, *14*(6), 863–892.

Poutsma, E., & Huijgen, F. (1999). European diversity in the use of participation schemes. *Economic and Industrial Democracy*, *20*(2), 197–224.

Ramsay, H. (1977). Cycles of control: Worker participation in sociological and historical perspective. *Sociology*, *11*, 481–506.

Robinson, A. W., & Wilson, N. (2006). Employee financial participation and productivity: An empirical reappraisal. *British Journal of Industrial Relations*, *44*(1), 31–50.

Rousseau, D., & Shperling, Z. (2003). Pieces of the action: Ownership and the changing employment relationship. *Academy of Management Review*, *28*, 553–570.

Weitzman, M. L., & Kruse, D. (1990). Profit sharing and productivity. In A. Blinder (Ed.), *Paying for productivity: A look at the evidence* (pp. 95–139). Washington, DC: Brookings Institution.

Welz, C., & Macias, E. F. (2007). *Financial participation of employees in the European Union: Much ado about nothing?* Report, European Foundation for the Improvement of Living and Working Conditions.

APPENDIX A: SUMMARY STATISTICS OF ECS DATA USED IN MODEL 1

Variable	Fraction 0.00	Fraction 1.00	Mean	Std. Dev.	Min.	Max.
Proportion of female employees			36.99	28.62	0.00	100.00
Proportion of high-skilled workers			21.09	26.47	0.00	100.00
Small	44.21	55.79	0.56	0.50	0.00	1.00
Medium	71.91	28.09	0.28	0.45	0.00	1.00
Large	83.87	16.13	0.16	0.37	0.00	1.00
Southern Europe	91.65	8.35	0.08	0.28	0.00	1.00
Western Europe	57.98	42.02	0.42	0.49	0.00	1.00
Baltic region	94.09	5.91	0.06	0.24	0.00	1.00
Iberia region	88.37	11.63	0.12	0.32	0.00	1.00
Nordic region	88.16	11.84	0.12	0.32	0.00	1.00
CEE region	79.74	20.26	0.20	0.40	0.00	1.00
Construction	87.59	12.41	0.12	0.33	0.00	1.00
Electricity	99.16	0.84	0.01	0.09	0.00	1.00
Financial sector	97.67	2.33	0.02	0.15	0.00	1.00
Wholesale and trade	78.23	21.77	0.22	0.41	0.00	1.00
Real estate and transport	83.93	16.07	0.16	0.37	0.00	1.00
Other services	90.07	9.93	0.10	0.30	0.00	1.00
Manufacturing	63.34	36.66	0.37	0.48	0.00	1.00
Trainings last year	39.08	60.92	0.61	0.49	0.00	1.00
Teamwork	15.38	84.62	0.85	0.36	0.00	1.00
Employee representation	55.22	44.78	0.45	0.50	0.00	1.00

APPENDIX B: GOODNESS OF FIT TESTS

B.1 ECS

Model 1.

	Specification 1. a	Specification 1. aa	Specification 1. b	Specification 1. bb
Number of observations	17,697	16,804	17,491	16,804
Number of groups	4	4	4	4
Hosmer-Lemeshow chi2 (8)	3.82	0.74	1.16	1.92
Prob > chi2	0.1483	0.6892	0.5601	0.3823

The respective *p* values of Hosmer and Lemeshow's goodness-of-fit test indicate that the model specifications fit the data well.

B.2 EWCS

Model 2.

	Specification 2.a	Specification 2.b
Number of observations	37,920	37,890
Number of groups	4	4
Hosmer-Lemeshow chi2(8)	2.40	1.83
Prob > chi2	0.3019	0.4008

The respective *p* values of Hosmer and Lemeshow's goodness-of-fit test indicate that the model specifications fit the data well.

APPENDIX C: SUMMARY STATISTICS OF EWCS DATA USED IN MODEL 2

Variable	Fraction		Mean	Std. Dev.	Min.	Max.
	0	1				
Sex	0.48	0.52	0.54	0.50	0	1
Age	–	–	38.73	11.76	15	99
Years at the company	–	–	8.01	8.70	0	60
Permanent	0.24	0.76	0.79	0.41	0	1
Training	0.75	0.25	0.28	0.45	0	1
B_C	0.74	0.26	0.24	0.43	0	1
D_E	0.98	0.02	0.02	0.12	0	1
F	0.91	0.09	0.09	0.29	0	1
G_I	0.73	0.27	0.28	0.45	0	1
H	0.95	0.05	0.05	0.22	0	1
K	0.96	0.04	0.05	0.21	0	1
J_L_M	0.94	0.06	0.08	0.28	0	1
N_O_S_T_U	0.87	0.13	0.09	0.28	0	1
P_Q_R	0.92	0.08	0.09	0.29	0	1
Small	0.33	0.67	0.67	0.47	0	1
Medium	0.80	0.20	0.20	0.40	0	1
Large	0.87	0.13	0.13	0.34	0	1
PS	0.89	0.11	0.11	0.32	0	1
ESO	0.97	0.03	0.03	0.16	0	1
Year_2000	0.72	0.28	0.28	0.45	0	1
Year_2005	0.71	0.29	0.29	0.46	0	1
Year_2010	0.57	0.43	0.43	0.50	0	1
Southern	0.91	0.09	0.07	0.26	0	1
Baltic	0.90	0.10	0.06	0.24	0	1
Western	0.65	0.35	0.48	0.50	0	1
Iberia	0.90	0.10	0.10	0.29	0	1
Nordic	0.88	0.12	0.12	0.33	0	1
CEE	0.76	0.24	0.16	0.37	0	1
Management	0.75	0.25	0.25	0.44	0	1
Worker	0.25	0.75	0.75	0.44	0	1

CHAPTER 9

FINANCIAL AND DECISION-MAKING PARTICIPATION OF MARGINALIZED SMALL FARMERS THROUGH THE PRAGATHI BANDHU MODEL IN INDIA

Sudha Kornginnaya

ABSTRACT

Purpose – *To describe the Pragathi Bandhu Groups (PBG) Model and portray the performance of PBG farmers encouraged by their financial and decision-making participation in micro financing and labor sharing, as well as to analyze the factors that influenced participation of small farmers in PBG.*

Design/methodology/approach – *The empirical study is confined to the small farmers and laborers of PBG functioning in the coastal districts of Karnataka State in India. The study is conducted in Belthangady and Bantwal Taluks of Dakshina Kannada (DK) Districts-Udupi taluk of Udupi District in the State of Karnataka. Primary data from 100 farmer members, selected at random in each of the Taluks, is collected through*

Sharing Ownership, Profits, and Decision-making in the 21st Century
Advances in the Economic Analysis of Participatory & Labor-Managed Firms, Volume 14, 217–258

ISSN: 0885-3339/doi:10.1108/S0885-3339(2013)0000014010

personal interview by administering semi-structured interview schedules and open discussion. In addition, the data on the functions and the performance of PBG in the State of Karnataka in India are also collected from the official records of Shri Kshetra Dharmasthala Rural Development Project (SKDRDP) and their field-level functionaries through informal discussions. Factor analysis is performed with principal component analysis followed by Varimax rotation to analyze the factors that influenced participation of small farmers in PBG.

Findings – *Results show that the implementation of PBG Model, through the collective participation of small farmers in micro financing, free labor sharing, financial and decision-making activities underlying the functions of PBG Model, has helped them to achieve robust performance in terms of increased savings mobilization, loan utilization, and value of free labor sharing and acres of land brought under cultivation with the help of irrigation facilities created by them. The factor analysis has derived four factors that influenced the participation of farmers in PBG (agriculture development, financial participation, capacity building, and other benefits) which explain 63.701 of total factor variance.*

Practical implications – *The findings of this paper can benefit the small farmers and laborers in replicating the PBG Model and its initiatives that address shortages of labor and credit, as well as the high cost of labor, particularly in the unorganized sector in the agrarian economy.*

Originality/value – *The insights offered are likely to be beneficial to the distressed small farmers, development agencies, and agriculture policy makers to solve the agrarian crisis caused due to shortages of labor and farm credit.*

Keywords: Small farmers; Pragathi Bandhu groups; financial participation; free labor sharing; agriculture development; decision making

JEL classifications: J43; Q14; P32

INTRODUCTION

India is a land of 490 million small farmers with an average land size of 1.3 hectares. They are the largest producers of food in India, assuring food security, rural employment, and the generation of revenue and foreign currency through exports. However, small farmers face a multitude of barriers in eking out a livelihood. Debt and drought have emaciated them, causing a loss of confidence in the viability of their livelihood. Lack of access to formal channels of credit has made them rely on money lenders requiring very high interest rates, leading to their high suicide rate. Thus, India lost 256,913 farmers over the past 16 years due to farm suicides, and around 100 million farmers are living on less than a dollar per day (Yashwanth, 2010).

Lack of employment opportunities both within agriculture and outside it, low profitability, high cost of production, lack of rain and irrigational facilities, and other problems have compelled resource poor farmers to quit their traditional livelihood activity, resulting in a large scale exodus of farmers to the urban areas (Viswanathan, Thapa, Routray, & Ahmed, 2012). Forty percent of small farmers are being forced to leave the agriculture and are migrating to towns and cities, causing a labor shortage in agriculture (Yashwanth, 2010). During the last decade, in Punjab 200,000 small holders have opted out of farming and 22% of them joined the rank of agricultural or other laborers (Singh, Singh, & Kindra, 2009). Thus, increasing rural–urban migration, feminization of agriculture, high cost of labor, growing landlessness, aging farm population with dislike for farming among youngsters, and the multidimensional challenges confronting small holders have jeopardized the future of smallholder farming as a livelihood (Chand, Laksmi Prasanna, & Singh, 2011; Rawal, 2008; Vepa, 2005; Vishwanathan et al., 2012).

Against this backdrop, this paper describes the Pragathi Bandhu groups (PBG) Model and portrays the performance of smallholder farmers encouraged by their financial and decision-making participation in micro financing and free labor sharing underlying the PBG Model, and analyses the factors influencing their participation in PBG. The results of this research will contribute to the body of knowledge on the application of the team-based PBG Model that acts as a means for achieving agricultural transformation by addressing the problem of shortages of labor and credit. This is the first such study on the PBG Model on the facet of financial and decision-making participation in micro financing and labor sharing of small farmers.

The rest of the paper is organized as follows: The second section provides a literature review. The third section describes the PBG Model. The fourth section explains the research method. The fifth section presents the portrait of PBG Participation. The sixth section outlines the factors that influenced the participation of PBGs. The seventh section presents the policy implications and the eighth section concludes the paper.

LITERATURE REVIEW

Overview of Current Status of Small Farmers and Agriculture Workers in India

According to India's Planning Commission's estimates of poverty in the work segment, nearly 50% of agricultural laborers are poor and 40% of other laborers are below the poverty line. This estimation is based on the spending on health, education, and calorie intake (*The Hindu Business Line*, 2012). Based on the Tendulkar Committee norm, a minimum 0.8 hectares of land area is needed to keep a farm family above the poverty line, if this family lives only on agricultural income. This implies that 62% of farmers in India, who own less than 0.8 hectares of cultivable land, fall under poverty if they do not get income from nonfarm sources. This figure is going to rise further with the ongoing division of landholdings (Agarwal, 2011; Bhalla & Singh, 2009; Chand et al., 2011; Dhingra, 2011).

Since the early 1990, the process of globalization and the structural transformation from agriculture- to services-led growth have contributed to the agrarian crisis through decreased public investment in agriculture and the stagnation of production, productivity, and incomes of small and marginal farmers. Structural transformation has not helped to move any sizable population of cultivators to nonagricultural occupations. The share of agriculture and allied sectors in the gross domestic product (GDP) has come down significantly in the last 60 years, now standing at less than 20% whereas more than 50% of the workforce is still engaged in agriculture (Chand et al., 2011; Kannan & Pushpangadan, 1988; Mishra & Puri, 2011). The imbalances in structural change in output and occupations, the disparity between per worker income in agriculture and nonagriculture, and the slowdown in the growth rate of agriculture after the post-reform period have all put serious strain on the income and livelihood of smallholders (Chand et al., 2011; Vishwanathan et al., 2012).

National Sample Survey Office (NSSO, 2004–2005) data show that more than 40% of rural households are landless and inequality in landownership has worsened. On the one hand, increasing urbanization and industrialization, acquisition of land for dams, roads and other projects, and land purchases by corporations have caused severity of landlessness. On the other, the rising cost of farming and perennial indebtedness have caused distressed farmers to losing their land that had been used as collateral for borrowing (Basole & Basu, 2011; Dogra, 2007; Vishwanathan et al., 2012).

Some of the causes for the marginalization of the farming community are lack of organization among farmers, lack of connection with the market, repeated crop failures, absence of adequate social support infrastructure, inadequate and costly institutional credit, exploitation in the marketing process, high expenditures on health, lack of nonfarm sources of income (Dev, 2005; ILO, 2007), and weak bargaining power, resulting in lower prices received by the small farmers (Agrawal, 2000).

The increasing rural–urban migration and large scale retreat of young people from the farming sector have compelled women and the elderly to take farming responsibilities. Feminization of agriculture has posed many challenges to the women as they have poor access to land, productive assets, technology, training, and credit. In India, about 33% of cultivators and 47% of agricultural workers are women (Vepa, 2005). Further, almost 65% of all women workers and 83% rural female workers in India are women (NSSO, 2004–2005).

From the last decade, distressed farmers' segment has been a cause of concern to the Government of India. The loan waiver program by the government to relieve their debt has helped only 22.5% of such farmers, who have borrowed from the formal institutional credit system and have holdings up to five acres of land. This neglected 75% of farmers who have resorted to informal channels Kumar & Paramanand, 2010) were a considerable part of the lot who committed suicides. The relief compensation given by the government did not reach their families. The government support to farmers in terms of minimum support prices has also not provided effective relief.

India has seen over a quarter of a million farmers' suicides between 1995 and 2010, which underscores the growing agrarian crisis and its manifestation in economic and social dimensions. Maharashtra, Karnataka, Andhra Pradesh, Madhya Pradesh, Punjab, and Chhattisgarh are the most affected states in India. Analysis of the 2010 data shows that the majority of the suicide victims are in the age group of 30–59, and around 15% suicide victims are women members (Jodhka, 2006; Mohanty & Shroff, 2004; Sainath, 2011; Sarma, 2004; Shah, 2012; Singh, 2006; Bharathi, 2011).

Thus, a large body of extant literature reveals that the smallholder agriculture segment faces multidimensional challenges on account of demographic, socioeconomic, structural, and institutional factors. An analysis of these factors will help in identifying the purpose and locating the space under which the PBG Model can be applied at the grassroot level to enable collective action of small farmers; the current study is an attempt in this regard.

Prior Studies on the Development Strategies for Marginalized Farmers and Agricultural Laborers

A plethora of studies were undertaken on the various government-initiated development strategies/programs adopted for poverty alleviation and self-reliance of farmers and agriculture workers. Several official and individual scholars have conducted evaluation studies of various government measures implemented under the different plans including: minimum wages, abolition of bonded labor, providing land to landless laborers, provision of housing sites and asset creation, special agencies for development (Small Farmers Development Agency, Marginal Farmers and Agriculture Laborers Development Agencies), micro credit through self-help group (SHG) formation, the Mahatma Gandhi National Rural Employment Guarantee Scheme, creation of alternative sources of employment, Self-Employment Programs that provide productive assets financed by subsidies and credit (Swarnajayanti Gram Swarozgar Yojana), Wage Employment Programs (National Food For Work Program, Sampoorna Grameen Rozgar Yojana), and the National Social Assistance Program. The findings of the evaluation studies of these programs have revealed that the beneficiaries have not significantly benefitted in terms of increase in income, employment, and asset formation for many reasons, including lack of participation, structural imbalance, a dependency culture of the poor on the government subsidy, planning and implementation deficiencies, in-built limitations of the strategies, weak institutions and faulty National Policies, poor quality delivery systems, and corruption (Agrawal, 2000; Agarwal, 2011; Chand et al., 2011; Chand, Raju, & Pandey, 2007; Datt & Ravallion, 2010; Dhingra, 2011; GOI, 2008; Gopalappa & Rao, 2004; Hirway, 1985; ILO, 2007; Mishra & Puri, 2011; Pandey, Chand, & Raju, 2007; Parthasarathy, 1985; Rath, 1985; Srivastava, 1999).

Some of the scholars have discussed the efficacy of the emerging practices that help small farmers in terms of direct linkage to the markets (domestic and export) through private agencies, NGOs, and Parastatal agencies like Cooperative Marketing Federation, linkage to the supermarket chain growth, and interface with corporate agribusinesses through contract farming (Acharya, 1997; Dev, 2005; Kumar, 2006; Singh, 2012). However, the studies have also revealed that small holders are excluded from the commercialization, vertical coordination of agriculture, and contract farming due to reasons like ineffectiveness of formal contracts and their enforcement, high transaction costs, tighter control, quality standards, business attitudes and ethics, discriminatory practices, and the weak bargaining power of small growers (Kirsten & Sartorius, 2002; Kumar, 2006; Narayanan, 2012; Singh, 2005).

A few of the empirical studies on the participatory strategies have examined the success factors of farmers' collective action. The success factors include:

(a) The formation of farmers' collectivities for the purpose of joint approach in agriculture production, marketing, group farming, joint investment, and labor and skill pooling. The factors attributed to their success are voluntariness, participatory decision making, group affinity, and equitable benefit sharing. For instance, formation of agricultural cooperatives, collective tea cultivation in West Bengal, Sangam self-help groups of Deccan Development Society in Andhra Pradesh (Ahluwalia, 1990; Agarwal, 2010; Dev, 1967; Dwivedi, 1982; Ganesan, 1969; Goyal, 1966; Hajela, 1976; Krishnaswami, 1976; Lin, 1990; Neb, 1998; Puri, 1979; Swain, 1985; UNRISD, 1975; Vaidyanathan, 2013);
(b) Labor Banks that tackle the labor shortage problems faced by the farmers, which is practiced in Kerala (Kannan, 2011);
(c) Participation of Kudumbashree self-help groups (state sponsored) in Kerala in the lease land group farming on fallow land termed as "Harithashree" enabling them to earn income and contribute to agricultural production (Jacob, 2009; Kenneth & Seena, 2012; Nidheesh, 2009; Oommen, 2007; Reed & Reed, 2013);
(d) The organized rights-based movement of tribal farmers and farm laborers for the food and land in Kerala (Sreerekha, 2012) and Punjab (Bharathi, 2011);
(e) Collective farming and occupational diversification strategy (Jodhka, 2006, 2012; Lindberg, 2005);
(f) Collective action of backward groups in Joint Forest Management and Watershed Development Programs in the State of Andhra Pradesh (Chopra, 2002; D'Silva & Pai, 2003); and
(g) Inclusive participatory communication strategies that empower the poor to take their own decisions and actions, such as in the Kheda Communication Project, Application of Services and Technology for Rural Areas (ASTRA) (Jagadish, 1995; Joshi & Bhatia, 1995; Tucker, 1999).

The above-mentioned collective participatory approaches sponsored either by the state or nongovernmental organizations have ensured poor farmers access to land, credit, and extension activities and infrastructure, and provided greater diversity of skills and knowledge, good bargaining power and decision making, social capital, enhanced productivity, and viable livelihoods. However, geographical confinement, lack of funds and continued support from the promoting agencies, lack of trust within communities and consequent noncooperation of the members, policy distortions, mismanagement of funds, interference of vested interest, lack of accountability and factions are some of the causes for the improper functioning of the collective actions (Agarwal, 2010; Agvekar & Borude, 1992; Chopra, 2002; D'Silva & Pai, 2003; Krishnaswami, 1976; Shah, 1996).

Some scholars have also conducted studies on the role played by the Shri Kshetra Dharmasthala Rural Development Project (SKDRDP) on different dimensions like implementation of the PBG Model (Chatterjee, 2012; Manjunath, 2010), micro financing activities (Babu & Sahu, 2007), and inclusive growth (D'Souza, Chidananda, Udayachandra, & Devaraja, 2012).

Based on the literature review that describes the range of measures initiated for the development of small holders and farm workers and their effectiveness, it is apparent that there are few studies on the participatory strategies that address the problems of shortages of labor and credit. Empirical studies have been conducted on the functioning of self-help groups of women in micro credit and lease land farming, but there has been a dearth of research with empirical evidence on the collective action of self-help groups formed predominantly by men for free labor sharing and micro credit leading to the financial and decision-making participation of disadvantaged farmers. Hence, this study attempts to bridge the gap and intends to analyze the factors influencing the participation of PBG farmers.

PRAGATHI BANDHU MODEL (PARTNERS FOR PROGRESS)

The Pragathi Bandhu Model based on the concept of labor sharing was evolved by the SKDRDP under the leadership of Dr. D. Veerendra Heggade in Dakshina Kannada (DK) District of Karnataka State in India. It was developed in the year 1991 and linked to a micro credit program in 1995. The PBG Model is now approved by the National Bank for Agriculture and Rural Development (NABARD) and adopted for the implementation of Joint Liability Group (JLG) for MFI credit. The model has been replicated in other states like Bihar, Uttar Pradesh, and Himachal Pradesh.

PBGs are self-help groups comprising five to eight small and marginal farmers in each group, who own from a few cents to 2 hectares of land in the same village. The members of the group not only participate in the group transactions, but also help each other in times of crisis. PBGs are predominantly formed by men although a few women members also join the group. The important features of PBGs are:

1. Participating in compulsory labor sharing for individual as well as community works.
2. Organizing and empowering small and marginal farmers.
3. Strengthening financial participation leading to secured livelihoods.
4. Developing the habit of savings and thrift.
5. Accessing micro credit facilities required for land development and agriculture.
6. Developing self-confidence, self-reliance, and leadership among the members.
7. Transferring the governance to the village level federations of SHGs (SKDRDP, 2009).

Functions

Following are the functions of PBG members:

Planning farm activities: Members prepare a five-year plan called an "Investment Plan" or "Farm Plan" along with budget estimates based on their landholdings and cropping patterns. Each plan has a long-term component to be implemented over a period of five years and a short-term component for the current year. Members are trained by field-level functionaries in the effective implementation of the vision plan through the judicious utilization of the credit. Five elements are given due importance while preparing the plan: (1) land development (levelling, fencing, cleaning), (2) irrigation development, (3) agriculture development (integrated farming – from mono cropping to multiple cropping by using intensive practices and organic inputs), (4) ancillary activities (dairy, poultry, beekeeping, sericulture, floriculture), and (5) infrastructure development (house repair, mechanization, improving farm infrastructure).

Labor sharing: The group meets once a week and works on each individual member's farm on a rotational, participatory labor sharing basis free of cost. They decide the date, place, work schedule, and the task to be performed. On the day of the labor sharing, hospitality becomes the host's responsibility. Group members usually work for 8–9 hours on the labor-sharing day to complete the planned task.

Participation in Micro Financing and Decision Making

After the group formation, the PBG members get trained by the field functionaries on aspects like conducting meetings, writing accounts, lending policies, and handling funds which gets them adapted to fund flow management. The extent of the financial and decision-making participation of the members and their repaying capacity indicates the grades of their group which in turn specify their eligibility for getting loans from the project. Only those groups with grade A or B are entitled to get a loan. They record their weekly meetings, the decisions they have taken, the labor sharing effected, and the extent of their participation in savings and the credit, which will be verified by the heads of the groups, their representatives in the federations, and the project officials.

The group members save (₹10 or more) on a weekly basis and thus build a corpus fund and take up financial transaction among themselves. Their additional financial requirements are addressed through SKDRDP's financial assistance called as "Pragathinidhi," repayable within three to five years on a weekly installment basis. The groups which have completed 12 weeks of successful savings can apply for Pragathinidhi. Members can borrow initially to the extent of ₹10,000 per member, which will be increased based on their need. Members can obtain loans from the group based on their savings and the purpose set out in the investment plan. For instance, a member can obtain up to ₹25,000 or 10 times the savings for emergency purposes, and ₹50,000 or 20 times the savings for taking up income generating activities or for infrastructure development purposes.

The group generates the loan applications after discussing with the members and sends the same for the approval of the village level federation of the PBGs, which constitutes a subcommittee for recommending the loan. SKDRDP will finally sanction the loan based on the recommendation of the subcommittee (SKDRDP, 2010). Thus, the active participation of the farmers in planning, financial, and decision making both at the grassroots level and at the federation level is paramount for achieving the targeted agriculture development specified in the investment plan.

Participation in Capacity Building Initiatives

The members visit various research stations, model farms, and universities, and attend various extension programs that include farmers' field schools, training camps, annual farmers' fair, study tours, and workshops that expose them to agricultural technology and better farming practices (SKDRDP, 2009).

RESEARCH METHODOLOGY

This study is descriptive and exploratory in nature and is based on an empirical survey conducted during 2010–2012 (March). Both primary and secondary sources of data are used in the study. The study is confined to the small farmers and laborers of PBG functioning in the coastal districts of Karnataka State in India.

On the basis of the inventory of literature and the data obtained from the Office of the Sub-Registrar of Charitable Trusts, Government of Karnataka, Belthangady Taluk, DK District, the researcher has chosen Shri Kshetra Dharmasthala Rural Development Project, popularly known as SKDRDP, registered under the Charitable Trust Act of 1920 in the year 1991. It is located in DK District on the Western Coast of the State of Karnataka. The SKDRDP encompasses all aspects of enriching the rural life. The study is conducted in Belthangady and Bantwal Taluks of DK District-Udupi taluk of Udupi District which has diverse socioeconomic conditions, geophysical features, and demographic factors. These factors affect the working of the SKDRDP that influence their efforts in developing the PBG farmer members.

The purpose of the study is to understand how the PBG Model facilitates financial and decision-making participation of farmer members rather than to build up any estimates. Hence, a cross-section sample of group of farmers is selected at random in each of the Taluks. However, care was taken to select representative sample to include gender, literacy, age, occupation, and location. A total of 100 farmer members were interviewed.

Primary data from the PBGs functioning in the two districts are collected through personal interviews that included semi-structured interview schedules and open discussion. In addition, organizational data of SKDRDP relating to the current state of PBG initiatives and their coverage in the State of Karnataka are also collected from official records that include annual reports, balance sheets, bye-laws, manuals, newsletters, and magazines, and from personal interviews with the field-level functionaries of SKDRDP. Observation technique was employed wherever live demonstration was accessible. Statistical methods such as scaling technique, percentages, averages, chi-square, correlation, factor analysis, and

Table 1. KMO & Bartlett's Test.

Kaiser–Meyer–Olken Measure of Sampling Adequacy		0.807
Bartlett's Test of Sphericity	Approx. Chi-square	341.357
	Degrees of freedom	120
	Significance	0.00

Note: $p < 0.001$ V.H.S.

nonparametric statistics are used in the analysis, interpretation, and presentation of the data.

Analysis

During the field survey an attempt is made to probe into experience-based perceptions of the participant members toward PBG initiatives. The study explores the important factors (variables) that influenced the farmers' participation in PBG Model, having a bearing on their financial and decision-making participation. The important variables (16) are coded with a five-point Likert scale. In order to test the suitability of the data for factor analysis, the correlation matrix is computed and examined. The results indicated that there are enough correlations to justify the application of factor analysis. Data are tested by Bartlett's test of sphericity and Kaiser–Meyer–Olkin (KMO) measure of sampling adequacy (MSA) (Table 1). The KMO measure value for individual variables is found to be sufficiently high for all variables. Overall MSA is found to be 0.807 (>0.50) that indicates (values between 0.50 and 1.00) the appropriateness of the sample. Bartlett's test of sphericity showed statistically significant number of correlations among the variables ($p < 0.001$), which indicates that our data is suitable for factor analysis (approx. Chi-square = 341.36, df = 120, significance = 0.00). The factor analysis is performed with principal component analysis as the extracted method followed by Varimax rotation using SPSS Version 15.0.

PORTRAIT OF PBG PARTICIPATION

Table 2 shows the progress of PBGs in the State of Karnataka in India in terms of groups formed, families involved, savings mobilized, loans utilized, and value of labor sharing. The PBG Model is now working in nine districts of Karnataka State in India with 32,018 groups covering 224,511

Table 2. Progress of PBG in the State of Karnataka.

Performance	2011–2012	Since Inception (1995)
Groups formed	8,395	32,018
Families involved	53158	224,511
Savings mobilized (₹in millions)	69.3	674.2
Loans utilized by the members		
Numbers	42553	594,960
Amount (₹in millions)	593.5	5731.80
Amount repaid (₹in millions)	894.2	4866.80
Labor sharing		
No. of man days	3.39 million	38.6 million
[a]Value@ ₹150 per day	₹509.30 million	₹5780 million

Source: SKDRDP. [a]Labor sharing is done free of cost and its value is estimated at the current rate of ₹150 per day.

families. With cumulative savings of ₹674 million, members have utilized a loan amount of ₹5,731 million for farming and infrastructure development activities, thus improving their lives and livelihoods. Since inception till 2011–2012, the members have shared free labor worth of ₹5,780 million thereby helping them to save significant amounts of labor cost.

Table 3 shows the performance of PBGs and their families in agriculture development, the irrigation facilities generated through free labor sharing, and their involvement in non-farming allied activities. In total, 705,225 PBG groups have cultivated varied cash crops and horticultural crops in 1.686 million acres since inception of the Model in 1995. About 70,280 groups have created 16,535 acres of irrigated land through ground water sources such as wells, bore wells, and pump sets. The joint efforts of the PBGs have helped in stabilising the output and yield thereby reducing the adverse impact of monsoon failure. This demonstrates that by effective fund flow management and concerted collective efforts, it is possible to substantially increase the area under cultivation. Thus, Table 3 shows how the model successfully spreads and covers a large number of farmers and acres under cultivation.

The participatory labor technique has helped thousands of small farmers to achieve important farm tasks such as fencing, land levelling, digging wells, and house/shed construction at an affordable cost. The PBG innovation looks at daily income of the farmer and encourages him to take up several non-farming allied activities and enterprises which increases his income (Table 3). PBG members have actively participated in constructive

Table 3. Agriculture Development Programs Achieved by PBGs as on March 31, 2012.

S. No.		2011–2012			Achievement (Since Inception (1995))		
		No. of groups	No.of families	Area (in acres)	No. of groups	No. of families	Area (in acres)
2.1	Coconut cultivation	7,778	17,460	9567	36,229	75,848	47,512
2.2	Arecanut cultivation	10,611	22,376	16848	52,161	113,335	82,891
2.3	Cashew	1,610	3,170	2236	17,335	42,425	35,070
2.4	Rubber	3,033	7,098	6391	10,547	24,868	26,165
2.5	Cocoa	1,118	3,501	1395	4,074	10,961	5,651
2.6	Cardamom	1,310	2,583	1488	4,695	6,755	3,884
2.7	Coffee	4,126	11,969	11499	13,952	23,682	21,057
2.8	Paddy	18,224	36,914	38713	55,633	137,821	156,653
2.9	Sugarcane	7,407	20,046	25134	17,569	41,544	51,452
2.10	Grams	9,839	25,900	29935	32,528	78,152	76,156
2.11	Cotton	4,452	11,661	16281	15,234	25,895	48,109
2.12	Corn	12,141	26,177	37345	35,703	75,388	101,720
2.13	Onion	5,020	12,903	23131	15,282	35,593	49,026
2.14	Oilseeds	5,944	14,700	16801	21,672	50,495	50,086
2.15	Tuber crops	12,054	27,177	29709	36,569	87,861	67,882
2.16	Vetiver grass (Lavancha)	116	304	110	1,564	1,069	3,375
2.17	Vegetables	17,771	37,267	27635	70,235	159,652	97,313
2.18	Banana cultivation	10,247	20,082	13,593	41,024	88,130	46,391
2.19	Fruiticulture	3,370	5,680	4,312	14,889	34,858	26,813
2.20	Jasmine and other floriculture	3,422	5,700	2,998	15,585	28,213	11,557
2.21	Beekeeping	654	909	189	4,413	6,357	5,686
2.22	Vanilla	116	229	264	2,998	2,792	4,314
2.23	Beetle	1,892	3,819	737	9,870	19,367	4,569
2.24	Pepper	5,132	10,942	5,441	18,878	45,768	15,368
2.25	Dairying	16,686	30,479	889	51,470	109,232	11,288
2.26	Vermi-compost	1,016	1,308	100	7,669	12,622	1,178
2.27	Compost	3,768	6,663	560	19,753	36,269	3,289

2.28	SRI system	6,951	13,828	13,068	16,263	29,909	27,766
2.29	Animal husbandry	6,032	13,381	107	19,918	45,106	9,122
2.30	Green grass	4,882	8,434	3,176	24,357	56,942	14,412
2.31	Integrated farming system	447	674	1,055	3,944	5,274	6,938
2.32	Floriculture	1,081	2,058	1,035	4,209	6,449	4,249
2.33	Medicinal plants	21	35	9	1,097	297	163
2.34	Others	574	814	648	7,901	13,319	569,538
	Total	18,8845	406,241	342,396	705,225	1,532,248	1,686,642

S. No.	Program	2011–2012			Achievement (Since Inception)		
		No. of groups	No.of families	Area (in acres)	No. of groups	No. of families	Area (in acres)
Details of irrigation facilities created							
2.35	Dugwell	1,599	2,121	11	16,639	25,811	2,137
2.36	Borewell	1,859	2,615	6	8,735	11,891	95
2.37	Pumpsets	3,112	4,926	10	18,639	33,014	2,948
2.38	Irrigation system	3,741	5,879	1,835	19,857	36,544	9,374
2.39	Tillers	358	411	0	2,564	2,050	1,650
2.40	Harvesters	171	259	20	1,465	855	221
2.41	Others	325	511	20	2,381	2,357	111
	Total	11,165	16,722	1902	70,280	112,522	16,535
Details of non-farming allied activities generated							
2.42	Purchase of vehicle	8,337	12,844		27,627	41,807	
2.43	Business	20,878	44,286		66,224	112,466	
2.44	Industry	1,008	1,488		5,334	7,034	
2.45	Service	794	1,573		7,540	11,095	
2.46	Food products	382	594		2,394	3,032	
2.47	Chemical products	143	292		631	1,169	
2.48	Tailoring	3,660	6,234		11,644	18,258	

Table 3. *(Continued)*

S. No.	Program	2011–2012			Achievement (Since Inception)		
		No. of groups	No.of families	Area (in acres)	No. of groups	No. of families	Area (in acres)
2.49	Poultry	1,281	2,274		4,388	7,554	
2.50	Other	231	354		1,171	4,214	
	Total	36,714	69,939	0	126,952	206,629	0
	Grand Total	*236,724*	*492,902*	*344,298*	*902,456*	*185,1399*	*1,703,178*

Source: SKDRDP. *Note*: The total includes multiple responses.

Table 4. Investment by the PBG Members in Infrastructure Development (in Nos.).

S. No.	Particulars	2010–2011	2011–2012	Since1995 till 2011–2012 March
1	Construction of new houses, house repair and electrification	24,082	28,614	334,800
2	Sanitation units constructed	14,163	20,327	76,800
3	Installation of solar lighting equipments	216	925	2800
4	Installation of renewable energy gas system	923	1,054	4,400
5	Drinking water	247	212	1,972
6	Rural roads	67	46	415

Source: SKDRDP.

infrastructure development activities with the construction and renovation of 334,800 houses, 76,800 sanitation units, 7,200 solar lights and renewable gas energy systems, 1,972 drinking water facilities, and 415 rural roads (Table 4). The strong performance of PBGs in their livelihood promotion owes to their regular exposure and active participation in the extension programs. During the year 2011–2012, 224,511 families have participated in 6,529 programs and planted 125,480 saplings. Around 18,330 families have undertaken 19,753 watershed development programs organized by SKDRDP. They have also attended 485 de-addiction programs.

FACTORS THAT INFLUENCED PBG PARTICIPATION

Using the statements in the question no. 4.8 in the interview schedule (in the appendix) the study identifies 16 important variables (Table 5) to measure PBG members participation. Factor analysis was applied to the responses of all 100 farmer respondents on 16 variables measured on a five-point Likert scale. A principal component analysis with Varimax rotation was done and it has derived four factors with each having Eigen values greater than 1. The Eigen values of four factors are 5.979, 1.866, 1.256, and 1.091 and explain 63.701 of total factor variance. This is acceptable and thus establishes the validity of the measures.

Table 6 shows the results of rotated component matrix (RCM) for the 16 variables using the level of importance attached to each variable. The 16

Table 5. Statements Related to the Perception of Members about PBG.

A1	PBG provides economic benefits (increased income, emergency loan)
A2	Provides social benefits (education, medical facilities)
A3	Promotes farm development (seeds, implements, irrigation)
A4	PBG facilitates free labor sharing
A5	Improves awareness and skill through training, field visits
A6	Helps to learn debt and cash flow management (micro credit)
A7	Helps in generating income through regular livelihood and allied activities
A8	Helps in creating assets (livestock, land, and other assets)
A9	Develops decision-making ability
A10	Increases investment (increased savings and other investment)
A11	Develops organising ability (group management and federation activities)
A12	Infrastructure development (renewable energy system, drinking water, and electricity)
A13	Reduce cost of operation
A14	Helps in utilising agriculture technology
A15	Helps in reducing poverty
A16	For community participation

Table 6. Results of Rotated Component Matrix.

	1	2	3	4
Economic benefits				0.747
Social benefits				0.724
Farm development	0.802			
Labor sharing	0.739			
Awareness and skill development			0.774	
Management of cash flows		0.757		
Income generation		0.713		
Asset creation		0.632		
Decision making			0.761	
Investment		0.563		
Organising ability			0.652	
Infrastructure development	0.610			
Reduced cost of operation	0.623			
Utilising agriculture technology	0.582			
Poverty reduction				0.630
Community participation	0.523			
Eigen values	5.979	1.866	1.256	1.091
Cumulative percentage	37.370	49.032	56.882	63.701

Note: All factor loadings above 0.50 are considered.

variables are grouped under four derived factors depending upon Eigen values of each factor and are shown in Table 7.

The first factor, denoted as "agriculture development," explains 37.37% of variance and includes farm development with factor loading (0.802); labor sharing (0.739); infrastructure development (0.610); reduced cost of operation (0.623); utilizing agriculture technology (0.582); and community participation (0.523). The second factor "financial participation" contributes 11.662% of variance and consists of components such as management of cash flows with factor loading (0.757); income generation (0.713); asset creation (0.632); and investment (0.563). The third factor "capacity building" contributes 7.850% of variance and consists of variables measuring awareness and skill development with factor loading (0.774); decision making (0.761); and organizing ability (0.652). The fourth factor, denoted as "Other benefits," contributes 6.819% of variance and consists of variables such as economic benefits with factor loading (0.747); social benefits (0.724); and poverty reduction (0.630).

Interpretation

The data collected through interview schedules and open discussions with the farmer respondents helped in understanding the dynamics of collective financial participation in micro credit and labor sharing underlying the PBG Model. The four Cs – convenience, cost, commitment, and the collective efforts – have galvanized the small farmers to choose the PBG Model initiated by SKDRDP. The integrated approach that combines both farming and non-farming activities coupled with social security and capacity building measures adopted by the project has been instrumental for retaining the marginalized farmers in agriculture in the study area. Respondent farmers assert that the model provides a direction, lays down guidelines, and also constitutes a source of legitimacy that justifies their collective efforts. About 15% of the respondent farmers affirmed that PBG acted as a means for reverse migration to rural areas, assuring them not only livelihood security but also a decent income.

All of the farmer respondents (100%) joined PBG for the purpose of agriculture and infrastructure development with the help of micro credit, labor sharing, increased internal inputs, and agriculture technology (such as a system of rice intensification, tillers). A combination of sustainable long-term commercial crops with the income generating short-term crops is practiced to ensure economic stability. The long-term loan taken for the

***Table* 7.** Clubbed Variables.

Factor Name	Clubbed Variables					
Agriculture development	Farm development	Labor sharing	Infrastructure development	Reduced cost of operation	Utilizing agriculture technology	Community participation
Financial participation	Management of cash flows	Income generation	Asset creation	Investment		
Capacity building	Awareness and skill development	Decision making	Organizing ability			
Other benefits	Economic benefits	Social benefits	Poverty reduction			

Source: Survey Data.

cultivation of major food crops is repaid in weekly instalments out of the income generated from the cultivation of short-term crops. Thus, adoption of mixed cropping has ensured regular returns and liquidity to 87% of farmers, freeing them from debt and making them resilient to face the adversities of weather and the market.

The increase in wages for agricultural work has been much faster than the increase in labor productivity, turning agriculture into a non-lucrative activity. So the loss of agricultural income owing to a rise in the cost of cultivation and market imperfections is mainly responsible for the farmers' distress (Kannan, 2011). But, in the current study, all the respondent farmers reaffirmed that the free labor sharing technique has reduced their cost of farm operations and dependence on external farm inputs substantially, leading to the enhanced agricultural productivity. Besides rice cultivation, they have also ventured into rubber, floriculture, horticulture, livestock rearing, and bee-keeping. However, the unexpected crop loss and the lack of marketing facilities are still the major hindrances for the PBG members.

Most of the farmers (90%) have adopted water conservation techniques, innovative methods of cultivations, diversification, and mixed and multiple cropping leading to their economic stability, sustainability, and economic well-being. Their investments in water resources, infrastructure development, farming operations, and exposure to extension activities have enabled them to achieve sustainable farming. With the help of the labor cost saved through free labor sharing, the farmers have been able to procure improved agricultural seeds, agricultural implements, and livestock leading to the enhanced agricultural productivity and income. Some of the groups act as custodians of agricultural machines which are rented out to other members in times of need. Collective efforts are also mobilized for the community participation resulting in the creation of community infrastructure such as community halls, rural roads, canals, roadside plantations, medicinal forests, and decent houses for the group members.

The sense of ownership and the active participation of farmers (87%) in savings, management of cash flows and debt, keeping records, and optimal utilization of funds and resources for productive purposes have empowered them to manage their economic affairs and have improved their asset base which is vital for their poverty reduction. Besides, some of the farmers have taken up non-farming allied activities as an alternative sources of income generation (87%) and created logistic facilities for marketing their farm products in the cities (13%). About 60% of farmers work as farm laborers during spare time to make additional income in the agricultural season, and 14% of the respondent farmers have become entrepreneurs. The marked increase in the involvement of farmers both in the planning and execution of work at the group level and federation level has enabled them to rise to the higher stature in the local governance bodies. About 35% of PBG farmers have actively participated in federations and 18% in Panchayat Raj institutions (Village Governance Bodies). All these speak of their confidence, decision-making abilities, leadership, and organizing caliber.

All the respondent members have obtained credit under different schemes such as income generation fund, infrastructure fund, group activities fund, and Swagruha fund (used for house construction/repair). Very few respondents (17%) have taken loans under revolving fund schemes meant for personal or emergency purposes. The total savings of the entire farmer respondents for the last seven years amounted to ₹757,000 and the total amount of loans borrowed was ₹4,388,000. They utilized ₹586,000 worth of man days through labor sharing. The repayment of the loan was regular and the loan amount was used for the productive purposes due to regular follow-up measures taken by the group heads. The net earnings of the farmer respondents per annum range between ₹9,000 and ₹235,000 for the year 2011–2012.

Renovation of their houses, construction of the sanitation units (100%), installation of solar lighting and renewable gas system (85%), access to drinking water, updated information and agriculture extension programs provided by the NGO (100%) are some of the success factors that appeared as a means to fulfil the long cherished desires of disadvantaged respondents, who had earlier experienced exclusion and isolation. PBG farmers get good social security benefits provided by SKDRDP that include Sujnana Students Scholarship, Jeevan Madhura Insurance Scheme, National Pension Scheme, Asset Insurance and Health Insurance (Sampoorna Suraksha). For a nominal premium of ₹1050 per annum, the scheme Sampoorna Suraksha covers a family of five members against expenses related to hospitalization, maternity, death, calamity, and accidents. Thus PBG members get economic and social benefits and an assured livelihood opportunity leading to their socioeconomic well being and improved quality of life.

POLICY IMPLICATIONS

The study findings have policy implications worth considering given the need for the development of marginalized small farmers through financial and decision-making participation. For the large number of small farming families in India, it is important to focus on improving their productivity through financial and social inclusion measures in terms of access to hassle-free long-term credit and financial services, agriculture inputs, health care, extension services, and technology as practiced in the case of PBG. This can help serve as a remedy for the high rate of farmers' suicides as described earlier.

The PBG model appears very successful and could be replicated across India, but it could be more effective with supportive policies. PBG members lack access to market linkages and logistic support that facilitate value addition, so they are often forced to sell their farm products at lesser rates to the middlemen, giving poor returns to the farmers and impeding their financial participation. Hence, there is a need for State Governments and Local Panchayats to provide effective marketing linkages with fair pricing, market information and mobile markets (on wheels) that are essential for their economic empowerment and poverty reduction. Inclusive financial participation of poor farmers necessitates a supportive socioeconomic and political environment for their prosperity. Integrated support of the government, NABARD and other financial institutions through policy initiatives, investment, and programs oriented to agriculture development are paramount for the smooth implementation of the PBG initiatives. The success of this model indicates that the Pragathi Bandhu concept should be integrated with the development agenda of India, and become an operational mandate for all the state governments and local governance bodies. If marginalized farmers are to achieve their goals of full employment and self-reliance that assure them work, income, food and social security, it is valuable for them to organize into farmers' collectives that function with financial autonomy and participatory democracy.

CONCLUSION

Based on the surveyed data, this paper has examined the functions and progress of PBGs in terms of groups formed, savings mobilized, loans utilized, number and value of labor sharing effected, agriculture development achieved, non-farming allied activities generated, and investment in infrastructure development. The paper explains how the model facilitates the poor small holder farmers in financial and decision-making participation through micro credit and free participatory labor sharing strategies. It also analyses the four factors influencing the farmers' participation in PBG – agriculture development, financial participation, capacity building, and other benefits. The study reveals how the participatory labor sharing provide farmers new forms of livelihood, income and savings, and employment within the village in terms of allied activities and sense of participation in agriculture development, helping to counter the problem of shortage of labor. The success of PBG owes to the committed financial and decision-making participation of farmers in terms of thrift and micro credit that make them bankable by diversifying income sources and facilitating labor sharing.

The important implications for future research are: to analyze the problems and challenges faced by the PBG members in the current marketing context; to look into more dimensions of PBG participation in terms of its impact on their socioeconomic development and capacity building; and to analyze participation of small farmers in micro credit and labor sharing strategies across space and time.

ACKNOWLEDGMENT

An earlier version of this paper was presented at the 16th IAFEP Conference on the Theme "Financial and decision-making participation of low-income, historically disadvantaged, or marginalized populations," School of Management and Labor Relations, Rutgers University, NJ, July 13–15, 2012.

REFERENCES

Acharya, S. S. (1997). Liberalization of agricultural produce markets and role of marketing organization. *Indian Journal of Agricultural Marketing*, *11*(3), 151–159.

Agarwal, A. N. (2011). *Indian economy – Problems of development and planning*. New Delhi: New Age International Pvt. Ltd. Publishers.

Agarwal, B. (2010). Rethinking agricultural production collectivities. *Economic and Political Weekly*, *45*(9), 64–78.

Agrawal, R. C. (2000). *Perspectives for small farmers in developing countries: Do they have a future?* Forum zur Gartenkonferenz. Retrieved from http://userpage.fu-berlin.de/garten/Buch/Agrawal(englisch).htm

Agvekar, K. S., & Borude, S. G. (1992). Study of member participation in village cooperatives in Ratnagiri District. *The Maharashtra Cooperative Quarterly*, *75*(3), 145–152.

Ahluwalia, M. (1990). Policies for poverty alleviation. *Asian Development Review*, *8*(7), 111–132.

Babu, N. Y. M., & Sahu, A. K. (2007). *A case of Shri Kshetra Dharmasthala rural development project linking micro finance with livelihood augmentation*. Retrieved from http://thelivelihoodschool.in/publication/

Basole, A., & Basu, D. (2011). Relations of production and modes of surplus extraction in India: Part1 – Agriculture. *Economic and Political Weekly*, *46*(14), 41–56.

Bhalla, G. S., & Singh, G. (2009). Economic liberalisation and Indian agriculture: A statewise analysis. *Economic and Political Weekly*, *44*(52), 34–44.

Bharathi, V. (2011). Indebtedness and suicides: Field notes on agricultural labourers of Punjab. *Economic and Political Weekly*, *46*(14), 35–40.

Chand, R., Laksmi Prasanna, P. A., & Singh, A. (2011). Farm size and productivity: Understanding the strengths of smallholders and improving their livelihoods. *Review of Agriculture, Economic and Political Weekly*, *46*(26/27), 5–11.

Chand, R., Raju, S. S., & Pandey, L. M. (2007). Growth crisis in agriculture-severity and options at national and state levels. *Economic and Political Weekly*, *42*(26), 2528–2533.

Chatterjee, S. (2012). Pragathibandhu self-help groups (PBG). An agricultural project for development of marginal and small farmers in Karnataka. In M.V. Rao (Ed.), *Research highlights – 2009–2010* (pp. 52–55) Hyderabad: National Institute of Rural Development.

Chopra, K. (2002). Social capital and development processes: Role of formal and informal institutions. *Economic and Political Weekly*, *37*(28), 2911–2916.

Datt, G., & Ravallion, M. (2010). Shining for the poor too. *Economic and Political Weekly*, *45*(7), 55–60.

Dev, S. K. (1967) *Sahakari Samaj: The cooperative commonwealth*. New Delhi: Asia Publishing House.

Dev, S. M. (2005). Agriculture and rural employment in the budget. *Economic and Political Weekly*, *40*(14), 1410–1413.

Dhingra, I. C. (2011). *The Indian economy – Environment and policy*. New Delhi: Sultan Chand and Sons Educational publishers.

Dogra, B. (2007). Landless farmers demand a piece of the action. *IPS NEWS*. Retrieved from http://ipsnews.net/news.asp

D'Silva, E., & Pai, S. (2003). Social capital and collective action. Development outcomes in forest protection and watershed development. *Economic and Political Weekly*, *38*(14), 1404–1415.

D'Souza, S., Chidananda, H. L., Udayachandra, P. N., & Devaraja, T. S. (2012). BC model for inclusive growth – Study on performance of SKDRDP. *IRJC*, *1*(10), 254–262.

Dwivedi, R. C. (1982). *Democracy in cooperative movement: An Indian profile*. New Delhi: National Cooperative Union of India.

Ganesan, K. (1969). Member satisfaction with working of agricultural primary credit societies. *Cooperative Information Bulletin*, *4*(3), 23–26.

Gopalappa, D. V., & Rao, V. M. (2004). Agricultural growth and farmer distress. *Economic and Political Weekly*, *39*(52), 47–52.

Government of India (GOI). (2008). *Planning commission*. Eleventh Five-Year Plan (2007–2012), Vol. 1, pp. 2–11.

Goyal, S. K. (1966). *Cooperative farming in India* .Bombay: Asia Publishing House.

Hajela, T.N. (1976). *History of economic thought*. Agra: Shivlal, Agarwala and Co.

Hirway, I. (1985). Garibi hatao, can IRDP do it? *Economic and Political Weekly*, March 20, p. 562.

International Labor Organization (ILO) (2007). *India decent work country programme – 2007–2012*. Geneva: ILO.

Jacob, J. (2009). *A Study on Kudumbashree project – A poverty eradication programme in Kerala. Performance, impact and lessons for other States*. Retrieved from http://planning commission.nic.in/reports/sereport/ser/ser_kudu.pdf

Jagadish, K.S. (1995). Generating appropriate rural technologies: The ASTRA experience. In V. Padaki (Ed.), *Development intervention and programme evaluation-concepts and cases*. New Delhi: Sage.

Jodhka, S. S. (2006). Beyond crisis: Rethinking contemporary Punjab agriculture. *Economic and Political Weekly*, *41*(16), 1530–1537.

Jodhka, S. S. (2012). Agrarian changes in the times of (Neo-Liberal) crisis. Revisiting attached labour in Haryana. *Economic and Political Weekly*, *47*(26/27), 5–13.

Joshi, S.R., & Bhatia, B.S. (1995). The Kheda communication project. In V. Padaki (Ed.), *Development intervention and programme evaluation-concepts and cases*. New Delhi: Sage.

Kannan, K. P. (2011). Agricultural development in an emerging non-agrarian regional economy: Kerala's challenges. *Economic and Political Weekly*, *46*(9), 64–70.

Kannan, K. P., & Pushpangadan, K. (1988). Agricultural stagnation in Kerala: An exploratory analysis. *Economic and Political Weekly*, *23*(39), 120–128.

Kenneth, K., & Seena, P. C. (2012). Socio-economic changes of women through Kudumbashree – A Study from Puthenvelikkara (Gp) of Kerala State, India. *International Research Journal of Social Sciences*, *1*(2), 1–7.

Kirsten, J., & Sartorius, K. (2002). Linking agribusiness and small-scale farmers in developing countries: Is there a new role for contract farming. In S. Singh (Ed.), *New markets for smallholders in India. Economic and Political Weekly*, *47*(52), 95–105.

Krishnaswami, O.R. (1976). *Democracy in action*. New Delhi: Somaiya Publication.

Kumar, P. (2006). Contract through agribusiness firms and state corporation: A case study in Punjab. *Economic and Political Weekly*, *52*(30), 5367–5375.

Kumar, A.T., & Paramanand, S. (2010). *Globalisation-inclusive growth and Indian economy: Issues and policies*. New Delhi: Regal Publications.

Lin, J. Y. (1990). Collectivisation and China's agriculture crisis in 1959–1961. *Journal of Political Economy*, *98*(6), 1228–1252.

Lindberg, S. (2005). Whom and what to fight ? Notes and queries on Indian farmers' collective action under liberalisation and globalisation. In J. S. Agrarian (Ed.), *Changes in the times of (neo-liberal) crisis. Revisiting attached labour in Haryana. Economic and Political Weekly*, *47*(26/27), 5–13.

Manjunath, L. H. (2010). *Financing small farmers – An innovative methodology*. Retrieved from http://www.indiaenvironmentportal.org.in/

Mishra, S.K., & Puri, V.K. (2011). *Indian economy – Its development experience*. New Delhi: Himalaya Publishing House.

Mohanty, B. B., & Shroff, S. (2004). Farmer suicides in Maharashtra. *Economic and Political Weekly*, *39*(52), 5599–5606.

Narayanan, S. (2012). Inflections in agricultural evolution – Contemporary commodity complexes and transactional forms in interior Tamil Nadu. *Economic and Political Weekly*, *47*(52), 84–94.

National Sample Survey office (NSSO). (2004–2005). *Employment and unemployment situation in India* (July 2004–June 2005), NSS 6th round, National Sample Survey Organisation, Government of India, New Delhi.

Neb, D. P. (1998). Active member participation – A pre condition for success of cooperative organization. *Cooperative Perspective*, *33*(3), 49–52.
Nidheesh, K. B. (2009). Study on changing process of Kerala women through Kudumbashree in Kerala. *International NGO Journal*, *8*, 352–361.
Oommen, M. A. (2007). *Kudumbashree of Kerala: An appraisal.* Institute of Social Sciences. Retrieved from http://www.kudumbashree.org
Pandey, L. M., Chand, R., & Raju, S. S. (2007). Growth crisis in agriculture. *Economic and Political Weekly*, *42*(26), 2528–2533.
Parthasarathy, G. (1985). Reorientation of rural development programmes: A note on some basic issues. *Economic and Political Weekly*, November 30, pp. 2125–2128.
Puri, S.S. (1979). *Ends and means of cooperative development*. New Delhi: NCUI.
Rath, N. (1985). Garibi hatao, Can IRDP do it? *Economic and Political Weekly*, *20*(6), 245.
Rawal, V. (2008). Ownership holdings of land in rural India: Putting the record straight. *Economic and Political Weekly*, *43*(10), 43–47.
Reed, A. M., & Reed, D. (2013). *Taking solidarity seriously: Analyzing Kudumbashree as a women's social and solidarity economy experiment.* Draft paper prepared for the UNRISD conference – Potential and limits of social and solidarity economy, May 6–8, 2013, Geneva. Retrieved from http://www.unrisd.org
Sainath, P. (2011). In 16 years, farm suicides cross a quarter million, *The Hindu*, October 29, p. 5.
Sarma, E. A. S. (2004). Is rural economy breaking down? Farmers' suicides in Andhra Pradesh. *Economic and Political Weekly*, *39*(28), 3087–3089.
Shah, U. M. (1996). Problems and strategies of cooperative development. *The Tamil Nadu Journal of Cooperation*, *88*(4), 11–16.
Shah, E. (2012). A life wasted making dust: Affective histories of dearth, death, debt and farmers' suicides in India. *The Journal of Peasant Studies*, *39*(5), 1159–1179.
Singh, S. (2005). Contract farming system in Thailand. *Economic and Political Weekly*, *40*(53), 5578–5586.
Singh, S. (2006). Credit, indebtedness and farmer suicides in Punjab: Some missing links. *Economic and Political Weekly*, *41*(30), 330–331.
Singh, S. (2012). New markets for smallholders in India – Exclusion, policy and mechanisms. *Economic and Political Weekly*, *47*(52), 95–105.
Singh, K., Singh, S., & Kindra, H. S. (2009). Agrarian crisis and depeasantisation in Punjab – Status of small/marginal farmers who left agriculture. *Indian Journal of Agricultural Economics*, *64*(4), 585–603.
SKDRDP. (2009). *Annual report*. Retrieved from http://www.skdrdpindia.org
SKDRDP. (2010). *Rural development*. Retrieved from http://www.skdrdpindia.org
Sreerekha, M. S. (2012). Illegal land, illegal people. The Chengara land struggle in Kerala. *Economic and Political Weekly*, *47*(30), 21–24.
Srivastava, A. (1999). Nongovernmental organisations and rural development. *Social Action*, *49*(1), 27–44.
Swain, N. (1985). *Collective farms which work?* Cambridge: Cambridge University Press.
The Hindu Business Line. (2012). *Poverty level dipped to 29.8% in 2009–10: Plan panel. The Hindu Business Line*, March 19, p. 4.
Tucker, V. (1999). Role of NGOs in participatory communication. *Social Action*, *49*(1), 15–26.
UNRISD. (1975). *Rural cooperatives as agents of change: A research paper and a debate* (Vol. 8). Geneva: UNRISD.

Vaidyanathan, A. (2013). Future of cooperatives in India. *Economic and Political Weekly*, *48*(18), 30–34.

Vepa, S. (2005). Feminisation of agriculture and marginalisation of their economic stakes. *Economic and Political Weekly*, *40*(25), 2563–2568.

Viswanathan, P. K., Thapa, G. B., Routray, J. K., & Ahmed, M. M. (2012). Agrarian transition and emerging challenges in Asian Agriculture: A critical assessment. *Economic and Political Weekly*, *48*(4), 41–50.

Yashwanth. (2010). Farmers India – Sasya Syamalam – Solidarity to 490 millions of small farmers. Retrieved from http://farmersindia.blogspot.in/

APPENDIX: INTERVIEW SCHEDULE FOR THE FARMER MEMBERS

This study aims to analyze the factors that influence the participation of farmer members in PBG Model and the extent of their participation in PBG initiatives. Hence kindly complete this schedule. Your response will be kept confidential and will be used exclusively for research purpose.

- Please do not omit to answer any question.
- Please give your frank opinions.
- Do not write your name/sign.
- Please feel free to ask for any clarification while answering the questions.
- Please tick(√) the correct answer in the appropriate box.

Name and address of the PB Group

I Personal Profile:

(a) Place of dwelling: Village ____________ Town ____________

(b) Duration of being a member:

Below 5 Years	
5–10 years	
10–15 years	
15–20 years	
Above 20 years	

(c) Other status: Present: ___________ Previous: ___________

(d) Membership in other organizations:

1.	
2.	
3.	
4.	

(e) Status in other organization:

1.	
2.	
3.	
4.	

(f) Distance between residence and SKDRDP staff's office:

0–10 km	
10–20 km	
20–30 km	
Above 30 km	

II Family Profile:

No.	Relationship	Age (Yrs.)	Education	Occupation	Monthly Income (Rs.)	Association of family with SKDRDP
1.	Respondent					
2.						
3.						
4.						

III Knowledge and Perception on Participation:

3.1 To whom does the PBG belong?

(a)	Government	
(b)	SKDRDP	
(c)	Members	
(d)	Others (specify)	
(e)	Don't know	

3.2 Who motivated you to take membership?

(a)	Self	
(b)	Friends/relatives	
(c)	Family members	
(d)	SKDRDP	
(e)	Others (specify)	

3.3 What is your opinion about becoming a PBG member. Explain in detail:

(a)	It is necessary	
(b)	It is not necessary	
(c)	It improves the status	
(d)	It gives me many opportunities	
(e)	It helps me to avail facilities	
(f)	Provides livelihood	

3.4 Are you associated with any of the local organizations?

	Organization	Position/Capacity
(a)		
(b)		
(c)		

3.5 How often the group members meet? Explain the purpose.

(a)	Daily	
(b)	Weekly	
(c)	Monthly	

3.6 What is discussed in the group meetings? Explain.

3.7 How do you prepare the invest plan? Explain.

3.8 What are the objectives you specify in the investment plan?

3.9 How is the labor sharing done? Explain the modalities.

3.10 Explain in detail the record keeping and financial participation.

3.11 How many times you have taken micro credit? Explain the purpose.

3.12 What is the amount of loan borrowed?

3.13 Have you repaid the loan promptly?

3.14 How do you manage to repay the debt?

3.15 Explain the various types of crops you cultivate.

3.16 Explain the water resources generated after joining PBG.

3.17. How many acres are brought under cultivation?

3.18 How do you market your farm products?

3.19 Have you taken up any other income generating activities? Explain.

3.20 Give an account of infrastructure development activities taken with the help of PBG.

(a) Construction/repair of the house
(b) Electrification
(c) Construction of the sanitation units
(d) Installation of solar lights? Renewable energy systems
(e) Drinking water facility
(f) Roads

3.21 Do you know about the following related to PBG?

		Very Well	Well	Something	Nothing
(a)	Your group members				
(b)	Federation				
(c)	Financial participation				
(d)	Structure and functions				
(e)	Facilities/services offered				
(f)	Financial activities and performance				
(g)	Documentation				
(h)	Meeting procedures				
(i)	Planning				
(j)	Labor sharing				
(k)	Micro credit				
(l)	Financial management				
(m)	Record keeping				
(n)	Agriculture development				
(o)	Fund flow management				
(p)	Income generating				

IV Extent of Participation:

4.1 How often do you visit your federation?

Frequency			Purpose	
Regular			To avail and repay loan	
Sometimes			To attend meetings	
Rarely			Get together	
Never			General body meeting	
			Election	
			Others (specify)	

4.2 How far do you depend on PBG to meet your needs?

Nil	
1–25%	
25–50%	
50–75%	
75–100%	

4.3 What is the amount of deposits you hold?

Nos.	Amount

4.4 What is the extent of utilization of SKDRDP service?

Nil	
1–25%	

25–50%	
50–75%	
75–100%	

4.5 Explain the amount of loans utilized:

₹10,000–50,000	
50,000–100,000	
100,000–200,000	
200,000–500,000	
500,000–1,000,000	
>1,000,000	

4.6 Explain the purpose of availing micro credit:

Agriculture development	
Non-farming allied activities	
Infrastructure development	
Purchase of vehicles	
Self-employment	
Household consumption	
Repair/construction of the house, sanitation units	
Irrigation facilities	
Education purpose and health care	
Personal reasons	
Revolving fund loan	
Livestock and other assets	
Any other (specify)	

4.7 What is the extent of your participation in the following? Explain in detail:

		Very High Extent	High Extent	Moderate Extent	Less Extent	Never
1.	Availing financial services					
2.	Farm planning and development					
3.	Decision making					
4.	Weekly meeting					
5.	Labor sharing					
6.	Extension activities					
7.	Interaction with other members					
8.	Interaction with field workers					
9.	Irrigation activities					
10.	Availing micro credit and thrift					
11.	Infrastructure development					
12.	Record keeping					
13.	Non-farming allied activities					
14.	Utilizing agriculture technology					
15.	Federation activities					
16.	Repayment of loan					
17.	Income generation activities					
18.	Community participation					
19.	Group enterprises					

(*Continued*)

		Very High Extent	High Extent	Moderate Extent	Less Extent	Never
20.	Cash flow management					
21.	Capacity building initiatives					
22.	Asset creation					
23.	Investment activities					
24.	Local governance bodies					
25.	Availing insurance services					

4.8 Please respond to these questions based on your experience in PBG. Explain in detail (perception of members about PBG):

1. Strongly disagree
2. Moderately disagree
3. Neither disagree nor agree
4. Moderately agree
5. Strongly agree

(a)	I joined PBG for the purpose of farm development	
(b)	Free labor sharing has motivated me to join PBG	
(c)	Training, field visits have improved my awareness & skill	
(d)	I learnt to reduce the cost of operation through interaction in PBG	
(e)	I learnt to manage the debt and cash flow (micro credit)	
(f)	I increased my income after participating in PBG activities	
(g)	I get medical insurance, educational facilities for my family	
(h)	I am empowered to take decision on my own	
(i)	Helped me repair my house and construct sanitation units	
(j)	I have increased my savings	
(k)	I learnt nuances of group management and federation activities	

(l)	Learnt the agriculture technology, new method of cultivation	
(m)	It has reduced my poverty as I have sustainable livelihoods	
(n)	Rural roads are made possible through group efforts	
(o)	It has helped to install solar & renewable gas system	
(p)	I have raised loan for emergency needs	
(q)	I joined the PBG out of compulsion	
(r)	It has helped me to pursue other allied activities	
(s)	I derived a minimal benefit from PBG	
(t)	I get drinking water and electricity	
(u)	I get seeds and implements	
(v)	Helped me to have livestock and other assets	
(w)	Provided livelihood opportunities	
(x)	Reduced poverty	
(y)	For community participation	
(z)	Any other (specify)	

4.9 Have you attended any extension programs:

Yes	No

4.10 If yes, what prompted you to participate? Rank according to your perceived level of importance:

1.	Improve awareness	
2.	Enhance productivity	
3.	For socioeconomic gain	
4.	For social acquaintance	
5.	Exposure to current practices.	
6.	Entertainment	

7.	For participation	
8.	Any other (specify)	

4.11 Give a list of capacity building program you have attended:

S. No.	Year	Nature of Program	Who Conducted	Place	Duration	Who Paid	Impact
1.							
2.							
3.							

4.12 Did you find the above programs useful? If yes, Explain

Yes	No

4.13 In what way you found extension activities useful? Explain rank according to your perceived level of importance:

1.	Increased awareness	
2.	Functional competence	
3.	Increased income	
4.	Built up confidence	
5.	Improved human relation	
6.	Social responsibility	
7.	Increased participation	
8.	Needy service	
9.	Any other (specify)	

4.14 What is your perception of the utility derived from the activity attended?

Very great extent	
Great extent	
Some extent	
Little extent	

4.15 How is your relation with the group members? Explain:

Very good	
Good	
Average	
Not so good	
Poor	

4.16 Do you discuss your needs and problems with the group members? Give example:

Yes	No

4.17. Have you shared your experiences of your participation in PBG activities with the non participants/public? Explain:

Yes	No

4.18 Have you encouraged them to participate?

Yes	No

4.19 Feel free to add your suggestions if any, for making PBG initiatives effective.

PART III
THEORY AND POLICY

CHAPTER 10

DEMOCRATIC DIFFERENCES: HOW TYPE OF OWNERSHIP AFFECTS WORKPLACE DEMOCRACY AND ITS BROADER SOCIAL EFFECTS

Mark J. Kaswan

ABSTRACT

Purpose – *To examine how different types of ownership, including investor-owned, employee-owned, and mixed models, affect the dynamics of participatory practices in the workplace, and the broader social effects of these differences.*

Design/methodology/approach – *Brings together literature from democratic theory and empirical research in workplace participation and employee ownership. The first step is to articulate the range of democratic practices from nondemocratic to strongly democratic. The essay then discusses the different forms that participation can take and the threshold for what can be considered democratic participation. It then*

Sharing Ownership, Profits, and Decision-making in the 21st Century
Advances in the Economic Analysis of Participatory & Labor-Managed Firms, Volume 14, 261–294

ISSN: 0885-3339/doi:10.1108/S0885-3339(2013)0000014011

considers different models of ownership and the impact of ownership type on participatory practices.

Findings – *It is found that investor-owned firms cannot be considered strongly democratic and that worker cooperatives are more likely to be strongly democratic and cannot fall below the threshold of weak democracy. However, strong democracy is not necessarily a feature of worker cooperatives.*

Originality/value – *Little work has been done to consider the way the type of ownership affects the kind or degree of democratic practices that may be present in an enterprise.*

Keywords: Employee participation; workplace democracy; ESOPs; worker cooperatives; self-managed firms; democratic theory

JEL Classifications: J54; J83; M14; M54; P12; P13; P14

INTRODUCTION

Democratic theorists often begin from the fundamental premise that democracy is a good thing, and that we should have more of it. As Held puts it, "democratic ideas and practices can in the long run be protected only if their hold on our political, social and economic life is *extended* and *deepened*" (Held, 1996, p. 4). While some hold that economic democracy refers to greater equality in economic outcomes (Abrahamsson, Broström, & Knocke, 1980), an increasingly popular perspective is that it implies the extension of democratic practices and principles to economic enterprises (Dahl, 1989, Chaps. 22–23).

A parallel, and older, track has been followed in management science and industrial relations studies that begins with the premise that worker participation in decision-making in the workplace is a good thing, and that enterprises can benefit substantially from it. As Strauss puts it, the notion of worker participation "provides a win-win solution to a central organizational problem: how to satisfy workers' needs while simultaneously achieving organizational objectives" (Strauss, 2006, p. 778).

The distinction between "democracy," the principal concern of democratic theorists, and "participation," the primary object for management studies, is an important one for this essay. It should be noted that the arguments of democratic theorists are often accompanied by arguments for various forms of worker ownership (see, e.g., Alperovitz, 2011; Dahl, 1985, 1989; Ellerman, 1999; Rothschild, 2000; Rothschild & Whitt, 1986). Indeed, some theorists are quite dismissive of the possibility of worker self-management outside of worker ownership (e.g., Rothschild & Ollilalnen, 1999), although this is by no means a consensus position (see, e.g., Dahl, 1985; Pateman, 1970). In management science, however, democracy is much less likely to be discussed, and the traditional model of investor ownership is generally assumed. The result is that the question of the interaction between forms of ownership and democratic (not merely participatory) practices is rarely examined.

This essay, written from the perspective of democratic theory, is concerned with the ways in which ownership and participatory practices in the enterprise interact, and the larger social consequences of this interaction in promoting the extension and deepening of democratic practices and principles. The basic premise of this essay is that different forms of enterprise ownership will be associated with different kinds of participatory practices, some of which may not be properly considered "democratic," and, as a result, will have different kinds and degrees of effects in terms of the expansion of democracy within a society.

The first part of the essay will discuss democracy and its requirements, including recognition that there are stronger and weaker forms. The second section will consider different elements of participation and the threshold of what can and cannot be considered democratic participation. The third section will examine different forms of ownership and how participation may differ between these forms, as well as the impact the presence of a union may have. Woven into this will be a discussion of the larger social effects of these participatory practices – including those that may not be considered democratic – on the broader society. It should be noted at the outset that, because worker cooperatives may stake a claim to being inherently democratic (as will be seen), somewhat more detailed attention will be given to this ownership type than to the others.

STRONG AND WEAK DEMOCRACY

Democracy is one of those terms that gets used a lot without much attention to the variety of meanings that it carries. It is not without reason that Gallie includes it as a prime example in his seminal paper on essentially contested concepts (1955–1956). He contrasts the ancient Greek conception of democracy as direct rule by the people with the modern conception, in which democracy is basically a set of procedures whereby representatives are selected and held accountable to the people. These two systems include, for my purposes, one essential point in common and one essential difference. The point in common is that, in both the ancient Greek and the modern model, what is assumed is that democracy is a form of rule. The point of difference has to do with the nature of participation.

Breaking the term "democracy" into its Greek roots, *demos* and *kratia*, "democracy" means, literally, "the people rule," or "the rule of the people." As Gallie shows, this can mean different things to different people. From the time of the ancient Greeks until the modern era, democracy meant the direct involvement of the people in decision-making, generally through assemblies, even as these coexisted with representative or other institutional structures of governance such as the Boule in Athens or the Roman Senate.[1] As is commonly noted, a democratic system in which participation is limited to the periodic election of representatives is a fairly recent development. This distinction between a direct form of democracy, in which rule is exercised directly by the people, and a representative form in which the people's self-rule functions through the intermediary of elected representatives, can be recognized as a primary distinction between different types of democracy. The difference between direct and representative democracy, then, has to do with the form of *participation* in rule, in that in the first case it is direct and in the second case mediated by representatives.

A major critique of the representative system is that it limits the people's participation to that of merely selecting representatives; political participation beyond this point is either not encouraged or even actively discouraged.[2] However, while representative systems may be considered participatory to a greater or lesser extent, the gap between representative and direct democracy can never be completely bridged because ultimately, in a representative system, governance is the function of the representatives – the people may have "input," but ultimately, decision-making is up to the elected representatives.[3] This does not mean that the two systems are incompatible, however, and one way of measuring the strength of democracy is by the extent of the opportunities for participation. Because citizens do not participate in any direct way in decision-making, representative systems are perforce less participatory than ones based on direct democracy, although various factors may affect the degree of participation within the representative model (e.g., in the extent to which mechanisms exist for effective communication between citizens and representatives). So, the level of participation within the representative model can vary fairly substantially.

As will be discussed in detail in the next section, direct democracy in the workplace may also be more or less participatory depending on the particular practices through which workers are able to participate in decision-making – for example, if they are organized into highly participatory self-directed work teams, as opposed to, say, when managers simply call assemblies when they see fit. What this shows is that, regardless of the underlying form, participation is not an either-or proposition, but something that varies depending on various factors. A system might be considered "weakly" participatory when workers have few opportunities to have input or "strongly" participatory if their involvement is extensive. Either way, however, questions of the degree or nature of participation are largely distinct from questions about the degree to which workers may be said to rule.

By "rule" what I mean is effective control, which involves power.[4] In a formal sense, power in the enterprise is based on legal authority, which, regardless of the specific form of ownership, is based on the investment of capital (although sometimes only particular kinds of capital).[5] This, however, is not the only source or form of power in a firm, and various factors influence the degree of power exercised by owners and management – including the existence or lack of a participatory framework for employees. For their part, workers may have more or less power, although generally speaking, absent a union, in a traditional capitalist enterprise they may only exercise what authority they have at the pleasure of management (which exercises its authority at the pleasure of the board of directors, if there is one). So rule, like participation, is not a simple either/or proposition, making it possible to refer to "weak" versus "strong" forms of democratic rule.

What emerges from this is a two-dimensional understanding of democracy, with two scalar variables, participation and rule. Thus, four classifications can be identified: nondemocracy, where the people have neither participation nor rule (or only very weak versions of both); two types of weak democracy, where they have either strong participation but weak rule, or strong rule and weak participation; and strong democracy, which combines both strong participation and strong rule. These are not fixed categories, but general descriptions of points of relative strength or weakness depending on the degree of presence or absence of the two variables. Fig. 1 provides a graphical representation of this arrangement.

The two forms of weak democracy can be more fully described as follows. Where participatory institutions do not include final decision-making power, then they may be said to be *consultative*: Their purpose is to advise

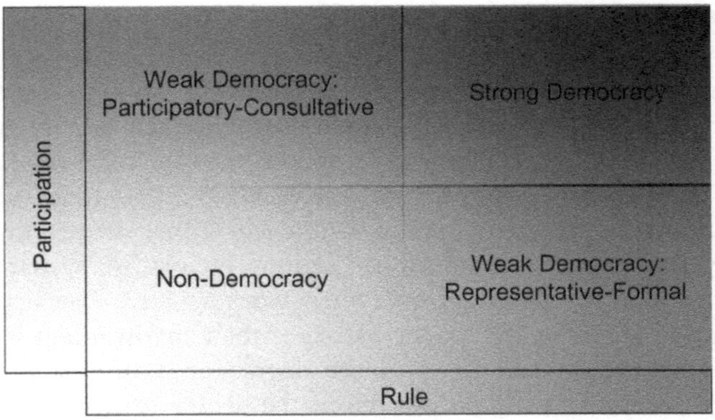

Fig. 1. Forms of Democracy.

or inform the rulers as to the preferences of the people, but they cannot be said to rule in a formal sense. The greater the degree to which this participation may be said to be effective, the closer it gets to strong democracy. This is the most common form of workplace participation in traditional enterprises. In some cases workers may have the feeling of control over substantial matters, but, as will be discussed below, limits imposed by management – including the ability to revoke the participatory system itself – and the structural conditions imposed by a hierarchical structure mean that even with highly participatory and democratic procedures, in a final sense the role of the workers is only consultative, not decisive.

The other weak form comes in the shape of representative institutions where the people's (or workers') voice is, at least in some sense, final, but their participation is limited to electing representatives and little more besides the electoral mechanism for holding them accountable. I call this *formal democracy*, because the people do rule, but only in an indirect and formal, and not in a practical, sense. Again, however, the greater the opportunities for participation, the closer this gets to strong democracy. This form may be seen, for example, in ESOPs or worker cooperatives in which workers are given the ability to elect all or some portion of the board of directors but have little say over operational decision-making.

For the purposes of this essay, the distinction between different domains of decision-making – governance versus operations – is an important, but largely technical distinction. The distinction is significant to the degree that, "Participation at the top can protect and broaden participation on the plant floor. Participation at the bottom increases the interest and support workers give to their representatives on the top ... and strengthens the representatives' positions vis-à-vis directors" (Bernstein, 1982, p. 53). The degree to which workers' participation is *decisive* is relevant, because the lack of decisiveness will undermine the democratic character of the procedures.[6] What matters here is the form that participation takes. The distinction between governance and operations is significant in that governance, or decision-making at the macro level, has broader-scale impacts that generally involve everyone at the firm, but is more episodic. Operations, or decisions at the micro level, only affect specific workers or groups of workers and are more of an on-going activity. This means that, generally speaking, different forms of participation will be more appropriate in one setting than in the other. However, regardless of the context (governance or operations), there are a number of factors that may be considered, including the way workers' preferences are communicated, the level of intensity, whether participation is direct or indirect, and so on. These questions will be discussed in the next section.

WORKPLACE PARTICIPATION

Democratic theorists have not been at the forefront of research on workplace participation; in fact, the field has been largely silent on the question.[7] Rather, most research in this area has been driven by economic concerns, particularly regarding performance and competitiveness. Worker participation in decision-making began to be promoted in the 1940s and 1950s as a means of improving productivity and morale. It became popular in the United States thanks to the work of two American expatriates, Edward Deming and Joseph Juran, who developed models of workplace participation in Japan in the 1970s and 1980s (Rothschild, 2000, p. 198). These models, quality circles and total quality management (TQM), were primarily geared toward quality control, but they gained attention in the United States as Japanese companies began capturing ever-increasing market share in areas that had been dominated by U.S. firms. Following an agreement between General Motors and the UAW in 1973 to explore ways to "enhance the quality of working life," so-called "QWL" programs and joint labor–management committees became fairly common. These were replaced by TQM, which, more recently, according to Rothschild, "is being displaced by the 'self-managing team' and the 'high performance team.' In the most recent estimates [as of 2000], some 85 percent of Fortune 1000 firms are said to be using some type of team, circle, or other employee-involvement approach" (Rothschild, 2000, p. 198).

Justification

This brief history of workplace participation reveals much about its principal motivations. Increasing profits by promoting greater productivity, quality control, and cost savings is the primary concern. There is no pretense regarding normative claims about worker empowerment[8] and expanding democratic practices. As Rothschild notes, to the extent that the language of empowerment is used at all, it is "set out as the main carrot to get employees to 'buy into'" participatory practices (Rothschild, 2000, p. 198). Programs that promote worker empowerment and participation, then, are offered as part of management science as a means to extract more value from employees – as critics often complain. Hodson quotes a study of Japanese industrial worker participation programs: "Toyotism is, therefore, not an alternative to Taylorism but rather a solution to its classic problem of the resistance of the workers in placing their knowledge of production in the service of rationalization" (Hodson, 2001, p. 177).

Clearly, the kinds of arguments used to sell participatory practices to upper management, based on profit enhancement, are different from the empowerment-based arguments used to sell the idea to workers. However, workers' participation cannot be just for show. In order for it to work, employees' participation needs to be *meaningful* – they have to *feel* empowered. Some refer to this as an "ownership culture" in which employees are given the sense that they are truly invested in the enterprise, whether or not they actually have an ownership stake. The need for the development of this sort of culture takes on greater significance when employees do, in fact, have an ownership stake, either through an ESOP or other sort of stock-ownership program. The issue in this case is most acute where employees have minority ownership, although the issue of developing an ownership culture may also arise in fully employee-owned ESOP companies, especially in a firm undergoing a conversion from a traditional structure, where upper management may be used to a more hierarchical, top-down system (see, e.g., Rosen & Rodgers, 2011).

For their sake, democratic theorists extend two kinds of arguments. Normative arguments assert that the principles of a democratic society ought to be extended to the workplace. As Dahl puts it, "*If* democracy is justified in governing the state, then it must *also* be justified in governing economic enterprises; and to say that it is *not* justified in governing economic enterprises is to imply that it is not justified in governing the state" (Dahl, 1985, p. 111). David Ellerman bases his argument for workplace democracy on "a descriptive and a normative theory of property," based on juridical principles of aligning rights with responsibilities (1999, p. 111). A different sort of argument is advanced by Pateman and others, based on the broader social and political effects of democratic practices in the workplace. Schur sums up this perspective nicely, saying that, in this argument, "making workplaces more democratic can increase employees' civic skills, interest in politics and feelings of efficacy, which increase participation in the broader society" (2003, p. 752). Empirical research generally supports this claim (Verba, Schlozman, & Brady, 1995, pp. 309–317), although, as Schur notes, "The relationship between workplace decision-making and political participation ... is not a simple one," in part because of the variety of forms that political participation can take, and the fact that the demands of the workplace itself may inhibit some forms of political participation (2003, p. 753).

The normative arguments help to support claims for strong forms of workplace democracy, but the consequentialist arguments support broader forms of participation even if relatively weak, because their ultimate concern has to do with the ways in which practices in the workplace support higher levels of political activity *outside* of the workplace. Thus, even forms of participation that do not rise to the level of democratic participation may be significant to the extent to which they "incubate civic skills" (Verba et al., 1995, p. 310). Indeed, weakly democratic practices may be more significant in some ways than strongly democratic practices if they are easier to implement and, therefore, more widespread. Then again, there may be a tradeoff between widespread yet shallow effects and narrower but deeper effects. But that will have to be considered at a later point.

Forms of Participation

Workplace participation may be defined as "the range of mechanisms used to involve the workforce in decisions at all levels of the organization – whether direct or indirect – conducted with employees or through their representatives" (Gollan, Poutsma, & Veersma, 2006, p. 499). It varies based on a number of different factors, including the nature of the work, the size of the enterprise, the type or level of the employees involved (or the degree to which employees at different levels are involved), and so on.

Bernstein identifies 3 different dimensions of participation, 16 specific areas of decision-making, and 7 different models of participation. The three dimensions are: "(1) the *degree* of control employees enjoy over any particular decision; (2) the *issues* over which that control is exercised; and (3) the organizational *level* at which their control is exercised" (Bernstein, 1982, p. 53). The areas of decision-making range from the local (the "worker's own work") to the long-term goals of the company. This includes a middle range of the means by which the company seeks to attain its goals (Bernstein, 1982, p. 57). The models of participation range from very weak (a suggestion box) to very strong (fully self-managed firms) (Bernstein, 1982, p. 58).

Additional dimensions of participation can be identified that help to provide a fuller sense of the different forms that participation can take. A number of categories can be easily recognized: Formal versus informal, small-group versus large-group, open versus closed, and so on. *Formal* systems would, for example, provide for regularly scheduled meetings with clearly identified participants, and could even be codified in some way in an organization's regular operating procedures. An *informal* system of participation could include ad hoc meetings called by a supervisor, or so-called "management by walking around," in which managers are expected to make a habit of walking around the shop floor or office to connect with workers and give them an opportunity to discuss their work in a meaningful, direct way (Miller, Hartwick, & Le Breton-Miller, 2004, p. 8). A system based on *small groups* (such as workgroups) may be task-oriented, while a *large-group* system would bring all of the employees of an enterprise, or perhaps even a subunit, together for more general purposes. *Open participation* would include systems in which participation is voluntary and available to anyone, whereas a *closed* system has defined participants and is considered a part of the employees' duties. One might also recognize a difference between *horizontal* and *vertical* participation, the former incorporating employees who are all at the same level within the hierarchy of the organization, and vertical including people from different levels.

Distinguishing between Mere Participation and Democratic Participation

As Bernstein points out, not all participatory practices may be recognized as "democratic." The question then becomes one of identifying the particular criteria by which a practice is understood as democratic versus merely participatory. He argues that, "Minimally, democratization begins with the establishment of an upward flow of criticisms and suggestions from the managed to the managers" (Bernstein, 2012/1976, p. 47). However, the existence of this communication flow does not make a system democratic: a suggestion box, for example, which involves no face-to-face discussion or regularized communication so employees can know when or even why their proposals are accepted or rejected, falls below the threshold. Even in the presence of apparently democratic procedures, if employees' initiatives are consistently rejected by management, workers will likely lose interest in participating, and the veneer of democracy will become too thin to support claims of a democratic workplace (Bernstein, 2012/1976, p. 49).

For Bernstein, the fundamental criterion for a workplace to be considered democratic is that the normal status of employees as "managed and ruled" is disrupted, and workers become, in at least a limited sense, co-managers (Bernstein, 2012/1976, p. 48). Pateman's position is similar; as she puts it, "The whole point about industrial participation is that it involves a modification, to a greater or lesser degree, of the orthodox authority structure ... where decision making is the 'prerogative' of management, in which workers play no part" (Pateman, 1970, p. 68). In other words, the standard hierarchical relationship between workers and managers is altered such that workers are no longer merely subordinates of managers. This means that the employees must have a meaningful impact on decision-making, which is to say that they must be able to exert power or influence on the outcome of the decision-making process.[9] If they do not have this, then their participation cannot be considered democratic.

Dahl provides some further detail on what this might entail, as he articulates a set of standards for democratic procedures. Dahl suggests five criteria: effective participation, equality in voting, enlightened understanding, ability to control the agenda, and inclusion (1998, p. 38). Dahl admits that it is unlikely that any association would ever be able to meet these standards in any complete sense (1998, p. 42), which means that there is substantial flexibility in the degree to which they may be implemented while retaining their democratic character. However, the presence of a set of criteria does imply that some forms of participation can be identified as clearly not democratic. Bernstein's suggestion that participation initiated by managers who "retain full power to accept or reject the employees' decision" falls "below the threshold of ... democratic participation" (1982, p. 58) is certainly consonant with Dahl's procedural definition. The notion of "effective participation" implies, at the least, that the participation of workers is meaningful, which is to say that it has a demonstrable impact on decision-making.

Nondemocratic Participation

As one final point, it may be noted that the types of participation considered by Bernstein and Dahl are all *positive* forms of participation in which workers are given opportunities to directly and intentionally engage with management in decision-making processes over some aspect of the enterprise in which they work. But if the criterion for participation is the ability of workers to affect managerial decision-making, this raises the question of whether *negative* forms of participation might also be considered relevant. Such practices as absenteeism, shirking, sabotage, and even exit are not only ways of expressing dissatisfaction, but also affect decision-making.[10] Negative participation, such as exit, may be considered political to the extent that it involves an assertion of power (the power of exit). Warren adds that not only is exit an exercise of power, but it also has considerable communicative value, even if the actual content is not explicit (Warren, 2011). While usually understood as isolated, individual actions, they do have a collective effect. As has been pointed out by numerous observers, the fact that most enterprises employ various levels of managers to oversee workers imposes great costs on those companies (see, e.g., Bowles & Gintis, 1993; Veblen, 1904). So, if the purpose of participation is to influence the decision-making of management, clearly negative participation does this by creating the need for supervision. Indeed, the desire to address this condition is what inspired the TQM movement, which sought to establish forms of positive participation precisely in order to address the impacts of negative participation.

Regardless of its collective effects, the fact that negative participation is, generally speaking, uncoordinated, informal, and individualistic appears to preclude it from being considered a form of *democratic* participation. The idea that employees "vote with their feet" does not seem to rise to Dahl's standard. "Vote" implies the presence of some kind of democratic procedures, or at a minimum a level of explicit coordination that is missing in this case.[11] The metaphor, therefore, obscures the nature of the participation. Indeed, a procedural definition of democracy implies, even mandates, positive participation, and the lack of such participation – or, negative participation in the form of absence from engagement with the system (i.e., apathy) – is generally understood to undermine democracy and reflect its failures. My argument that at least some systems of workplace participation can, in fact, be understood as weakly democratic does depend on a procedural definition of democracy as the mechanism through which workers are given a voice, so negative participation cannot be counted as democratic participation.

Another practice that sometimes gets included as a form of participation, and is even referred to as "democratic," is the provision of information by management to workers, which may include any information related to governance, such as strategic planning, but especially in the form of financial performance information.[12] It is not immediately clear, however, why the passive receipt of information is considered participatory. But while the provision of information may not in itself be participatory, much less democratic, it does affect the power relations to some degree. Knowledge, it is often said, is power, and increasing workers' knowledge about the company's functioning or plans both reduces the power of managers and increases the power of the workers. This relates, in a way, to negative participation, because if workers are unhappy about the managers' performance as revealed in the information provided to them (e.g., they are concerned about risky behavior or excessive compensation for top executives), they are more likely to engage in such practices as shirking or sabotage. So, the provision of information has a kind of democratic effect by affecting the inequalities between management and workers, a point that will be discussed further below.

ADDITIONAL DEMOCRATIC FACTORS

A number of different specific factors may have a substantial impact on the nature and form of any participatory practices and their broader effects. Here I will focus on two: size and equality (perhaps better understood as the degree of inequality). These will affect the character of any participatory scheme, regardless of the type of ownership.

Size

Size is probably the most significant factor to consider with regard to the specific form that participatory practices take. Simply put, in an organization with thousands of members, it would be difficult – although not impossible – to function as an assembly, certainly not in operations and only with some difficulty in governance. Forms of direct democracy could be practiced through ballots, but in all likelihood these would be fairly limited, and mostly only with respect to governance. That said, as was discussed above, the establishment of small workgroups would make it possible for employees to meet together for operational decision-making. By the same token, in a small organization of only five or six members, it would be difficult to enact a representative system. Informal, ad hoc decision-making may be the order of the day, at least at the operational level. Functions of governance typically must be formalized, but in a small outfit this can still be practiced in a direct manner in assembly form.

Another important factor having to do with size has to do with its effect on the nature of the relationship among the employees, and the relationship between employees and management. A smaller enterprise will be characterized by higher levels of interdependency among employees and a better understanding of their relationship to one another and to the enterprise as a whole. Increasing size leads to the establishment of epistemic distance, as the complexity of the operation increases and, as a result, few employees outside of management have a complete grasp of what all the other employees contribute to the firm and how each relates to all the others. This, along with increased distance, both epistemic and physical, between the owners and top managers of the company on one side, and the nonmanagerial employees on the other, may lead to a greater sense of alienation on the part of the workers both from each other and from the firm itself.

Equality/Inequality

The degree of equality, understood as equal capacity to determine the outcome of decision-making, is the ultimate measure of how democratic a system is. Measuring the degree of equality, however, is not a simple matter. Equality may be measured across a number of dimensions, including economic status, power, and social status. Factors related to identity such as gender, race, ethnicity, age, religion, or sexual preference, may have a strong impact on people's position with respect to these dimensions.[13] Formal equality may mask substantive inequality, making that inequality difficult to address. In particular, because financial, political, and social status are intertwined to a great extent (i.e., those with higher status have more power and more money), those who benefit in some way from this inequality are generally in a position to maintain it, and may use the fact of formal equality to justify a system that provides unequal rewards.

This means that even enterprises that make efforts to enforce high levels of equality across multiple dimensions will find that it cannot be eliminated entirely. As Rothschild and Whitt note, "Inequalities in influence persist in the most egalitarian of organizations .... Because authority resides in the collectivity as a unit, the exercise of influence depends less on position and more on the personal attributes of the individual. Members who are more articulate, responsible, energetic, glamorous, fair-minded, or committed carry more weight" (1986, p. 70). Further, as Mansbridge notes, "Egalitarian organizations ... pose a problem for conflict management." In particular, "Face-to-face assemblies provoke anxieties and tensions that rarely arise when a citizen simply walks into a voting booth and pulls a lever ... that subtly influence the way decisions are made" (Mansbridge, 1982, pp. 126–127). Mansbridge (1982) details a number of ways in which the very sorts of close personal relationships that might make a consensus-based, nonhierarchical model highly egalitarian, participatory, and deeply democratic can also serve to limit and even distort participation, especially for those who are less closely connected to the group. Conflict in such situations can be particularly damaging. These factors lead some to argue that systems of formal representation that involve secret ballots and the like may be more effective at overcoming identity-based inequalities in a democratic system than do systems that rely on face-to-face encounters (Sirianni, 1994).

THE OWNERSHIP FACTOR

It is fairly obvious that different kinds of enterprises will engage in different sorts of participatory practices – what is appropriate for workers in a factory, for example, will be different from what is appropriate for a retail operation. It is also the case, however, that different forms of ownership will be associated with different kinds of participation, and that within the domain of democratic participation, different forms of ownership will be more or less amenable to either strong or weak forms. The essential questions have to do with the relationship between the owners and the employees, which is mediated by two factors: The type of ownership, and the presence or absence of managers who oversee operations on behalf of the owners. The broad universe of different forms of ownership can be narrowed for my purposes to just a few: Traditional forms of ownership, which includes private ownership, whether publicly traded or privately held; ESOPs, of which there are three types, minority, majority, and fully employee owned; and worker cooperatives.[14] An important additional factor involves the role of unions, but as this may affect any of these ownership types it will be discussed separately at the end.

Traditional Forms of Ownership

Despite David Ellerman's eloquent arguments to the contrary,[15] decision-making authority in private enterprise is generally understood to flow from property rights, which means, in effect, the investment of capital. In a small business directly controlled by an individual entrepreneur it is difficult to say anything of a general nature, because the presence and character of any participatory practices in this setting depend, in many ways, on the temperament of the owner and the degree of his or her involvement in the company. In some cases, the owner is directly involved in operations and operational decision-making. While these may be among the most likely sites for relatively high levels of employee participation, it is also one in which the relationship between ownership and authority is clearest and the most difficult to alter.

In other firms, including all those owned by investors (whether publicly traded or privately owned by a small group, such as a venture capital firm or other form of partnership), the owners limit themselves to governance and hire a manager who makes the operational decisions. This does not alter the fundamental association of ownership and authority, but the interposition of a managerial layer between owners and workers may create somewhat greater room for various forms of employee participation in decision-making, including the establishment of democratic procedures, because the delegation of operational decision-making to managers may enable their further delegation to employees. With the exception of legally mandated codetermination arrangements, common in Europe, as long as governance rights are firmly associated with property rights, the workers' role in decision-making will necessarily be at the pleasure of the owners (or their agents, the executive managers) and, as a result, tenuous, because any decision made by the workers may be overruled by the owners, even to the point of the participatory arrangements being suspended or discontinued.

Ultimately, then, from the employee perspective, strong democracy is virtually impossible in the context of investor-owned companies, although this does not preclude the establishment of various forms of weak democracy, including those that approximate strong democracy, such as the kinds of "high-performance teams" mentioned above. A number of factors will affect the nature of participation and its potential democratic effects in these kinds of businesses. As suggested above, one of these has to do with size: A small enterprise in which all employees are in close contact with one another and have a strong feeling of interdependency is more likely to develop a participatory ethos that will have a fairly strongly democratic character. In fact, the size of the enterprise may be less significant than the way an enterprise is organized: A large company with smaller and largely autonomous units may offer similar conditions. The smaller the group, the more likely that participation will be direct rather than representative. Larger organizations are more likely to function through representatives, although this is not incompatible with smaller, self-directed workgroups that function in a directly participatory manner.

The degree to which these sorts of participatory schemes contribute to a more democratic society is debatable. As Schur notes, "Directly participating in workplace decisions seems to have positive effects on feelings of efficacy and non-voting forms of political participation," although it appears to have little effect on voter turnout (2003, p. 753). The positive effects may be felt even with weakly democratic systems, as the experience gained of analyzing information, articulating one's position, and engaging in deliberation may have the kinds of beneficial effects Pateman and others predict. However, there may be some downsides that could undermine the positive impacts. One has to do with the development of conflict due to the different interests of different groups of employees – for example, between white collar and blue collar employees, or older and younger workers (Hansmann, 1993, pp. 592–593). This sort of conflict, under some conditions, could lead to at least some employees gaining a distaste for democratic procedures if they are perceived as being overly conflict-ridden, inefficient as a model for decision-making and ineffective if employee conflict leads to management reasserting its authority or overriding employees' decisions.

These negative effects may be most severe in large organizations where the participation is indirect and management's commitment to making participation work is weakest. Small groups are not immune to problems, however. Mansbridge notes that hierarchy may provide a kind of "protective distance" that limits conflict between individuals in the group. "Eliminating hierarchy," however, "eliminates the institutional buffer zone that otherwise protects workers from one another" (Mansbridge, 1982, pp. 125–126). The inherent authority structure of the investor-owned firm may help to ameliorate some of those problems by giving employees a way of avoiding conflict by giving them recourse to an authority that exists outside of the group. However, this is not a positive result in terms of increasing people's political skills or an inclination to want to participate more broadly.

ESOPs

An ESOP is a means by which employees may have a share of ownership in the company where they work, up to and including full ownership. Most ESOP companies – between 60% and 70% – are minority-owned (i.e., employees own less than 50% of the company). Only about 3% of ESOPs are in publicly traded companies (NCEO, 2012). ESOPs are principally structured as retirement plans and a means for affecting a broader distribution of the net assets of a company both as a matter of equity but also in hope that giving employees a stake in the company will help improve productivity. As the National Center for Employee Ownership (NCEO) puts it, "ESOPs are most commonly used to provide a market for the shares of departing owners of successful closely held companies, to motivate and reward employees, or to take advantage of incentives to borrow money for acquiring new assets in pretax dollars. In almost every case, ESOPs are a contribution to the employee, not an employee purchase" (NCEO, n.d.-b). For the purposes of this essay, it is important to note that while ESOPs may be formed as a way of addressing inequities of wealth, they are not usually established as a means of empowering workers or establishing participatory or democratic workplaces – although this has been mentioned as a "fundamental value worth pursuing, and ultimately may represent the most compelling justification for ESOPs" (Murphy, 2005, p. 667, quoting McDonnell, 2000, p. 241).

The fact that employees have an ownership stake in their company does not mean that they therefore control the company either at the governance or the operational level. At the operational level, there is nothing about the ESOP model that necessarily affects the management structure of the firm: In fact, most ESOPs retain a hierarchical structure indistinguishable from a traditionally owned corporation. With respect to governance, there may not be much difference, either: In most ESOPs the employees are minority owners, and in some cases their share of the company may be quite small. Furthermore, an ESOP is a kind of a trust, so employees do not own their shares individually as other shareholders do, but own shares in the ESOP, which are managed by a trustee on their behalf. In most cases, the trustee is selected not by the employees, but by the board of directors, and the trustee is the one who has a role in governance. Employees' rights are limited to providing direction to the trustee, but only on a very narrow set of issues having to do with the legal form of the enterprise (e.g., in cases of sale or merger). With respect to other governance issues, the trustee acts as fiduciary for the plan, usually acting "at the direction of management" (NCEO, n.d.-a),[16] although, as fiduciaries for the plan, trustees are legally obligated to vote shares in the interests of the beneficiaries (i.e., the employees). ESOPs that are majority or fully owned by employees may be more likely to have a significant say in governance, including electing members of the board of directors.

The issue of inequality arises in employee-owned firms in two ways: In the hierarchical structure of most companies, ESOP or not, not only is power concentrated at the top, but also financial reward. Research shows that employee ownership "does little to mitigate effects of occupational segregation on job access, wealth accumulation, and access to power, and, in some cases, exacerbates the effects of other workplace inequality mechanisms" (Meyers, 2011a). In the typical ESOP, shares are allocated on the basis of tenure and earnings, which means that those at higher levels in the hierarchy, who have been around longer, and who earn more, also are allocated more shares. When it comes to governance, in most ESOPs in which elements of democracy have been implemented (e.g., pass-through voting for directors), voting proceeds on the same basis as in traditionally capitalized firms – that is, on the basis of shares held. Thus, the inequality lower-ranked employees experience in operations is replicated with respect to governance, and, rather than providing a mechanism whereby it can be addressed, inequality is reinforced.[17] This issue leads Dow to argue that most ESOPs should not be considered labor-managed firms, even when owned by a majority of the employees (2003, p. 81).

Two points may be made in response to this. First, ERISA rules, which govern ESOPs, limit the degree of inequality somewhat,[18] and companies may establish more egalitarian distributions if they so choose. Also, longevity matters, too, so a low-level but long-tenured employee may own more shares than much more senior but newer employees. Second, it could be said that within the hierarchical structure of a typical mid- or large-sized company, each level enjoys about the same degree of ownership because those lower in the scale have greater numbers. Much like the Electoral College, which functions to balance out the population differences among states (albeit imperfectly), the unequal allocation of shares based on compensation helps to balance out differences between the different levels of the hierarchy. Therefore, managers might be wary of a one-person-one vote rule, because this would introduce a different kind of inequality whereby lower levels, which are typically more populous, have more power than the higher levels. In fact, within the context of the firm, two elements in particular would mitigate these concerns: First, much has been written about the kinds of collective action problems that larger groups face in comparison to smaller groups (see, e.g., Olson, 1965). The second (which is acknowledged in the collective action literature) is the advantages in information, expertise, and communications that senior managers enjoy. The function of unions as a way of addressing these advantages will be discussed below, but in their absence, inequalities based on the distribution of power and the distribution of shares will affect the democratic character of an ESOP.

In terms of their broader social effects, ESOPs can be expected to be similar to traditional firms in most respects. However, ESOPs do help to democratize society, affecting the distribution of wealth by giving workers the opportunity to accumulate some assets who would otherwise be unlikely to be able to do so.

Worker Cooperatives

> I believe that someone who believes in cooperativism is much more likely to actively participate in the social and democratic processes outside the cooperative. If you are not willing to be pushed about in your job, you are not willing to be pushed about by a politician, by a policeman, by anybody else who thinks that they've got power. (Susanne Bradtmueller, Mondragón Language Coop, quoted in Dworkin & Young, 2012)

Worker cooperatives are enterprises that are wholly owned by their workers and are democratic by definition on the basis of one-person-one-vote. However, even here there is variation with respect to just how democratic they may be. Issues such as size and the presence of inequalities have different dynamics than in traditional firms and ESOPs, but they are still present. In comparison to ESOPs and traditionally owned firms worker cooperatives are more likely to have strong democratic systems simply because workers necessarily have a role in governance, but if participation is limited to governance, then they may embody the other sort of weak democracy, in which participation is limited to a formal role in electing representatives and little else.

The strongest form of democracy may be found in those cooperatives that Rothschild and Whitt refer to as "collectivist-democratic organizations" (1986, p. 50). Contrasting an "ideal-type" collectivist-democratic organization with an ideal-type bureaucratic enterprise characterized by hierarchy and formalism, the collective is characterized by collective decision-making with an absence of hierarchy, bureaucracy, or other formal decision-making structures. Decisions are generally made on an ad hoc basis through a consensus process without a reliance on formal, established rules, and any rules that have been established are always subject to renegotiation and change. Every effort is made to maintain equality on all levels, so not only is there little differentiation in pay, but also in influence and authority. Job rotation and cross-training help to ensure that no member can claim authority on the basis of a particular position or expertise (Rothschild & Whitt, 1986, pp. 50–61).

Such organizations would generally need to be quite small. The "negative relation between size and participation is most pronounced where the motivation of members is based on identification with system goals rather than on individual material rewards" as in a more traditional hierarchical structure where workers advance in authority, prestige, and pay based on performance (Rothschild & Whitt, 1986, p. 92, citing studies by Ingham and Rosner regarding an inverse relationship between size and participation). Various factors will affect the optimal size with respect to ensuring the greatest degree of equal participation. In fact, the notion of an "optimal size" may be paradoxical because of the various trade-offs involved between functioning as an effective organization and maintaining maximal participation. Thus, with respect to their participatory character, it may be a matter of "a curve of diminishing returns – a slow erosion of democracy" (Rothschild & Whitt, 1986, p. 92).

Rothschild and Whitt acknowledge that "the limited size of such organizations may reduce their impact on the surrounding society and their value as demonstrations of alternative organizational principles" (1986, p. 95). In fact, their small size is not the only factor that may affect their impact on society. As was noted above, the attempt to establish a purely egalitarian workplace may be a chimera, because the factors that introduce inequalities may have to do with the personal qualities of individuals. The attempt to enforce equality may even undermine the survival of an enterprise, leading to a dilemma of choosing between "organizational permanence" and "democratic process" (Rothschild & Whitt, 1986, pp. 76–84).[19] These factors will tend to undermine the ability of such enterprises to contribute to the democratization of society in a couple of ways. In the first place, the oppositional character of many of these "alternative institutions" may create an "us-versus-them" mentality that leads to withdrawal from "mainstream society" rather than engagement (Rothschild & Whitt, 1986, pp. 116–117). Setting the standard for what constitutes democracy too high may paradoxically lead to apathy on the part of those who either dismiss existing institutions as insufficiently democratic, on the one side, or find the standard too demanding, on the other. Finally, organizations that disband due to their inability to function effectively will not only not have a positive impact, but may in fact have a negative impact if the former members of the group become disenchanted or cynical about the potential for strengthening democracy more broadly.

Indeed, not all worker cooperatives are of the sort that Rothschild and Whitt describe,[20] and it is worth examining what happens in larger organizations. It turns out that the development of formalized systems is often a consequence of growth. In a recent study, Meyers examines two worker cooperatives, both of which started small in the 1970s as the sort of collectivist-democratic organizations Rothschild and Whitt describe, only to evolve in different ways as they grew to substantial size – one, a bakery, had 100 employees at the time of her study (2002–2003), while the other, a grocery, had 234. Although both developed significant elements of formality and structure, the bakery, though smaller, developed a more formal and fairly traditional hierarchy, with different members of the board of directors elected by managerial and nonmanagerial employees. The grocery maintained a much flatter and more participatory structure based on decentralized teams, laid on top of a representative system that includes various elective "coordinating and consulting committees" that deal with matters of governance as well as conflict-resolution and problem-solving (Meyers, 2011b, pp. 18–20). But while both companies could be described as bureaucratic, with formal rules to address a wide variety of conditions, the grocery retained a highly egalitarian workplace where equality was enforced by the existence of and adherence to a complex array of rules. The hierarchy of the bakery, however, enabled a managerial mindset to develop that established and, in some ways, enhanced differences in status between employees and undermined the democratic procedures that were in place, although the fact that managers could exercise discretionary authority meant that there were, generally speaking, fewer rules (Meyers, 2011b, pp. 21–26).

In fact, the larger the organization, the more likely it is that it will take on the dynamics of a traditionally owned firm, with the exception that workers retain at least a formal a role in governance. The struggles of Mondragón, the world's largest worker cooperative (in fact a conglomerate of over 111 cooperatives with over 80,000 employees around the world) are well-documented (Arando, Freundlich, Gago, Jones, & Kato, 2011; Cheney, 1999; Kasmir, 1996).

A major issue faced by Mondragón is the presence of large numbers of nonowner employees, mostly due to rapid expansion in the 1990s through acquisition.[21] The existence of nonowner employees in worker cooperatives is a common issue that threatens to undermine, to a degree, the democratic character of these companies by establishing a two-tiered system in which some employees enjoy a role in decision-making while others are excluded. This condition is not uncommon. Probationary employees may be fairly ubiquitous in this regard, but these are only temporarily excluded, and cooperatives may allow employees to choose whether to join or remain as nonmember employees, which poses no great difficulty unless internal rules or dynamics establish conditions that make it more difficult for particular classes of employees to join.[22] Some cooperatives, however, permanently exclude whole classes of workers, including, for example, administrative support staff and even top management (NCF, 2006, p. 20). The exclusion of top managers certainly inverts the traditional structure, although it also reifies the division between governance and operations management, with one being weakly democratic (especially if governance is by an elected board) and the other (potentially) nonparticipatory. Indeed, if the number of nonmembers is much larger than the number of owners and parallels a division between say, professional and administrative support staff, the company becomes more like a traditional partnership, such as a law firm, than a cooperative.

The impact of worker cooperatives in terms of their democratizing effect on the broader society depends, as the foregoing discussion reflects, on several factors. One of these is the intensity of the democratic practices inside the firm. If participation is limited to periodic votes for members of the board of directors, they may have little impact. At the other end of the scale, if participation is exceptionally intensive, the members may expend so much of their energy on internal issues that they have little time for participation in political or social institutions on the "outside," particularly if those outside institutions are derided for being insufficiently democratic and therefore not worthy of participation. As they grow, even a cooperative that puts participatory mechanisms in place may slowly devolve into a thin, representative model, especially with the rise of a class of professional managers that exercises operational control. Over time, fewer and fewer members may attend meetings, deferring decision-making to elected workers councils and a board of directors (who may defer to the judgment of the professional managers). Eventually, participation in elections may decline to a point where only a few members are involved even at that level.

In addition, there is no particular reason to assume that worker cooperatives would have any positive effect on their society. Some take it on faith that worker cooperatives contribute to a more democratic society (see, e.g., Wright, 2010), and without question many do, but this cannot be taken for granted. Indeed, there is no particular reason why, understood as autonomous enterprises, cooperatives would be any different from any other sort of enterprise. What Gonzales says with respect to Italian worker cooperatives could be said about them more generally: "Though guided by strong ethical commitments to solidarity and democratic control, at heart, cooperatives are business enterprises dedicated to serving the collective through the private interests of their members" (2010, p. 230). Worker cooperatives, like all businesses, must operate in a competitive environment that presents them with ethical dilemmas on which a business' very survival may hang. As one research subject put it, "Democratic participation in management is all well and good, but people around here don't always realize: no profit, no cooperative. Just like that, your social values are irrelevant" (quoted in Schoening, 2006, p. 297). If workers in a cooperative tend to have a higher level of concern for the local community,[23] this may be a matter of selection bias (where the kind of people who join cooperatives are likely to be less self-interested and more socially conscious) or acculturation in the cooperative culture. If it is the latter, this would point to the possibility that the growth of worker cooperatives would have a strongly positive impact on the democratization of their communities, as their spread would increase the number of people who spend a significant portion of their lives – while at work – immersed in a cooperative culture.

The Effect of Unions

Unions can have a democratizing effect in several ways. In terms of the broader society, the most direct is through voter mobilization efforts, which is both substantial and well-documented (see Zullo, 2008 and the literature reviewed therein). Unions have also been historically understood as a means by which to counterbalance the autocratic structure of traditional corporations, which they accomplish by constraining the ability of management to act unilaterally (McCarthy, Voos, Eaton, Kruse, & Blasi, 2011, p. 28; Zullo, 2008, pp. 23–25). Internally, most unions can be characterized as weakly democratic at best; despite regulatory moves in the 1950s to improve the internal practices of unions, as recently as 2000 one author was moved to comment, "we are no closer to the democratic ideal of active membership involvement and contested elections, let alone two-party systems (Estreicher, 2000, p. 247).

Besides – or rather through – their ability to counterbalance the hierarchical corporate power structure, unions can affect operational practices within a firm by establishing joint union–management programs. These programs, which are common in the automobile and telecommunications industries, as well as other industries with relatively high levels of union representation, provide a setting by which workers and management can engage in communication and problem-solving, and protect workers' rights (Hodson, 2001, pp. 178–179).

Although early in their history unions experimented with employee ownership (see the Olsen paper in this volume), over time their attitude became skeptical, especially as worker ownership came to be used by management not as a means to benefit workers but as a way of saving a failing company or fighting off a hostile takeover. More specifically, union leaders may be concerned that employee ownership would lead to workers identifying more closely with management, loosening their commitment to the union (McCarthy et al., 2011, p. 34). Over time, however, their perspective has become more positive (Yates, 2006, p. 710). With respect to ESOPs with unionized workforces, Yates found the full range of cases, including those in which the union members owned a majority, a minority, or were excluded entirely from ownership. The firms that established majority-employee-owned ESOPs "moved from a rather traditional management approach to equal or surpass other employee-owned companies in the use of participatory management techniques" while, in contrast, the companies that excluded union members "changed the least" – even less than non-unionized ESOPs (pp. 719–720).[24] Majority-owned unionized ESOPs also showed the highest level of employee interest in decision-making. Yates suggests that "Involvement and interest can interact in a self-reinforcing spiral where interest leads to more involvement and involvement leads to more interest," although "It is difficult to say which comes first" (pp. 726–727). She concludes that, "after their ESOPs were established, the unionized, majority-employee-owned companies created a considerably better working life for their unionized employee-owners, with more equality, better communication, more training, more opportunities to participate, and a more cooperative relationship between employees and management." Unionized companies that were minority employee-owned showed less improvement, and those that excluded the union had the lowest scores on all of these measures (p. 728). Among nonunion firms, those that were majority-employee-owned showed more improvement on these measures than did minority-employee-owned firms, but the difference was not as dramatic as for the unionized firms.

Yates notes that, "Entry into employee ownership is not always a free choice for employees," as it may be initiated by management to avert a takeover or enable a tax-friendly succession for the prior owners (2006, p. 710). In some cases employees are faced with the choice of buying a failing company or face closure and the loss of their jobs. The advantage of an active, involved union is the ability for the union to exercise its bargaining power to negotiate a favorable contract that incorporates employee participation along with the ESOP – a power it has to the greatest extent in those cases where the ESOP is the majority owner (Yates, 2006, p. 731). Based on Yates' research, it appears that unionized, employee-majority-owned ESOPs can take on a strong-democratic form, in some cases exceeding the level of participation in some worker cooperatives.

Unions in worker cooperatives are uncommon. Berry and Schneider's study (2011) of the relationship between Cooperative Home Care Associates (CHCA, the nation's largest worker cooperative with over 1,700 members) and the Service Employees International Union (SEIU) finds that their relationship is generally positive and cooperative, based on their shared goals of providing good jobs and a supportive work environment, although some tensions are evident. In fact, CHCA saw unionization as helpful in organizing and educating their membership, providing leadership training and opportunities, and even enabling employees to pursue a college education (pp. 85–86).

A unique collaboration between Mondragón, the Ohio Employee Ownership Center (OEOC), and the United Steelworkers (USW) has developed recently in which Mondragón will develop manufacturing facilities in the United States in which the worker-owners will also be union members (Witherell, Cooper, & Peck, 2012). The "Union Co-op Model" defines a union co-op as "a unionized worker-owned co-operative in which worker-owners all own an equal share of the business and have an equal vote in overseeing the business" (p. 6). The authors note that worker cooperatives elect a board of directors to "look out for the interests of the worker-owners as owners," but what they rarely do is "elect people to look out for the … interests of workers as workers" (p. 6). So, in addition to taking part in annual general assemblies and the election of a board of directors, nonsupervisory employees would be organized into a bargaining unit, which would represent them in negotiating a collective bargaining agreement and would form a union council that would have formal bargaining authority (p. 7).

Unions appear to have the potential to play a positive role in maintaining the democratic character of cooperatives, particularly where large size may lead to more formal and hierarchical structures. As with traditional companies, the union can counteract the "oligarchization" that Rothschild and Whitt warn against (1986, pp. 23–24) and that appears to have arisen in Mondragón.

CONCLUSION

This paper has explored, from a largely theoretical perspective (supported by empirical evidence where present), the impact of different types of ownership on the strength of democratic practices within firms and on the democratization of the broader society. The results are not categorical – that is, it is not possible to simply say that traditionally owned firms are necessarily and always less democratic than are, for example, worker cooperatives. In other words, employee ownership – partial or complete – is neither a sufficient nor a necessary condition for a strongly democratic workplace. However, there is no question that the provision of ownership rights to workers establishes conditions more amenable to democracy than if worker ownership is lacking. After reviewing the six components necessary for democratization, Bernstein notes that "at least two contain rights traditionally reserved to owners," including "the owner's right to *manage* the firm at his sole discretion, and … the owner's right to have *first claim on the profits*" (1982, p. 77). The worker cooperative model, in which ownership rights are equal for all members, is therefore more amenable to a strong-democratic form than the other types of ownership.

Democracy will tend to be stronger in worker cooperatives because the two most significant dynamics, size and the presence of inequality, work in their favor: They are more likely to be small, and the degrees (and forms) of the various inequalities that may be present in the workplace – based on authority, wage differentials, etc. – are likely to be much reduced. The ownership structure addresses one of the most fundamental of those inequalities, because, in a formal sense with respect to governance, at least, all employees are equal – in fact, members of a worker cooperative enjoy a higher degree of equality in this sense than do the owners of an investor-owned firm.

However, the formal equality in the worker cooperative may mask substantive inequalities. The fact of equality with respect to governance does not always translate into equality with respect to operational decision-making, and it is in the on-going practice of operational decision-making that participation is most directly experienced. What is true for worker cooperatives is true for any enterprise: Small size will tend to make it easier to have high levels of participation in operational decisions, but as an enterprise grows, as differentiation between different parts or even divisions increases, epistemic distance grows, and effective participation becomes more difficult – at least unless and until smaller units are able to act with fairly high levels of autonomy.

The fact that hierarchical frameworks and a managerial mindset can develop in worker cooperatives means that, although they may never go below the level of weak democracy, they also cannot be assumed to be strongly democratic. Investor-owned firms present the inverse case: they may approach strong democracy, but, lacking a formal governance role for workers, can never quite cross the threshold into fully democratic workplaces. ESOPs fall into a middle ground: Although few enable workers to have an effective role in governance, some do, and in this case they may make it all the way into strongly democratic systems.

The kinds of democratic practices that take place within a company will affect the kind and degree of the "spillover effect" in terms of the democratization of the broader society. Here the results are decidedly mixed. Intensively democratic practices such as in the collectivist-democratic organizations may paradoxically have less of a spillover effect, for at least a couple of reasons: First, because the very intensiveness of the practices in the firm may sap the energy of its members for participating in political activity on the outside – and it may set a standard for democratic practices that is so difficult to meet that lesser forms of political action may be treated with apathy and disdain. By the same token, people who are engaged in these practices may approach democratic practice with an almost religious zeal and become active advocates to the point of proselytizing.[25] However, the small size of these companies will limit the reach of this kind of activity.

While the intensiveness of strong democratic practices may limit the extent of their social effects, the weaker sorts of democratic practice may have broader, though less intensive, reach. The basis for the claim here is primarily quantitative: The few thousand members of worker cooperatives must be compared to 11 million worker-owners in ESOPs (NCEO, 2012) and an unknown number – perhaps tens of millions – of employees in traditionally owned companies that incorporate some form of employee participation in decision-making. Those types of worker participation in decision-making that least challenge existing power structures are precisely the sort that are most likely to be implemented. But because they are weaker, their democratizing effect can be expected to be less, as well.

For those whose normative commitments lead them to advocate for the extension of democratic practices into the workplace, it is valuable to have a sense of the ways in which different forms of ownership establish the conditions for democratization to take place and that affect the strength of the kinds of systems that may be established. It is simply not possible to establish something like a collectivist-democratic system in an enterprise that is owned by investors, and to attempt to do so is destined to failure. By the same token, understanding how growth may affect the democratic character of a strongly democratic worker cooperative may make it possible to identify warning signs of a weakening system and establish mechanisms to better retain and sustain strongly democratic systems. Finally, the analysis presented here suggests that there are good reasons to support weakly democratic systems if they are widespread.

NOTES

1. And as significant portions of the population, such as women and slaves, were excluded from these assemblies.
2. For critiques, see, for example Barber (2003) and Pateman (1970, Chap. 1).
3. For further discussion of this point, see Kaswan (2011).
4. This essay is not the place for an extended discussion of the nature of power, but for a detailed discussion see Lukes (2005).
5. For example, public corporations may limit ownership rights to those who own certain types of stock. Similarly, a worker cooperative may accept capital investment by nonmembers, but only members may purchase shares that give them rights of ownership.
6. This will be discussed at greater length in the following section.
7. I say "largely silent," but not entirely so. Important early contributions include Pateman (1970) and Dahl (1985). More attention has been given to these ideas recently, with somewhat greater urgency since the start of the Great Recession (see, e.g., Alperovitz, 2011; Wright, 2010). However, the field is dominated by managerial science, not democratic theory.
8. Indeed, an interesting feature of the literature is the tendency to refer to "employees" rather than "workers." Perhaps the latter term is seen as carrying too much ideological freight.
9. Pateman distinguishes between "power" and "influence," where the former refers to the ability to *determine* the outcome of a decision-making process and the

latter refers to a weaker condition, limited to the ability to *affect* the outcome. Only the former, in her view, constitutes full participation; the latter she refers to as "partial participation" (Pateman, 1970, pp. 69–70). While there is clearly a difference here, both of these meet the weaker criteria of being democratic as Bernstein defines it, as long as employees have the sense of empowerment and managers have a sense that their decision-making is directed by the employees at least to some extent.

10. My research on which this discussion is based focused on the public administration literature, where bureaucracy is particularly prevalent and large in scale (see, e.g., Brehm & Gates, 1997; Hirschman, 1970; O'Leary, 2006). However, there is no reason to expect the character of negative participation to be different in private enterprise (see, e.g., Hodson, 2001, pp. 124–131).

11. The exception here would be the types of collective action usually associated with unions, such as strikes, slow-downs, sick-outs, and the like.

12. Logue and Yates (2001) is a good example of this.

13. Much has been said about issues of equality as pertains to these identity factors, but even these proceed from an assumption of fundamental equality or, as Thomas Jefferson put it, that "all men are created equal." The issue of equality connects to that of identity to the extent that people who either identify themselves or are identified by others as having certain attributes feel that their condition in life is in some way determined by their identity.

14. One further type of ownership includes public (state) ownership, by which I mean ownership by a federal, state, or local governmental unit. However, from a theoretical perspective there are a great number of complexities that make this particular form both especially interesting but also difficult to address in a constrained manner. An effective discussion of the issues involved would require a separate paper, so this ownership category will be excluded here.

15. In essence, Ellerman (1999) argues that based on the legal principle of responsibility, which assigns responsibility based on de facto control, employees should by right control the assets and liabilities of the enterprise in which they work, which implies democratic control of the enterprise.

16. This mostly applies to ESOPs in privately held companies. Employees have more voting rights in publicly traded companies, but these are a small minority of ESOPs.

17. Two recent essays examine this question in detail: Buchele, Kruse, Rodgers, and Scharf (2010) and Carberry (2010).

18. There are various limits with respect to the amount that any one participant can receive in a year ($49,000 or 100% of salary, whichever is less) and the tax deductibility of contributions (NCEO, n.d.-a).

19. Rothschild and Whitt's research was done in the 1970s, during the heyday of collectivist-democratic workplaces. As Meyers notes, of the estimated 5,000 such organizations that began in the 1970s, few survived (2011b, p. 6).

20. A recent survey by the U.S. Worker Cooperative Federation found that, of 270 cooperatives (which they estimate to be an undercount by approximately 10–20%), the vast majority – 195 – are small, with under 15 employees. Only nine cooperatives were considered "large" (50–199 employees), and four "jumbo" size, with over 200 employees (Melissa Hoover, personal correspondence, 2013).

21. This condition, which at its peak meant that there were more nonmember employees than members in the company, has abated substantially as some of the acquired firms have been converted into cooperatives (Arando et al., 2011). The current level of worker-owners is close to 80%.

22. As was, in fact, the case, in one of Meyers' cases (Meyers, 2011b).

23. I am unaware of any formal research on this question, but anecdotal evidence would suggest that this is the case.

24. While the types of participation that are included in Yates' study include what here are considered nondemocratic forms, such as suggestion boxes, the unionized, majority-owned sites also were more likely to use the more intensively democratic forms. These were also much more likely to give employees a bigger role in governance (Yates, 2006, p. 721).

25. Just by the way of illustration, a friend once described some former roommates, heavily involved in their worker cooperative, as "cultish" – to the point that it gave him a negative impression of cooperatives. The language of evangelism was, in fact, used in an early stage of the cooperative movement in Britain in the early 19th century (Carpenter, 1832).

ACKNOWLEDGMENTS

The support the author has received as a J. Robert Beyster and Michael W. Huber Fellow through the Rutgers School of Management and Labor Relations, including the opportunity to present some of these ideas in Beyster Fellows Workshops and Beyster Symposia has been vital to the development of this paper, and for this the author is most grateful. He also thanks Mary Ann Beyster and the Foundation for Enterprise Development for supporting this research. Finally, the author thanks Doug Kruse and an anonymous reviewer for their helpful comments and suggestions.

REFERENCES

Abrahamsson, B., Broström, A., & Knocke, W. (Eds.), (1980). Announcing a new journal. *Economic and Industrial Democracy*, 1(1), i–v.

Alperovitz, G. (2011). *America beyond capitalism: Reclaiming our wealth, our liberty, and our democracy*. Boston, MA: Dollar & Sense and the Democracy Collaborative Press.

Arando, S., Freundlich, F., Gago, M., Jones, D. C., & Kato, T. (2011). Assessing Mondragon: Stability and managed change in the face of globalization. In E. J. Carberry (Ed.), *Employee ownership and shared capitalism: New directions in research* (pp. 241–271). Champaign, IL: Labor and Employment Relations Association.

Barber, B. R. (2003). *Strong democracy: Participatory politics for a new age* (20th Anniversary ed.). Berkeley, CA: University of California Press.

Bernstein, P. (1982). Necessary elements for effective worker participation in decision-making. In F. Lindenfeld & J. Rothschild-Whitt (Eds.), *Workplace democracy and social change* (pp. 51–81). Boston, MA: Extending Horizons Books.
Bernstein, P. (2012/1976). *Workplace democratization: Its internal dynamics*. Chelsea, MA: Educational Services Publishing.
Berry, D. P., & Schneider, S. (2011). Improving the quality of home health aide jobs: A collaboration between organized labor and a worker cooperative. In E. J. Carberry (Ed.), *Employee ownership and shared capitalism: New directions in research* (pp. 59–89). Champaign, IL: Labor and Employment Relations Association.
Bowles, S., & Gintis, H. (1993). The revenge of homo economicus: Contested exchange and the revival of political economy. *Journal of Economic Perspectives*, *7*(1), 83–102.
Brehm, J., & Gates, S. (1997). *Working, shirking and sabotage: Bureaucratic response to a democratic public*. Ann Arbor, MI: University of Michigan Press.
Buchele, R., Kruse, D. L., Rodgers, L., & Scharf, A. (2010). Show me the money: Does shared capitalism share the wealth?. In D. L. Kruse, R. B. Freeman, & J. R. Blasi (Eds.), *Shared capitalism at work: Employee ownership, profit and gain sharing, and broad-based stock options* (pp. 351–376). Chicago, IL: University of Chicago Press.
Carberry, E. J. (2010). Who benefits from shared capitalism? The social stratification of wealth and power in companies with employee ownership. In D. L. Kruse, R. B. Freeman, & J. R. Blasi (Eds.), *Shared capitalism at work: Employee ownership, profit and gain sharing, and broad-based stock options* (pp. 317–350). Chicago, IL: University of Chicago Press.
Carpenter, W. (1832). Proceedings of the third cooperative congress owenism and the working class: Six pamphlets and four broadsides, Arno Press, New York, NY, pp. 1821–1834.
Cheney, G. (1999). *Values at work: Employee participation meets market pressure at Mondragón* (Updated ed.). Ithaca, NY: Cornell University Press.
Dahl, R. (1985). *A preface to economic democracy*. Berkeley, CA: University of California Press.
Dahl, R. (1989). *Democracy and its critics*. New Haven, CT: Yale University Press.
Dahl, R. (1998). *On democracy*. New Haven, CT: Yale University Press.
Dow, G. K. (2003). *Governing the firm: Workers' control in theory and practice*. Cambridge: Cambridge University Press.
Dworkin, M., & Young, M. (Writers). (2012). Shift change. In M. Dworkin & M. Young (Producer). Oley, PA: Bullfrog Films.
Ellerman, D. (1999). The democratic firm: An argument based on ordinary jurisprudence. *Journal of Business Ethics*, *21*(2/3), 111–124.
Estreicher, S. (2000). Deregulating union democracy. *Journal of Labor Research*, *21*(2), 247–263. doi:10.1007/s12122-000-1046-8
Gallie, W. B. (1955–1956). Essentially contested concepts. *Proceedings of the Aristotelian Society*, *56*(New Series), 167–198.
Gollan, P. J., Poutsma, E., & Veersma, U. (2006). Editors' introduction: New roads in organizational participation? *Industrial Relations 45* (4), 499–512.
Gonzales, V. (2010). Italian social cooperatives and the development of civic capacity: A case of cooperative renewal? *Affinities: A Journal of Radical Theory, Culture, and Action*, *4*(1), 225–251.
Hansmann, H. (1993). Worker participation and corporate governance, *University of Toronto Law Journal*, *43*, 589–606.
Held, D. (1996). *Models of democracy* (2nd ed.). Stanford: Stanford University Press.

Hirschman, A. O. (1970). Exit, voice, and loyalty: Responses to decline in firms, organizations, and states. Cambridge, MA: Harvard University Press.

Hodson, R. (2001). *Dignity at work*. Cambridge: Cambridge University Press.

Kasmir, S. (1996). *The myth of mondragon: Cooperatives, politics, and working-class life in a Basque Town*. Albany, NY: State University of New York Press.

Kaswan, M. (2011). A bridge to nowhere: Connecting representative and radical models of democracy. *International Journal of Organization Theory and Behavior*, *14*(4), 514–536.

Logue, J., & Yates, J. (2001). *The real world of employee ownership*. Ithaca, NY: ILR Press.

Lukes, S. (2005). *Power: A radical view* (2nd ed.). New York, NY: Palgrave MacMillan.

Mansbridge, J. J. (1982). Fears of conflict in face-to-face democracies. In F. Lindenfeld & J. Rothschild-Whitt (Eds.), *Workplace democracy and social change* (pp. 125–137). Boston, MA: Porter Sargent Publishers.

McCarthy, J. E., Voos, P. B., Eaton, A. E., Kruse, D., & Blasi, J. (2011). Solidarity and sharing: unions and shared capitalism. In E. J. Carberry (Ed.), *Employee ownership and shared capitalism: New directions in research* (pp. 27–57). Champaign, IL: Labor and Employment Relations Association.

McDonnel, B. (2000). ESOPs' failures: Fiduciary duties when managers of employee-owned companies vote to entrench themselves. *Columbia Business Law Review*, 199–260.

Meyers, J. S. M. (2011a). Employee ownership, democratic control, and working-class empowerment. In E. J. Carberry (Ed.), *Employee ownership and shared capitalism: New directions in research* (pp. 113–145). Champaign, IL: Labor and Employment Relations Association.

Meyers, J. S. M. (2011b). Unpacking bureaucracy: An intersectional theory of gendered organizations. Paper presented at the Beyster Fellows Workshop, Rutgers University New Brunswick.

Miller, D., Hartwick, J., & Le Breton-Miller, I. (2004). How to detect a management fad – And distinguish it from a classic. *Business Horizons*, *47*(4), 7–16.

Murphy, M. E. (2005). The ESOP at thirty: A democratic perspective. *Willamette Law Review*, *41*, 655–705.

NCEO. (2012, February). *A statistical profile of employee ownership*. Retrieved from http://www.nceo.org/articles/statistical-profile-employee-ownership. Accessed on April 28, 2013.

NCEO. (n.d.-a). *A comprehensive overview of employee ownership*. Retrieved from http://www.nceo.org/articles/esop-employee-stock-ownership-plan. Accessed on April 28, 2013.

NCEO. (n.d.-b). *How an employee stock ownership plan (ESOP) works*. Retrieved from http://www.nceo.org/articles/esop-employee-stock-ownership-plan. Accessed on April 28, 2013.

NCF. (2006). *Worker cooperative toolbox: In good company: A guide to cooperative employee ownership*. Minneapolis, MN: Northcountry Cooperative Foundation.

O'Leary, R. (2006). *The ethics of dissent: Managing guerrilla government*. Washington, DC: CQ Press.

Olson, M. (1965). *The logic of collective action: Public goods and the theory of groups*. Cambridge, MA: Harvard University Press.

Pateman, C. (1970). *Participation and democratic theory*. Cambridge, UK: Cambridge University Press.

Rosen, C., & Rodgers, L. (2011). *Fundamentals of ownership culture: Practical ideas for creating a great employee ownership company*. Oakland, CA: National Center for Employee Ownership.

Rothschild, J. (2000). Creating a just and democratic workplace: More engagement, less hierarchy. *Contemporary Sociology*, *20*(1), 195–213.

Rothschild, J., & Ollilalnen, M. (1999). Obscuring but not reducing managerial control: Does TQM measure up to democracy standards?. *Economic and Industrial Democracy*, *20*(4), 583–623.

Rothschild, J., & Whitt, J. A. (1986). *The cooperative workplace: Potentials and dilemmas of organizational democracy and participation*. Cambridge: Cambridge University Press.

Schoening, J. (2006). Cooperative entrepreneurialism: Reconciling democratic values with business demands at a worker-owned firm. *Research in the Sociology of Work*, *16*, 293–315.

Schur, L. (2003). Employment and the creation of an active citizenry. *British Journal of Industrial Relations*, *41*, 751–771.

Sirianni, C. (1994). Learning pluralism: Democracy and diversity in feminist organizations. In F. Fischer & C. Sirianni (Eds.), *Critical studies in organization and bureaucracy* (pp. 554–576). Philadelphia, PA: Temple University Press.

Strauss, G. (2006). Worker participation – Some under-considered issues. *Industrial Relations*, *45*(4), 778–803.

Veblen, T. (1904). *The theory of business enterprise*. New York, NY: Charles Scribner's Sons.

Verba, S., Schlozman, K. L., & Brady, H. E. (1995). *Voice and equality: Civic voluntarism in American politics*. Cambridge, MA: Harvard University Press.

Warren, M. (2011). Voting with your feet: Exit-based empowerment in democratic theory. *American Political Science Review*, *105*(4), 683–701.

Witherell, R., Cooper, C., & Peck, M. (2012). Sustainable Jobs, Sustainable Communities: The Union Co-op Model: United Steelworkers, Ohio Employee Ownership Center and Mondragon International USA.

Wright, E. O. (2010). *Envisioning real utopias*. London: Verso.

Yates, J. (2006). Unions and employee ownership: A road to economic democracy? *Industrial Relations*, *45*(4), 709–733.

Zullo, R. (2008). Union membership and political inclusion. *Industrial and Labor Relations Review*, *62*(1), 22–38. doi:10.2307/25249183

CHAPTER 11

THE LABOR MANAGED FIRM – A THEORETICAL MODEL EXPLAINING EMERGENCE AND BEHAVIOR

Anthony Jensen

ABSTRACT

Purpose – *This article describes the practical and theoretical implications relating to the labor managed firm (LMF), which has been formed from an insolvent company purchased by its workers. The research focuses on an international comparison and the cultural context of six LMFs – two each in the United States, Spain, and Italy where legislation supports worker buyouts from insolvency. Adopting a critical theoretical approach it draws on the scholarship of industrial relations and human resource management, grounded in a historical analysis to predict when a transformative or integrative LMF will be formed.*

Design/methodology/approach – *Taking a case study methodology to enable an in-depth understanding of the firms internal processes and relationships the use of semi-structured interviews of blue- and white-collar workers (with the use of a translator) and the administration of a*

Sharing Ownership, Profits, and Decision-making in the 21st Century
Advances in the Economic Analysis of Participatory & Labor-Managed Firms, Volume 14, 295–325

ISSN: 0885-3339/doi:10.1108/S0885-3339(2013)0000014020

structured questionnaire are used to gather and triangulate qualitative and quantitative data. The research limitations relate to the small number of respondents in each firm, which prevented more rigorous analysis, and calls for further research with larger numbers of respondents.

Findings – *The results reveal that at macro level the theoretical model predicts that the LMF will have a propensity to emerge when there are market failures, when there is support from the state and the labor movement. The type of LMF was found to depend on the national context of industrial relations. At the micro level a core set of practices were found to work together to lead to high member commitment and positive behavioral outcomes.*

Social implications – *The research has important social implications by informing public policy aimed at redressing the injustice to employees when a business fails and jobs and entitlements are lost.*

Originality/value – *The article advances an understanding of the theoretical nature of the LMF.*

Keywords: Insolvency; worker self-management; high performance work system; participatory work practices; industrial democracy; theory of the labor managed firm

JEL classifications: J54; D23; P130

INTRODUCTION

The scarcity of the labor managed firm (LMF), despite a number of studies pointing to its theoretical and empirical advantages over the investor managed firm (IMF) within Western market capitalism, has resulted in vigorous debate and research among academics and practitioners for the last 30 years (Ben-Ner, 1988; Clarke, 1984; Dow, 2006; Perotin, 1999). In light of the global financial crisis and the search for sustainable models of corporate governance there is continuing interest in the LMF as a vehicle for industrial democracy.

Accompanying this debate there has been a call for a new theoretical model going beyond standard economic theory to include the motivations of the entrepreneurs (Perotin, 1999); history, culture, institutions, and politics (Dow, 2006); and an evolutionary perspective (Borzaga, Galera, & Tortia, 2009). While scholars of the LMF agree that a new theoretical model of the firm is required along with empirical data, little has been said about the epistemology, theory, and methodology used to develop and test a new model.

This paper takes up this challenge and sets out to explain the development of a theoretical model and present empirical data, which will assist an understanding of the emergence and subsequent behavior of the LMF from insolvency. The paper argues that it is the management of the tensions involved in this process and subsequent trajectory, determined by different cultural contexts, which is the essential condition for success.

THE DEBATE

The development of an understanding of how the LMF can play a role in market capitalism has evolved over the last 150 years out of a series of intense debates and practical actions. This debate can be seen to consist of four arguments: the Sceptics; the Revisionists; the Contextualists; and the Evolutionists.

The Sceptics

Arguments that the LMF is an unsustainable business model within capitalism have drawn support from sceptics from the left and the right. The essence of a political economy argument began with the undialectical Marx and later Lenin and Luxembourg who argued that the LMF is "an island in a sea of capitalism" and is not sustainable because of the logic of capitalism in which market forces and democratic values are not compatible and the LMF will therefore degenerate. The Webb and Webb (1920) in their monumental work on industrial democracy concluded that an LMF where management was responsible to the worker owners would not have a viable governance system. Likewise neoclassical economists, basing their argument on individual *homo economicus*, argue that the demise of the LMF is inevitable due to workers' rent-seeking aspirations resulting in underinvestment and a propensity to hire nonmember workers. Further Ostrom (1990) points to the predictions that principals will not engage in mutual monitoring and select a mutually beneficial strategy resulting in LMF demise. Ward's (1958) seminal paper criticizing collective ownership and collective objectives was a highly influential paper in this vein. This paper invoked an important debate, but left many questions related to ownership and control unanswered.

The Revisionists

The revisionists however challenged these views, especially in the area of governance and design, with empirical evidence of the long-term sustainability and success of representative governance of worker cooperatives in Spain (Oakeshott, 1973) and Italy (Oakeshott, 1978; Zevi, 1982). Jones (1978) challenged the data and criticism of the Webbs and found them ideologically blinkered.

The flaw in the LMF design exposed by Ward (1958) was addressed by Domar (1966) and Vanek (1975) in their extension of the collective model. Mygind (1986) however argued that an LMF, which included both individual and collective ownership and objectives, would be superior to the neoclassical firm.

Further conceptual clarity was brought by Clarke (1984, pp. 99–100) in describing the opposing orientations between alternative modes of cooperative production; the incorporative model of worker ownership and the transformative model of worker cooperatives. Clarke (1984, p. 99) argued that in reality LMFs were hybrids, which were subjected to almost unbearable contradictions and tensions.

The tension was explored further by Eagan (1990) who then produced an analysis of the dialectical Marx and concluded Marx conditionally approved of worker cooperatives provided they were part of the labor movement, did not hire nonmembers, and contributed funds to the advancement of the cooperative sector.

Two important contributions added to our understanding of LMF scarcity. Perotin (1999) diagnosed the issue as one of either entry in accessing resources or exit related to degeneration and failure of the LMF. Ben-Ner (1988) supported this analysis arguing scarcity resulted from the disadvantage that an LMF faces in the start-up stage in acquiring necessary resources, but once the LMF is established it is able to demonstrate superior efficiency. Ben-Ner (1988, pp. 308–310) then argued that factors emerging later in the life cycle of the firm and the capitalist system are likely to cause the LMF's demise due to failure to invest and the propensity to hire nonmember workers.

Dow and Putterman (1999) added to these insights, arguing that the IMF outnumbers the LMF because of key efficiencies: work incentives, monitoring, overcoming shirking are more efficient in a KMF (capital managed firm); workers lack finance; workers are risk averse; the LMF cannot deal with asset specificity; and collective choice in an LMF is costly. Dow (2006) later added a new dimension in arguing that the external asymmetrical relationship between capital and labor will be reflected internally.

The Contextualists

A further critique was provided by the contextualists who argued that firm entry and behavior are dependent on the political culture, the variety of capitalism, and the resources supporting different models in different national cultures. Poole (1986, p. 28) went further and systemized the main institutional forms of industrial democracy listing the ideological positions and institutional forms, arguing that the LMF was an output of the country's industrial relations system: liberal pluralism associated with collective bargaining and codetermination; syndicalism and anarchism associated with producer cooperatives; and modern capitalism associated with autonomous work groups and employee share holding. Buyouts in the 1980s were most common in Italy and Spain (the two countries chosen for the case studies) followed by France and the United Kingdom with Germany well down the scale. Borzaga and Tortia (2006, p. 19) argued contextual influence is a necessary extension of a new theory of the firm. This focus on cultural context is the point of departure for this research from Clarke's work as it extends our understanding of the LMF emergence and behavior beyond that of economic models by drawing on history, industrial relations, and comparative political economy.

The Evolutionists

Finally, another new dimension from an institutionalist perspective was added by the evolutionists who argued that LMF behavior and success could only be explained from a dynamic life cycle model perspective as opposed to the black box, equilibrium seeking model of the neoclassical economists. The LMF was now seen to be either in a state of degeneration or renewal. Ben-Ner (1988), Lichtenstein (1986) and Borzaga and Tortia (2006) independently argued that the internal dynamic of an LMF has a unique life cycle and trajectory. Both Batstone (1983) and Lichtenstein (1986) developed life cycle models of the LMF, an evolutionary model based on the dialectics of the democratic process rather than on Ben-Ner's (1988) economic rationalism. They distinguished three phases: (i) start up, (ii) early maturity, and (iii) late maturity, and argued that it is the firm's trajectory through these phases that determines the record of success and failure.

Lichtenstein (1986, p. 55) then developed the concept of the LMF as a learning organization and argues that a new set of skills and values needs to be acquired, where "personal and interpersonal growth and development are uniquely linked to organizational viability." The LMF becomes an institution that fosters the "phenomenon of human learning" and has to "succeed both economically and pedagogically" (Lichtenstein, 1986, pp. 55–56).

These three critiques, going beyond the sceptics, have given fresh insights into the factors underpinning the success of the LMF in a cultural specific context. These have enabled Clarke's (1984) theoretical model to be enriched. The plausibility and potential value of these key theoretical insights will be explored using the empirical data collected through the case study research.

THE THEORETICAL MODEL

The theoretical model proposed here has some similarities with Clarke's (1984) framework but extends this model regarding contradictory tensions to focus on the importance of the contextual framework as a determinant of the type and trajectory of LMF that emerges. The theoretical model also explores the internal and external dynamics of the LMF where it is the management of the tensions between commercial viability and democratic control, namely the forces seeking to integrate the LMF with the market system versus the values seeking to transform the LMF into an alternative organization (Clarke, 1984, p. 100), that constitute the essential causal dynamic.

Integral to this is the need to address the sustainability of the LMF and the prediction that individuals will not commit to devise and monitor their own rules to obtain joint benefits (Ostrom, 1990, p. 45). However, LMFs do exist where these tensions have been resolved, where developmental individualism and cooperative maximizing behavior overcome degenerative tendencies ensuring LMF sustainability. Trying to understand how firms do this becomes a key theme of this research. Further as most organizations are hybrids, Clarke's (1984) model shows how the political economy of the LMF is a mixture of economic rationalism and democratic processes. The theoretical model advanced in this paper extends our understanding of these issues by defining six factors, both macro and micro, that affect the emergence and subsequent trajectory of the LMF.

The *three macro* contextual factors which determine the type of form the LMF takes and its emergence are: (i) the state, (ii) the market, and (iii) the labor movement, as the key institutions that affect workers' ability to take the initiative and conduct a worker buyout. The macro factors impact on the type of LMF that forms and the rate of emergence. They are either inhibitors to or enhancers of the formation of worker buyouts initiated by workers themselves. Here we draw on the varieties of capitalism literature (Hall & Soskice, 2004) and contrast the liberal market economy (LME) or unmediated capitalism where there is a weak labor movement and a poorly developed consciousness of egalitarian and collective consciousness, with the coordinated market economy (CME) or mediated market economy where socialist values of cooperation and solidarity and a strong labor movement proposing an alternative society are apparent. The macro factors of the state, the market and the labor movement go beyond Clark's typology in that LMF emergence is both contingent on them and shape their internal structure. Where these macro forces align positively, the result is an exercise of collective power by workers to take control of a situation threatening their jobs and to procure the business.

The *micro factors* were selected from the theoretical debates as being the key issues which affect the performance and success of the LMF. These propose an alternative perspective to the political economy factors of Clarke (1984) as they endeavor to explain the LMF business model. These are: (i) the design of the legal structure of the LMF's ownership, (ii) the governance architecture, and (iii) the development of the human resource motivational system creating a learning organization that is entrepreneurial and has an evolutionary life cycle.

Here we can address the question as to whether the constitutional design, the governance, and the human resource practices that can transform the LMF into an evolutionary learning organization result in a high performance workplace brought about by employees owning the firm. This links with Winther's (1998, p. 10) Theory O where ownership transforms workers into partners, another form of High Commitment Management (Wood, 1996), where both have in common a high identification by employees with the firm (Boxall & Purcell, 2003, p. 62) a prerequisite for high performance.

Table 1 goes beyond Clarke with its intention to address the national political economy context of different economies and explain the different types of LMFs that emerge and evolve toward a collectivity of

Table 1. The Six Factors Influencing the Emergence and Success/Failure and Type of Labor Managed Firm.

	Worker Ownership Commercial viability Integrative	Worker Cooperation Democratic control Transformative
Macro factors		
1. Role of state	Liberal pluralism	Class paradigm
2. Role of trade union/ labor movement	Collective bargaining	Syndicalism and anarchism
3. Nature of market	Unmediated liberal market economy	Mediated market economy
Micro factors		
4. Organizational design	Individual ownership and objectives	Collective ownership and objectives
5. Governance architecture	Representative	Participative
6. Human resource management and life cycle of the learning organization	Bureaucratic Disengagement/extrinsic satisfaction Incorporation or degeneration	Purposeful Intrinsic satisfaction Alternative Evolutionary and democratic

entrepreneurs in these contexts. The table illustrates that each of these factors is subject to a tension between the incorporation forces of commercial viability and the transformational tendencies of democratic values.

The playing out of this tension, in a national context, results in either an integrative LMF, described as worker ownership, or a transformative LMF, known as a worker cooperative.

On a *macro* basis, the model predicts that workers will take the initiative to form an LMF when there has been a business failure either due to the cyclical swings of capitalism, or due to the nature of the business itself where jobs are threatened and there are no other jobs available. In this situation workers may be propelled to act to take over the business to save their jobs. While it may be highly problematical to make this decision, they will be more likely to do so if they are assisted by the state through enabling legislation, finance, and advice, and a labor movement that has solidarity or a consciousness of organizing at the firm level. The type of LMF that emerges will reflect the national context of industrial relations in terms of collective bargaining, codetermination, syndicalist, or anarchistic ideologies. It will also reflect the relational principles of the variety of capitalism model, namely the Anglo Saxon market model or the European networked model. These macro factors work together: a transformative LMF is more likely to occur when there is a class paradigm, the labor movement has a history of syndicalism or anarchism, and there is a mediated market economy while an integrative LMF is more likely to occur when the state is based on liberal pluralism, trade unions are focused on collective bargaining, and there is an unmediated market economy.

At the *micro* level the model predicts that success, failure, and trajectory of the LMF can be explained by the internal core set of practices, which develop commitment from employee owners. Like other HR models such as the Warwick model, this model "maps the connections between the outer (wider environment) and inner (organizational) context and explores how the practices adapt to the context" (Bratton & Gould, 2012, p. 22). The model considers how an integrated set of LMF key features – collective and individual ownership, a participative governance architecture and a bundle of high-performance HRM policies – work together in combination, to lead to high employee commitment, high quality and high flexibility with positive behavioral outcomes (e.g., increased effort, cooperation, and organizational citizenship). This is an organic bottom-up process leading to the maximising of human potential arising out of a solidaristic and collective orientation (Bratton & Gould, 2012, p. 23).

In conclusion the theoretical model enables us to predict when a LMF will emerge and the type of LMF that results. The model also enables us to predict that the LMF that combines all the features of democratic control will become a successful transformative HPWS; the firm that combines the integrative features will be commercially successful and degenerate; while the firm that mixes the features will fail due to unmanageable tensions.

METHODOLOGY

The objective of the research was to compare worker buyouts in Italy, the United States, and Spain in order to throw light on the theoretical debates and add to the empirical evidence. The three countries chosen provide rich historical contrasts and demonstrate the continuum of regulatory regimes and legal models supporting LMFs in both an LME and Mediterranean market economies (Hall & Soskice, 2004, p. 21).

This paper argues that the different corporate governance models in these three countries will deliver different outcomes in terms of work culture, alienation, conflict, involvement, and hence performance. All the three countries chosen had successful legislative interventions to specifically assist the formation of employee buyouts: the 1970s ESOP tax legislation in the United States, the 1985 Sociedades Laborales (SAL) Act in Spain, and the 1985 Marcora Law in Italy.

Within each country there are hubs of successful employee buyouts. Two successful LMFs, one unionized the other nonunionized, were selected in each country from a hub with the assistance of senior personnel from key institutions that support LMFs. All LMFs were manufacturing firms in the metal industry, which both simplified and standardized the comparison by eliminating an important variable – industry type. They were subject to different levels of exposure to international competition. Of the six firms, five were small, ranging from 30 to 56 workers, while one was a medium-sized business of 300 workers. The percentage of employees who are owners or partners varied among the firms: in the United States both had 100%, followed by Italy with 73% and 93%, and finally Spain with 72% and 44%. This reflects a compromise with the market and the varied nature of the departure from the ideal of open membership and the aspiration of having over 90% of workers as members.

All had been formed out of a crisis situation and struggled to overcome significant obstacles and, in one case, corruption. They were not randomly chosen but selected because they were successful in terms of longevity. As such, they are not used to formally test the model (which would require a comparison with non-surviving LMF's), but rather to explore how the conditions and characteristics of successful LMF's are consistent with and help inform the theoretical model.

The Case Study Firms

The government policy motivation and design of these three legal structures were somewhat different in the three countries. While aiming to produce a new "species of worker," one who would collectively engage in entrepreneurial activities and risk to preserve their job, there were different overriding objectives: in the United States to turn the worker into a capitalist who would benefit from the wider distribution of wealth; in Italy to support the emergence of a form of nonspeculative mutual sector; and in Spain to introduce a new form of corporation which featured a model of industrial democracy prevalent in Europe.

The United States
Brainard Rivet is a manufacturer of cold-headed fasteners for the automobile industry situated in Gerrard, Ohio. The company was established in 1917 to make rivets for strapping on wooden barrels. Camcar/Textron purchased it in 1995 and in 1996 it earned $2.1 million with its 45 hourly and 20 salaried workers paying excellent wages and benefits (*Owners at Work*, 1997). Following a three-day strike by the trade union the business was shut down and put up for sale, This created a substantial community backlash led by the local US senator, the city council, and employees who fought to keep the plant open. They were joined on the picket line by other unions. The plant was eventually bought by the employees, through a loan from Fastner Industries, that was repaid, and Brainard Rivet became part of the Fastner Industries employee-owned group.

Marland Mold was founded in Pittsfield, Massachusetts by two men in a garage in 1946 and quickly established a reputation for making quality moulds which were used for a range of plastic items (The *Berkshire Eagle*, 1992). They sold the company in 1968 to the conglomerate Tredegar Industries. Following a restructure by Tredegar Industries in 1991 Marland Mould faced closure. Pittsfield, like many industrial cities, was facing decline – it had lost 43% of its manufacturing jobs in the 1980s and was concerned at the prospect of another closure and the loss of another 42 jobs. A concerted community action plus the trade union enabled the workers to buy the company (*The Berkshire Eagle*, 1992).

Italy
The two case studies in Southern Italy, Trafilcoop and SOCAM, are worker cooperatives, the former unionized and the latter nonunionized and these were linked to and given direction by the Compagnia Finanziaria Industriale (CFI) set up by the Marcora Law. This institution, which financed the buyout, provided investment and board representation. The CFI was also linked to the left-wing LEGACOOP as were the two cooperatives typifying the European networked governance model (Hall & Soskice, 2004).

Trafilcoop is a market leader in the manufacture of wire products. The cooperative was formed out of a failed company, owned by four brothers who employed 100 workers and also had a number of other companies. The firm had reached a stage in its life cycle where the owners, according to a manager, did not want to work. The corporate collapse was triggered by the failure of one of the companies. The new company that emerged in 1985, using the Marcora Law, originally employed 70 workers, of who 10 left in the first year. There are now 56 partners and 4 workers on temporary contracts.

SOCAM is a cooperative situated near Naples and founded after World War II in the state encouragement of industry. This cooperative produces high quality high-end market designer office furniture with state-of-the-art machinery. The design and marketing of the furniture are contracted out. Of the 60 workers only 20 wanted to be in the cooperative; it started with 6 or 7 workers and gradually reemployed all 20. Now there are 28 workers, 22 partners, and 6 employees. It was founded using the protocol of the Marcora Law. The formation of the cooperative was protracted over three years hindered by intransigency in the local bankruptcy court.

Spain

Betsaide is the fourth largest foundry and also the largest SAL in Spain with 296 workers. It is situated 50 kms from the town of Mondragon, the headquarters of the Mondragon Cooperativa Corporacion (MCC). It is deeply embedded in the supply chain of the highly competitive automotive industry producing castings for clients such as VW, MAN, EVACA, and Ford. It recently invested Euro150 million in a fully automated warehouse planned by two members of the company over two years. Betsaide has diversified producing three product groups – water valves, castings for lorries, and cars and "miscellaneous," which included products for trains as well as hand tools. The company went bankrupt in 1989 after it had been losing money for 11 years. The founders were no longer involved in the business; they were either deceased or retired, and there was no leadership or clear direction. The business was overstaffed with 236 workers and had lost direction with three different factories.

Torniplasa is a manufacturing company also in the Basque country located in Vittoria, the large capital city of the region. It supplies the automotive industry with screws, with clients including Citroen, Peugeot, and Renault. It started in 1957 as a family-owned company and was acquired by a Belgian/Dutch consortium, based in Madrid, in 1991 The company had brought with them a very important manager who was to play a key role in the transformation. With the car industry in deep recession in 1991–1993 the company faced bankruptcy and closure and had to enter into difficult negotiations with the workers over working hours to save their jobs. In 1993 the workers took over and were given the company in preference to a cash handout. The company was said to have no value, due to its debts, except for the potential to create jobs (Table 2).

Table 2. Theoretical Model Applied to Case Studies.

Contradictory Tensions	Commercial Viability Capital and labor asymmetrical	Capital and labor symmetrical	Democratic Practices Labor and capital asymmetrical
Country	The United States	Spain	Italy
Typology	Employee ownership	Worker democracy	Worker cooperative
Macro factors			
State	Liberal pluralism	Democratic socialism	Corporatism
Market	Liberal market	Mediated market	Coordinated market
Labor movement	Collective bargaining	Anarchism	Syndicalism
Micro factors			
Legal design	Employee share ownership plan	Sociadades Laborales (SAL – labor corporation)	Worker cooperative
Governance	Representative	Self-management	Oligarchical
Human resource management	Pluralism/consultation bureaucratic incorporation degeneration	Radical/self-management alternative evolutionary	Cooperativism/joint coexistence purposeful intrinsic satisfaction

The ESOP, the worker cooperative and SAL provide different solutions across three jurisdictions to engaging workers in ownership and governance to address social problems and job preservation. They vary in the allocation of control and return rights to workers, as vehicles to create the LMF and allocate power.

Research Design

A case study approach was chosen to study these 6 firms, using a mixed methodology of semi-structured interviews and a structured questionnaire survey administered to workers in the firms. This was supplemented by a historical analysis of the LMF emergence and development in each jurisdiction.

The case study approach was chosen as it enables a broad holistic approach to be taken whereby the "inner connection" and the "complex web of internal relations," and the tensions within the firm, can be explored (Best & Connolly, 1976, p. xiii in Giles & Murray, 1997, p. 87) and placed within whole patterns of industrial relations. It also enables examination of workers' attitudes to specific aspects of their work.

Semi-Structured Interviews
Around 7–11 interviews of 1 hour's length using mainly open-ended questions were conducted in each company. Interviews were conducted with blue-collar workers, the CEO, and the chairman as well as personnel from senior management, accountancy and marketing plus middle management and team leaders. This resulted in 53 interviews across the six firms, which were transcribed and then analyzed using the NVIVO software to identify key words, phrases, and themes. In Spain and Italy the author was accompanied by an interpreter for the interviews.

The Survey – Structured Questionnaire
About 25–30 questionnaires were distributed to employees in each of the six companies, totaling a potential survey population of approximately 150 out of 500 employees. The objective was to spread this randomly over the workforce in each firm on the basis of approximately 20% to middle management, 20% to administration/quality control, and 60% to blue-collar shop floor workers. Management was asked to randomly select the actual participants. Response rates varied between the firms but were generally quite high – 137 questionnaires were returned representing 91% of the distributed questionnaires and 27% of the total 500 employees of the six firms. The analysis of the surveys was used to triangulate the interview data.

RESULTS

Macro – External Factors

The theoretical model posits that the ability and potential for working people to successfully conduct a worker takeover and establish a successful LMF is dependent on three macro factors: the role of the market, the influence of the labor movement, and the position of the state. In the 1980s and 1990s these three factors provided the problematical context for the buyouts in this study.

Nature of Market
The market downturn in the 1980s and 1990s ushered in a period of recession and stagflation reflecting the restructuring of capital and labor due to

international market forces. The resulting slump in output, high unemployment, and lower corporate profitability weakened manufacturing firms in particular. This resulted in a spate of company closure and restructuring – the context in which the case study firms were taken over. However, the coincidental upswing in the market in the mid-1990s, especially in the automobile market, resulted in these firms entering a period of recovery and in some cases significant success.

Labor Movement

Three of the case study firms were unionized – one in each country. Labor unions did not have a coherent response to the strategy of the employee buyout to plant closure. In the three firms with a trade union presence, the union was supportive and assisted the buyout playing a collaborative and transformative role grounded in ideological support. In the three firms without a union there was an antagonistic relationship with the buyout arising out of animosity between the LMF leadership and the local union representatives who were not convinced that this strategy advanced the labor movement.

In the United States in LMF1 the trade union suggested the buyout and provided a loan to finance the purchase. The president of the IUE, a radical union dedicated to democratic unionism and collective bargaining, stated:

> Our goal is to save jobs. If a buyout will do it, we are interested. We have been involved in some successful efforts, and we have also looked at other opportunities and decided not to participate because they would not have worked for us. (The *Berkshire Eagle*,1992).

The union provided a loan of $900,000 to assist in the purchase of the firm. In the nonunion LMF2 the closure came after a three-day strike and the desire of management to move the plant to a nonunion area. The union opposed the buyout.

The pattern was repeated in Europe. In Italy, despite deep roots from their syndicalist past, unions had changed their focus to collective bargaining in the 1980s as skilled workers had seen private companies as a better route to career progression than the worker cooperative. In this ambiguous context, in nonunion LMF3 the union tried to "create terror" and "workers felt betrayed by the union" (Jensen, 2012, p. 207). In LMF4 the union representative in the firm of the radical left-wing union Confederazione Generale Italiana del Lavro, the most important of Italian Trade Unions, suggested and assisted the buyout and subsequently provided members for the management team.

In Spain the ambiguous position continued where workers build SALs "sometimes from union positions and sometimes in spite of unions" (Vidal & Vilaplana, 1999, pp. 5–10). The unions did not have a model for constructing a relationship between the SAL and the union except to offer unconditional support "as it was important to make room in the economy for worker self-management" (Secretary General, CGT, interview, 2006). In the unionized LMF6 the CGT assisted with the buyout. It was one of the four unions in the firm. In LMF5 the workers voted, under the guidance of the manager, to exclude the union because "being an owner and a worker you know how to defend your own rights" (blue-collar foreman).

Role of the State

The state played a key role in the successful emergence of all the case studies. However, the strategy varied along a continuum from the voluntarist individualistic position of the United States, to the enabling state of Spain and the collectivist regulated position of Italy.

In the United States in both cases local political figures became involved. Entrepreneurial leadership and managerial expertise in developing business plans came forward to assist planning and the raising of finance. The president of LMF1 commented:

> The amount of cooperation it took to make this happen was amazing. Everyone was involved: the IUE (the union), the City, the state, the chamber, The First Agricultural Bank, management, labor. (The *Berkshire Eagle*, 1992)

It became a *cause célèbre* for the local community, which forced the hand of the owners to sell to the workers. US Senators and city politicians put pressure on the parent company. In the LMF2 case another employee owned company put forward the necessary finance resulting in LMF2 becoming an autonomous subsidiary in an expanding employee-owned company conglomerate.

In Europe a corporatist framework supporting employee buyouts had been put in place by the state. This enabled advisory support and finance to be obtained. In Italy, within a Syndicalist tradition of building a "socialist state within a state" both companies accessed finance and support through the 1985 Marcora Law and its financial institution CFI, supplemented by a "lump sum" payment capitalizing three years of future unemployment benefits. LMF3 initially was antiunion but successfully accessed finance through the Marcora Law after overcoming corruption in the bankruptcy court, and later joined the LEGACOOP (LEGA). LMF4 is a "red cooperative" linked to the LEGACOOP and was initiated by a trade union leader in the firm.

In Spain, where anarchy and a state of continuous revolution had deep roots, the practical examples of worker buyouts and takeovers were role models and part of labor consciousness. Both LMF5 and LMF6 successfully accessed finance and support through the SAL infrastructure supplied by ASLE (the local association of the Spanish Association of Employee Owned Businesses). The support came from local financial and advisory institutions supplemented by access to three years of capitalization of unemployment benefits or "lump sum" payments to support the formation of autonomous worker-owned and run firms.

These worker buyouts demonstrated "the favorable conjunctures" model whereby the factors of the depressed market and declining job opportunities, a confident labor consciousness concerning democratic opportunities, and an enabling state and community support to access finance came together in a particular historical moment. It can be concluded that these labor-owned manufacturing firms came into existence by overcoming the barriers identified by Ben-Ner (1988): the need for premeditation and planning by entrepreneurs, the assumption of risks and losses, the provision of capital, and the bearing of set-up costs (Ben-Ner, 1988, p. 289). This was done in a moment of crisis and opportunity to take over the assets of the bankrupt firm.

Micro – Internal Factors

The macro factors in a national context were seen to affect the emergence of a specific type of LMF with specific internal characteristics. The theoretical model predicts that the internal mechanisms of the LMF – namely the design, governance and HR processes – are linked to the culture and performance where the key issue is managing the tension between democratic values and market forces.

Legal Design

The design of the three firms, using Dow's (2006) typology, is seen clearly in a continuum from the asymmetrical KMF in the United States through the asymmetrical state – labor partnership LMF in Italy, to the symmetrical LMF in Spain reflecting how the tension between democracy and market values is configured in each culture.

The US ESOP democratizes ownership but not control, and is management driven. Ownership is structured as a company pension fund linked to a collectively owned Employee Share Ownership Trust (ESOT) which acquires all or part of the equity of a company for the employees. Management appoints trustees to the ESOT. The ultimate decision to set up the ESOP also rests with management. Membership can be restricted but must not discriminate in favor of key employees. Return rights are limited to a profit share of up to 25% of employee's salary per annum. Employees do not have a say regarding the payment of dividends. Control rights by employees are limited. US legislation makes no requirement to pass decision-making power to the worker owner except on supermajority issues such as mergers, acquisitions, and sale of the company. Management generally selects the board of directors. However, in both case studies, employees elected a minority of directors and approved managerial suggestions for the appointment of directors.

The Italian cooperatives ownership is both collective and individual in that workers have their own individual ownership portfolio of the firm which accumulates dividends as well as the cooperative having nondivisible collectively owned capital. The constitution is based on the seven principles of the International Cooperative Alliance. Control rights are vested in all employee members on the basis of personal rights of one-person one-vote and open membership. The cooperative is regulated by the state in a number of ways. Return rights in the form of dividends are limited by statute, capped at not greater than 6.55% of an individual member's capital. Return on labor is also capped: only 20% of the residual or the surplus can be used to supplement salaries and cannot be more than 30% of the wages. A further requirement states that 30% of the profits must go to indivisible locked assets, discouraging demutualization, while 70% can be divided among the workers as dividends, individual capital or cash. The cooperative exists as part of a "state within the state" demonstrating an asymmetrical relationship where labor employs capital in a mediated economy, where support for nonspeculative mutual organizations is enshrined in the 1945 Italian Constitution.

The Spanish SAL is a Limited Labor Company, legally regulated and formed by wage and salary earners featuring individual and collective capital accounts. Control rights are property rights, based on one share one vote, are not restricted, and are based on two types of members: shareowners who have an employment contract and those who only invest. Control is held by the workers who must hold a majority (51%) of the shares of equity capital. One partner must not hold more than one-third of the stock, except for public authorities which can own 49%. Degeneration is discouraged by offering new shares to nonmember employees and limiting nonmembers to 15% for companies with 25 or more partners. The workers elect the president and the assembly board to which they delegate executive powers. There are no restrictions on the decisions that the assembly can consider. The board meets with management on a monthly basis. Return rights are in reality not capped even though SALs are required to invest 25% of profits in a collective special reserve fund to offset losses. This can be released however to workers on the advent of a sale. A further 10% of profits can be distributed as dividends. There is a symmetry between labor and capital.

The design of the LMF, the way tension is managed and its subsequent trajectory is reflected in the comment of Charny (1999): "The crucial issue is how much power to give worker directors," which is influenced by the role that the market and national culture play in the choice of design. Worker participation was emasculated in the US ESOP design; control was uncapped in Italy but return rights were capped; while in Spain in reality neither control nor return rights were capped.

Governance

The flow from this continuum of legal structures was a continuum of governance models, where workers evolved a range of culturally specific democratic practices. The illuminating feature was that each of the two firms in their national context were remarkably similar to each other in the governance model that they chose: consultation in the United States, joint coexistence in Italy, and worker self-management in Spain.

These structures will now be examined through the work of Westenholtz (1986, pp. 144–149) focusing on direct democracy at both the level of the firm and at the level of the shop floor. They represent a continuum from participatory work practices to industrial democracy.

Governance at the Level of the Firm. In the United States the legal design of the ESOP established a representative model of governance, or consultation, which resulted in workers being excluded from everyday decision making and in the institutions of governance. They could be consulted and offer comments. Managers in both LMFs advised: "You will find frustration here. People believe they should be involved in decision-making." The CEO reinforced the emasculated decision making at LMF1:

> Unfortunately, we cannot make these decisions based on democracy. We will never make a decision if we always put these decisions to the vote. We will never move forward.

The ESOP is therefore seen as a consultation model whereby three workers were elected to the board – two blue collar and one white collar – who were in a minority, mainly participating in information sharing and consultation. In LMF1 the worker owner assembly was simply a mechanism for reporting the annual results to members in a restrained manner. There was no debate or discussion over major issues. In both LMF1 and LMF2 workers reported in the interviews a perception that the ESOP had been oversold.

In Italy a model of joint coexistence was found in both cooperatives. Workers elected the board and the president every three years. The cultural compromise in Italy was to defer to an oligarchic leader in a stewardship role rather than adopt a principal agent model. In both firms the CEO had been in place since the takeover (for about 25 years), and had been continuously reelected as is common in Italy (Hancock, 2007, p. 73).

In Italy workers were also comfortable with their power in the assembly, where major decisions were discussed and decided and where they conceded managerial power on a daily basis in exchange for the ability to scrutinize managers in the assembly where decisions were made. A worker described democracy in LMF3:

> There is no kind of dictatorship. All the decisions that are made by the managing team are always passed through the assembly. When there are very important decisions from the managing team they are passed to the assembly where they are discussed.

However, the workers in LMF4, after 25 years, in a drawn out and acrimonious decision-making process which involved the LEGA interviewing all members, asserted their democratic rights, and replaced the long serving president, demonstrating a resurgence of democracy.

In Spain both firms demonstrated a very similar trajectory in assertive worker self-management's ultimate test – they regularly replaced their managers. The worker assembly, the presidency and the board, were powerful institutions, dominated by the blue-collar worker where all major decisions were discussed and decided. Here they exercisied strong control over the general manager. The quality control manager at LMF6 commented on whether the assembly was democratic:

> Totally. There is no other way to work. Because all important issues are decided in these meetings so there is always participation. We don't see any other way to do it. We have all the same shares so no one can stand out and say "I am the boss and what I say goes." It's for the best of all our interests.

Worker members elected the board and the blue-collar president who was rotated every three years. The general manager was selected by the board and ratified by the assembly. There have been five general managers in LMF6 and three in LMF5.

Governance on the Shop Floor. The governance on the shop floor again saw democratic cultural imperatives in conflict with market demands. Compensating for the lack of participation at the corporate governance level in the United States, both case study firms had established worker self-management on the shop floor. They asserted that self-managing work teams had been established where the workers organized production and maximized job autonomy. A worker describes the situation at LMF1 which was also reflected at LMF2:

> We are self-directed. We can decide how we are going to do something. For the most part we decide the hours we are going to work based on our workload and what we need to get through there, and we are in control of grinding wheels [and] downloads. If we need a special tool we put in a special request – we go talk to Brian or Jim and say this is what we need. That's what I like about it. You can make a lot of red tape if you want, or very little if you want to.

In Italy we move beyond liberalism into a culture steeped with solidarity and syndicalism where the concept of collective solidarity transcends the liberal notion of autonomous work groups, worker autonomy, and self-management. A worker in LMF3 stated:

> I feel there should be collaboration between the head of the department and someone who works for the head of the department. But they should not forget who is head of the department and who is the worker. You need a little bit of dictatorship to keep law and order amongst the workers, even in a cooperative.

In Spain both case study firms went further in responding to the pressure of international competition – they both chose to implement high performance, high engagement work systems where democracy was extended to all levels of the firm. Both firms developed team-based production on the shopfloor and throughout the factories. In the smaller LMF5 the European Federation of Quality Management System (EFQMS) was in place operating through 15 processes that focused on continuous quality improvement for the customer.

In LMF6 workers operated in teams, both in the foundry and extending to include the customer as well as design and production personnel. Worker participation and high involvement management had been integrated into all levels of decision making (Mason, 1982, p. 172). A worker at LMF6 describes this:

> Of course we do not make up our own minds and can do it one way or the other. We have to agree [on] this with our supervisor and then agree on a basic approach or to do

> whatever we need to do. This type of working – this type of methodology – makes us feel important in the decision making process. Our opinions are well respected and acknowledged. We feel our opinion is important and we add to the value of the company.

Hard legalistic forms of these firms' constitutions were complemented by soft cultural norms. These cultural mechanisms steered these firms from the "grab strategy" to the "cooperative maximizing strategy" as will be seen.

Human Resource Management and the Evolution of the Learning Organization

Understanding the success of the LMF requires an appreciation of its life cycle. Batstone (1983) argues that to be successful a firm needs to traverse a life cycle of start up, maturity, degeneration, and renewal on its journey to become what Lichtenstein (1986) describes as a learning organization – one that succeeds economically and pedagogically, transcending the neo-classical paradigm. The LMF however is a hybrid and as such may straddle both individualistic and collectivist models of HRM best practice, for example, a unitarist contractural HRM system would base recruitment and selection on a system of meritocracy while the Italian relational model would look to offer jobs to family and local community in the first instance. We now look at examples from the six case studies demonstrating their progress through the life cycle.

Start Up

All six firms made a successful start when the workers, propelled by a falling market for jobs, acquired the firms by accessing all the resources they required through the state and labor movement. This was a moment of communal effort and primitive democracy where expectations were raised of "reducing managerial control and enhancing self control" (Stryjan & Hellmark 1985, p. 18). The views of such a transformation were highlighted in the local paper describing LMF1 in the United States:

> That distinction, management and worker, vanished yesterday when everyone became an owner. "It's just like the early days at [LMF1] when we all worked together." (The *Berkshire Eagle*, 1992)

However, it was the issue of leadership where successful emergence was enhanced by the fortuitous circumstances of having the right manager in place to lead the buyout. The general manager at LMF5 in Spain states:

> He was very important, this manager. Giving us confidence. Inyake was the one behind the whole pushing. He was the one behind the leap of faith.

Having traversed the start up moment these firms blossomed. In the process of insolvency or closure the workers had overcome the barriers described by Ben-Ner (1988) and Dow and Putterman (1999): they overcame their adversity to risk; they invested their own capital from the "lump sum" or borrowed it; insolvency enabled them to overcome problems of asset specificity and acquire capital intensive assets and machinery; and initially they had effective highly motivating primitive collective democratic decision-making processes.

Early Maturity

After a period of sacrifice and with rising markets these firms prospered, buoyed by the enthusiasm and commitment of their worker owners to their goals of job preservation and job satisfaction. They demonstrated the features that Ben-Ner (1988, p. 291) argues can enable LMF firms to demonstrate superior performance to the KMF: allocative efficiency and technological efficiency. They dealt with the forces of decline in different ways.

In the United States, LMF1 had been transformed "from an ugly duckling" to "a company with sustained profits, a trebling of its share price and good stable jobs for its owners" according to *Equity Report* (2000, p. 13). Worker owners had reengineered "an unwanted plastics maker into a dynamic and profitable enterprise." Sales have doubled and jobs had increased from 42 at the time of the takeover to 93, with 100% worker ownership. However, in this case the seeds of the firm's demise also became apparent. The role of the management was skewed toward a defensive cycle associated with the decline of the firm. It could be described as reactive and risk averse. A blue-collar worker stated:

> From the very beginning the board of directors instructed the management to "get all our eggs out of one basket" and diversify the business.

The firm's management failed to diversify through aquisition and remained at the mercy of the destabilizing forces of the market. In contrast at LMF2 the parent Fastner Industries had responded to worker owner demands for expansion. A dynamic growth strategy was adopted and the firm expanded through acquisition and start up, carving out a niche in the market where stabilizing forces were in the ascendency.

Again in Spain it was the fortuitousness of having the right manager in place. In LMF6 the key issue was the visionary manager affecting the turnaround and rationalization strategy, switching product markets. Importantly they also demonstrated the capacity for persistence, which not all companies have. This process of establishing teams for continuous improvement was described in the other Spanish LMF5:

> We started to work in European Federation of Quality Management (EFQM) here, and it's very important to work by processes. It is very difficult. It is not easy – a lot of societies start by working these processes but at the end they can't. They finish a lot of paper documentation but not in their practice.

The translating of their worker ownership into democratic governance and becoming a team based learning LMF, while advancing the cooperative maximizing strategy against the grab strategy (Charny, 1999), required an intense effort in communicative and emancipatory learning.

Late Maturity – Renewal or Decline

In late maturity the forces that can result in compromise or extinction had become an issue for each of the firms, and here the results of the contextual influences, design, and governance came to the fore and can be explained by the theoretical model.

The two ESOPs in the United States were hybrid models demonstrating contradictory tensions arising from an integrated ESOP governance structure and transformative worker self-management on the shop floor. In LMF1 this tension became unbearable and the firm was sold to another investor in the upswing following the global financial crisis and failure to expand by acquisition. The firm also demonstrated goal displacement and had become an archetypical integrated LMF where owners were more interested in the stock price. In the other firm LMF2 the tensions had been ameliorated by being in the Fastner Group, which provided a democratic shelter and market niche and enabled the transformative shop floor initiative of the semiautonomous teams to coexist with the embedded consultative democratic processes in the Fastner Group.

In the Italian cooperatives these tensions were also dealt with differently. Both were commercially successful and embarked on or planned expansionary strategies such as a new factory or joint venture. LMF4 preserved its membership at a high level – 90% – while in LMF3 there was a decline to 75%. Stabilizing forces advancing commercial values had appeared to prevail in both firms with the long-term stewardship of the president personifying continuity and stability. Differences among members and tensions over controversial issues had been accommodated. In LMF3 the oligarchical governance structure – the Italian cultural phenomenon of joint coexistence between the long serving president and the worker assembly –

remained in place as did the tension over management issues, but it was not unbearable. However, in LMF4, the transformative "red cooperative," the tension over oligarchical governance did finally become unbearable and the workers with the assistance of the LEGA removed their long serving president and asserted their democratic rights, regenerating the cooperative's transformative mission.

The Spanish SALs retained their commitment to pursuing both democratic and commercial goals. They retained their dynamic democratic spirit of worker self-management, exemplified by having recently changed their managers. Both became highly successful commercial learning organizations achieving the characteristics of the High Performance Work System. LMF5 was awarded the Gold ISO 9000, and LMF6 acquired another foundry and expected to become the largest foundry in Spain. Both continued to be transformative LMFs.

They however made compromises in adopting the core periphery model of industrial production: membership at LMF5 was 74% of total employment while in LMF6 it was only 45% (they acknowledged that this was the minimum level they could tolerate). What becomes clear is that both firms had evolved to high performance work systems where democracy and efficiency worked in a dialectical manner to create the optimum-learning organization. The extension of democratic values, from command and control to self-management, while meeting the intense demands of the international motor vehicle market provided these firms unique competitive advantage. This, states Westenholtz (1986, p. 149), is a "phenomenon that can teach us something new." Lawler (1992, p. xi) also believes that this is creating the "ultimate advantage" – the "high involvement organization" which he describes as "revolutionary" (Lawler, 1986, p. 17).

These conclusions assist in gaining a deeper understanding of the polarity within the human resource scholarship surrounding the nature of the HPWS, its rarity, the contentious debate regarding its practices and outcomes and the factors leading to success.

Tensions and resistance were present across all firms but were contained and managed and did not become unbearable in five of them. Both Spanish firms acknowledged the need to manage dissent and resistance. At LMF5 the foreman, who identified a pocket of resistance, stated:

> I worry about a crisis that occurs internally. Being a good company I can't understand why there is a problem with parts. I can't point to the source of the problem. I worry about it. It's an internal crisis. It keeps occurring. Some people are too comfortable. This may be the origin. Young people add to solving the problem. Got to solve it. [Shrugs shoulders] Not good enough.

This, then, raises the issue that the workplace is still contested terrain a potential zone of tension. This is an issue beyond the scope of this research but reveals a darker side of worker self-management, the possibility of dissent in the face of workers' desire "to bargain for greater freedom, self actualization and dignity" (Hodgson, 1984, p. 735).

The SAL however is susceptible to demutualization and a return to the private sector as a consequence of the life cycle of the firm and its relation to the capitalist system. National results indicate that around 50% of SALs demutualize – but the benefits of their job creation and preservation generally remain.[1]

Navigating the three stages of the life cycle of the alternative firm is a requirement for success. The interviews illuminated tensions within the LMFs and found them related to procedural and distributive justice. The interviews uncovered discourses concerning equality and participation that contained paradoxes where tensions, resistance, and debate had not been resolved but had not become destructive except in US LMF1. The HRM system contained tensions and paradoxes which the successful European LMFs resolved through the process of democracy: the debate over collective and mutual values versus individualistic and instrumental values. This was manifested in sharing the bonus equally, of having access to information, of recruitment based on friendship, family, and sociopolitical values of sharing the load of potential redundancies, and of participating in decisions.

Importantly in five of the six case study firms the five forces of decline identified by Lichtenstein (1986) were overcome. The creation of participative learning organizations with double loop learning embedded in their representative governance and shop floor participation processes overcame the forces of routinization and organizational rigidity that prevent experimentation and adaptability. The firms were still dedicated to their goals of job preservation and job satisfaction based on meaningful participation. Market shocks had not destabilized them. The firms had invested heavily in new machinery and infrastructure and had maintained their high levels of cooperative spirit and commitment with five firms accommodating resistance. Finally the classical self-extinction force of employing nonmembers had been pragmatically resolved despite a significant compromise and deference to the market in LMF6.

In all these firms the road to transform a conventional business into worker self-management within the capitalist market system was a precarious social experiment involving contradictory tensions as the cynics predicted. However, those tensions need not be unbearable. It seemed clear that the Spanish firms had been transformed into LMFs that were a "durable organizational form well suited to ongoing transitions" (Gordon, 1999, p. 318) but also susceptible to integration back into the capitalist system.

CONCLUSIONS

The proposition that the entry level of LMFs can be increased via the strategy of the worker buyout of an insolvent company has been shown to have definite possibilities of success, but is contingent on a range of factors being in place which assist in overcoming the disadvantages facing the LMF in the start-up phase. These factors include access to finance and advice, support from the state and trade unions, and the more problematical presence of quality management that can carry out the entrepreneurial function. The multifactor theoretical model proposed here, based on the scholarship of the fields of study of industrial relations and human resource management, provides a vehicle to explain and predict the mystery of the emergence and subsequent behavior of a LMF where these two issues are inexorably linked in a path dependent way through national contextual factors. This study has added to our understanding of the issues that affects whether the LMF succeeds or fails.

Central to the study is the management of tension as a major determinant of success, across the six key factors of the LMF model within national industrial relations contexts. The result of managing these tensions is a LMF that is either incorporated within capitalist relations by abandoning its democratic values, or one that seeks to transform them by preserving democratic values. The national context is crucial to this understanding. Here we are contrasting two radically different assumptions underlying what motivates human behavior: those based on market values of individualistic rational economic man as opposed to those based on democratic values centered on solidarity principles of reciprocity, trust, and social preferences. Here we find a different rational construct where success is related to workers choosing to forgo individual immediate gain for the preference of the good of the collective and where success can no longer be explained by rational individual goal seeking market maximizing behavior or legal structures based on neoliberal constructs.

This paper explores a new theoretical model of the labour managed firm. At the macro level the "favorable conjuncture" concept explained the worker buyout phenomenon of the 1980s and 1990s where LMF emergence was associated with market recession resulting from the oil shock, labor assertiveness to preserve jobs, and a sympathetic state. In the contemporary situation job-saving worker buyouts continue to emerge in specific national constructs where deteriorating markets, an assertive labor movement, and sometimes a sympathetic state infrastructure exist as in France, Italy, and Argentina. Recommendation J of the Nuttall Report (2012) in the United Kingdom has resulted in a pilot project to investigate the feasibility of employee buyouts from insolvency.

At the micro level the theoretical model points to the conclusion that we are dealing with "an entity that cannot be subsumed by the classical firm concept" (Stryjan & Hellmark, 1985, p. 22) and that a developmental rationality or developmental individualism, nurtured by leadership deep within the firm, pervades the culture rather than a possessive individualism or instrumental rationality. Reflecting the power relationships of the macro culture a combination of legalistic and soft cultural forms determine the firm design and subsequent governance architecture. It was within these altered power relationships that workers were able to evolve and construct progressively more democratic and participative models across the continuum from the United States, Italy, and to Spain, which contributed to meeting the commercial rigors of the globalized market. Here we saw a progressive loosening of the legislative constraints on worker control and return rights along a continuum from the LME of the United States to the mediated Mediterranean economy (MME) of Italy and finally maximized in Spain where the MME saw the LMF embedded in a socialist political culture suitable for the emergence of a fully developed high performance work system of collegiate worker self-management. The emergence of spontaneous worker self-management on the shop floor of the US ESOPs raised interesting issues for the labor movement as to the prospect of more appropriate and sustainable models for the extension of democratic worker ownership.

In conclusion it seemed clear that Marx's conditional support for the LMF and worker self-management as a long term sustainable transforming vehicle had the best chance of success in the MME of Italy where the LMF was connected to the labor movement, funds were contributed to the cooperative movement, and nonmember labor was minimized. Further research is now required in other jurisdictions and varieties of capitalism to determine the usefulness of the multifactor theoretical model in predicting and charting sustainability of the LMF and contributing to policy formation surrounding the role of the High Performance System in rejuvenating mature industrial economies.

NOTE

1. Conversation with general manager of Madrid chapter of Spanish Association of Worker Owned Businesses (2005).

ACKNOWLEDGEMENTS

The author wishes to thank Professor Bradon Ellem, Professor Greg Patmore and Adjunct Professor Ron Callus from the University of Sydney for their comments on this article. The author is also indebted to Professor Doug Kruse of Rutgers University for his advice on shaping the article. This research was conducted as the basis for the author's Doctoral dissertation.

REFERENCES

Batstone, E. (1983). Organisation and orientation: A life cycle model of French co-operatives. *Economic and Industrial Democracy*, *4*(1), 39–161. London: Sage.

Ben-Ner, A. (1988). The life cycle of worker-owned firms in market economies. *Journal of Economic Behavior and Organisation*, *10*, 287–313. North Holland: Elsevier Science Publishers.

Best, M., & Connolly, W. (1976). *The politicized economy*. Lexington, DC: Heath.

Borzaga, C., Galera, G., & Tortia, E. (2009). Towards a new development paradigm. The potential of social enterprises, In Aa.Vv., *Social ministry* (2nd ed., pp. 176–193). Tangaza Occasional Paper No. 23. Pauline's Publications Africa, Nairobi.

Borzaga, C., & Tortia, E. (2006). *An evolutionary perspective in the theory of social enterprises*. Provisional version presented at the IFEPA Conference, Mondragon.

Boxall, P., & Purcell, J. (2003). *Strategy and human resource management*. Hampshire: Palgrave Macmillan.

Bratton, J., & Gould, J. (2012). *Human resource management: Theory and practice*. New York, NY: Palgrave Macmillan.

Charny, D. (1999). Workers and corporate governance – The role of political culture. In M. Blair & M. Roe (Eds.), *Employees and corporate governance* (pp. 91–120). Washington, DC: Brookings Institution Press.

Clarke, T. (1984). Alternative modes of cooperative production. *Economic and Industrial Democracy*, *5*, 97–129. London: Sage.

Domar, E. (1966). The Soviet Collective farm as a producer cooperative. *The American Economic Review*, *56*(4), 734–757.

Dow, G. K. (2006). *Creative destruction in the theory of the labor managed firm*. Keynote address. IAFEP conference. Department of Economics, Simon Fraser University, British Columbia, Canada.

Dow, G., & Putterman, L. (1999). Why capital (usually) hires labor: An assessment of proposed explanations. In M. Blair & M. Roe (Eds.), *Employees and corporate governance* (pp. 17–57). Washington, DC: Brookings Institution Press.

Eagan, D. (1990). Towards a Marxist theory of labor-managed firms: Breaking the degeneration thesis. *Review of Radical Political Economics*, *22*, 67–86.

Giles, A., & Murray, G. (1997). Industrial relations theory and critical political economy. In J. Barbash & N. M. Meltz (Eds.), *Theorizing in industrial relations: Approaches and applications* (pp. 77–120). Sydney: Australian Centre for Industrial Relations Research and Training.

Gordon, J. (1999). Employee stock ownership in economic transitions: The case of united and the airline industry. In M. Blair & M. Roe (Eds.), *Employees and corporate governance*. Washington, DC: Brookings Institution Press.

Hall, P., & Soskice, D. (2004). *Varieties of capitalism: The institutional foundations of comparative advantage*. Oxford: Oxford University Press.

Hancock, M. (2007). *Compete to cooperate: The cooperative district of Imola*. Coop, Agave-Imola.

Hodgson, G. (1984). *The democratic economy*. Harmondsworth, UK: Penguin.

Jensen, A. (2012). *Insolvency, employee rights and employee buyouts: A strategy for restructuring*. Unpublished doctoral thesis, University of Sydney, Australia.

Jones, D. C. (1978). Producer cooperatives in industrialised western economies: An overview. *Annals of Public and Cooperative Economy*, *49*(2), 149–161.

Lawler, E. (1986). *High-involvement management*. Princeton, NJ: Jossey-Bass.

Lawler, E. (1992). *The ultimate advantage: Creating the high involvement organisation*. San Francisco, CA: Jossey-Bass.

Lichtenstein, P. M. (1986). The concept of the firm in the economic theory of 'alternative' organizations: Appraisal and reformulation. In S. Jansson & A.-B. Hellmark (Eds.), *Labor-owned firms and workers' cooperatives* (pp. 51–72). Aldershott, UK: Gower Publishing Company Limited.

Mason, R. (1982). *Participatory and workplace democracy: A theoretical development in critique of liberalism*. Carbondale, IL: Southern Illinois University Press.

Mygind, N. (1986). From the Illyrian firm to the reality of self-management. In S. Jansson & A.-B. Hellmark (Eds.), *Labor-owned firms and workers' cooperatives* (pp. 73–104). Aldershott, UK: Gower Publishing Company Limited.

Nuttall Report. (2012). Sharing Success – Nuttall Review of Employee Ownership. Department for Business Innovation and Skills. Retrieved from http://www.bis.gov.uk/assets/biscore/business-law/docs/s/12-933-sharing-success-nuttall-review-employee-ownership.pdf

Oakeshott, R. (1973 [1975]). Mondragon: Spain's oasis of democracy. In Vanek (Ed.), *Self-management: Economic liberation of man*. London: Penguin.

Oakeshott, R. (1978). *The case for workers' coops*. London: Routledge & Kegan Paul.

Ostrom, E. (1990). *Governing the commons*. Cambridge: Cambridge University Press.

Owners at Work. (1997). *Newsletter of the Ohio Employee Ownership Association*.

Perotin, V. (1999). Why there are not more labor managed firms. Paper presented at the Yaraslov Vanek Memorial Conference. Columbia University, New York, NY.

Poole, M. (1986). *Industrial relations: Origins and patterns of national diversity*. London: Routledge & Kegan Paul.

Stryjan, Y., & Hellmark, A. B. (1985). *Beyond ownership*. Sweden: Swedish Centre for Working Life.

The Berkshire Eagle. (1992). *The Berkshire Eagle*, October 3 (Vol. 101, Issue 48). Retrieved from http://www.berkshireeagle.com

Vanek, J. (1975). *Self-management: Economic liberation of man*. Harmondsworth, UK: Penguin.

Vidal, I., & Vilaplana, A. (1999). *Perspectivas empresariales de las sociedades laborales en la U.E.* Barcelona: FESALC.

Ward, B. N. (1958). The firm in Illyria: Market syndicalism. *American Economic Review*, *48*, 566–689.

Webb, S., & Webb, B. (1920). *Industrial democracy*. London: Longmans Green and Co.

Westenholtz, A. (1986). Democratic management and efficiency. In S. Jansson & A.-B. Hellmark (Eds.), *Labor-owned firms and workers' cooperatives* (pp. 140–154). Aldershott, UK: Gower Publishing Company Limited.

Winther, G. (1998). Theory O – Is the case closed? Paper presented at the 9th International Conference Economics of Participation International Association of the Economics of Participation, Bristol.

Wood, C. (1996). High commitment management and unionisation in the UK. *The International Journal of Human Resource Management*, *7*(1), 41–58.

Zevi, A. (1982). The performance of Italian producer co-operatives. In D. C. Jones & J. Svejnar (Eds.), *Participatory and self-managed firms*. Lexington, MA: Lexington Books.

CHAPTER 12

THREE THEMES ABOUT DEMOCRATIC ENTERPRISES: CAPITAL STRUCTURE, EDUCATION, AND SPIN-OFFS

David Ellerman

ABSTRACT

Purpose – *The purpose of this paper is to delve into three themes about democratic enterprises.*

Design/methodology/approach – *(1) The first theme is the question of capital structure where labor-managed firms (LMFs) are often pictured as having "horizon problem." Yet this is only a minor technical problem which is solved by the system of internal capital accounts as in the Mondragon cooperatives.*

(2) The second theme concerns the attempt to implement participative management and the related ideas of active learning in educational theory in the workplace. The point is that the democratic firm is the natural setting to implement these ideas, not the conventional firm where the staff have the legal role of "employees" rented by the company.

Sharing Ownership, Profits, and Decision-making in the 21st Century
Advances in the Economic Analysis of Participatory & Labor-Managed Firms, Volume 14, 327–353

ISSN: 0885-3339/doi:10.1108/S0885-3339(2013)0000014012

(3) The third theme is the old canard the cooperatives are incompatible with entrepreneurship. My rethinking of the issue was inspired by the analysis of the late Jane Jacobs who emphasized that the primary means of growing economic "biomass" is through economic offspring (e.g., spin-offs) – in analogy with the biological principle of plentitude. Yet the conventional form of ownership operates as a fetter on this process since the ownership and management wants to expand its empire and maintain "ownership" of any potential offspring. But that constraint against spin-offs is absent in democratic firms, and the Mondragon complex has indeed illustrated how to catalyze this process of growth through offspring.

Social implications – *A public policy to encourage all companies to grow by affiliated and perhaps democratic spin-offs would create more jobs (through filling extra niches) and more stability (through the agility of separate companies).*

Keywords: Capital accounts; participative management; spin-offs

JEL classifications: J54; L2; M13; P13

INTRODUCTION

My topic is a set of themes where I think the experience of the Mondragon cooperatives is particularly relevant. In my opinion, these themes are also not widely understood even by advocates and practitioners of the various forms of worker ownership and cooperative enterprise. The first topic of capital structure is notoriously difficult and controversial, and yet it is an area where the Mondragon cooperatives have in their system of internal capital accounts made a social invention of the first order. But the practice has preceded the theory so this accomplishment is little understood.

Education has always played a leading role in the cooperative movement and particularly in the Mondragon experience. My point here is to mine a broader theme in the philosophy of education which has been the topic of a recent book (Ellerman, 2005a), and to relate that theme to the structure of a democratic firm (e.g., a worker cooperative). Education works best when it is structured not as the pouring of knowledge into learners as passive vessels but as the indirect facilitation of learners taking an active role in constructing and appropriating knowledge. In this sense, education should be the cognitive version of the producers appropriating the fruits of their own labor. That fruits of their labor principle is only implemented in a firm where the members of the firm are the producers, the managers, and workers of the firm. Thus in a democratic firm (as opposed to a conventional employment firm), we have a unique coincidence of structures; the legal structure of the firm respects the autonomy and responsibility of the workers as producers, and this should naturally carry over to their role as active learners or appropriators of knowledge – but this is by no means an "automatic" process. The legal role of the workers as members does not automatically transform people socialized as "employees" to active participants in a democratic process.

And finally this brings me to the third theme. Critics of workplace democracy as well as some sympathetic observers have often raised the question of entrepreneurship. In the conventional economy of employment firms, entrepreneurs play an important innovative role in fact (and an even more important role in the ideology of the system). Hence the advocates of workplace democracy need to take the question of entrepreneurship seriously. Three decades ago, I tried to approach this question by studying the Empresarial Division of the Caja Laboral Popular (since reorganized as a separate cooperative, LKS). I argued that the Empresarial Division was a "factory factory" that represented the "socialization of entrepreneurship" (Ellerman, 1982, 1984). I now think that this analysis was not well taken. Hence in the third part of the paper, I would like to develop a new approach that still recognizes the role of the Empresarial Division and its successors but which has a different angle on the question of entrepreneurship.

CAPITAL STRUCTURE IN AN EMPLOYMENT FIRM AND A DEMOCRATIC FIRM

The Horizon Problem

Most people who have taken a serious look at the idea of a democratic firm has grasped the idea that membership rights in such a firm cannot be a market commodity that could be purchased by any "shareholder." Whether they use the language or not, they will have grasped the idea that one must qualify for membership in a democratic firm by working there on a long-term basis (in additional to other requirements, one of which may be paying in membership fee). Membership in a democratic firm is a personal right like citizenship in a political democracy, not a property right that can be bought or sold on a stock market.

The controversy arises concerning the issue of what might be loosely called "the value of the firm." The treatment of membership rights as personal rights could be legally implemented using the legal structure of a nonprofit corporation where the members cannot recoup any of the "value of the firm." This structure was typical in many of the traditional worker cooperatives in Europe, in the late Yugoslav self-managed firms, and in the common ownership firms of the United Kingdom. The members of such a firm always face the decision of splitting their net income into a portion currently paid out as wages and salaries, and a portion retained in the firm. They will not be able to recoup their share of the retained earnings if they leave the firm in the near future. If an individual would remain with the firm for the lifetime of the investment, then the inability to recoup the undepreciated retained earnings would not matter since the investment would have been depreciated. But workers have different time horizons with the firm so this created what was called the "horizon problem for labor-managed firms." The problem was treated in much of the literature as some intrinsic and fatal flaw in the very idea of labor management rather than as a merely technical issue that could be readily solved (Ellerman, 1986).

The other nonsolution to the capital structure problem (aside from the nonprofit or social equity nonsolution) was to have membership shares that would also serve the dual purpose of carrying the typical member's portion of the capital value. One needed to own a membership share (in theory) to work in the firm, but one had to buy such a share from a retiring or exiting worker. This retained the connection between working in the firm and being a member, and it was supposed to recognize each member's share of the capital value. This sort of structure was used in some of the older worker cooperatives in the United States (e.g., the plywood cooperatives) and it unfortunately seems to be the model used in many of the Spanish SAL (*Sociedad Anonima Laboral*) firms. The value of a membership share was determined by what the market would bear, but the "market" was restricted to the workers who might replace a retiring worker. There were two tendencies. If the exiting workers insisted on a value comparable to their undepreciated past retained earnings and investment, not whatever entering workers could pay, then soon or later the older members would "broaden the market" by forcing the sale of the whole company as a conventional corporation to any buyers. The other tendency is for the company to browbeat the exiting workers to accept whatever the entering workers can pay in order to preserve the firm as being worker-owned.

It is interesting that for both these nonsolutions, the technical problem was so often transformed into a "moral" problem. With the nonprofit nonsolution, the net earnings of the firm that could have been paid out as personal income were seen as being somehow transformed into "social property" or "common ownership" when they were reinvested in the firm. Then it was seen as a moral impropriety to want to take a share of "social property" upon exit or retirement. Or with the nonsolution of the dual-purpose membership share, the retiring workers who expected back some reasonable value were pictured as being morally derelict. These are two examples of a somewhat broader tendency on the left of "premature moralization" of a technical problem.

In this case, the capital structure problem for democratic firms has a solution which has been discovered at least four times but is still little understood. The solution is to have a system of what are called "internal capital accounts" for the members. Based on a pure rental model for a labor-managed firm (LMF), Jaroslav Vanek arrived at the notion of "external funding" as opposed to "self-financing" for LMFs and suggested that external support agencies might play that role. But then Vanek noted that an internal redeemable savings account would be counted as "external" – all of which amounts to an internal capital account (Vanek, 1975). I personally was involved in working out the internal capital account idea in the context of the work of the Industrial Cooperative Association, whose acronym ICA also coincidentally could stand for "Internal Capital Accounts." The ICA quickly found out that the same idea had already been developed in practice in the Mondragon cooperatives and it was thereafter presented as the "Mondragon solution" to the problem. The fourth and even older solution was in the system of partner capital accounts to be found in law partnerships and other professional partnerships. Sometimes partners have to invest a share of partnership earnings (or out of pocket) to make some capital acquisition (e.g., a new building) and these investments were kept track of in a separate capital account that was eventually paid out. Each partner's share in the profits or vote was independent of the amount in the internal capital account.

Parsing the Corporate Ownership Rights

In the conventional corporation, there is a "bundle of rights" attached to the common equity shares. Our task is to show precisely how these rights are split apart, transformed, and reassigned in a democratic firm. We simplify down to the essentials: the voting rights (to elect the board to select the management and to vote on any other questions put to the stockholders) and the economic value rights which can now be parsed into the net asset value and the (economic) profits rights. The net asset value is for the current time but the voting and profit rights need to be broken down into the current rights and future rights after the current time period. Thus we have the following taxonomy:

Corporate Ownership Rights

A. Voting rights
   - A.1 Current voting rights
   - B.1 Future voting rights

B. Value rights
   - A.1 Profit rights
     - B.1(a) Current profit rights
     - B.1(a) Future profit rights
   - B.1 Net asset value.

In the conventional joint stock company, these corporate ownership rights (voting + value rights) are property rights represented by the common voting shares that may be owned and freely transferred as any other property rights.

In a democratic firm, the corporate ownership rights are not only rebundled but are assigned on a different basis. The rights structure is derived from first principles which have been detailed elsewhere (see Ellerman, 1992). The voting rights are assigned on the basis of democratic principle of self-government. The people working in the firm are the only people under the management of the firm's managers so by the democratic principle, the voting rights to elect those managers (perhaps indirectly through board election) should be assigned to the people working in the firm. Note that this assignment to those people is based on the assumption that those people are playing a certain functional role, that is, working in the firm. They do not "own" the voting rights as property rights to be held or sold independently of their functional role. It is the same with political rights in a democracy. We call rights assigned to a functional role *personal rights* (but one can use whatever label so long as the concept is clear).

The workers in the firm change so the assignment of the voting rights will change with the workforce. The future workers, like the future citizens in a political democracy, do not have to buy their voting rights from the present holders. Hence the separation of the (A) voting rights into the

(A.1) current voting rights and (A.2) future voting rights. It is the (A.1) current voting rights that are part of the bundle of *membership rights* attached to the functional role of currently working in the democratic firm. The (A.2) future voting rights would be assigned to the future workers.

The second normative principle (here called the *responsibility principle*) is just the standard jurisprudential norm of assigning to people the legal responsibility for the results of their deliberate and intentional actions. In rather abstract terms, the intentional actions L of the people working in the firm produce the outputs Q by using up the nonlabor inputs K. In vector terms, the product of the human activity L is (Q,−K,0). Since the so-called "capitalist" system hypostatizes this human activity L as a service "owned" by the workers and "used up" in production, we can parse the product of this human activity as:

$$\begin{aligned}\text{Labor Product} &= (Q, -K, 0) = (0, 0, L) + (Q, -K, -L)\\ &= \text{Labor Services} + \text{Whole Product}\end{aligned}$$

Since the workers already "own" their labor (0, 0, L), by imputing labor's product to the workers, the responsibility principle would additionally be imputing the whole product (Q,−K,−L) to the workers. The value of the whole product is the current profit so this is precisely the (B.1(a)) current profit rights. Thus those rights would also be in the bundle of membership rights assigned as personal rights to the functional role of working in the firm (where "working in the firm" in the current time period means producing the current labor product). As one might expect, the (B.1(b)) future profits rights represent the future whole products that would be assigned to the future workers who produce them.

Thus on the basis of the first principles of democracy and responsibility, we have accounted for all the rights except the (B.2) net asset value rights. In terms of the point-in-time versus time-period distinction (e.g., balance sheet vs. income statement), the net asset value is a current value relating to a point in time, while votes are cast and profits are earned in each time period. There is no reason to assume that the net asset value is supplied by or produced by the current workers. Current workers will, to be sure, use up the capital services derived from the capital assets of the company as part of the nonlabor inputs K and that is why they are held legally responsible for the liabilities −K, but we are now concerned with the rights to the net asset value. This value represents property rights accumulated by production and exchange in the past so the claims on the value by past and present members would be determined by the history of past transactions.

The system of internal capital accounts is quite simply the means of keeping track of that history so that the net asset value is in whole or part owed in varying amounts to current and past members. They contributed to that value through any membership fees paid in and through any profits (or losses) retained in the firm rather than being paid out (or assessed in the case of losses). These claims could be thought of as a form of "internal" debt (like a shareholder's loan) subordinate to all other (external) debts. Indeed, the internal capital accounts should be interest bearing. The balance is a property right, not a personal right. One test to distinguish personal and property rights is inheritability. If a member dies, the voting and profit rights (like political voting rights) do not pass to the person's estate, but the internal capital account balance would be a debt of the company to the estate of the deceased member.

Thus we have seen how all the corporate ownership rights are rebundled and assigned in a democratic firm. The current voting and profit rights are bundled together as the *membership rights* attached to the functional role of working in the firm (in practical terms, usually after a certain probationary period) so the future voting and profit rights would go to future members, and the remaining net asset value rights are captured in the system of internal capital accounts held by the current members. The accounts of past members would be closed and elevated into an external debt of the company to the ex-member. The rights structure in the so-called "capitalist corporation" and the democratic firm can now be compared point-by-point (Table 1).

Origins of Internal Capital Accounts

There has been some controversy about how the net asset value should be treated. One widespread socialist belief was that the net asset value must be

Table 1. Comparison of Rights Structures.

Rights Structure	"Capitalist" Corporation	Democratic Corporation
Current membership rights (A.1 + B.1(a))	Owned as property rights by shareholders	Assigned as personal rights to the current workers
Future membership rights (A.2 + B.1(b))	Owned as property rights by shareholders	Assigned as personal rights to the future workers
Net asset value rights (B.2)	Owned as property rights by shareholders	Owned as property rights by the current workers

collectively owned as in the English common ownership firms or the former Yugoslav self-managed firms – a holdover from the mistaken view that "capitalism" was based on the "private ownership of the means of production" rather than on the employment contract. To analyze this view, it must first be recalled that the voting and profit rights have been partitioned away from the rights to the net asset value. The phrase "private ownership of the means of production" usually does include specifically the rights to control and reap the profits from the means of production. But those rights have been restructured as personal rights assigned to labor in the democratic firm. Hence the remaining right to the net asset value does *not* include the control and profit rights traditionally associated with "equity capital" or with the "ownership of the means of production."

Let us suppose that it is still argued that any private claim (e.g., by past workers) on the net asset value of a democratic firm would be "appropriating social property to private uses." Now some net asset value might come from a historical endowment that should not be appropriated by whoever happens to be the current workers. Very well, that endowment could be captured in a separate (bearing interest to reflect its scarcity) "collective account" (as in the Mondragon cooperatives). But what about that portion of the net asset value that comes from retained earnings in the past or from paid-in membership fees?

In a democratic firm, the past workers could, in theory, have used their voting and profit rights to pay out all the net earnings instead of retaining any in the firm, assuming they could cover any financing needs by borrowing (as in the academic model of the "pure rental" LMF). Suppose they retained some earnings to finance a machine. Why should those workers lose their claim on that value – except as they use up the machine? Why should the fruits of their labor suddenly become "social property" simply because they choose to reinvest it in their company?

Consider the following *gedanken* experiment in a "social property" LMF. Instead of retaining the earnings to finance a machine, suppose the workers paid out the earnings as bonuses, deposited them all in one savings bank, and then took out a loan from the bank to finance the machine using the deposits as collateral. Then the workers would not lose the value of those earnings since that value is represented in the balance in their savings accounts in the bank. And the enterprise still gets to finance the machine. Since the finance was raised by a loan, there was no private claim on the social equity capital of the enterprise. The loan capital is capital hired by labor; it gets only interest with no votes and no share of the profits. This hired capital satisfied Jaroslav Vanek's (1975) idea of "external" finance as opposed to self-finance.

Now we come to the point of the thought-experiment. How is it different *in principle* if we simply leave the bank out and move the workers' savings accounts into the firm itself? Instead of going through the whole circuitous loop of paying out the earnings, depositing them in the bank's savings accounts, and then borrowing the money back – suppose the firm directly retains the earnings, credits the workers' savings accounts in the firm, and buys the machine. The capital balance represented in the savings accounts is essentially *loan* capital. It is hired by labor, it receives interest, and it has no votes or profit shares. This was the conceptual route followed by the ICA to develop the idea of internal capital accounts (before learning about the Mondragon accounts), and Jaroslav Vanek seems to have followed a similar route since he explicitly noted that his notion of "external" funding would include such capital accounts.

> Into our concept of external funding we also include redeemable savings deposits of members, bearing a market rate of return paid, as to other creditors, prior to the distribution of labor incomes. To the extent that our analysis comes out in favor of external funding, it also favors this type of individualized funding by members. (Vanek, 1975, p. 445)

Prior to Vanek's and ICA's development of the internal capital account concept, they were developed in the Mondragon cooperatives, and prior to that in the capital accounts of legal and other professional partnerships.

The separate treatment of the membership rights (current voting and profit rights) as personal rights, and net asset rights as property rights recorded in the internal capital accounts solves the so-called "capital structure problem" for democratic firms. Some older forms of employee ownership use one instrument (the membership share) to serve the two different purposes and thus led to problems such as the mule firm tendencies (failure to reproduce as a worker-owned company). As the carrier of the net asset value, the membership shares might obtain such a high value that new workers could not afford a share so would be hired as a nonmember. And then an external market would be sought for the high-priced shares of the founding cohort, so the company would end up converting to a conventional firm in the course of a generation. The Mondragon-style capital structure solves these "mule-firm" problems.

ACTIVE LEARNING IN A WORKPLACE DEMOCRACY

From the Employment Relation to the Membership Relation

Let us now turn from the legal structure of a democratic firm and the principles behind it to the relationship between the managers and workers that would be appropriate for a democratic firm (but could be approximated or simulated in other types of firms). We have approached the questions of legal structure from first principles that treat persons as being inalienably decision-making and responsible beings – in contrast to things. The basic idea is to treat people as persons rather than as things which is essentially the Kantian principle to treat people always as ends in themselves and never solely as a means. This means treating people as being autonomous – as being the source of decisions and responsibility ("*auto-nomos*" or self-law) in contrast to be subjugated or dominated and ruled from the outside.

How does this translate into the internal management of a firm? Some of modern participative management theory in the human relations school has been concerned with the problem of organizing the hierarchy of decision-making and action within a firm so that people's capacity as autonomous beings will not be undercut and they will not just be treated as instruments.

One of the earliest and best management thinkers on the topic was Douglas McGregor who wrote in the middle of the 20th century. He outlined two broad approaches to management which he called "Theory X" and "Theory Y." Theory X was the more usual approach to management, top-down and manipulative with the extrinsic motivation of pay and bonuses being assumed as the primary motivators. Theory Y actually represented a Copernican revolution in management thinking by rebuilding the whole theory of management based on the assumed integrity, intrinsic motivation, and self-control (or autonomy) of the people working in the firm.

McGregor describes Theory Y as being based on the principle of integration and self-control where "integration" refers to the situation where an individual "can achieve his own goals *best* by directing his efforts toward the objectives of the enterprise" (1960, p. 61). Management's task is not to provide incentives; the "task is to provide an appropriate environment – one that will permit and encourage employees to seek intrinsic rewards *at work*" (1967, p. 14). The contrasting Theory X is based on the principle or philosophy of direction and control using the type of incentives that management can provide, that is, extrinsic or external incentives ("*hetero-nomos*" or external-law).

Theory X is based on conventional economics that sees the worker as *homo economicus* motivated by extrinsic considerations that can be engineered by management to bring about the behavior desired by management. In economics, this view of the manager–worker relationship is based on the employer–employee relation and is sometimes called the "principal–agent relationship." Since the natural home of the alternative Theory Y is outside the employment relationship, I will use alternative terminology of manager as "helper" and worker as "doer." The helper–doer terminology will allow us to draw some later analogies between McGregor's Theory Y and the teacher–learner relationship in active learning and constructivist theories of education.

McGregor starts with the common problem where someone in an organization (the doer) is facing a certain problem to better do their job. What is the role of the manager as helper, facilitator, coach, or catalyst? Starting with the doer's problem within the organization and seeing the problem through the doer's eyes, the helper can then offer knowledge and experience to help the doer find the best way to further the doer's own intrinsic ends while addressing the organizational problem. The helper is not to "teach" the doer what the helper considers the best solution.

Ortega y Gasset stated the matter very clearly: "He who wants to teach a truth should place us in the position to discover it ourselves" (1961, p. 67). In McGregor's words: "*A's* [Helper's] objective is to utilize his skill to create a situation in which *B* [doer] can learn, and to make his knowledge available so that *B* may utilize it to augment his own need satisfaction in ways consistent with the achievement of organizational objectives" (1966, p. 163). Or again, "Fundamentally the [helper] ... must create a situation in which [the doers] can learn, rather than one in which they are taught" (1966, p. 161).

McGregor's references to the doers' "own goals" and "intrinsic rewards *at work*" goes well beyond the conception of many economists and managers that workers are motivated primarily by extrinsic considerations of pay and benefits. Early in the 20th century, the economist Dennis Robertson expressed a broader vision:

> A high wage will not elicit effective work from those who feel themselves outcasts or slaves, nor a low wage preclude it from those who feel themselves an integral part of a community of free men. Thus the improvement of this element in the supply of labour is an infinitely more complex and arduous task than if it depended upon wage alone, but at the same time a task more possible of fulfillment by an impoverished world. (Quoted in Whyte, 1955, p. 5)

The passage above was quoted by the late William Foote Whyte about the time that the first Mondragon firm of ULGOR was founded – quite early in his long and illustrious career. Bill Whyte throughout his career searched for models of the new vision of work based on the participation, autonomy, and intrinsic motivation of the workers that we have illustrated with McGregor's Theory Y. Later in his life, Bill Whyte learned about the Mondragon experience and spent his remaining years studying it in great depth. Bill Whyte and his wife Kathleen summarized their findings about Mondragon with insight and sensitivity in their 1991 book *Making Mondragon*.

My point here is basically the same; the vision of work based on participation, autonomy, and intrinsic motivation finds it natural home not in employment firms but in the democratic firm as illustrated by the Mondragon cooperatives.

From Passive Instruction to Active Learning in Education

The basic principles we see exemplified in the Mondragon experience have a broader reach than governance, property rights, and management relationships. Just as we juxtaposed the conventional firm and the democratic firm or McGregor's Theory X and his Theory Y, so we find two rather opposite visions or philosophies of education: the one is teacher-centered with the instructed student in a passive role, and the other vision is more learner-centered with the teacher playing a more indirect catalytic role (the teacher–learner version of the helper–doer relationship). John Dewey (1859–1952) as well as Father Arizmendiarrieta could be taken as representatives of the latter tradition.

These two visions or pedagogies might even be traced back to two opposing metaphors for the mind itself as a passive mirror or as an active lamp. With the first pedagogy, the student is described as being essentially passive: a wax tablet on which knowledge is stamped, a mirror or reflector for knowledge (Plato, Locke), a vessel or cistern into which knowledge is poured (Cudworth, Coleridge, Dewey), a phonographic record onto which knowledge is recorded (Dewey, Gramsci, Ryle), and so forth. In this model, the teacher supplies the knowledge that is imprinted into the student, crammed into the student as into a bag (Maritain), forced into the student through a "funnel" (Buber), drilled into the student as into hard and resisting rock (Dewey), or forced into the student using a "grease gun" (McGregor).

The other pedagogy sees the student's mind as taking a more active role represented by metaphors such as lamp, fountain, or projector – or often by organic metaphors of a growing plant. The teacher then has a more subtle indirect role of a guide, coach, or midwife to foster and nurture the student's active search for and appropriation of knowledge. Some of the subtlety of the teacher's indirect role can be expressed using the metaphor of the internal fountain. Impediments can obscure or block the flow of the fountain (like turning off a faucet or hose). External enabling help can then unblock the fountain or open the faucet but the subtle point is that external help cannot directly supply the pressure to make the fountain flow. That pressure has to come from within.

This can't-push-on-a-string asymmetry is reflected in the distinction between extrinsic and intrinsic motivation. Extrinsic motivation can override and crowd out intrinsic motivation to control behavior, but removing the former will not automatically supply the latter. One cannot extrinsically bring about intrinsically-motivated action just as opening a faucet cannot itself supply water pressure. The oft-repeated metaphor for this insight is: "[W]hile we may lead a horse to water we cannot make him drink" (Dewey, 1916, p. 26). While real learning thus cannot be an imposition, neither can it be a gift. Father Arizmendiarrieta contrasted what could be obtained by "paternalist catapults" with what might result from the "need and opportunity to be able to resort to and count on one's own resources or personal abilities" (n.d., p. 116).

The reliance on extrinsic rewards or punishments may yield conforming behavior and a rote learning[1] but has little educative or transformative effect. Indeed, the threat to autonomy may lead to an adverse reactance effect. "His instincts of cunning and slyness may be aroused, so that things henceforth appeal to him on the side of evasion and trickery more than would otherwise be the case" (Dewey, 1916, p. 26). An autonomy-compatible educational program needs to engage the person's more natural and intrinsic motivation.

> When we confuse a physical with an educative result, we always lose the chance of enlisting the person's own participating disposition in getting the result desired, and thereby of developing within him an intrinsic and persisting direction in the right way. (Dewey, 1916, p. 27)

The students' active interest and involvement is a necessary component so one must consider the roots of engagement. Students do not construct knowledge in a void. Learning is contextual; it builds upon the context of previous knowledge, experience, and problems. Hence Father Arizmendiarrieta's pragmatism: "We build the road as we travel" (n.d., p. 158).[2] Hence Dewey's "pragmatic" emphasis was placed on learning in the context of the "social environment," albeit simplified and ordered in a school, so that the student would have a natural or intrinsic incentive to learn. Hence Paulo Freire's (1970) emphasis on dialogue as the prelude to, as well as the means of, learning. By formulating a literacy campaign in terms of the peasants' daily concerns, the peasants are motivated to be involved and take ownership of the process. The cases, examples, and questions can be couched in terms that make sense from the student's viewpoint and are relevant to the student's interests. With this preparation, the student can take responsibility for actively reconstructing and appropriating knowledge with occasional prodding and questioning from the teacher as midwife. Knowledge obtained in this active way is truly the student's own; it is neither an imposition nor a gift.

Here again we see the cooperatives are the natural home for this sort of active learning.

> The cooperative movement is an economic effort that is translated into an educational action, or, it is an educational effort that uses economic action as a vehicle of transformation. (Arizmendiarrieta, n.d., p. 174)

The Mondragon cooperative complex was founded and built on Father Arizmendiarrieta's educational vision, a vision that is very much in line with the philosophy emphasizing the active role of the learner based pragmatically on the type of problems that arise in the business and social environment. This vision has been carried through the Escuela Politecnica to today's Mondragon University.

The overall point is that the democratic firm provides the ideal and natural setting for autonomy-respecting management methods (e.g., McGregor's Theory Y) and active learning (e.g., John Dewey and Paulo Freire). None of this is to suggest that these difficult transformations from "employees" to active participant-members are somehow automatic in a democratic firm. Human relations programs have a more important substantive and positive role in democratic firms since the structure of the firm then supports rather than opposes those transformations. In conventional firms, those programs often boil down to trying to get the staff to "act like owners" when they are not.

ENTREPRENEURSHIP AND DEMOCRATIC FIRMS

Existing Firms as Schools for Business Training

My earlier work on entrepreneurship and Mondragon (1982, 1984) contrasted the "socialization of entrepreneurship" in the Empresarial Division of the Caja Laboral Popular (now the separate second-tier cooperative LKS) with the conventional stories of the heroic individuals starting companies in their garages.[3] But an intensive study of the work of the late Jane Jacobs forced me to rethink the issue of entrepreneurship from scratch.

This, in turn, lead me to appreciate a different connection between entrepreneurship and democratic firms, an aspect that is also illustrated by the Mondragon cooperatives.

Every company has two products: its products and itself. By "itself" is meant the company as an organization of people trained in the systems necessary to run the business and in the technologies necessary to produce the products or services of the company. While some skills are already possessed by people when they join the organization, the company still has to have the training capacity to specialize those skills to the systems and technologies specific to the firm. And as people leave or retire, the company has to recreate those human capabilities within the firm.

While the company's ordinary products may be protected by patents and trademarks, there is generally no such exclusive rights over the human capabilities developed in the company. When those capabilities leave the company, then it is a positive externality. In A. C. Pigou's classic book on normative economics, he noted that the businesses in a country provided the positive externality (meaning their social product exceeded their private product) of training people in business:

> One very important indirect service is rendered by the general economic organisation of a country in so far as, in addition to fulfilling its function as an instrument of production, it also acts, in greater or lesser degree, as a training ground of business capacities. (1960, p. 204)

Modern economics texts seem to have lost sight of this fundamental point that existing businesses are major training grounds for entrepreneurial and managerial capability and major incubators for new businesses. Yet the conventional business sees this social product as no part of its corporate goals. Quite to the contrary, businesses want to grow by expansion rather than by spin-offs and they want to retain their potential future managers rather than lose them to new businesses.

In a vibrant entrepreneurial environment, such as Silicon Valley in California or Silicon Gulch in Taiwan, people routinely leave companies, often together with some colleagues, to start new companies. But these are rather exceptional cases.

The Biological Principle of Plentitude: Growth through Offspring

In biological terms, there are two ways in which the biomass is increased: existing life getting bigger or existing life having offspring. Diminishing returns set in as companies get bigger and the same happens to biological organisms. The limits of increasing biomass by existing creatures getting larger in size are soon reached. Most of the biomass that covers the globe comes from the second strategy of having offspring; that is the biological principle of plentitude. Indeed, biology gives little choice. While organisms can grow larger within certain limits, the organism must eventually die and so the DNA can only survive by having offspring. These ideas have been used in the economic development thinking of Jane Jacobs in *The Economy of Cities* (1969) and in *Cities and the Wealth of Nations: Principles of Economic Life* (1984).[4]

Corporations are subject to various forms of diminishing returns to increased size (e.g., in management's ability to monitor and comprehend events) but they have no natural limitation on lifetime. Hence the first tendency of companies is preserve their "business DNA" by growing bigger and having more layers in the hierarchy rather than fostering offspring. In this sense, the company's "second product" (its trained people) is sterile – particularly in a less-than-vibrant business environment; the company may grow but it does not breed. Indeed, some companies only grow through the "reverse offspring" of acquisitions. Hence there is relatively little increase in the "economic mass" and the business environment stagnates. That is the conundrum faced by conventional companies. Their structure mitigates against the principle of plentitude.

This conundrum pointed out by Pigou gives grounds for some public policy support to schemes that try to improve the social role of existing businesses as spawning new businesses. Pigou also recognized that some organizational forms more than others might lend themselves to this social role. In particular, "associations of workers combined together in small copartnership workshops" would constitute the "first school in which this capacity can be developed" and thus such companies would contribute to the community not just "boots and shoes" but the second product of "well-trained competent" people (Pigou, 1960, pp. 205–206).

The basic point is that in a worker cooperative or a democratic firm, there is no unified "ownership" that has the power to block the second and most potent "off-spring" way of increasing economic biomass. The workers in each part of a company have their own standing as members of the company. This does not mean that the workers in cooperatives are automatically oriented to taking entrepreneurial risks with spinoff cooperatives. The most common attitude in most businesses, cooperative or conventional, is try to stabilize, improve, and perpetuate one's position with the company. The point is that with a cooperative, there is no structural constraint against the economic analogue of the biological principle of plenitude, growth through offspring.

There at least four ways that a company, conventional or cooperative, might accelerate the production of its "second product" (trained people) to foster offspring.

Four Ways to Promote Growth through Spin-offs

1. *Sheltered or associated spin-offs of routine products and services as separate companies.*

Inside any medium to large-sized company, there are routines products or services provided for the company such as printing, graphics design, catering or food services, trucking, and cleaning services. These could be organized first as a separate profit-center and then as a "sheltered spin-off" majority locally or cooperatively owned with a multiyear contract with the mother firm. But as a quasi-separate firm (associated with the original firm or group of firms), it would be free to do business with other companies to expand its market. There is only so much printing that is needed by any one company. That will create job growth to serve the expanded market. Moreover, it will build entrepreneurial and managerial skills on the part of the people leading the spin-off.

This strategy should be differentiated from "outsourcing" where the purpose is to reduce the payroll of the mother company and introduce competition in the supply of those services, not to expand the market and jobs in the business unit. The spin-off could remain associated with the original company perhaps even carrying part of its name, for example, Acme Printing, Acme Food Services, or Acme Trucking as spin-offs from Acme Company. It should have a multiyear sole-source contract to counteract any suspicion that it was just an "outsourcing" scheme.

Eventually a group of companies might form around the original mother company. The group might sponsor a second-tier organization to help spawn more offspring.

A slight variation on this theme occurs when a production company wants to eventually upgrade machinery. Given limited space, they may scrap the old machinery and replace it with the new equipment. But there might be several years of effective operation in the old equipment which could be moved off-site to a more disadvantaged area as a job-creation scheme. Some workers in the factory might take that as an opportunity to start their own production shop with low start-up costs and some guaranteed sales but where they have the possibility to finance other machines and produce parts for other clients. This type of urban-to-rural spin-off helped to fuel the rural industrial development in township-village enterprises in China.

2. *"Light touch" franchising: Seconding entrepreneurs to learn about a business.*

Most entrepreneurs do not start from scratch. They have worked in companies and learned how companies operate first hand before striking out on their own with some colleagues. But in many cases an entrepreneurial individual may not have had that relevant experience so an economic development agency could sponsor secondments in an existing company (e.g., by paying most of the salary of the seconded person). The seconded person would work with the manager and various departments to learn about their functions. Since the existing company would not want to be training new competition, the new company would have to commit to operate in a noncompeting zone, for example, in another city outside the business region of the original company. If the new company develops well, there might be future business partnerships with the original company where the entrepreneurial received the training.

This could be thought of as an "ad hoc" or "light-touch" franchise. A franchise also tries to replicate the business systems and procedures of an existing company and to insure that such clones will be in noncompeting niches. But franchising requires a rather sophisticated legal system to enforce all the intellectual property rights. And franchising is a rather top-heavy system due to the large up-front fees and strict rules since all the franchisees will be advertising under the same name and should be enforcing the same quality standards. Hence this light touch franchising scheme tries to use as a development tool the enterprise multiplication or replication part of the franchise idea without all the other top-heavy parts of the system.

3. *Spin-offs of new products using an existing technology.*

When a company learns or imports into a country the technology or know-how X to produce product A, then often with minor new knowledge, the technology can also be used to produce other products B and C. But those other products may have a different customer base, require different suppliers, and be outside of the original business focus of the company. Hence companies will not pursue those other feasible products in order not to confuse the strategy and dilute the managerial attention span of the company. But a few individuals might very well spin off from the company to produce B or C. This is particularly feasible in the information technology industries where the capital requirements to produce the other products may be minimal. This sort of spin-off is commonplace in the business environment of Silicon Valley in California or in a Silicon Gulch in Taiwan. In Taiwan, there is the saying that the people leading the spin-off would "rather be the head of a chicken than the tail of an ox."

In an ordinary company, there might be some resistance to fostering spin-offs since talented and already-trained people will be leaving the original company. And, more to the point, it reduces the "empire" under the direct control of the management of the mother company.

In the case of the Thermo-Electron group (www.thermo.com), there is a rule that every new product must be produced in a new company. The mother company owns a portion of the "spin-out" to help alleviate the tendencies to resist spin-offs. Now the children have had children on the same principle so the Thermo group has some 80-odd companies. It is doubtful that such creativity and growth could have been released if it had been confined to one company. Yet this is the exception, not the rule, in conventional companies due to the desire to maintain the ownership and control of the "empire" and any hidden profit potential it might have. Think of how many companies there would be in the "MicroSoft Group" if every new product meant a new related spinoff.

Most companies would rather try to exploit such opportunities in a multi-divisional structure. Such a structure could facilitate some growth (e.g., the 3M company – now nicknamed the "Mutation Machine from Minnesota" – is a rare example) but it seems that the growth opportunities would be maximized from the social (job creation) viewpoint if the new products were produced in a new company that was not just a division or controlled subsidiary of the mother company.

4. *Import replacement via spin-offs.*

Often a company may grow by "import replacement," that is, by starting to produce itself what had previously been an input produced by other domestic or foreign companies. Taking the unit of economic activity as a city region, Jane Jacobs has emphasized the process of import replacement as a mechanism for growth and development. Cities can grow through a process of dynamic interaction with each other through direct or indirect rivalry. To play in the "game," a city must produce something which it can export – perhaps based on its natural endowment. The export earnings can then buy imports from other cities that were not produced in the given city. In the rivalry between cities, a manufactured import is like a "slap in the face," an "insult," or a challenge; the city has to buy the import because it cannot produce it itself. If the other exporting cities were not too advanced, then the import will present a plausible challenge to be replaced through learning and improvisation and perhaps improved upon by the importing city. Since the wealth to buy the imports might have been earned productively (not a gift), the city might already have some productive capacity that might begin to improvise and differentiate to produce and replace the import.

In the meantime, the other cities might be replacing the original exports of the city; its temporary advantage might be competed away. Now the domestic and perhaps improved version of the originally imported products can then be reexported perhaps to the original supplier city or more likely to other cities "down the line" that are less developed or have different specializations. The new export earnings will then purchase other more challenging imports, and the process can repeat itself ratcheted up at a higher level. In this matter, a diversified group of innovative and versatile cities can through trade learn from each other and not only grow but *develop* "on one other's shoulders" (Jacobs, 1984, p. 144) – which we might call climbing *Jacobs' Ladder*.

It should be particularly noted that the Jacobs' Ladder mechanism works best between competitors at a roughly comparable level of development.[5] Her theory provides a rationale for regional trading blocs between countries at roughly the same level of development, not for free importing from the most advanced countries. "Science fiction" imports from advanced countries (largely to feed the conspicuous consumption habits of the elites[6]) would stop the rivalrous process in the same way that allowing a heavyweight to box in a lightweight class would stop the rivalry and stop the associated process of learning and improvement through competition – leaving aside any other damages. Enforcing "level playing field" competition between "heavyweights" and "lightweights" – that is, between advanced and underdeveloped countries – would be tantamount to "kicking away the ladder" (Chang, 2002) that the developing countries could climb.

Our point here is that import replacement is not done by firms that appear out of nowhere; it is usually done by the firms that purchased the imports and that have the option of organizing the new production as a related spin-off. Often some of the technological knowledge needed in the offspring is already present in the mother firm which also supplies the initial market for the off-spring's products.

Workplace Democracy and Job Creation

All of these schemes could be promoted by companies themselves or by local development agencies or ministries with appropriate financial incentives. One theme running through these examples is that economics should imitate biology in the sense that existing businesses are the best sources and incubators for new businesses. Biomass expands primarily by old life spawning new life, not by old life getting bigger. The ideas broached above are ways to similarly increase the economic diversification and biomass in a country by getting old firms to spawn new firms.

The enemies of diversification are not just one-sided economic theories that denigrate "import substitution" and emphasize the deepening of old work (e.g., Adam Smith's division of labor) rather than the creation of new work (to put it in Jacobs' terms). Empire-building proclivities also thwart diversity, and those tendencies are evident both politically and economically. But the political grip of those proclivities will depend on the form of government. In an autocracy where power comes from above, the sovereign will seek to maintain and perhaps even expand the realm.[7] But if power comes from below as in a political democracy (leaving aside the half-free and half-slave antebellum America), there are few grounds to deny the expressed wish of the bulk of the population in a part of a country to become autonomous or to secede. Jacobs cites the early twentieth century peaceful secession of Norway from Sweden as an example (the separation of Singapore from Malaysia might also be mentioned), and she viewed the possible secession of Quebec with equanimity if not support (Jacobs, 1980).

The same dynamics of power and legitimacy are at work in an economic organization. In a conventional company, where power comes from above, management has little reason to sponsor spin-offs and would have little cause to accede to any expressed desires coming from below to use the firm's technological and business capabilities for new enterprise creation through spin-offs and breakaways. When the preconditions of a Silicon Valley are present or in labor-intensive service sectors, then it may happen anyway – not because of the form of business but in spite of it.

In a democratic company (e.g., an industrial cooperative) where power comes from below, then management has less of a leg to stand on to oppose new enterprise creation through spin-offs and breakaways.[8] That has certainly been the experience of today's best example of cooperative development, the Mondragon group of cooperatives in the Basque region of Spain. The Mondragon companies produce a rather full variety of high value-added consumer products, intermediate goods, and capital goods including the first robots and computer numerically controlled machinery designed and built in Spain. Since the firms are all cooperatives, it was all done with no foreign ownership. The group started with a single company in the mid-1950s producing a kerosene heater. Then it systematically implemented the economic principle of plenitude by filling out the backward linkages through import replacement, producing the machines to make the heaters and then the machines to make those machines. Through multiproduct diversification (new products using existing technologies), it started producing other consumer durables (stoves, refrigerators, and washing machines) and all the things to produce those things. Each bottleneck called forth new energies to solve problems, for example, a bank to help finance new enterprises, an applied technological research institute to systematically learn new technologies and turn them into new products, a consulting company to help catalyze the process of spinoffs, an insurance company for members, and a polytechnic university.

Since the firms were cooperatives and had as a group the express goal of developing good jobs in the Basque country, the positive externality of having spin-offs and break-aways was fostered rather than opposed. The original company did not have the option of "owning" a spin-off or preventing the spin-off if the mother company could not capture all the benefits. The new company would also be a cooperative that would have to "rest on its own bottom" or "walk on its own two feet" – within the group.[9] Thus the headquarters of the whole group encouraged groups within existing firms to coalesce around ideas to produce adjacent products in a spin-off. The managers and workers might be from a village or small region without much industrial development so by doing the spin-off near their homes they satisfied both economic and social goals.

In a similar context, Jacobs noted that such "division would be a normal, untraumatic accompaniment of economic development itself, and of the increasing complexity of economic and social life" (1984, p. 215). Since the spin-off process was carried out in an organized and socially approved way, precautions could be taken so that it did not disrupt the original mother firm. It became part of how the group evolved.

The focus of economic policy for job creation should not be expecting jobless individuals to create jobs or expecting existing companies to expand their current businesses to create jobs. The focus should be to get existing companies to indirectly create jobs by fostering spin-offs of routine segments, as-if franchises, spin-offs putting existing technologies to new uses, or spin-offs to replace imports. Each company's second product, its production of a staff trained in doing business, has potentially significant positive externalities for the local economy so there are grounds for governments to create incentives to increase those positive spillover effects.

It is in light of these potential dynamics that I would now reevaluate the work of the Empresarial Division of the CLP or its successor cooperative LKS. It was not "socializing" the entrepreneurial function which was otherwise "individualized." It was working with the natural school for training in business capacity, namely existing firms, and it was following the biological principle of plenitude by catalyzing the process of increasing economic biomass (e.g., job creation) through the various types of spin-offs. It is a process that would tend to be blocked by the managers and owners in conventional companies, but which fits naturally into cooperatives and democratic firms.

CONCLUDING REMARKS

Elsewhere (Ellerman, 1992) I have argued for democratic firms based on the first principles of inalienable rights to self-determination and to the fruits of one's labor. In this paper, I wanted to touch on three "side arguments" or themes about democratic firms. In the first part, I considered the idea that LMFs have an inherent flaw called the "horizon problem." My point was that while the horizon problem is actually only a technical problem that has a simple solution in internal capital accounts. The solution has been rediscovered several times but the best known implementation is in the capital accounts of the Mondragon cooperatives. There is no excuse for the proponents or critics to continue the obsolete "debate" which assumes that democratic firms must be structured either as nonprofits (where members have no recoupable claim on retained earnings) or as employee-owned companies that conflate the personal rights to membership based on labor and the property rights to retained earnings (which leads to "mule-firm" problems).

In the second part of the paper, I considered the modern human relations school of participative management (taking Douglas McGregor as the primary example). This school tries to implement in the workplace the ideas stemming from the educational theory of activist and constructivist learning which emphasizes the internal motivation and autonomy of the learners. While these ideas can to some extent be implemented in conventional companies, my point was that this was in spite of (rather than because of) the employment relation that characterizes those companies. The natural setting for participative management schemes and for the workplace as a site of active learning is the democratic company where the workers are full-fledged members of the company rather than rented "employees." Participative and empowering human relations programs then have the substantive role of enabling people socialized as "employees" to become active participants in a democratic work community (often with attendant spillover effects in the external political community). Here again, these educational ideas can be found in the writings of Father Arizmendiarrieta and they supplied part of the original rationale for structuring the firms in the Mondragon group as cooperatives.

And finally, I revisited the old canard that cooperatives are inconsistent with entrepreneurship. This view is the result of the conventional mythology that sees entrepreneurs as heroic individuals who appear out of nowhere and who are primarily motivated by the possibility of "owning" any company that they single-handedly create.[10] Following the remarkable work on Jane Jacobs, I tried to reconceptualize this issue by starting with the fact that the main school for training in business and technological capacity is existing firms – particularly in that "nursery of firms," the small and medium-sized firm sector. While the possibility of "owning" a new company may indeed provide an incentive for some potential entrepreneurs, that conventional notion of ownership is what typically in the first place prevents companies from implementing the principle of plentitude by spinning off new firms.

While entrepreneurial people have many motivations other than "ownership," there seems to be no way to systematically overcome conventional ownership as a fetter on the principle of plentitude. There are exceptional examples such as the Thermo-Electron group, and there are exceptional circumstances such as Silicon Valley where growth through spin-offs is the main means of increasing economic biomass. But they are the exceptions that prove the rule.

Far from being a fetter on entrepreneurship, a cooperative structure is the natural setting to economically implement the principle of plenitude of growth through offspring. Here again, we see the Mondragon complex as illustrating this possibility by developing second-tier cooperatives to foster and catalyze the entrepreneurial process of growth through spin-offs in niche-filling small and medium-sized firms.

NOTES

1. If repeating a truth was a real appropriation of the truth, then Father Arizmendiarrieta quipped that "it could be said that also a recorded tape can be Christian" (n.d., p. 75).

2. This phrase has even been taken as the title of a book on Mondragon (Morrison, 1991). A similar pragmatic philosophy for education and social change is expressed in a book with a similar name: "We make the road by walking" (Horton & Freire, 1990).

3. See Ruef (2010) for an authoritative recent study exploding that myth.

4. For more of this background, see Ellerman (2004, 2005b).

5. See Chapter 10 "Why Backward Cities Need One Another" in Jacobs (1984).

6. Even imported "factories" such as the BMW and Mercedes assembly plants in South Africa will largely serve only the purpose of gratifying the elites. Moreover by soaking up much of the local demand for cars by those who can afford them, such plants will crowd out and foreclose on the possibility of there being a genuinely African car with all the technological ramifications that would follow from it.

7. Jacobs has noted the connection between top-down power and empire-building: "The biggest and most thoroughly centralized governments have always, finally, required the special environment of oppression to continue to maintain themselves. And some could never have attained their great size at all had they not grown in that environment" (Jacobs, 1980, p. 77).

8. In biological terms, the more that power is bottom-up in a firm, the more it is like an organism with reproductive cells under decentralized control throughout the organism rather than under central control in one specialized part.

9. In a democratic firm, where "corporate governance" is more than an oxymoronic phrase, the quality of the self-governance deteriorates as the firm gets larger so firms will tend to naturally subdivide anyway to keep the membership at workable levels. The upper limit might be between several hundred and a thousand members depending on the technologies involved.

10. The political analogy is that the leader of a revolution should become the new monarch (or its modern equivalent of the "lifetime maximum leader" such as Fidel Castro and many other communist revolutionaries) rather than a "George Washington" or a "Nelson Mandela" who could lead a revolution without trying to "own" the new entity.

REFERENCES

Arizmendiarrieta, D. J. M. (n.d.). *Reflections of Don Jose Maria Arizmendiarrieta*. Mondragon: Otalara.

Chang, H.-J. (2002). *Kicking away the ladder*. London: Anthem Press.

Dewey, J. (1916). *Democracy and education*. New York, NY: Free Press.

Ellerman, D. (1982). *The socialization of entrepreneurship: The empresarial division of the caja laboral popular*. Somerville, MA: Industrial Cooperative Association.

Ellerman, D. (1984). Entrepreneurship in the Mondragon cooperatives. *Review of Social Economy*, *XLII*(December), 272–294.

Ellerman, D. (1986). Horizon problems and property rights in labor-managed firms. *Journal of Comparative Economics*, *10*(March), 62–78.

Ellerman, D. (1992). *Property & contract in economics: The case for economic democracy*. Cambridge, MA: Blackwell. Retrieved from www.ellerman.org

Ellerman, D. (2004). Jane Jacobs on development. *Oxford Development Studies*, *32*(4), 507–521.

Ellerman, D. (2005a). *Helping people help themselves: From the world bank to an alternative philosophy of development assistance*. Ann Arbor, MI: University of Michigan Press.
Ellerman, D. (2005b). How do we grow? Jane Jacobs on diversification and specialization. *Challenge*, *48*(5), 50–83.
Freire, P. (1970). *Pedagogy of the oppressed.* New York, NY: Continuum.
Horton, M., & Freire, P. (1990). *We make the road by walking: Conversations on education and social change* (B. Bell, J. Gaventa & J. Peters, Trans.). Philadelphia, PA: Temple University Press.
Jacobs, J. (1969). *The economy of cities*. New York, NY: Random House.
Jacobs, J. (1980). *The question of separatism: Quebec and the struggle over sovereignty*. New York, NY: Random House.
Jacobs, J. (1984). *Cities and the wealth of nations: Principles of economic life*. New York, NY: Random House.
McGregor, D. (1960). *The human side of enterprise*. New York, NY: McGraw-Hill.
McGregor, D. (1966). *Leadership and motivation*. Cambridge: MIT Press.
McGregor, D. (1967). The professional manager. In C. McGregor & W. Bennis (Eds.). New York, NY: McGraw-Hill.
Morrison, R. (1991). *We build the road as we travel: Mondragon, a cooperative social system*. Philadelphia, PA: New Society Publishers.
Ortega y Gasset, J. (1961). *Meditations on Quixote*. New York, NY: Norton.
Pigou, A. C. (1960). *The economics of welfare* (4th ed.), London: Macmillan.
Ruef, M. (2010). The entrepreneurial group: Social identities, relations, and collective action, *Kauffman Foundation Series on Innovation and Entrepreneurship*. Princeton, NJ: Princeton University Press.
Vanek, J. (Ed.). (1975). The basic theory of financing of participatory firms. In *Self-management* (pp. 445–455). Harmondsworth: Penguin Books.
Whyte, W. F. (1955). *Money and motivation: An analysis of incentives in industry*. New York, NY: Harper & Row.
Whyte, W. F., & Whyte, K. K. (1991). *Making Mondragon* (2nd rev. ed.). Ithaca, NY: ILR Press.

CHAPTER 13

POLITICAL METAPHORS AND WORKPLACE GOVERNANCE

Christopher Mackin

ABSTRACT

Purpose – *Political institutions and contemporary workplaces operate according to different rules. The seeming contradiction between these two spheres, one democratic and the other something else, presents an opportunity for productive speculation about the possibilities for reconciliation. The purpose of this paper is to provide a guide for future research investigation of this perennial topic.*

Design/methodology/approach – *The discussion of whether the workplace can catch up with the democratic achievements of political life requires an understanding of the status quo, the prevailing frames or metaphors that govern our understanding of organizational life. Four metaphors are put forward to describe the prevailing spectrum of thought. In addition to metaphors, analogies are introduced as an interpretive tool to help guide the imaginative transition between political and workplace domains.*

Sharing Ownership, Profits, and Decision-making in the 21st Century
Advances in the Economic Analysis of Participatory & Labor-Managed Firms, Volume 14, 355–379

ISSN: 0885-3339/doi:10.1108/S0885-3339(2013)0000014013

Practical implications – *Democratic political cultures are supported by structures and institutions which encourage the expression of individual and collective voice. Workplaces, comprised of the same citizens who participate in the governance of communities, do not, with some important exceptions, offer the same opportunities for democratic participation. If a general analogy between political and workplace sphere is found persuasive, it should be possible to import and adapt democratic traditions from the former to the latter.*

Originality/value – *Discussions of workplace democracy often suffer from a certain naiveté, a bias against structure and toward informal consensus. Insofar as democratic workplaces are by definition smaller scale than political communities, this bias is defensible. This paper concludes however by asserting certain minimal "acid test" challenges to those who would promote the goal of workplace democracy.*

Keywords: Metaphor; analogy; workplace governance; workplace democracy; unions; employee ownership

JEL classifications: J53; J54; K20; K31; L23; P40

INTRODUCTION: METAPHORS AND ANALOGIES AT THE WORKPLACE

Given the centrality of the institution of work to social and economic life, it should be no surprise that the study of the workplace comprises a significant percentage of academic research. The consulting profession and much of the remaining popular book trade in publishing, depend upon on a seemingly inexhaustible appetite to understand the world of work. The breadth and complexity of the world of work warrants the use of certain considered intellectual shortcuts, "heuristics" that can help us break through layers of received, conventional wisdom and into a fresh consideration of previously neglected themes.

This paper makes use of a specific and familiar heuristic, that of the metaphor, to help describe how work is understood. In the service of our general argument that the workplace deserves consideration as a political as well as a technical arena, we introduce an implicit developmental scheme charting the progression of four familiar workplace metaphors from a simple and familiar starting point (the workplace as family) through two familiar intermediate models (workplace as bureaucracy and workplace as contested terrain) toward a morally and technically complex endpoint (the workplace as democratic social institution).

The choice of these specific metaphors is idiosyncratic and explained further in the text. The choice of metaphors as a heuristic device however is also deliberate. It is premised both upon the capacity of metaphors to motivate discussion and on the ubiquity of metaphors as a "real life" method people actually use to make sense of or "frame" (Lakoff, 1995) discussions of their circumstances – in this case their experience of the workplace.

> We may not always know it, but we think in metaphor. A large proportion of our most commonplace thoughts make use of an extensive, but unconscious, system of metaphorical concepts, that is, concepts from a typically concrete realm of thought that are used to comprehend another, completely different domain. Such concepts are often reflected in everyday language, but their most dramatic effect comes in ordinary reasoning. (Lakoff, 1995)

The typology of workplace metaphors introduced in this paper are "ideal types" that can be expanded upon over time. They are introduced here to help start a discussion. A second order treatment of the idea of metaphors, introduced later in the paper and deserving of more complete treatment in future work, comes through the introduction of the concept of analogies. If metaphors are the photographic frames of this discussion, analogies are the movie, a more elaborate motion picture of ideas that can achieve a narrative arc than cannot be fully communicated through the use of metaphors.

In a paper entitled *Political Metaphors and Workplace Governance*, the narrative destination of that arc should not be difficult to imagine. The author believes that with assistance provided by the study of history and political science (MacPherson, 1977) that a useful analogy can be drawn between understanding the emergence of democratic ideas and practices in the political sphere – or polity – and the possibilities for the same developmental emergence in the workplace – or economy. Democratic states evolved from feudal states. By analogy, democratic workplaces should be able to evolve from the feudal workplaces that dominate the economic landscape of our time. Mapping specific steps or stages of that developmental process is a key objective of this paper.

POLITICAL METAPHORS

Reviewing the variety of frames that are revealed by workplace metaphors one is reminded of the range of purposes that work fulfills. Work has been described variously (Kohn, 1969; Lempert, 1998; Weber, 1978) as an instrumental sphere, where people trade their labor for economic value in order to survive, an associative sphere where people find – or do not find – community and as a developmental sphere, a social crucible where adolescents and adults develop competence, character and capability, qualities that are passed down through the child rearing process and shape the outlook and prospects of later generations.

Work and workplaces have also been described as a political sphere (Dahl, 1985; Derber, 1970; Ferreras, 2012; Pateman, 1970) where people deliberate in normative terms about their fortunes as individuals and as a group. Whether or not deliberation is encouraged or sanctioned by formal structures of involvement, it happens as a matter of course in the workplace. Workplaces function as miniaturized societies where relationships and careers are developed or thwarted, where discussions involving matters of fairness and justice are routinely conducted. Workplaces also function as miniaturized economies where scarce resources of time, talent, capital, and imagination must be "managed" for success or failure under conditions of external competition.

Though contemporary usage in both the popular and academic press tends to strip the term of its political content and associate it with technical competence and the display of individual genius, the word "managed" as applied within the workplace also serves as a proxy for the word power. The exercise of managerial discretion in the workplace is a routine but often obscured example of the exercise of power. That power may be exercised effectively with subtlety and wisdom, through the use of persuasion and compelling argumentation, or effectively in a second sense of the word with force, through the power to marginalize, eliminate, or fire opponents.

Persons in positions of power in corporations do not descend from the sky. They arrive at those positions through one or more at least partially plausible creation narratives we will discuss below. In that sense, managers almost always manage with some form of legitimacy. They may rule poorly or well. Under most prevailing corporate governance frameworks, their exercise of power operates largely unchecked. The central point is that however credible the path may have been that lead them to their jobs and however capable they may be in the exercise of their duties, management is a term interchangeable with the power to rule in day to day organizational life. Insofar as management is a profession involving the conduct of power, it should not be difficult to understand why political metaphors may shed some useful and previously neglected light on the world of work.[1]

Under the standard textbook scenario associated with Jensen and Meckling (1976) that dominates the fields of economics and law, capital hires labor. Having established that basic fact, that standard model then elaborates rituals of corporate governance that one might presume to be pregnant with accounts of power and deliberation *within* the workplace as taking place *outside* the workplace largely between management and external shareholders. Management may or may not have been a party to the provision of capital by shareholders that is seen as the originating "at risk" event from which all authority must follow. However, it is the narrow occupational circle of management which is typically considered to be the sole agent of capital whose interests should be aligned with shareholders in order to "maximize shareholder value." Without some form of independent representation usually associated with unions, workers are essentially spectators in this narrative, a variable cost to be "rented" in order to execute the production of tasks that create value for shareholders.

This organizationally and morally denuded depiction of the role of workers in the design of the firm that dominates textbook discussions may simplify the conversation about corporate governance but it does little to accurately describe what transpires in the contemporary workplace. Indeed, if the standard narrative derives from the above described structural premise that capital hires labor, then it should be possible to imagine an alternative model that could reset the corporate governance conversation. If labor institutionally hires capital, a scenario that is not entirely imaginary when considering examples such as Mondragon (Whyte & Whyte, 1991), we might expect a more complete account of the actual dynamics of a workplace. Within that reimagined abstraction that situates labor in the lead role of the corporate governance narrative, we might be able to find a truer account of the complexity of what actually transpires. If such a reversal of accepted frames is allowed then it should bring with it a broad enough definition of "labor" to include all parties centrally involved in actual workplace deliberation, management, and workforce alike. Using this new perspective we can expect to uncover a more descriptively rich account of what takes place within the workplace than is provided by the dominant model.

The use of political metaphors to understand or describe workplace governance which animates this effort is not entirely new but is something of a departure for contemporary organizational studies. Recent work by

Ferreras (2012), for example, builds upon earlier work by Hirschman (1970), Pateman (1970), Piore and Sabel (1984) and others to elaborate an explicit theory of how employee voice at the workplace might be institutionalized. Ferreras appeals to a theory of economic bicameralism involving institutionalized dialogue between a "house of labor" and a "house of capital." Other schemes (Bernstein, 1979; Dahl, 1985) draw upon familiar insights from the political sphere regarding the doctrine of a separation of powers between executive, legislative, and judiciary bodies within a firm. A particular adaptation put forward by Ellerman (1988) regarding the need for an internal "legitimate opposition" at work introduces a welcome level of complexity to the naïve embrace of the democratic firm as an oasis of interpersonal consensus. It is discussed at some length at the conclusion of this paper.

MORE ON THE METAPHOR METHOD

The account that follows makes use of a sequence of selected metaphors. This choice works backwards from a declared normative stance evident in the final metaphor, which in addition to being a metaphor also doubles as an "ideal type" (Weber, 1978) less clearly observable in the contemporary economy than the alternatives that precede it, of the workplace as a democratic social institution.

As previously admitted, this entire method is a shortcut. The panorama of possibilities offered here is a prime example of what Kaldor (1961) referred to in another context as an arrangement of "stylized facts" in support of theory development, in this case an emerging theory of democratic workplaces. Such a method must admit to limits. The choice of metaphors is limited. Few organizations can be seen as fitting absolutely within one category. In fact most workplaces make use of blends of these various types.

In addition to admitting to not having captured the full range of possibilities, there must be a further admission regarding a claim implied here for the existence of a developmental sequence of workplace metaphors from the relatively simple toward the more complex. Developmental sequences typically suggest two internal dynamics. First, that later stages incorporate or assimilate the achievements of earlier stages and second that higher stages while incorporating earlier achievement are nonetheless somehow higher or better (Kohlberg, 1984). Typically, the province of individual psychological research exploring individual reasoning structures and patterns of persons, the export of the developmental method to organizations (Mackin, 1984) is fraught with peril. Organizations do not reason. Only individuals do. Individuals can, however, serve as "informants" with respect to the organizations they inhabit. Their stories about what takes place within their organizations can reveal the norms and values of their members. Further "objective" ethnographic evidence in support of the presence of one or more workplace metaphors can be derived from documents and from participant observation of meetings where relevant statement can be recorded and analyzed. This evidence can corroborate claims that an organization resides within one or more of these metaphorical constructs.

Nothing in this litany of admissions and qualifications should suggest that what is presented here is an empirical investigation. Our use and choice of metaphors is admittedly conjectural. It does not make use of primary research data. It is entirely possible that research efforts informed by this account could be undertaken but that is a task for another time. Our journey begins with what the author believes are familiar frames or metaphors that guide workplace life. It is there where the act of persuasion toward democratic ideas must begin.

WORKPLACE AS FAMILY

Arguably the most familiar and enduring workplace metaphor with explicit associative overtones is that of the family. Family life and family authority relationships constitute a near universal experiential background to organizational life (Entin, 1993). It should be no surprise, therefore, that an easily accessible inventory of family metaphors is where we are prone to turn in order to make sense of the workplace. Though applied to large as well as small organizations, the family metaphor makes more intuitive sense in face to face organizations of fewer than 200 members, a size range which statistically comprise the largest percentage of workplaces. Regardless of the size of the organization to which it is applied, the "workplace as family" narrative is prominent but highly problematic.

The workplace as family metaphor can be found in strong or weak forms. Where strong, we can find uses that are disturbingly literal. In these settings grown adults willingly invoke norms, values, and strategies to please, flatter, and protect workplace "parents" – owners and/or senior management of companies – even when the persons who may have founded the firm – the natural owners – may no longer serve in positions of authority. Authority and expertise in these kinds of organizations are described in personal rather than professional terms. Workplace relationships are deferential. Advancement is more likely to take place through criteria of loyalty rather than merit. Personal norms dominate over professional norms.

A second, more benign and widespread use of the family metaphor can be distinguished in other organizations. In this "weaker" use, the narrative of parental authority is de-emphasized but often latent. What are emphasized instead are bonds of affection, reminiscent of family relations, that have developed over time in the pursuit of common goals in a workplace. This use suggests a certain communitarian ethos where authority relations are vague but presumably more consensual. While preferable, this model lacks structure and certainty. Without enforceable and consensually arrived at rules and procedures that can support its implicitly democratic norms, the positive qualities of this model hang in the breach, perpetually threatened by crises that will reveal its underlying structure. Under stress, the benign organizational family may remain consensual or it may revert to the traditional-strong family model. Fate rests not in objective evaluations, transparent rules and processes of deliberation but in the subjective judgments of "parental-like" organizational leaders.

For better or for worse, the ubiquity of the family frame has made it the default frame for understanding workplace norms. Among its various important characteristics the feature most relevant to this discussion is the implicit claim the family metaphor makes with regard to the possibilities of unity. A family is presumed to be a unified group. The same aspiration can be found in most corporate vision statements. The critical question to explore is how effectively norms of unity that are relatively easy to evoke in the context of the family can translate to the more rough and tumble world of the workplace. Though the resilience of the workplace as family metaphor is evident, it remains a disturbingly simple and subjective frame for organizing the work lives of adults. Over time other frames have emerged to challenge this unified family frame and its hold on the organizational imagination.

WORKPLACE AS BUREAUCRACY

Bureaucracy is a concept that first emerged in discussions of government and the management of political power. It later migrated to workplace organizations, particularly larger scale organizations where face to face management practices became impractical or impossible. Formally bureaucratic organizations can, from certain vantage points, be seen as a developmental advance from the "family" metaphor. In these organizations, power, status and advancement are presumed to derive from more from objective criteria of merit, rationality and efficiency as opposed to subjective personal relationships and judgments. In a recent review of a book that attacks the foibles of bureaucracy, Rob Horning reminds us that "The hope of some of the French revolutionaries was that paperwork (and bureaucracy) would rationalize the state, that it would depersonalize power and destroy the corrupt networks of aristocratic influence."[2] Less evocative as a pure workplace metaphor than the concept of family, the bureaucratic idea nonetheless is regularly invoked to describe life within large and complex organizations.

Contemporary characterizations of bureaucracy are overwhelmingly negative and associated with impersonality and sluggishness. These critiques may be warranted but they tend to dismiss the laudably "scientific" and objective ideals of bureaucratic organizations. Weber (1978) described the promise of bureaucracy as the rule of knowledge over personal power. The historical context for the emergence of bureaucracy was essentially feudal; societies emerging from administration by royal edicts. Bureaucracy was therefore the name given to modern efforts to "objectively" administer power. The concept of "civil service" in government administration represented the clearest example of its positive manifestation.

Outside the realm of the state, within the private economy, bureaucratic norms and practices accompanied the growth of large scale workplaces. Legendary research based organizations such as Bell Labs and IBM were once lauded as positive models of corporate bureaucracy involving hierarchy based upon expertise. The modern critique of bureaucracy at the workplace (Heckscher & Donnellon, 1994) generally acknowledges its superiority to familial, "personal" rule but critically challenges certain core bureaucratic assumptions about the need for hierarchy in favor of lateral networks and decision making through consensus rather than command. Knowledge based organizations have tended to move in this post-bureaucratic direction. However, even in these more advanced organizations fundamental questions of governance and power remain ambiguous.

WORKPLACE AS CONTESTED TERRAIN

Academic accounts of life in the workplace, particularly in the fields of management or organizational studies, tend to be stories told through the lens of leadership. A central theme of these disciplines is the management of people through coherent and unified corporate cultures. So is the mastery of technology, finance, and contending with external threats of competition. Most of these accounts share an implicit premise that management as we know it is a legitimate and necessary role with attendant powers. Those powers may be exercised softly or firmly. In either case there is no questioning the so-called right to manage.

The legitimacy of management is usually traced to a specific creation narrative regarding the origins of a particular workplace or company. Those stories take place against a set of assumptions about the workings of a capitalist economy we have referred to as the standard model where capital hires labor where the central concerns of the organization revolve around deliberations between capital and their agents in management. Labor is regarded as a variable cost, hired in at will to achieve the aims of shareholders.

A common thread justifying the standard model describes an original act where one or more parties put "at risk" capital to work on a business idea. In order to implement the business idea, employees are hired to produce it. By virtue of their original risk taking, founding owners and their successors in management are seen not only as the rightful appropriators of profit. They are also entitled to serve as the architects of the organizational culture to be worked within and the arbiters of any and all terms and conditions of employment. Under this relatively frictionless creation narrative, the only constraints these leader/founders must endure are those imposed from without by labor market conditions and by local, state and national law. In the US context, employment is generally classified as "at will" and at the service of employers. Employers not obliged to retain employees or include them in decision-making.

After several intriguing but largely overlooked decades of experimentation in the late 19th century with its own narrative of originating employment through democratically organized cooperative firms (Jones, 1984; Leikin, 2005), a new institutional actor began to assert claims in the early 20th century. That actor was the American labor movement. It complicated matters. With the arrival of union structures, the idea of a unitary and presumably harmonious organizational culture, be it familial or bureaucratic, was for the first time challenged.

This challenge took the form of a second claim of allegiance for employees chosen by and working for employers. Unionization fostered the development of a workers culture distinct from, though not necessarily in opposition to the culture of the firm. The union role was both to represent the heretofore unrecognized voice of the work and through bargaining to extract a larger share of the economic rewards primarily through higher wages and more generous benefits. The act of securing the rights to represent workers has almost always involved an independent grassroots campaign acting against the preferences of management.

With the possible exception of a post-World War II (1950–1970) epoch marked by heavy industrialization and successful unionization drives that lead to density of as much as 30% of private sector employment, the arrival of labor into the creation narrative of American capitalism has never been accepted by the management profession.

The arrival has generally been considered an intrusion. The concerns of labor, providing a voice to workers, being an advocate for justice and reaping a fair share of the rewards of common effort have been duly if somewhat begrudgingly noted and subsequently internalized by the curriculum of our modern business schools. It is generally presumed that these concerns are now the responsibilities of management. The success of union drives is therefore judged to be the failure of management. Judging by recent trends in private sector unionization in the United States, where union representation has dropped to 6.9%, the cultural divide introduced by the appearance of labor into the capitalist creation narrative would seem to have been averted.[3] The divide is now considered by many in the management profession to have been a several decade long cultural detour now residing safely in the rear view mirror of history.

Whatever other moral or practical advantages unions may bring to the lives of working people, it is hard to dispute the simple fact that the introduction of labor unions into established workplaces disturbs the normatively simple culture of capitalist enterprise. The presence of a union introduces a second and competing cluster of allegiances; a "workers culture" that must coexist alongside a "company culture." The competition between these two cultures creates a workplace metaphor of internal complexity, the "contested terrain" that labor economist Rick Edwards vividly described in his 1979 book of the same title.[4]

Where they are successful in breaking in to pre-existing company cultures, unions also complicate the creation narrative that lends considerable weight to the legitimacy of management authority. By occupying an independent platform for the workers within a firm and by persistently making the case that workers should share more fully in the profits that their labor makes possible, unions suggest an alternative and overwhelmingly *implicit* narrative whereby the workers should be viewed as the true and legitimate *owners* of the firm.

However, compelling this case may sound, it is seldom made overtly. Union leaders are generally aware that other factors are also responsible for success. Technology, capital, and managerial talent are three such factors that labor cannot, under conventional circumstances, claim as their contribution. Overreaching on the claims that labor might make toward the success of an enterprise can also bring labor dangerously close to a role that they are typically reluctant to fill. Ownership implies responsibility, a responsibility that unions are generally not equipped and in most cases not disposed to exercise. Conventional collective bargaining may have its limits but it at least offers the prospect of near term increases in wages and benefits. It is rational, therefore, for a union to restrict the reach of its claims, to stay on the near side of a cultural continental divide they enforce with management where they willingly accept a more limited role as bargaining agent and potential critic of managerial authority.

WORKPLACE AS DEMOCRATIC SOCIAL INSTITUTION

We have so far described a simplified progression of workplace metaphors that started with the family, moved through the idea of bureaucracy and while retaining elements of both familial and bureaucratic culture arrived somewhat awkwardly at the contested terrain that unions have introduced to the organizational dynamic where union cultures compete with company cultures for the loyalty of a given workforce.

The next step in this progression moves beyond a standoff between competing cultures of workers on the one side and managers/owners on another and presumes that the cultural divide unions enforce in conventionally owned organizations has actually been overcome in favor of the workforce as a whole.

What happens if the workforce as a whole, workforces that almost always are statistically dominated by "workers" over managers, actually becomes the firm?[5] What if they become its legal owners, or, in an alternative framing we discuss below, become the full fledged "members" of the firm with requisite corporate governance power? Does such a change simply return us to the simple organizational metaphor of the single culture family or does something more complex take its place? Does that more complex organizational metaphor resemble something analogous to our understanding of political democracy, consisting of structures and practices that do not merely tally votes but that also manage power? If they manage power then they presumably do so through an array of countervailing structures and institutions that have been developed in the political realm that are designed to disperse that power and promote freedom of thought even if that thought is potentially critical of incumbent leadership. To be more concrete, in these ostensibly democratic settings, how should budgets be decided? how should compensation be set? how should the power to include (hire) and exclude (fire) be managed?

These are questions that should be explored at both the level of practice, by examining experimental evidence produced in the field, and at the level of theory where an appeal to political metaphors and analogies to the evolution of political democracy should prove useful.

PRACTICAL EXPERIENCE WITH DEMOCRATIC MODELS

The realm of practice offers some compelling evidence for the workplace as democratic social institution model. Research by Quarrey and Rosen (1987) and Kruse and Blasi (2000) has established a clear link between the legal fact of broad based employee ownership, usually through an Employee Stock Ownership Plan or ESOP, and corporate performance. The key intermediate variable that Quarrey and Rosen's research in particular isolated was the extent of participatory management in those firms. Those employee ownership firms with participatory management grew 8–11% per year faster than they would have been expected to grow.

Specific accounts of what constitutes participatory management are difficult to come by and are not uniform across companies. They typically involve some structure for participation in decision-making by employees. Those structures may be permanent or temporary. Those staffing the structure may be appointed by management or elected by employees. The subject matter for employee involvement in these settings to date more likely than not involves immediate work process or work environment issues and does not typically include issues related to either compensation or corporate governance. The structures themselves in most cases are removable by management with no due process or appeal. In these and other ways, the standards for what constitute employee voice would seem to fall short of those established by unions in conventionally owned settings.

Comparisons of employee involvement practices within employee ownership firms and union representation structures should also, however, take into account very different originating circumstances. Union representation is typically a "grassroots" bottom up phenomenon usually resisted by management and aided by external union organizations. Where successful, they are then protected by a body of external labor law and administrative procedure enforced by government. Employee involvement practices, in or outside of employee ownership settings, are more likely to be top down initiatives inspired by a range of motives including an interest in common economic success, in realizing employee potential and, in some cases, helping to reduce the appetite for external union representation.

Leaving aside the historical era alluded to earlier when 19th century American unions explicitly advocated for and supported the growth of cooperatives, there are rare contemporary cases where unions have initiated worker ownership. A formal alliance announced in 2009 between the United Steelworkers and the Mondragon Cooperatives of Spain is the most significant such development.[6] This is a welcome development for a variety of reasons including the fact that by taking on this challenge unions, whose experience implementing participatory agreements with employers is considerable, will be forced to directly confront the distinctive challenges that democratic ownership structures bring to their traditional inventory of ideas.

How will the union as organizational architect adjust its role when its members comprise the firm? The familiar role of serving as an external critic of management efforts will no longer be sufficient. Ellerman (1988) warns unions against adopting a "Jekyll and Hyde" attitude toward ownership where workers are thought of as employees by day – protected by conventional collective bargaining provisions – and owners at night where their representatives on a Board of Directors may expand the conversation to more complicated matters. In a democratic firm, there should be no place to hide. He writes that under a democratic governance form "every topic is fair game: 'management prerogatives', investment, marketing, sales, productivity, cost control, business planning and corporate strategy"(Ellerman, 1988, p. 439). If this is the case, then more elaborate ideas of democracy, beyond the confines of a collective bargaining agreement and beyond the purview of existing legal frameworks imagined by the National Labor Relations Act (NLRA), must be introduced.

DEMOCRATIC THEORY: THE USE OF POLITICAL ANALOGIES

As the world of practice involving broad based employee ownership proceeds with experimentation, it may be useful to appeal to theory for guidance. Pioneers in this endeavor include Pateman (1970), MacPherson (1977), Dahl (1985), and Ellerman (1992). The primary contribution that the political theorists mentioned have made to extending the democratic metaphor has been at the system level, arguing for economic democracy as an analogue to political democracy. A straightforward assertion made by the eminent Yale political scientist Robert Dahl in his 1985 book A Preface to Economic Democracy is representative of this discussion. In a chapter titled *The Right to Democracy within Firms* Dahl states "If democracy is justified in governing the state, then it must also be justified in governing economic enterprises; and to say that it is not justified in governing economic enterprises is to imply that it is not justified in governing the state" (Dahl, 1985). In this context Dahl proceeds to defend his use of political analogies against the likely objections of critics. He addresses objections regarding supposedly impaired property rights, exit rights of employees, and differential expertise.

The focus of this paper however is at a more micro level, in particular on how democratic distinctions proposed at a system level might translate at the level of an organization, clarifying what democracy means at the level of the firm. The primary analytical tool we have employed thus far to effect this translation is the metaphor. Dahl and others introduce a related and more sophisticated tool, the analogy. A complete discussion of the difference between metaphors and analogies as analytical tools is beyond the scope of this paper. Provisionally, we would claim that analogies serve as extended metaphors. While both tools serve the purpose of enabling translation or comparison from one sphere, in this case, political institutions, to a second sphere, economic institutions, analogies allow for more sweeping translations or comparisons. Metaphors provide a snapshot comparison. Analogies, particularly those informed by historical narrative, provide the movie.[7]

As described at the outset of this paper the introduction of political metaphors and analogies in the workplace finds particular resonance when the practice of management is understood to extend beyond the narrow administrative function described in mainstream economic literature (Jensen & Meckling, 1976). An alternative description of management extends the principal-agent descriptions of that literature to include what is essentially a political role. Management continues its traditionally understood role of husbanding the allocation of scare resource inputs. But it also and more centrally extends to include that political role, as the party that exercises power over the work lives of employees. Those functions and that role may be performed well or poorly. How might they be framed in light of democratic theory?

The primary concerns of democratic theory involve the design of structures and practices that effectively disperse or balance power. Emerging in modern times from the shadow of self perpetuating, divinely justified feudal rule, democratic theory concerns itself with how to direct power to the "people" and the people's representatives as opposed to the sovereign. The democratic firm has similar ambitions. In place of the people at large, it recognizes the workplace community of blue and white collar worker/employees in discrete firms as the members in whose interest power should be exercised. Once again, the central question that this paper takes up is how that democratic workplace can be viewed as distinct from the prior workplace metaphors that dominate organizational life. How, if at all, is a democratic firm an advance beyond the standard of a family metaphor, a bureaucratic metaphor or the metaphor of the workplace as a contested terrain?

A common challenge when considering these questions in the context of the workplace might be characterized as the temptations of naïve democracy. Champions of workplace democracy regularly fall prey to vague aspirational proclamations of self proclaimed democratic organizations to "listen" to their workforces. Few, if any, structural demands (e.g., the right to vote for boards of directors, the right to influence policy, the right to a free press) are made upon those who choose to make use of the democratic label. Instead of taking to heart the demanding path that architects of democracy in the political sphere have taken to define and describe a credible democratic ensemble of ideas that contend with the challenges of power, many workplace democracy enthusiasts, often enamored with the illusory power of consensus decision-making practices, are willing to accept the lowest common denominator of espoused democratic intent.[8]

OVERCOMING NAÏVE DEMOCRACY: THE UNION AS LEGITIMATE OPPOSITION

In a largely overlooked paper published in 1988 in the journal *Economic and Industrial Democracy*, David Ellerman (1988) sketches out an extensive analogy from democratic political institutions of the firm as a democratic social institution. The first step in his argument addressed to would be democratic firm advocates invokes Michels (1962) familiar warning about the "iron law of oligarchy" that consumes democracies that submit to any form of single party rule. Without checks and balances provided by countervailing institutions that may keep the executive branch of a democratic firm in check, that branch will naturally, over time, identify itself with the "General Will," engineer its own permananance and tend to close ranks around critics. The result is a form of one party democracy that is difficult to distinguish from personalized, "family" organizational cultures.

In the course of specifying a series of measures that can work against the oligarchic temptation, Ellerman advocates for a constitutional model of the firm that revolves around his core thesis that "the acid test of democracy is the existence of a legitimate opposition ... an independent power base for those who seek to express opinions and policies at variance with the current powers that be" (1988, p. 438). Such a function is not, according to Ellerman, presumed to be adversarial. In a democratic firm after all, management itself has theoretically been appointed to their posts by a democratically elected board of directors and so enjoys that board's – and by extension – the "people's support. A legitimate opposition does not exist in hopes of toppling management. It exists to keep that management, the executive branch of an industrial government, honest.

The obvious candidate for fulfilling this crucial democratic role of legitimate opposition is, in his judgment, a radically redesigned union or union-like organization, appropriate for what he calls medium to large organizations of over 50 persons. The union role in a democratic firm would, according to Ellerman, be inclusive of both white and blue collar workers, all of whom should be engaged in constructive debate with their elected leaders in management. Certain traditional union functions such as representing individuals in grievance disputes with the organization would remain intact. Where a union as legitimate opposition would depart from tradition would be the conduct of economic bargaining. Given the new reality of a firm owned by its blue and white collar workers, the core economic debate does not pit workers versus managers. It instead pits the present against the future. In a successful democratic firm the central economic question becomes how much value should extracted now in wages and benefits (technically advances on profits or what Mondragon calls "anticipos") and how much should be invested in the future for the benefit of present and future generations of worker/members.

Traditional concerns about distributive or relative fairness between management and a workforce do not disappear in these settings. In Mondragon however and in similarly inspired firms these concerns are channeled into transparent debates about the extent of the "solidarity ratio" between top and bottom salaries. The union as legitimate opposition would continue to weigh in on these kinds of conversations in the interest of fairness and viability. However the practice of slicing up the economic pie should only be one of the functions of a union in a democratic firm. More novel and more fundamental than the economic distribution conversation is a conversation about how this redesigned union structure should, according to Ellerman, help organize internal debates about the future of the enterprise, where and how it should invest, who it should do business with, how it should cope with issues such as technological change and international trade.

According to Ellerman, the union as legitimate opposition should be a structure that helps insure a thorough and healthy debate with management about the merits of their plans for the future of the enterprise. This new role, the union a "safe harbor" for the development and articulation of alternative views about the future of the enterprise, presumes an informed and trained leadership and membership. In order to keep current with management thinking Ellerman imagines that the leader of the opposition would sit as an "ex-officio" member of the democratic firms board of directors.

The conduct of debates about the future of the enterprise initiated by a newly configured union structure are presumed to not be disruptive, or adversarial. They should take place following a clearly deliniated process, focused on annual or quarterly membership meetings where debate about alternative approaches takes place in public. It should be entirely possible that as a result of these discussions and debates the opposition ends up agreeing with management and publicly voicing its support. The important point is that management, the indirectly elected executive leadership of the firm, understands and accepts that their views about the future path of the organization should not be be implemented without the discipline of prior, internal, constructive debate.

Ellerman describes two likely and less burdensome alternatives that advocates of a democratic firm might bring to the idea of an institutionalized opposition. He judges both as naïve. First, is the idea of a "pop-up" opposition where instead of speaking from within an abiding union-like structure that serves as a home for developing alternative frames, brave individuals, "pop-up heroes," can be counted upon to speak up at public assembly gatherings as necessary to challenge management. A second alternative also does without any abiding structures and relies on the virtues of the "good manager." Under this great man/good manager theory extraordinary leaders whose capacity for listening and resistance to self aggrandizement are beyond reproach can be plucked out of obscurity to selflessly serve. This second approach seems to be the default position of most modern business schools who identify managerial excellence with the kind of omniscient, super-human qualities that make structure unnecessary (Khurana, 2002). Neither of these alternative models enjoys what might be called conceptual gravitas.

A final and important structural element in the Ellerman model of the legitimate opposition is the existence of a free press which can serve as ready outlet for critical as well as praiseworthy opinion. Ellerman makes the important point that a genuinely free digital or physical news outlet should not be dominated by any group or faction within an organization. Most news outlets of this kind tend to be purely celebratory and lack critical seriousness. A regular column by the leader of the union or union-like legitimate opposition and/or a point/counterpoint debate feature can overcome that difficulty and win the respect of a workforce curious to learn what its fellow members are thinking on a regular basis. The John Lewis Partnership, a large (81,000 person) employee owned retail enterprise in England, features a weekly newspaper called the Gazette which serves this same general purpose. Employee owners are encouraged to submit anonymous letters to senior management raising critical issues. Senior management is committed to respond to each letter in writing in the subsequent issue of the paper with the exception of rare submissions that might be deemed libelous. The overwhelming majority of letters are serious. The guarantee of anonymity and responsiveness has earned the Gazette an unusual level of respect unlike what can be found for most company controlled publications.[9]

A reasonable challenge to Ellerman's model asks whether the specific functions he delineates, the ability to represent individuals and uphold a standard of due process for grievances, the ability to constructively challenge management plans and the ability to protect and promote free speech through an independent free press could be achieved through structures other than a union. This challenge should be welcome, particularly if existing union structures are not prepared to cross the "continental divide" that Ellerman's model envisions. Certainly existing labor law, conceived to assert and protect rights within the context of a very different property ownership model that generally excludes workers, does not provide a hospitable environment for playing a substantively different role. In light of these facts, experimentation with independent models of worker representation within democratic firms should be encouraged. This experimentation should not, however, neglect another kind of "acid test" of democratic representation. Any alternative models should be able to demonstrate how they can protect their indepedence both for the individuals that serve in representative roles and for the institution of representation itself. Until or unless there are constitutional protections, conceived and memorialized at the organizational level, that prevent leadership from dismantling these structures in good times or bad, the challenge of democratic representation that Ellerman posits will not have been met.

CONCLUSION

This paper has reviewed the role that metaphors – and in a more limited sense analogies – play in understanding life in work organizations. With the exception of the metaphor of the family that is readily cited for better or worse in organizations of varying sizes, our choice of terminology is an interpretation of how workers and managers view the workplace rather than an empirical reporting of alternative frames. The fleshing out of alternative frames is posed here as a necessary step in the project of imagining constructive alternatives. To break new ground, those frames should challenge status quo assumptions held to by both management and labor communities alike.

Despite the political character of much of our work lives where we readily engage in discussions of fairness and judge the conduct of managerial power, explicitly political metaphors remain outside the realm of most accepted workplace discourse. Wherever possible, management scrambles for vocabulary devoid of moral content, hoping to turn all workplace challenges into technical discussions of competitive necessity.

The late 19th and early 20th century entry of unions into the workplace in the United States and in most industrialized countries served as an exception that introduced a semblance of political dialogue and what might be called industrial government. In the United States however, collective bargaining between unions and mangagement introduced a ritualized, rule bound zone of deliberation that is clearly delimited in its democratic and political character. By common agreement between the parties, many of the larger issues of possible workplace deliberation, including investment plans and the selection and evaluation of company leadership have remained outside the tent in the realm of managerial prerogatives. Instead of bridling from this constraint, labor leaders from a variety of ideological perspectives, spanning from left to right, have often served as the enforcers of this continental divide as much as if not more than management.

Justifications for excluding political metaphors and excluding workers from exercising more control over the workplace can generally be traced to a standard model creation narrative celebrated and defended in our universites that restricts discussions of rights and power to founders who supply at risk capital and their agents in management. Workforces are technically considered by the law and by custom to be later stage guests invited to join these associations without the same rights as their counterparts in management and in the investment world who control the organizational conversation. While tolerated with more or less patience, workers are as likely to be considered interlopers in these conversations as they are to be considered partners.

The growth over the past 20 years of a sizeable worker or employee ownership sector of the American private enterprise economy has complicated this narrative and raised questions about how employee owners can and should join the workplace conversation. When labor or workers find their way inside the capitalist firm and begin to voice various claims or, even more clearly, when labor or workers decide to initiate and therefore become the firm, the glaciers begin to move. The seemingly iron logic of the standard model creation narrative begins to give way and an alternative institutional arrangement stars to come into focus. Instead of capital hiring labor, perhaps labor can hire capital. If that becomes the case, then new assumptions, new workplace norms can take effect.

Ellerman (2012) and Ferreras (2012) among others distinguish between the ownership of shares in corporations and various ways in which firms are governed by the apparent consent of different parties. A related movement favoring a "stakeholder" theory approach to corporate governance of corporations (Freeman, 2010) has also begun to contend with the standard model. Instead of narrowly focusing on shareholders, this model includes government, communities and employees it its vision of who should be the firm.

These thinkers provide the necessary scaffolding for a fundamentally alternative economic universe. The most far reaching difference they assert, made most explicit by Ellerman (1992), is that corporations should not be viewed as property. Corporations may own property but they themselves should not be viewed as a commodity that can be bought, sold and traded at will. Corporations are instead properly understood as social institutions engaged in commerce. Entry to and exit from those institutions should be governed by clear rules arrived at by their members. The same general rights we recognize in the political sphere should be extended to workers and managers to govern themselves in the economic sphere.

These are not merely aesthetic distinctions. It is difficult to think ones way through to alternative arrangements using conventional frameworks. The rights of economic democracy at the level of the firm should be considered personal rights based upon membership in the firm, not property rights based upon capital stakes.

Claims such as these become more persuasive when they can be linked to nonstandard models of economic structure and economic initiative, to creation narratives that are both fundamentally different from the standard model and economically viable. When groups of workers with access to appropriate sources of capital find themselves in the position to originate or purchase ongoing enterprises, when labor hires capital, an increased use of political metaphors in the workplace and a more widespread acceptance of democratic organizational arrangements should follow.

NOTES

1. Recent radical critiques of power in the workplace, celebrated by champions of the Occupy Wall Street movement under the term "horizontalism," appear to be refutations not only of management but also of most forms of organizational hierarchy. Though apparently successfully applied in certain smaller scale enterprises in Argentina and elsewhere, this approach is challenged by organizations of scale where representative forms of democracy may present a more realistic model for viability. Though sympathetic with the critique, this paper adopts a more incremental approach that does not preclude the existence of hierarchy or leadership, democratically bound.

2. *Dissent Magazine*, February 21, 2013. Book review of The Demon of Writing: Powers and Failures of Paperwork by Ben Kafka Zone Books, 2012 by Paul Horning.

3. United States Department of Labor, Bureau of Labor Statistics, Union Members Summary, January 27, 2012 – http://www.bls.gov/news.release/union2.nr0.htm

4. Unions and their supporters recognize this complexity and typically frame their response according to the ideological dispositions of their leadership. One "collaborative" faction seeks to form "high road partnerships" that recognize the legitimacy of management and legacy ownership groups and seeks to work together on matters of common interest in order for the firm to succeed in the marketplace. A second "extractive" faction works harder to dominate the cultural competition with management and legacy ownership groups with only modest attention to marketplace consequences. A third "class struggle" faction is similarly extractive but motivated by a point of view toward history that sees the workers they represented as the primary producers of value regardless of the legal facts of actually existing ownership. This point of view generally extends to the water's edge of worker control over decision-making without assuming overall economic responsibility for the affairs of the firm.

5. The circumstances described are not purely theoretical. There exists in most advanced industrial countries a cluster of firms that meet the criteria of being worker or member owned. In the United States, two starting points have given rise

to somewhere near 12,000 firms, collectively employing over 14 million workers organized on this basis. The first of these is the familiar worker cooperative structure that comes about through the deliberate decision of groups of workers to self-organize in a democratic fashion. The US Federation of Worker Cooperatives reports over 300 such firms, collectively employing over 3,500 people. A second, larger cluster of firms in the United States come about through conversions of conventionally owned firms to employee ownership through Employee Stock Ownership Plans or ESOPs. The National Center for Employee Ownership reports 11,400 ESOP firms that collectively employ 13.7 million workers make use of the ESOP structure. Of these, it is estimated that 40% of that total or approximately 4,500 firms own 100% of company stock. In Europe, Latin America, and Australia, firms that meet the general criteria of democratic ownership or membership can usually be found using the cooperative ownership structure. Of these, the case of the Mondragon in the Basque country of Spain with 256 companies that collectively employ approximately 84,000 workers is the most renowned and instructive with respect to internal structures.

6. Press release describing the United Steelworkers–Mondragon collaboration, October 27, 2009 – http://www.usw.org/media_center/releases_advisories?id=0234

7. Here the author refers to a manuscript under development called Proceed by Analogy: Imagining Economic Democracy (Mackin, 2015) that makes use of historical accounts of the development of political democracy to illuminate similar patterns in the evolution of workplace democracy. This work is inspired by C. B. MacPherson's (1977) book, *The Life and Times of Liberal Democracy*.

8. A notable recent effort to promote democracy in the workplace while remaining silent on clear structural characteristics that constitute democratic circumstances can be found by an exploration of a for-profit consultancy by the name of WorldBlu. This organization describes itself as "a global network" of democratic organizations that achieve their status by successfully completing a "WorldBlu Scorecard™" survey judged by the staff of this organization who originated the survey and whose revenue appears to be drawn primarily from conferences . The idiosyncratic nature of the WorldBlu endeavor is fairly captured by the account of how WorldBlu received its name. In the words of its founder, Traci Fenton, "Why the name WorldBlu? Blue is universally recognized as the color of freedom, so we decided on 'WorldBlu' as a way to capture our vision in a word."

9. The John Lewis Gazette is described at length in David Erdal's (2011) recent book *Beyond the Corporation: Humanity Working*.

ACKNOWLEDGEMENT

This paper was originally presented in July 2012 at a meeting of the International Association for the Economics of Participation, Rutgers University, New Brunswick, NJ.

REFERENCES

Bernstein, P. (1979). *Workplace democratization: Its internal dynamics*. Kent, OH: The Kent State University Press.

Dahl, R. (1985). *A preface to economic democracy*. Berkeley, CA: University of California Press.

Derber, M. (1970). *The American idea of industrial democracy*. Urbana, IL: University of Illinois Press.

Edwards, R. (1979). *Contested terrain: The transformation of the workplace in the twentieth century*. New York, NY: Basic Books.

Ellerman, D. (1988). The legitimate opposition at work: The union's role in large democratic firms. *Economic and Industrial Democracy*, *9*(4), 437–453.

Ellerman, D. (1992). *Property & contract in economics: The case for economic democracy*. Cambridge, MA: Blackwell.

Ellerman, D. (2012). Is Wall Street capitalism really 'The Model'? Retrieved from http://ssrn.com/abstract = 1988259

Entin, A. (1993). The workplace as family, the family as workplace. Paper presented at the Annual Convention of the American Psychological Association, Toronto, Canada.

Erdal, D. (2011). *Beyond the corporation: Humanity working*. London: The Bodley Head.

Freeman, R. E. (2010). *Strategic management: A stakeholder approach*. Cambridge, MA: Cambridge University Press.

Ferreras, I. (2012). *Governing capitalism? Economic bicameralism in the firm*. Paris: Presses Universitaires de France.

Heckscher, C., & Donnellon, A. (1994). *Post bureaucratic organization: New perspectives on organizational change*. Thousand Oaks, CA: Sage Publications.

Hirschman, A. O. (1970). Exit, voice, and loyalty: Responses to decline in firms, organizations, and states, *Cambridge, MA*: Harvard University Press.

Jensen, M., & Meckling, W. (1976). Theory of the firm: Managerial behavior, agency cost and ownership structure. *Journal of Financial Economics*, *3*(4), 305–360.

Jones, D. (1984). American producer cooperatives and employee owned firms: A historical perspective. In R. Jackall & H. M. Levin (Eds.), *Worker cooperatives in America*. Berkeley, CA: University of California Press. (Chapter 3).

Kaldor, N. (1961). Capital accumulation and economic growth. In F. Lutz & D. Hague (Eds.), *The theory of capital*. London: Macmillan.

Khurana, R. (2002). *Searching for a corporate savior: The irrational quest for charismatic CEOs*. Princeton, NJ: Princeton University Press.

Kohlberg, L. (1984). *The psychology of moral development*. San Francisco, CA: Harper & Row.

Kohn, M. (1969). *Class and conformity: A study in values*. Homewood, IL: Dorsey Press.

Kruse, D., & Blasi, J. (2000). *National Center for Employee Ownership*. Retrieved from http://www.nceo.org/articles/esops-improve-performance-employee-benefits

Lakoff, G. (1995). Metaphor, morality, and politics, or, why conservatives have left liberals in the dust. *Social Research*, *62*(2), 177–214.

Leikin, S. (2005). *The practical utopians: American workers and the cooperative movement in the gilded age*. Detroit, MI: Wayne State University Press.

Lempert, W. (1998). Individual morality and industrialized work: some theoretical considerations. *Economic and Industrial Democracy*, *9*(November), 475–496.

Mackin, C. (1984). *The social psychology of ownership: A case study of a democratically owned firm*. Unpublished doctoral dissertation, Harvard Graduate School of Education, Cambridge, MA.

MacPherson, C. B. (1977). *The life and times of liberal democracy*. New York, NY: Oxford University Press.

Michels, R. (1962). *Political parties*. New York, NY: Collier Books.

Pateman, C. (1970). *Participation and democratic theory*. Cambridge, UK: Cambridge University Press.

Piore, M., & Sabel, C. (1984). *The second industrial divide: Possibilities for prosperity*. New York, NY: Basic Books.

Quarrey, M., & Rosen, C. (1987). How well is employee ownership working. *Harvard Business Review*, *65*(September/October), 126–130.

Weber, M. (1978). *Economy and society: An outline of interpretive sociology*. Berkeley, CA: University of California Press.

Whyte, W. F., & Whyte, K. K. (1991). *Making Mondragon: The growth and dynamics of the workers cooperative complex* (2nd ed.). Ithaca, NY: ILR Press.

CHAPTER 14

WORKER OWNERSHIP AND COLLABORATIVE PRODUCTION

Charles Heckscher

ABSTRACT

Purpose – *To explore the challenges of worker ownership in complex and distributed collaborative production systems.*

Design/methodology/approach – *Review of emerging developments in the organization of economic production and conceptual exploration of their implications for the ownership regime, and for worker ownership.*

Findings – *Worker ownership research and advocacy usually take for granted* what *is to be owned: a factory or firm, exchanging on open markets. But this form of production, analyzed in the markets-hierarchy literature, is increasingly in question as more value is generated through flexible cross-boundary collaborations. As a result, the nature of ownership rights are contested from both within and without the business community.*

Practical implications – *This paper explores some implications of these developments on employee ownership as a practical ideal: what are the main possibilities for the evolution of "ownership" rights in collaborative processes?*

Sharing Ownership, Profits, and Decision-making in the 21st Century
Advances in the Economic Analysis of Participatory & Labor-Managed Firms, Volume 14, 381–396

ISSN: 0885-3339/doi:10.1108/S0885-3339(2013)0000014014

Worker owners need to consider their relation to, and distribution of rights among, other collaborative partners, including knowledge contributors and interdependent stakeholders.

Social implications – *Implies a need to move beyond markets-hierarchies frameworks, in which concern is focused on the governance of firms, to building a set of mechanisms for the organization and governance of production networks.*

Originality/value – *Poses a set of problems for the worker ownership field emerging from the changing nature of production and organization.*

Keywords: Ownership; collaboration; knowledge; stakeholders

JEL Classifications: D230; L230; M140; D740

The worker ownership literature generally assumes that economic production is organized in firms, with clear ownership of their products, and linked by market exchange. The question raised from that perspective is to what extent employees, rather than individuals or outside shareholders, should gain decision rights in the firm and financial returns from it. But economic developments over the last few decades have put the basic productive model in question, creating both theoretical and practical managerial problems that a shift toward worker ownership would not solve by itself.

The issue is that economic production is gradually shifting from a model centered in large, closed bureaucracies to more decentralized and fluid network forms. Production requires forms of collaboration that are organized *neither* in a classic employment relation *nor* through an arms'-length contract for the delivery of goods – relations in which people from different companies work together in ongoing task forces and initiatives. This creates enormous and so-far-unresolved difficulties in assigning the rights and accountabilities of ownership.

FOUR PROBLEMS

The worker ownership literature generally looks at only one slice of the problem: where workers enter into an employment contract to provide their labor, it makes the case that they should share rights in decision-making and economic returns (Ellerman, 1999). But there are at least four growing issues in economic production posing problems for ownership rights that would not be solved by transfer of ownership to workers.

Knowledge Production

Many have argued that the value added in economic production is increasingly based on knowledge rather than mass production (Grant, 1996; Nonaka, Toyama, & Nagata, 2000). Though the speed and extent of this shift are debated, there is little doubt that physical labor counts for less, and advanced knowledge counts for more, than in the past.

In the mass production model, knowledge was an occasional addition: that is, there were Research and Development (R&D) departments that would periodically create innovations that were then passed to the production side. Knowledge work was almost entirely internal to the firm: generated through internal conversations (known in the old Hewlett-Packard as "next-bench" innovation); most managers, and even the R&D people, rarely attended outside conferences. Thus knowledge could plausibly be said to be owned by the company, and could be governed by existing property rights, including employee ownership forms (partnerships, ESOPs) as well as public shareholding and private ownership.

But firms are increasingly reaching beyond their own boundaries for knowledge. This makes perfect sense from the point of view of production: if engineers in India know something relevant to a problem, the solution will be more easily found if they are involved. In knowledge-intensive companies, these sorts of collaborative cross-boundary processes are commonplace. Thus companies in practice are forming a wide range of relations that are outside the traditional ownership frame: alliances, partnerships, employee-sharing, consortia, and so on (Bøllingtoft, Donaldson, Huber, Håkonsson, & Snow, 2011; Gulati & Singh, 1998; Hagel et al., 2010).

Such relations are growing because the two traditional choices – market transfer and corporate takeover – are often ineffective. On one hand, knowledge cannot be transferred in the same way as goods or services: if I tell you what I know, we *both* know it – I don't stop knowing it myself. Even more important, knowledge in complex production is rarely just a definable commodity that can be bought in a market transaction: it is valuable only as part of an interactive collaborative process. What is sought is not a particular piece of information, but a general expertise that can contribute, through discussion and recombination, to the generation of new solutions.

On the other hand, knowledge is in many cases not best managed by bringing a person or company into the organization through hiring or takeover. First, the knowledge relevant to a given problem may not be relevant to the longer-term mission of the firm; thus an employment relation is often seen as too rigid. Second, buying a firm for its knowledge means that you are buying very fragile assets: they can walk out the door the day after the purchase. Finally, pulling the people into an existing firm often undermines the qualities that enables them to generate the knowledge in the first place: they are expected to spend much more time dealing with the internal hierarchy and less time interacting with their networks of outside colleagues.

In general, knowledge is a fluid and evolving resource; trying to rely on internal resources limits a process that inherently needs continual interactive sustenance. Hence the growth of relations that are neither based on market nor hierarchy. Perhaps the clearest instance is the interpenetration of traditional large companies, such as IBM and Apple, open-source software production. Open source products like Firefox and varieties of Linux are produced through networks of volunteers. The companies have found that even their legions of carefully chosen engineers cannot match the knowledge and innovativeness of these extended networks; so they have entered into collaborative relations, in which they create consumer interfaces that can be sold commercially in exchange for providing resources to the open-source community (Ferraro & O'Mahony, 2012; Lerner & Schankerman, 2010).

These forms of knowledge sharing and exchange are emerging pragmatically rather than through clear application of consistent principles. The legal system has tried to apply traditional ownership principles but has run into great difficulties. Battles over intellectual property have spiraled out of control. Judges have not yet agreed on principles. To take one instance, Apple has consistently tried to assert property rights over knowledge, arguing that it owns the "look and feel" of its software and hardware products. The results have been inconsistent and sometimes ludicrous. One case in 2012 declared that Samsung did not have the right to use rounded corners on its tablets because Apple owned that aspect of the design (*Apple, Inc. v. Samsung Electronics Co., Ltd.*, 678 F.3d 1314 (Fed. Cir. 2012)). Beyond Apple, there have been lawsuits, some of which have dragged on for years, claiming that ideas like the hyperlink belong to someone and that we should all pay every time we click on a link. These extremes become absurd, but the reality of wide-open use of intellectual property suits to claim complex knowledge is a real and constant issue.

All this is inefficient. It strangles innovation and effective production (Benkler, 2002). *The Guardian* reports, for instance, that "App developers withdraw from US as patent fears reach 'tipping point'":

> App developers are withdrawing their products for sale from the US versions of Apple's App Store and Google's Android Market for fear of being sued by companies which own software patents – just as a Mumbai-based company has made a wide-ranging claim against Microsoft, Apple, Google, Yahoo and a number of other companies over Twitter-style feeds, for which it claims it has applied for a patent. Software patent owners in the US have latched onto potential revenue streams to be earned from independent developers by suing over perceived infringements of their intellectual property.(Guardian.co.uk, July 15, 2011)

Companies are pushing their ownership claims ever further to try to control the fluid nature of knowledge. The spread of "non-compete" clauses in contracts, for example, essentially asserts rights over the ideas that people have in their heads even if they haven't said anything about them; there is strong evidence that this retards economic growth (Marx, Singh, & Fleming, 2010; Samila & Sorenson, 2011). Current efforts to assert property rights in human genes have similar negative effects (Williams, 2010).

One result is that a parallel economy is being built around open source, with an entirely different property regime. This has produced a set of property licenses essentially protecting ideas as common (the "General Public License," or GPL). These efforts, very foreign to traditional ideas of property and markets, have penetrated deep into the mainstream economy. Microsoft produced Internet Explorer with a traditional internal process; but Mozilla produced Firefox with an open-source process, with hackers from all over the world making contributions and no one claiming exclusive property rights. Google, meanwhile, has produced Chrome partly internally and partly building with open-source modules. Google and IBM have been leaders in exploring such hybrid forms, which has not yet solidified in practice or law (Lerner & Schankerman, 2010; Lessig, 2006).

The General Public License is not a form of worker ownership; indeed it is not ownership at all in any familiar sense. It has not been tested much in the legal arena, and lawyers have not developed a consistent point of view toward it. It brings back elements of ancient laws of commons, but also includes various novel twists such as limited exclusivity (Abramowicz, 2010).

More broadly, the issue of who owns knowledge is not helped by saying that workers should own it. The core problem is not who owns it but what it means for it to be owned. The answer must probably involve some rather deep transformation in our conception of the rights and privileges of property.

Value Chains

Even outside "knowledge" industries, there is very strong evidence that vertical integration, in which firms own all the factors of production, is declining in favor of a model in which separate firms perform specialized functions that come together only at the end of the process (Gereffi, Humphrey, & Sturgeon, 2005; Greenan, Kalugina, & Walkowiak, 2007). This development can be seen as just the latest evolution of the logic of the division of labor, articulated by Adam Smith as the core of modern capitalism, which suggests that the economy does best when people – and by extension, firms – specialize, and then link their specialized activities together in some form of cooperative relation. Value chains are composed of companies that focus on one particular element of production and build their policies around it, from recruitment to organization to marketing. Just as in Smith's famous example of the pin factory, these specialized actors or modules can do their particular modularized tasks better than more general-purpose ones.

The limiting factor in the division of labor has always been the ability to integrate or organize the modules. Large bureaucratic firms grew when product complexity and demand grew faster than the ability of markets and civil society to support them. They provided training, for example, because there were no good outside training systems that could prepare people for the difficulty of managing an automobile plant; and they financed a great deal of their own growth because of the inadequacy of traditional external financing mechanisms. But over time external mechanisms – training mechanisms, sophisticated market exchanges, wider-ranging capital institutions – have developed a great deal, making it more feasible to link formally independent businesses in integrated production processes. The benefits include those usually associated with the increased division of labor, including efficiency and innovation (Khanna & Palepu, 1997).

Value chains can be compatible with a worker ownership regime as long as there are clear market transfers of product along the way – so one company makes headlights, for example, and another wiring harnesses, and both sell their products through a market transaction to a third that puts them together into headlight assemblies. The problem is that this model is relatively inefficient, with high costs incurred in the contracting and transferring. The Japanese alliance networks, or *keiretsus*, have led the way to another approach in which employees of the different companies work together in an ongoing way to share plans and techniques, leading to higher quality and more rapid innovation (MacDuffie & Helper, 2006). Assigning of ownership rights is not a helpful tool in managing these collaborative processes. The Japanese handle them relatively well because their strong existing communal relations dampen the need to assign clear ownership rights to each stage.

"Nontraditional" Work

The rise of knowledge value has been a major cause, though not the only one, of the weakening of the connections between firms and employees. Worker ownership, by contrast, is generally seen as a way of attaching employees more strongly to firms. This makes sense in the context of firms that are relatively stable and bounded: the research evidence is convincing that in such circumstances, increased loyalty and security create economic as well as social value. The problem is that those circumstances are a declining part of the economy.

One key indicator is the weakening of internal labor markets in general. Large companies are engaging in much more "churn" than in the past – that is, economically healthy companies lay off sectors of their workforces every year and hire new people. Sometimes this is a "talent" strategy – getting rid of the worst performers; more often, however, it is a capability strategy, trying to keep up with adjustments in market demands and technology. Qualitative research in companies is very consistent in suggesting that at both blue-collar and – the truly novel element – white-collar levels there is much more willingness to get rid of people and also to take on new people who have not come up within the firms (Lawler, 2005; Tuna, 2009; Uchitelle, 2006). Quantitative evidence of this shift is difficult – the data are not collected consistently across companies – but the most rigorous recent studies have confirmed the trend over the last two decades (Farber, 2007; Hollister, 2011; Osterman, 2001).

The rise of contingent, and especially temporary, work, is a trend common to most of the advanced industrial world (Belous, 1995; Greenan et al., 2007; Kalleberg, 2000). In the United States, there is great debate about how extensive it is: most estimates are around 30% (US Government Accountability Office, 2006; Valenzuela, 2011). The temporary help industry has grown particularly rapidly in the last few decades.

One view of this shift is that it is driven by short-sighted managerial cost-cutting which undermines productivity beyond the short term. To the extent that this is the case, a worker ownership regime would benefit everyone by slowing or reversing a noxious trend. Yet there is considerable evidence for a contrary view: that at least, some of the shift is driven by the changing nature of production, which requires increased flexibility in fast-changing competitive environments. This would mean that the trend would be hard to slow and would be likely to accelerate. The likelihood is that the erosion of internal labor markets is due in part to both factors – but the importance of the second creates challenges for worker ownership models.

Without trying to build the whole argument here, I would note a set of solidly constructed arguments that the increased emphasis on flexibility is rooted in deep changes of late capitalism, especially the maturation of markets, increased sophistication of consumers, and increased education of workers. These factors lead both to more unstable demand and also to greater capability in responding to it. The stable, closed firm is unable to rise to this level of responsiveness, and the more open networked firm is better at it (Amable & Lung, 2008; Benkler, 2007; Boltanski & Chiapello, 2006; Deloitte Center for the Edge, 2011).

To the extent that this is true – and we don't need to make any extreme claims about the transformation of capitalism in this context – employee ownership may fail to deal with this important emerging trend. And for workers who expect the payoff to come many years in the future will be taking a major gamble that the forces of change will not overwhelm their investment.

The goal of creating a mutual bond of responsibility in the workplace is a worthy one, but one has to ask whether employee ownership creates problems by limiting that bond to the boundaries of a single firm; many mutual relations now cut across those boundaries.

External Stakeholder Claims

In recent decades there has been a substantial rise in demands on business by stakeholders other than workers. These most frequently include local communities and environmental groups, but may also include many others. The original "New Deal" compromise channeled these other societal needs through government, but as that deal has unraveled the groups are taking up their own causes (Beloe, Elkington, Hester, & Newell, 2003; Friedman, 2006). Some companies have established processes for dialogue with such stakeholder groups, usually within the framework of Corporate Social Responsibility (European Multistakeholder Forum on CSR, 2004; Spar, 2002; Wei-Skillern, 2004). A large academic literature has grown up around stakeholder management (Freeman, Wicks, & Parmar, 2004; Friedman, 2006), including some attempts at redefining the legal responsibilities of corporations to extend beyond shareholders (Leung, 1997). About half the states have passed laws enabling consideration of a broader range of stakeholders, and seven have (as of this date) permitted a form of incorporation that *requires* stakeholder responsiveness.

From the stakeholder point of view, employees are just one of a range of groups that are affected by corporate actions and that should have rights of some sort – and not necessarily the most important one. The consequences of corporate decisions range far beyond employees. There are many cases in which employees and managers have united to pursue goals that are contrary to the interests of other key stakeholders, and arguably against the public interest: auto workers who fought regulations on pollution and fuel economy, communications workers who sought to preserve monopolies. In general, workers and managers share interests in maximizing profits and minimizing competition, so a shift of ownership to the former would not reduce the tendency to externalize costs as much as possible.

Thus there is an emergent point of view rejecting the core idea that corporations are, or should be, merely market actors pursuing profits within market constraints. The alternative is to see them as part of a network of institutions contributing to a healthy society, with mutual obligations. The maximization of profits is beneficial to society some of the time under some circumstances, but not all the time in all circumstances. This, unlike the earlier points, is primarily a *moral* argument – that the good of society requires balancing productive requirements with other values.

Government regulation, the classic way of bringing "other" considerations to bear, is increasingly perceived as ineffective and clumsy; again, this is not just a US phenomenon but common throughout the advanced industrial world (Pharr, Putnam, & Dalton, 2000; WorldPublicOpinion.org, 2008). It appears once again that neither markets nor states are capable of organizing conflicting moral claims. Many have therefore argued the need for collaborative relations of one kind or another – stakeholder engagement through forums, or diverse representation on boards and other decision-making bodies (Freeman et al., 2004; Leviten-Reid & Fairbairn, 2011; Varughese & Ostrom, 2001).

These solutions may or may not be viable: so far there is little evidence of effective alternate models of stakeholder engagement on a wide scale.[1]

The point here, however, is that worker ownership does not help solve the problem. Existing conceptions of ownership in effect replace shareholders with employees as the primary stakeholder; they offer neither rights nor engagement to a broader range of stakeholder concerns. There is no reason that a worker-owned firm should be more environmentally sensitive, or more attuned to product quality, than a conventional firm; owners in both cases seek maximization of profit.[2]

THINKING ABOUT SOLUTIONS

The common thread through these problem areas – knowledge production, value chains, nontraditional work patterns, and stakeholder engagement – is that the familiar markets-hierarchies analysis is insufficient, *both* for narrow considerations of economic production *and* for social justice. Instead, or rather in addition, there is a need for collaborative networks in which multiple actors work together across boundaries. Knowledge is best developed through such networks; coordination of production often requires close cooperation along a distributed value chain; and the achievement of social welfare often requires direct engagement of stakeholders.

This presents profound problems for ownership as currently conceived. The existing legal concept of ownership is heavily grounded in master–servant law and assumes that there are clear lines of management responsibility; it has trouble dealing with situations of distributed responsibility and specialized contribution in team-like settings. In Marilyn Strathern's (1996) phrase, the existing framework requires "cutting the network" in ways that do not reflect the actual contributions of its various members.

The challenge is to develop a form of ownership that recognizes and encourages processes of flexible collaboration that often cross boundaries defined in the current legal and organizational regime, and that respond to multiple stakeholder concerns. Worker ownership certainly has a role in this evolution, but it faces the same challenges as traditional firms in dealing with collaborative networks.

Ownership is not an immutable natural principle; it is a more elastic and historically contingent concept than is often recognized. It has changed fundamentally in the past, so there is no reason to think it cannot change in the future. An equivalent moment is the problem caused by the rise of large corporations in the late 19th century. Property law at that time was conceived as applying to individuals: persons controlled the things they owned. This was true of businesses as well as land. The owner of a factory controlled the resources and people within it and could decide how to use them, within a few limitations. But when corporations started growing in size, helped by the mastery of bureaucratic techniques of organization, there were two new consequences: they gained power well beyond their markets, and they required financing beyond the holdings of an individual or small group.

These developments led to the development of the law of public corporations. One key was the separation of ownership from managerial control (Berle & Means, 1932). Another, less widely noted, was the abstraction of the *purpose* of corporations. Since they were now owned by a widely dispersed mass of people, corporations could no longer set their purposes from the personal desires of the owners; there had to be some more abstract and stable goal that would ground a contract with the large number of stock owners. This came to be defined over time essentially as the pursuit of profit.

This shift in the notion of ownership was highly contentious, leading to titanic battles both in the courts and in electoral campaigns. The courts led the way in giving expansive rights to corporations; the Greenback, Granger, and Populist movements arose to combat the perceived imbalance of power; Theodore Roosevelt raised the centrality of government regulation as a way to maintain the balance. It was not until at least the 1930s that a reasonably stable view of corporate property was established.

In simple terms, we can describe what happened over that period as a redefinition of property to encompass new productive forces. Prior to the mid-19th century production occurred primarily in small workshops which could easily be linked to property rights; this is certainly what Adam Smith had in mind. When it became clear that organization in large bureaucratic structures greatly increased productive capacity, a redefinition of property was needed to encompass that form.

If, as I have argued, we are currently in a phase in which collaborative networks frequently demonstrate greater productive capacity than large bureaucracies, then we need once more to redefine ownership in order to encompass them. How this is to be done is still to be worked out, and we may have new versions of Populist and Granger movements before we are finished. The legal profession is increasingly aware that the existing master–servant framework is inadequate, and there is lively debate about new doctrines such as "entrepreneurial responsibility" and "participation as theory of employment" (Bodie, 2013).

One particularly interesting current development is the "Benefit Corporation," a new incorporation statute recently written into statutes in 15 states. Corporations incorporated under this form are required to respond to multiple stakeholders – specifically employees, customers, local communities, and the environment, in addition to shareholders – and must be assessed annually on these dimensions by independent parties. In principle shareholders can bring action against these companies for failure to "adequately consider" those stakeholder interests (Clark & Vranka, 2012). That procedure has not yet been tested in court, and it is likely to cause some earthquakes when it begins to happen.

Some Benefit Corporations, though not all, are owned by their workers. But whether or not they have ownership rights, workers have rights in the statute of incorporation: treatment of employees is among the criteria that companies are measured on and that they can be held legally responsible for. In cases where workers are also owners, they bear responsibility to the same range of stakeholder criteria. In other words, their ownership rights are *different* from those of worker-owners incorporated under classic statutes.

This is far from a complete solution, even in theory, to the problems raised by the rise of collaborative production: it addresses only one piece, specifically the problem of balancing multiple stakeholders in interdependent relations. It does not solve the problem of "cutting the network" in assigning property rights to knowledge. The GNU General Public License (GPL) is one radical solution used for free software projects such as Linux: it requires mainly that anyone using or modifying the product *not* assert any restrictions on further use or sharing. This has caused a fierce reaction from such protectors of capitalist markets as Steve Ballmer of Microsoft, who has referred to it as a "cancer that attaches itself in an intellectual property sense to everything it touches" (Microsoft CEO takes launch break with the Sun-Times, 2001). Yet the GPL has in fact merged in many and complex ways with commercial activity: companies like IBM and Google make extensive use of open-source software and contribute to GPL-licensed code.

There are also other suggestions for new conceptions of property rights, such as the "Platform for Privacy Preferences" proposed by Lawrence Lessig (2006, p. 226ff); limited exclusivity (Abramowicz, 2010); public stakeholder funds (Oswald, 1998); and others. Some of these try to address the issue of how to assign rights in knowledge products developed in collaborative networks.

I am aware of very few efforts to define a new property regime as a whole. Turnbull's carefully worked-through model of stakeholder governance (2002) is one of the more complete, though it remains (perhaps necessarily) utopian, disconnected from the main economy, drawing examples from currently marginal cases.

In short, the problem of ownership in collaborative and interdependent networks is already giving rise to a host of new definitions of property rights. Most are still experimental, in the sense that they have not been fully tested in court and have not been integrated into a coherent property regime. But the rapid proliferation of forms of licensing and incorporation is an indication of the forces pressing against the constraints of firm-based, exclusive notions of property. Worker ownership from this perspective addresses a subset of the problem, focusing *one* key relationship under which people cooperate for production, and *one* stakeholder that has both moral and practical claims to involvement in managerial decisions. A full exploration of the rights of ownership, and their attribution to workers or others, requires a more complete understanding of the changing nature of economic activity.

NOTES

1. There have been some partial successes, such as the decisions over Shell's North Sea oil drilling after the Brent Spar disaster (Livesey, 2002; Wei-Skillern, 2004), but we are very far from a regularized institutional framework.

2. There have been some experiments with multistakeholder cooperatives, which do address the problem I describe (and have had some success) (Leviten-Reid & Fairbairn, 2011); but they necessarily dilute the ownership rights of workers.

REFERENCES

Abramowicz, M. (2010). Orphan business models: Toward a new form of intellectual property. *Harvard Law Review*, *124*, 1362–1421.

Amable, B., & Lung, Y. (2008). *The European socio-economic models of a knowledge-based society*. Groupe de Recherche en Economie Théorique et Appliquée. Retrieved from http://ideas.repec.org/p/grt/wpegrt/2008-26.html

Beloe, S., Elkington, J., Hester, K. F., & Newell, S. (2003). *The 21st century NGO: In the market for change*. London: SustainAbility.

Belous, R. S. (1995). Rise of the contingent work force: The key challenges and opportunities. *The Washington and Lee Law Review*, *52*, 863.

Benkler, Y. (2002). Coase's penguin, or, linux and the nature of the firm. *Yale Law Journal*, *112*(3), 369–446.

Benkler, Y. (2007). *The wealth of networks: How social production transforms markets and freedom*. New Haven, CT: Yale University Press.

Berle, A. A., & Means, G. C. (1932). *The modern corporation and private property*. New York, NY: Macmillan.

Bodie, M. (2013). Participation as a theory of employment. SSRN Scholarly Paper No. ID 2252725. Social Science Research Network, Rochester, NY. Retrieved from http://papers.ssrn.com/abstract=2252725

Bøllingtoft, A., Donaldson, L., Huber, G. P., Håkonsson, D. D., & Snow, C. C. (Eds.). (2011). *Collaborative communities of firms: Purpose, process, and design* (2012th ed.). Berlin, Heidelberg: Springer.

Boltanski, L., & Chiapello, E. (2006). The new spirit of capitalism. *International Journal of Politics, Culture, and Society*, *18*(3-4), 161–188. doi:10.1007/s10767-006-9006-9

Clark, W. H., & Vranka, L. (2012). *The need and rationale for the benefit corporation: Why it is the legal form that best addresses the needs of social entrepreneurs, investors, and, ultimately, the public*. Benefit Corp Information Center. Retrieved from http://www.benefitcorp.net/for-attorneys/benefit-corp-white-paper

Deloitte Center for the Edge. (2011). *The 2011 shift index: Measuring the forces of long-term change*. Deloitte Center for the Edge. Retrieved from http://www.deloitte.com/assets/Dcom-UnitedStates/Local%20Assets/Documents/us_tmt_2011shiftindex_111011.pdf

Ellerman, D. (1999). The democratic firm: An argument based on ordinary jurisprudence. *Journal of Business Ethics*, *21*(2–3), 11–124.

European Multistakeholder Forum On CSR. (2004). *European multistakeholder forum on CSR – Final results and recommendations*. Retrieved from http://circa.europa.eu/irc/empl/csr_eu_multi_stakeholder_forum/info/data/en/csr%20ems%20forum.htm

Farber, H. S. (2007). Is the company man an anachronism? Trends in long-term employment in the US, 1973–2006. In S. Danziger & C. E. Rouse (Eds.), *The price of independence: The economics of early adulthood* (pp. 56–83). New York, NY: Russell Sage Foundation Publications.

Ferraro, F., & O'Mahony, S. (2012). Managing the boundary of an "open" project. In J. Padgett & W. Powell (Eds.), *The emergence of organizations and markets*. Princeton, NJ: Princeton University Press.

Freeman, R. E., Wicks, A. C., & Parmar, B. (2004). Stakeholder theory and "the corporate objective revisited.". *Organization Science*, *15*(3), 364–369.

Friedman, A. L. (2006). *Stakeholders: Theory and practice*. Oxford: Oxford University Press.

Gereffi, G., Humphrey, J., & Sturgeon, T. (2005). The governance of global value chains. *Review of International Political Economy*, *12*(1), 78–104.

Grant, R. M. (1996). Toward a knowledge-based theory of the firm. *Strategic Management Journal*, *17*(10), 109–22.

Greenan, N., Kalugina, E., & Walkowiak, E. (2007). The transformation of work? D9.2.2 – Trends in work organisation. No. CIT3-CT-2005-006193. CEE, France.

Gulati, R., & Singh, H. (1998). The architecture of cooperation: managing coordination costs and appropriation concerns in strategic alliances. *Administrative Science Quarterly*, *43*(4), 781–784.

Hagel, J. I., Brown, J. S., Jelinek, M., Sitkin, S., Cardinal, L., & Bijlsma-Frankema, K. (2010). Relational networks, strategic advantage: New challenges for collaborative control. In S. B. Sitkin, L. B. Cardinal, & K. Bijlsma-Frankema (Eds.), *Control in organizations: New directions in theory and research* (pp. 251–300). Cambridge, UK: Cambridge University Press.

Hollister, M. (2011). Employment stability in the US labor market: Rhetoric versus reality. *Annual Review of Sociology*, *37*, 305–324.

Kalleberg, A. L. (2000). Nonstandard employment relations: Part-time, temporary and contract work. *Annual Review of Sociology*, *26*, 341–365.

Khanna, T., & Palepu, K. (1997). Why focused strategies may be wrong for emerging markets. *Harvard Business Review*, *75*(4), 41–48.

Lawler, E. E. (2005). Creating high performance organizations. *Asia Pacific Journal of Human Resources*, *43*(1), 10–17. doi:10.1177/1038411105050304

Lerner, J., & Schankerman, M. (2010). *The comingled code: Open source and economic development*. Cambridge, MA: MIT Press.

Lessig, L. (2006). *Code: Version 2.0*. New York, NY: Basic Books.

Leung, W. S. (1997). The inadequacy of shareholder primacy: A proposed regime that recognizes non-shareholder interests. *Columbia Journal of Law and Social Problems*, *30*, 589.

Livesey, S. M. (2002). The discourse of the middle ground: Citizen shell commits to sustainable development. *Management Communication Quarterly*, *15*(3), 313.

Leviten-Reid, C., & Fairbairn, B. (2011). Multi-stakeholder governance in cooperative organizations: Toward a new framework for research?. *Canadian Journal of Nonprofit and Social Economy Research*, *2*(2). Retrieved from http://anserj.ca/index.php/cjnser/article/view/78

MacDuffie, J. P., & Helper, S. (2006). Collaboration in supply chains. In C. Heckscher & P. S. Adler (Eds.), *The firm as a collaborative community: Reconstructing trust in the knowledge economy*. Oxford, UK: Oxford University Press.

Marx, M., Singh, J., & Fleming, L. (2010). *Regional disadvantage? Non-compete agreements and brain drain*. Unpublished working paper.

Microsoft CEO takes launch break with the Sun-Times. (2001). Retrieved from http://web.archive.org/web/20010615205548/http://suntimes.com/output/tech/cst-fin-micro01.html\. Accessed on June 1, 2001.

Nonaka, I., Toyama, R., & Nagata, A. (2000). A firm as a knowledge-creating entity: A new perspective on the theory of the firm. *Industrial and Corporate Change*, *9*(1), 1–20.

Osterman, P. (2001). *Flexibility and commitment in the United States labour market*. International Labour Organization. Retrieved from http://staging2.ilo.org/wcmsp5/groups/public/—ed_emp/documents/publication/wcms_142344.pdf

Oswald, L. (1998). Shareholders v. stakeholders: Evaluating corporate constituency statutes under the takings clause. The University of Iowa. *The Journal of Corporation Law*, *24*(1), 1–28.

Pharr, S. J., Putnam, R. D., & Dalton, R. J. (2000). A quarter-century of declining confidence. *Journal of Democracy*, *11*(2), 5–25.

Samila, S., & Sorenson, O. (2011). Noncompete covenants: Incentives to innovate or impediments to growth. *Management Science*, *57*(3), 425–438. doi:10.1287/mnsc.1100.1280

Spar, D. L. (2002). *Hitting the wall: Nike and international labor practices (Case study)*. Harvard Business School. Retrieved from http://harvardbusinessonline.hbsp.harvard.edu/b02/en/common/item_detail.jhtml?id = 700047&referral = 1076

Strathern, M. (1996). Cutting the network. *Journal of the Royal Anthropological Institute*, *2*(3), 517–535.

Tuna, C. (2009, May 11). Many companies hire as they fire – WSJ.com. *Wall Street Journal Interactive Edition*. Retrieved from http://online.wsj.com/article/SB124198904713604533.html

Turnbull, S. (2002). Stakeholder governance: A cybernetic and property rights analysis. *Corporate Governance: An International Review*, *5*(1), 11–23. doi:10.1111/1467-8683.00035

Uchitelle, L. (2006). *The disposable American: Layoffs and their consequences*. New York, NY: Knopf.
US Government Accountability Office. (2006). *Employment arrangements: Improved outreach could help ensure proper worker classification (No. GAO-06-656)*. Retrieved from www.gao.gov/new.items/d06656.pdf
Valenzuela, A. (2011). Non-regular employment in the United States: A profile. In *Non-regular employment – Issues and challenges common to the major developed countries*. The Japan Institute for Labour Policy and Training. Retrieved from http://eforum.jil.go.jp/english/reports/documents/jilpt-reports/no.10.pdf#page=95
Varughese, G., & Ostrom, E. (2001). The contested role of heterogeneity in collective action: Some evidence from community forestry in Nepal. *World Development*, *29*(5), 747–765.
Wei-Skillern, J. (2004). Sustainable development at shell. Harvard Business School Case, 9-303-005, pp. 1–21.
Williams, H. L. (2010). *Intellectual property rights and innovation: Evidence from the human genome*. National Bureau of Economic Research Working Paper Series, No. 16213. Retrieved from http://www.nber.org/papers/w16213
WorldPublicOpinion.org. (2008). *World public opinion on governance and democracy*. Program on international policy attitudes at the University of Maryland. Retrieved from http://worldpublicopinion.org/pipa/articles/governance_bt/482.php?lb=btgov&pnt=482&nid=&id

CHAPTER 15

DESTRUCTIVE TRADE AND WORKERS' SELF-DEFENSE THROUGH ECONOMIC DEMOCRACY: A RESEARCH NOTE

Jaroslav Vanek

It can be shown that the theory of free trade and comparative advantage, concluding that such trade will maximize world income, is partly incorrect. Under conditions closely resembling the situation in the world economy of today, free trade – especially between advanced and developing countries – will tend to suboptimal conditions and especially to unemployment of human labor. This is precisely what has been happening over the past two decades, and can be associated with the so-called Great Recession. I have written several articles on this subject (Vanek, 2010a, 2010b, 2011b) showing that a fundamental error of economic analysis is at stake, and it is not my intention here to go over the technical aspects of the argument.

Also, there is an extensive literature presented and summarized by Professor Samuelson's (2004) article dealing with a general equilibrium analysis of recent world trading situation pointing in a similar direction.

Since at the center of the discussion is the suffering of millions of American working families, I would like to indicate that there may be a

Sharing Ownership, Profits, and Decision-making in the 21st Century
Advances in the Economic Analysis of Participatory & Labor-Managed Firms, Volume 14, 397–399

ISSN: 0885-3339/doi:10.1108/S0885-3339(2013)0000014018

way out, where the suffering unemployed workers can "fight back" by their own efforts – with the assistance of a sympathetic government.

Under capitalist conditions in a severe recession the policy makers – for example, the central bank managers and the government budget designers – can find themselves in the well-known Keynesian "liquidity trap" which can make it extremely difficult to extricate the economy from the state of Great Recession. Actually, the central bank managers even go further than the usual liquidity trap, by promising that they will sit in it for two or even four years. Keynesian analysis may indicate that recession could be overcome through further deficit spending, but this may be difficult with gigantic public debt.

And what is most significant is, the stimuli of the type applied by the Obama government are themselves subject to destructive trade forces, where additional government spending itself can be turned into production abroad and not employment at home.

But the significant quality of democratic cooperative firms is that by definition, they cannot move to China and hurt domestic U.S. employment. They offer another alternative to deal with the effects of destructive trade: they can remain home and at the same time, where possible, can cooperate with or create firms in regions (such as Mexico or China) where wages are significantly lower. They can then cooperate with such "offspring" firms, for example, offering their own used equipment, giving employment, showing principles of democratic production, and so forth.

All this is not only the imagination of a dedicated theorist, but a real situation in the world of today where the "mother firms" are represented by the cooperatives of the Mondragon Cooperative Corporation, who started and are operating such satellite firms, without lowering domestic employment, in many parts of the world. This writer actually visited such "offspring" in the Czech Republic twice, near the city of Olomouc, and the solution is working perfectly satisfactorily, as shown in my article offered to the present association some years ago (Vanek, 2007).

Instead of relying on capitalist Keynesian stimuli of the Obama type, the stimulus funds could be employed to support creation of democratic support structures of the Mondragon type, forming domestic firms with possible assistance to low-wage foreign regions (thus being welcome there) and thus retaining jobs at home.

And not only that: such a program would not only be fighting back the forces of destructive trade, but also assisting the creation of a "third sector" of the economy based on democratic principles, and by definition keeping jobs at home. In addition, such "democratic" stimuli would greatly contribute to the formation of an economy which is sound ecologically (Vanek, 2011a).

Moreover – and finally – all this is not just a dream. Such a support structure in a small form of several worker bakeries has been formed in San Francisco, symbolically under the name of the founder of Mondragon, Arizmendi. Joseph Marraffino (2011) has reported on the San Francisco Arizmendi experience.

REFERENCES

Marraffino, J. (2011). *The replication of Arizmendi bakery: A model of the democratic worker cooperative movement.* American Worker Cooperative, March 2011. Retrieved from http://american.coop

Samuelson, P. (2004). Where Ricardo and Mill Rebut and confirm arguments of mainstream economists supporting globalization. *Journal of Economic Perspectives, 18*(3), 135–146.

Vanek, J. (2007). A note on the future and dynamics of economic democracy. *Advances in the Economic Analysis of Participatory and Labor-Managed Firms, 10*, 309–316.

Vanek, J. (2010a). From destructive to creative trade through economic democracy. *Advances in the Economic Analysis of Participatory and Labor-Managed Firms, 11*, 247–253.

Vanek, J. (2010b). Destructive trade and its effects on the global economy. *Atlantic Economic Journal, 38*, 317–324.

Vanek, J. (2011a). Capitalism, economic democracy, and ecological destruction of our planet. *Advances in the Economic Analysis of Participatory and Labor-Managed Firms, 12*, 289–298.

Vanek, J. (2011b). From great depression to great recession. *International Review of Economics and Finance, 20*, 131–134.